FREETHINKERS

FREETHINKERS

A HISTORY OF AMERICAN SECULARISM

SUSAN JACOBY

METROPOLITAN BOOKS

Henry Holt and Company, New York

[logo: m]

Metropolitan Books
Henry Holt and Company, LLC
Publishers since 1866
115 West 18th Street
New York, New York 10011

Metropolitan Books™ is a registered
trademark of Henry Holt and Company, LLC.

Library of Congress Cataloging-in-Publication Data

Jacoby, Susan, date.
  Freethinkers : a history of American secularism / Susan Jacoby.
    p. cm.
  Includes bibliographical references and index.
  ISBN 0-8050-7442-2
  1. Secularism—United States—History. 2. Freethinkers—United States—History.
  I. Title.
  BL2760.J33 2004
  211'.4'0973—dc22   2003059294

Henry Holt books are available for special promotions and
premiums. For details contact: Director, Special Markets.

First Edition 2004
Designed by Fritz Metsch

The image of Thomas Paine is from an engraving in Samuel P. Putman, *Four Hundred Years of
Freethought* (New York: Truth Seeker Company, 1984), and is used, along with the picture of
Robert Ingersoll's oration, courtesy of the Center for Inquiry/Council for Secular Humanism.
The cartoon of "Mad Tom" and the images of Ernestine L. Rose, Lucretia Mott, and Elizabeth
Cady Stanton appear courtesy of the New York Public Library. The image of George E. Mac-
donald and the frontispiece, "The Story of the Truth Seeker," originally appeared in Volume I,
Fifty Years of Freethought (1929), published by the Truth Seeker Company. The image of
Clarence Darrow originally appeared in Volume II, *Fifty Years of Freethought* (1931), published
by the Truth Seeker Company. The photograph of President George W. Bush in prayer was
taken by Eric Draper and is used with permission of the White House.

Printed in the United States of America
10 9 8 7 6 5 4 3 2 1

FOR ROBERT AND IRMA BRODERICK JACOBY

The most formidable weapon against
errors of any kind is reason.
—THOMAS PAINE, 1794

Contents

FREETHINKERS

INTRODUCTION

We have retired the gods from politics. We have found that man is the
only source of political power, and that the governed should govern.
— ROBERT GREEN INGERSOLL,
JULY 4, 1876

On the centennial anniversary of the signing of the Declaration of
Independence, Robert Ingersoll, the foremost champion of
freethought and the most famous orator in late-nineteenth-century
America, paid tribute in his hometown of Peoria, Illinois, to "the first
secular government that was ever founded in this world." Also
known as "the Great Agnostic," Ingersoll praised the framers of the
Constitution for deliberately omitting any mention of God from the
nation's founding document and instead acknowledging "We the People" as the supreme governmental authority. This unprecedented decision, Ingersoll declared, "did away forever with the theological idea of
government."[1]

The Great Agnostic spoke too soon. It is impossible to imagine
such a forthright celebration of America's secularist heritage today, as
the apostles of religious correctness attempt to infuse every public
issue, from the quality of education to capital punishment, with their
theological values. During the past two decades, cultural and religious conservatives have worked ceaselessly to delegitimize American secularism and relegate its heroes to a kooks' corner of American
history. In the eighteenth century, Enlightenment secularists of the

revolutionary generation were stigmatized by the guardians of religious orthodoxy as infidels and atheists. Today, the new pejorative "elitist" has replaced the old "infidel" in the litany of slurs aimed at defenders of secularist values.*

Since the terrorist attacks of September 11, 2001, America's secularist tradition has been further denigrated by unremitting political propaganda equating patriotism with religious faith. Like most other Americans, I responded to the terrorist assaults with an immediate surge of anger and grief so powerful that it left no room for alienation. Walking around my wounded New York, as the smoke from the ruins of the World Trade Center wafted the smell of death throughout the city, I drew consolation from the knowledge that others were feeling what I was feeling—sorrow, pain, and rage, coupled with the futile but irrepressible longing to turn back the clock to the hour before bodies rained from a crystalline sky. That soothing sense of unity was severed for me just three days later, when President George W. Bush presided over an ecumenical prayer service in Washington's National Cathedral. Delivering an address indistinguishable from a sermon, replacing the language of civic virtue with the language of faith, the nation's chief executive might as well have been the Reverend Bush. Quoting a man who supposedly said at St. Patrick's Cathedral, "I pray to God to give us a sign that he's still here," the president went on to assure the public not only that God was still here but that he was personally looking out for America. "God's signs," Bush declared, "are not always the ones we look for. We learn in tragedy that his purposes

---

*Throughout this book, I have taken the liberty of using the words *secularism* and *secularist*—even though the latter was not in common usage until the second half of the nineteenth century—to denote a concept of public good based on human reason and human rights rather than divine authority. The *Oxford English Dictionary* defines secularism as "the doctrine that morality should be based solely on regard to the well-being of mankind in the present life, to the exclusion of all consideration drawn from belief in God or in a future state." The term first appeared in print in 1851 and soon took on a political as well as a philosophical meaning, distinguishing the secular (a much older word than *secularist*) functions of government from the domain of religion. In eighteenth-century political discourse, the adjective *civil* was the closest equivalent of *secularist*, and many of the founders used the word to refer to the public, nonreligious sphere of government, as distinct from the private role of religion.

are not always our own. . . . Neither death nor life, nor angels nor principalities, nor powers, nor things present, nor things to come, nor height, nor depth can separate us from God's love. May he bless the souls of the departed, may he comfort our own, and may he always guide our country." This adaptation of the famous passage from Paul's Epistle to the Romans left out the evangelist's identification of Jesus Christ as God—an omission presumably made in deference to the Jewish and Muslim representatives sharing the pulpit with the president.

Bush would surely have been criticized, and rightly so, had he failed to invite representatives of non-Christian faiths to the ecumenical ceremony in memory of the victims of terrorism. But he felt perfectly free to ignore Americans who adhere to no religious faith, whose outlook is predominantly secular, and who interpret history and tragedy as the work of man rather than God. There was no speaker who represented my views, no one to reject the notion of divine purpose at work in the slaughter of thousands and to proclaim the truth that grief, patriotism, and outrage at injustice run just as deep in the secular as in the religious portion of the American body politic.

Bush's very presence in the pulpit attested powerfully to the erosion of America's secularist tradition; most of his predecessors would have regarded the choice of a religious sanctuary for a major speech as a gross violation of the respect for separation of church and state constitutionally required of the nation's chief executive. Franklin D. Roosevelt did not try to assuage the shock of Pearl Harbor by using an altar as the backdrop for his declaration of war, and Abraham Lincoln, who never belonged to a church, delivered the Gettysburg Address not from a sanctuary but on the field where so many soldiers had given "the last full measure of devotion."

It is one of the greatest unresolved paradoxes of American history that religion has come to occupy such an important place in the communal psyche and public life of a nation founded on the separation of church and state. The tension between secularism and religion was present at America's creation; a secular government, independent of all religious sects, was seen by founders of diverse private beliefs as the essential guarantor of liberty of conscience. The descendants of passionate religious dissenters, who had fled the church-state establishments of the Old World in order to worship God in a multiplicity of ways, were beholden to a godless constitution.[2] From the beginning of the republic, this irony-laden and profoundly creative relationship produced a mixture of gratitude and unease on the part of its beneficiaries.

Given the intensity of both secularist and religious passions in the founding generation, it was probably inevitable that the response of Americans to secularism and freethought—the lovely term that first appeared in the late 1600s and flowered into a genuine social and philosophical movement during the next two centuries—would be fraught with ambivalence. Beginning with the revolutionary era, freethinkers periodically achieved substantial influence in American society, only to be vilified in periods of reaction and consigned to the margins of America's official version of its history.

American freethought derived much of its power from an inclusiveness that encompassed many forms of rationalist belief. Often defined as a total absence of faith in God, freethought can better be understood as a phenomenon running the gamut from the truly antireligious—those who regarded all religion as a form of superstition and wished to reduce its influence in every aspect of society—to those who adhered to a private, unconventional faith revering some form of God or Providence but at odds with orthodox religious authority. American freethinkers have included deists, who, like many of the founding fathers, believed in a "watchmaker God" who set the universe in motion but subsequently took no active role in the affairs of men; agnostics; and unabashed atheists. What the many types of freethinkers shared, regardless of their views on the existence or nonexistence of a divinity, was a rationalist approach to fundamental questions of earthly existence—a conviction that the affairs of human beings should be governed not by faith in the supernatural but by a reliance on reason and evidence adduced from the natural world. It was this conviction, rooted in Enlightenment philosophy, that carried the day when the former revolutionaries gathered in Philadelphia in 1787 to write the Constitution.

Thomas Paine, the preeminent and much-admired literary propagandist of the Revolution, was the first American freethinker to be labeled an atheist, denigrated both before and after his death, and deprived of his proper place in American history. In 1776, Paine's clarion call for steadfast patriotism in dark times—"the summer soldier and the sunshine patriot will, in this crisis, shrink from the service of their country; but he that stands it *now*, deserves the love and thanks of man and woman"—had inspired his countrymen in every corner of the former colonies. But memories of Paine the patriot would long be obscured by denunciations of his heretical views. In *The Age of Reason* (1794), he put forth the astonishing idea that Christianity, like all other religions, was an invention of man rather than God. Paine died a pauper and, nearly eight decades later, would still be subjected to slurs by such eminent personages as Theodore Roosevelt, who dismissed him as a "filthy little atheist . . . that apparently esteems a bladder of dirty water as the proper weapon with which to assail Christianity."[3] Were it not for the unremitting efforts of Ingersoll, who, despite his nineteenth-century fame and notoriety, is ignored in standard American history texts, Paine's vital contributions to the revolutionary cause might have suffered the same fate. Unfortunately, no champion arose in the twentieth century to do for Ingersoll what Ingersoll did for Paine. In a country with less reverence toward religious institutions, Ingersoll might occupy the historical position of a Voltaire, to whom he was frequently compared by his contemporaries.

The only freethinkers who have received their due in American history are Thomas Jefferson and James Madison, in spite of the fact that they were denigrated by their Calvinist contemporaries as atheists, heretics, and infidels (then understood in its literal, original sense—*unfaithful ones*). It is impossible to consign former presidents or the authors of the nation's secular scriptures to a historical limbo.

Thus, Jefferson, Madison, and, to a lesser extent, George Washington, John Adams, and Benjamin Franklin pose a vexing problem for twentieth-century political, religious, and social conservatives intent on simultaneously enshrining the founding fathers and denying their intention to establish a secular government.

The long struggle over the role of religion in American public and cultural life has been a slow, uneven movement away from Americans' original definition of themselves as a Protestant Christian people, albeit leavened by a strong secularist bent that accommodated both non-Christians and the nonreligious at a time when compulsory state religion was taken for granted throughout the world. At the beginning of the twenty-first century, the American self-definition has been expanded to non-Christians in ways that were unimaginable only fifty years ago. Since the Second World War and the Holocaust, public officials have increasingly substituted "Judeo-Christian" for "Christian" when talking about the nation's religious and ethical heritage. Religious Jews (as distinct from Jews as an ethnic group), who make up just 1.3 percent of Americans, are now routinely invited to participate in ecumenical ceremonies like the one held in the National Cathedral. Muslims, in spite of their recent growth as a result of immigration and proselytizing among African Americans, are an even smaller minority—one-half of 1 percent—yet they, too, are represented on most important civic occasions. In areas of the country with large first- and second-generation communities of non-Christian immigrants, Hindus and Buddhists are frequently asked to join Christians, Jews, and Muslims on public platforms. The message is clear: we may be a multicultural people, but we're all respectable as long as we worship God in some way.

The one minority left outside the shelter of America's ecumenical umbrella is the congregation of the unchurched. Yet the secularist minority is much larger than any non-Christian religious group. According to a nationwide opinion poll of Americans' religious identification, conducted by the Graduate Center of the City University of New York, the fastest-growing "religious" group in the United States is composed of those who do not subscribe to any faith. From

1990 to 2001, the number of the unchurched more than doubled, from 14.3 million to 29.4 million. Approximately 14 percent of Americans, compared with only 8 percent in 1990, have no formal ties to religion. Sixteen percent, and it is reasonable to assume that they make up essentially the same group as the unchurched, describe their outlook on the world as entirely or predominantly secular.[4] It would be a mistake to conclude that none of the "predominantly secular" believe in God; less than 1 percent described themselves as atheists or agnostics, while the overwhelming majority simply said they had no religion. However, in view of the opprobrium attached to the words *atheist* and *agnostic* in American culture, I suspect that there are many more nonbelievers in this group than there are people willing to call themselves nonbelievers. But a secularist's specific metaphysical beliefs are politically irrelevant, because insistence on the distinction between private faith and the conduct of public affairs is precisely what distinguishes secularists from the religiously correct.

Even though more Americans may be viewing public issues through a secular lens, the influence of religion at the highest levels of government has never been stronger or more public. This contradiction has surfaced repeatedly in American history. Hard-core fundamentalist religion has always flourished during periods of increasing secularization, and its adherents tend to be much more singleminded than secularists: most secularists will vote for a religious believer who respects separation of church and state, but few fundamentalists will vote for a secularist who denounces religious influence on government. In 2004, it is impossible to imagine an avowed atheist or agnostic winning or being nominated for the American presidency. In a nationwide opinion poll released in the summer of 2003, fully half of Americans said that they would refuse to vote for an atheist for president—regardless of his or her other qualifications.[5] Lincoln, who refused to join a church even though his political advisers—clearly not all-powerful "handlers" in the modern sense—argued that formal religious affiliation would improve his chances of election, might well be unacceptable as a major party presidential candidate today. Ronald Reagan, whose record of religious observance during his Hollywood years was spotty at best, started turning up regularly at church services as soon as he was elected governor of California and set his sights on the presidency. When Senator Joseph Lieberman, a devout Orthodox Jew, was running for the vice presidency on the Democratic ticket in 2000, political pundits indulged in interminable self-congratulation about the growing tolerance of the American people. While the positive response to Lieberman's candidacy certainly attests to the diminution of anti-Semitism, it was Lieberman's open religiosity, not his ethnic Jewishness, that enabled him to mix so effectively with evangelicals, High Church Episcopalians, and Roman Catholic bishops. An avowedly secular, nonobservant Jew—one who considered himself Jewish in a cultural rather than a religious sense—would never have been selected for a major party's national ticket. Although Democratic presidents have been much more careful to separate their private religious views from public policy making, both Jimmy Carter, the first born-again Christian in the White House, and Bill Clinton, the first president to publicly ask God's forgiveness for adultery, contributed to the blurring of the distinction between private faith and public responsibility.

In the Bush White House, the institutionalization of religion has reached an apotheosis. His cabinet meetings routinely begin with a prayer, as the public learned from a startling front-page photograph in the *New York Times* several years ago. The intertwining of religion and government today goes far beyond the symbolic, although symbols are important in themselves. The battle over abortion, now extended to stem cell research, is the longest-running dispute in which not only private religious beliefs but the official teachings of various churches permeate public debate and influence legislation. The Republican majority, joined by a fair number of Democrats, not only supports government funding of religious charities but insists that churches should be able to use public money to hire only members of their own faith. For the first time in American history, the judicial and the executive branches of government have endorsed tax breaks for parents who wish to send their children to religious schools. Biblical authority is cited by politicians and judges as a rationale for the death penalty. Vital public health programs—the use of condoms to prevent the spread of AIDS, family planning aid to Third World countries, sex education for American teenagers (unless it preaches "abstinence only")—are held hostage by the religious doctrines of a determined conservative minority.

Yet the religiously correct continue to speak of a "naked public square," a space in which secular humanists supposedly have succeeded in muzzling the voices of faith.[6] In *The Culture of Disbelief*, Stephen L. Carter asserts that "the truth—an awkward one for the guardians of the public square—is that tens of millions of Americans rely on their religious traditions for the moral knowledge that tells them how to conduct their lives, including their political lives. They do not like being told to shut up."[7] But no one is telling them to shut up—not that anyone could. And no one denies that all public policy issues, whether they involve scientific research or the conduct of foreign affairs, have both a moral and a pragmatic component. For individuals, morality is never a matter of consensus: your countrymen may go to war, but you may not follow if your conscience forbids you to do so. For a democratic society, however, there must be a moral consensus, extending beyond and in some instances contradicting particular religious beliefs, to maintain the social contract. Both the abolition of slavery and the civil rights movement a century later exemplify the kind of consensus that transcends all religions and runs counter to some. It is often noted that religion played a major role in both the nineteenth-century abolitionist and the twentieth-century civil rights movements, but, as Lincoln pointedly observed, the Bible was used just as frequently to justify slavery as to support emancipation. In the 1960s, America's steps toward racial justice were ratified by a moral majority—with a small *m*—that included both the men and women of faith and the nonreligious humanists who had played a vital role in the civil rights movement. When President Lyndon Johnson proposed the Voting Rights Act of 1965 and declared, in his memorable Texas twang, "We *shall* overcome," he was articulating a moral

position that could and did command the respect of citizens of any or
no religion.

Not surprisingly, generations of social reformers, concerned about
alienating religious Americans who might otherwise support their
causes, have attempted to minimize the importance of the secularist
influence in their ranks and protect themselves from guilt by association with the ungodly. That strategy has consigned many nonreligious
and social progressives to a historical memory hole and is responsible
for widespread ignorance of secularist contributions to the abolitionist, feminist, labor, and civil rights movements. Elizabeth Cady Stanton, the eminent leader of the nineteenth-century woman suffrage
movement, was censured by her fellow suffragists and all but written
out of the movement's official record after the 1895 publication of her
Woman's Bible, which excoriated organized Christianity for its role in
justifying the subjugation of women. Only in the 1980s, when a new
generation of feminist scholars rediscovered Stanton, was her reputation revived. Today, a similar impulse to downplay secularist leanings
is at work among prochoice groups. Abortion rights activists love to
point to liberal ministers and rabbis, as well as to the dissident lay
group Catholics for a Free Choice, as evidence that being prochoice
need not mean being antireligious. And of course that is true, but it is
a measure of the defensiveness of secularists today that they are reluctant to forthrightly acknowledge the abortion rights movement as the
product of a secularist rather than a religious concept of personal liberty and social good.

This timidity—in sharp contrast to the boldness of proselytizing
freethinkers of the nineteenth century—has unquestionably played an
important role in the demonization of American secularism. Those
who cherish secularist values have too often allowed conservatives to
frame public policy debates as conflicts between "value-free" secularists and religious representatives of supposedly unchanging moral
principles. But secularists are not value-free; their values are simply
grounded in earthly concerns rather than in anticipation of heavenly
rewards or fear of infernal punishments. No one in public life today
upholds secularism and humanism in the uncompromising terms used

by Ingersoll more than 125 years ago. "Secularism teaches us to be good here and now," Ingersoll declared. "I know nothing better than goodness. Secularism teaches us to be just here and now. It is impossible to be juster than just. . . . Secularism has no 'castles in Spain.' It has no glorified fog. It depends upon realities, upon demonstrations; and its end and aim is to make this world better every day—to do away with poverty and crime, and to cover the world with happy and contented homes."[8]

These values belong at the center, not in the margins, of the public square. It is past time to restore secularism, and its noble and essential contributions at every stage of the American experiment, to its proper place in our nation's historical memory and vision of the future.

I

REVOLUTIONARY SECULARISM

The essential rationalism binding America's founding secularists to one another was memorably expressed by John Adams to Thomas Jefferson in an 1813 letter commenting on Britain's repeal of an old statute that made it a crime to deny the existence of the Holy Trinity. "We can never be so certain of any Prophecy," Adams wrote, "or the fulfillment of any Prophecy; or of any miracle, or the design of any miracle as We are, from the revelation of nature i.e. natures God that two and two are equal to four. Miracles or Prophecies might frighten Us out of our Witts; might scare us to death; might induce Us to lie, to say that We believe that 2 and 2 make 5. But We should not believe it. We should know the contrary."[1]

In their seventies, with a friendship that had survived serious political conflicts, Adams and Jefferson could look back with satisfaction on what they both considered their greatest achievement—their role in establishing a secular government whose legislators would never be required, or permitted, to rule on the legality of theological views. Trying to discern the true religious opinions of the founders from their voluminous writings is rather like searching for the real Jesus in the conflicting passages of the Scriptures. Jefferson's political opponents in the early 1800s were just as mistaken, and as hypocritical, to call him an atheist as his conservative modern rebaptizers are to claim him as a committed Christian. Adams's critics and admirers, then and now, have been equally misguided in their attempts to portray him as a man of orthodox faith. What did distinguish the most important revolutionary leaders was a particularly adaptable combination of political and religious beliefs, constantly subject to revision in an era when modern views of nature, science, and man's place in the universe were beginning to take shape. These views included skepticism vis-à-vis the more rigid and authoritarian religious sects of their day; the conviction, rooted in Enlightenment philosophy, that if God exists, he created human rationality as the supreme instrument for understanding and mastering the natural world; and the assignment of faith to the sphere of individual conscience rather than public duty. The logical extension of such beliefs was a civil government based not on the laws of God, as promulgated by self-appointed earthly spokesmen, but on the rights of man.

In the half century before the Revolution, an extraordinarily dynamic culture, characterized by the spread of both nonreligious freethought and religious dissent, provided fertile soil for the growth of secularist ideas that would be translated into a civic ideal in the 1789 Constitution. The proliferation of religious sects, and a hands-off policy toward religious pluralism on the part of many of His Majesty's governors, was a conspicuous feature of colonial society. Any pope or church-sanctioned king would have been taken aback by the thanksgiving services held in August 1763 in New York City to commemorate the British victory in the French and Indian War. There is of course nothing unusual in the annals of human conflict about the victorious sides thanking God. What was unusual, indeed unprecedented in a world of unquestioned union between church and state, was the religious diversity in evidence on the day of thanksgiving proclaimed by His Majesty's colonial governor. The services were held in Episcopal, Dutch Reformed, Presbyterian, French Huguenot, Baptist, and

Moravian churches. Even more extraordinary was the participation of Congregation Shearith Israel, representing the city's small community of Sephardic Jews. The Jewish thanksgiving sermon was based on Zechariah 2:10, "Sing and rejoice, O daughter of Zion: for lo, I come, and I will dwell in the midst of thee, saith the Lord."[2] George III undoubtedly approved of the political sentiments expressed by his colonial subjects on that day, but a king in possession of more wits might well have sensed a revolution brewing in the peaceful coexistence in the New World of religious believers who had only relatively recently ceased bloodying one another in the more enlightened parts of the Old World. The public inclusion of multiple Christian sects, even if all were Protestant, manifested a religious liberalism that not only set the colonies apart from their mother country but also underscored the difference between Puritan New England and the already sinfully cosmopolitan city of New York. The addition of Jews to the mix was far more radical, since Jews in the eighteenth century were commonly listed by many orthodox Christians in a litany of detested unbelievers—"Jews, pagans, infidels, heretics, deists. . . ." As defenders of monolithic state-established churches have always known, the presence of many religions, unchecked by the inquisitor's rack and pyre, tends to impeach the claim of any religion to absolute truth and spiritual authority. Moreover, many contemporary observers reported a widespread casualness toward formal religious observance by the beginning of the revolution. In 1780, Samuel Mather, a member of the famous family that produced the fire-breathing Puritan preachers Cotton and Increase Mather, complained that only one in six of his fellow Bostonians could be counted on to attend regular church services. This does not mean that the majority of Americans were unbelievers, but it does attest to the presence of powerful libertarian and noncomformist impulses in the new nation.

The religious pluralism of colonial America, which militated against a common cultural definition of religious heresy, also made room for freethought. As early as the 1750s, the spread of deism—often used by its detractors as a synonym for freethought and atheism—was considered a serious problem by orthodox clergymen. In 1759, the widely respected Reverend Ezra Stiles was already convinced that "Deism has got such Head in this Age of Licentious Liberty, that it would be in vain to stop it by hiding the Deistical Writings: and the only Way left to conquer & demolish it, is to come forth into the open Field and dispute it on an even Footing."[3] Stiles was writing a letter to express his disagreement with the president of Yale College, who had turned down a donation of a library from a Newport merchant on the already anachronistic ground that Rhode Island, having been founded by Roger Williams in response to Puritan persecutions in Massachusetts, was a schismatic state. The devout minister's acknowledgment of the futility of censorship was itself an indication of the influence of American freethought.

Expanding literacy, especially in the northern colonies, contributed to the spread of freethought beyond an educated elite to a larger audience of literate farmers, small businessmen, craftsmen, and, in growing numbers, their wives and daughters. "In no part of the habitable globe is learning and true *useful* knowledge so universally disseminated as in *our native country*," declared Bostonian John Gardiner in a Fourth of July oration on the eighth anniversary of the Declaration of Independence. "Who hath seen a native adult that cannot write? who known a native of the age of puberty that cannot read the bible?"[4] Even allowing for patriotic hyperbole, the connection between America's rising literacy rate and the wider dissemination of sophisticated social, political, and religious, as well as antireligious, ideas is obvious. Literate men and women did not need ministers to tell them how, and what, to think about God. (In this respect, the Roman Catholic opposition to Bible reading in the vernacular was much more protective of the church's interests than was the Protestant emphasis on reading the Scriptures in a language that could be understood.) Ordinary literate Americans might not have been reading Locke, Hume, Newton, Voltaire, Rousseau, and Diderot, but they did read secondhand accounts, in pamphlets and newspapers, of political and religious debates that drew on all of the Enlightenment thinkers. If large numbers of Americans had not been familiar with both the language and the philosophy of the Enlightenment, the secularist revolutionary leaders would not have used those concepts in the nation's founding documents. The Declaration of Independence and the Constitution were written to be understood by literate Americans of every social background. Paine's polemical pamphlets on behalf of independence, as well as his later antireligious arguments, were composed in the same straightforward language—a source of particular fury to clerics who could only reply with abstruse theological arguments.

The expansion of literacy in the late colonial era was accompanied by a growing interest in and respect for science—an important element of freethought in all countries affected by the Enlightenment. The leaders of the American Enlightenment were well aware of how inferior the American intellectual and scientific environment was to the elite established centers of learning in Europe, and they hoped to remedy this disadvantage after the achievement of independence. But those who knew Europe well were convinced that Europe's intellectual superiority applied only to the most privileged minority and that the majority of Americans were far better informed about science than their European counterparts. From Paris in 1785, Jefferson wrote that "in science, the mass of [European] people is two centuries behind ours." Jefferson conceded, however, that Europe's "literati" were half a dozen years ahead of Americans, because it took that long for important new books to cross the Atlantic and be thoroughly assimilated by American intellectuals.[5] Then as now, American scientific interest focused not on theory but on the immense practical benefits to be derived from discovering the secrets of the natural world—the subject of so many of Benjamin Franklin's popular scientific writings. But scientific curiosity was also rooted in the more general Enlightenment passion for rationality. Respect for the laws of science—*the Laws of Nature and of Nature's God*, as the Declaration of Independence put it—translated into the conviction that both government and religion should and could operate in a manner consistent with those laws.

By the time of the Revolution, it was impossible to dismiss the connection between emerging concepts of political freedom and religious freethought, although the most religiously orthodox patriots certainly wished to do just that. The fundamental ethos of the Revolution was opposed to divine as well as earthly despotism. "Who would imagine," the Revolutionary War hero Ethan Allen asked in 1784, "that the Deity conducts his providence similar to the detestable despots of the world? O *horrible* most *horrible impeachment* of Divine Goodness!"[6] To Allen, better known today as the leader of the Green Mountain Boys and an advocate of statehood for Vermont, rejection of the all-powerful Calvinist deity went together with rejection of the divine right of kings. The Reverend Timothy Dwight, who, as president of Yale, would play a leading role in a concerted effort to reestablish religious orthodoxy in the postrevolutionary nation, described Allen's *Reason the Only Oracle of Man* (1784) as "the first formal publication, in the United States, openly directed against the Christian religion."[7] A disorganized and stylistically clumsy writer, Allen never achieved the influence or notoriety that accompanied the dissemination of Paine's *The Age of Reason* a decade later. But his book, in spite of and also because of its rough-hewn style, offers considerable insight into the revolutionary connection between political and religious freedom. Allen embodied the anticlerical strain in early American freethought; although his antagonism toward ecclesiastical hierarchies was directed chiefly at hellfire-and-damnation Calvinist ministers, his many derogatory references to "priests" and "priest-craft" also reflected the strong influence of French Enlightenment thought on the American revolutionary generation.[8] Notions of the depravity of human reason, Allen argued, were cherished by priests because, if ordinary human beings were assumed to be perfectly capable of reasoning for themselves, the clergy would be out of work. Allen also noted that "while we are under the tyranny of Priests . . . it will ever be in their interest, to invalidate the law of nature and reason, in order to establish systems incompatible therewith."[9]

The link between political and religious freethought was not always so explicitly drawn, but it was always in the air. It should not therefore be surprising that, even before the end of the Revolutionary War, a radical new vision of absolute separation of church and state was set forward by freethinkers as the logical outgrowth of political independence. In 1779, Jefferson proposed a bill that would guarantee complete legal equality for citizens of all religions, and of no religion, in his home state of Virginia. Jefferson's was the first plan in any of the thirteen states to call for complete separation of civil and religious authority, and seven years of fierce debate and political bargaining would pass before a version of his bill was enacted into law. Virginia stood alone in marshaling a legislative majority that, as Jefferson observed, "meant to comprehend, within the mantle of its protection, the Jew and the Gentile, the Christian and Mahometan, the Hindoo, and infidel of every denomination."[10] It is impossible to overstate the importance of Virginia's 1786 Act for Establishing Religious Freedom, for, much to the dismay of religious conservatives, it would become the template for the secularist provisions of the federal Constitution.

When Jefferson first put forward a law to separate church and state, the Episcopal Church—the American branch having declared its independence from the Church of England—represented the official, or "established," religion of the state of Virginia. The issue remained on the back burner until the end of the war, when both freethinkers and dissenting evangelical Protestants renewed their objections to the existence of a state church. The battle was joined in 1784 when Patrick Henry introduced a bill in the Virginia General Assembly that would have assessed taxes on all citizens for the support of "teachers of the Christian religion." The proposal, which would have replaced the single established Episcopal Church with "multiple establishments," was eminently reasonable, even tolerant, if you happened to believe that the state government should be in the business of supporting Christian churches. James Madison was among those who did not, and he conveyed his views to the Assembly in his "Memorial and Remonstrance against Religious Assessments."

Madison's eloquent "Memorial," eventually signed by some two thousand Virginians, should be as familiar to students of American history as the Declaration of Independence and the Constitution. "Who does not see," he asked in a passage that delineated his concern for personal freedom *of* religion, "that the same authority which can establish Christianity, in exclusion of all other Religions, may establish with the same ease any particular sect of Christians, in exclusion of all other Sects? That the same authority which can force a citizen to contribute three pence only of his property for the support of any one establishment, may force him to conform to any other establishment in all cases whatsoever?" Madison's advocacy of government freedom *from* religious control is equally explicit:

> If Religion be not within cognizance of Civil Government, how can its legal establishment be said to be necessary to Civil Government? What influence in fact have ecclesiastical establishments had on Civil Society? In some instances they have been seen to erect a spiritual tyranny on the ruins of Civil authority; in many instances they have seen the upholding of the thrones of political tyranny; in no instance have they been seen the guardians of the liberty of the people. Rulers who wish to subvert the public liberty, may have found an established clergy convenient auxiliaries. A just government, instituted to secure and perpetuate it [liberty], needs them not.

Citing the "malignant influence" of religious hatred not only on individuals but on "the health and prosperity of the state," Madison conceded that even a law guaranteeing complete religious liberty might not be sufficient to extinguish ancient religious enmities. Nevertheless, he argued, a secular government's evenhandedness toward all forms of belief and nonbelief would serve "sufficiently" to minimize the worst effects of religious discord on civil society and government.[11]

In the mid-1780s, Jefferson was in Paris, serving as America's minister to France, so it fell to Madison to lead the political battle against tax assessments for the support of Christian churches. Henry's assessment plan had powerful support from affluent Episcopal landowners, who, though they had established an American church independent of the Church of England, were not at all averse to emulating their mother Anglican church by filling their coffers from the public trough. As the debate began, most dissenting Protestant sects, because they stood to benefit from the new tax levies, were equally enthusiastic about Henry's plan.

Then Madison's "Memorial" was inserted into the mix. It was a masterful piece of publicity on behalf of freedom of conscience, with an impact not unlike that of Thomas Paine's celebrated arguments, in "Common Sense," on behalf of independence. And although Madison was speaking from the perspective of an Enlightenment rationalist, his presentation of the pernicious possibilities for state interference with religion appealed powerfully to nonconformist Protestants, including small Quaker and Lutheran sects as well as the more numerous Baptists and Presbyterians, who had long resented the domination of the Episcopalians. Although evangelicals did not share Madison's and Jefferson's suspicions of religious influence on civil government—indeed, they wished to expand the scope of their own influence—they eventually became convinced that dissenting denominations could best flourish under a government that explicitly prohibited state interference with church affairs. And they were willing to renounce government money to ensure government noninterference.

The best account of this often overlooked episode in American history appears in Thomas E. Buckley's *Church and State in Revolutionary Virginia* (1977). Buckley, a Jesuit priest, presents a fairminded account of the secularist as well as the religious contributions to the passage of Jefferson's bill, underscoring the complementary and contradictory motives of both groups. For Virginia's minority religious groups, which included evangelical Baptists, Quakers, Presbyterians, and Methodists, theological conviction went hand in hand with their desire to thwart any attempt by the Episcopal Church to retain its privileged prerevolutionary position. Evangelical faith rested on a personal, unmediated relationship between God and man, and any union between church and state was seen not only as unnecessary but as an insult to the Creator, whose claims preceded those of any civil government. The "Memorial" passages most significant to evangelicals declared that "in matters of Religion, no man's right is abridged by the institution of Civil Society, and that Religion is wholly exempt from its cognizance. True it is, that no other rule exists, by which any question which may divide a Society can be ultimately determined, but the will of the majority; but it is also true, that the majority may trespass upon the rights of the minority."[12] While secularists like Jefferson and Madison were concerned mainly with limiting the influence of religious intolerance on civil government, the evangelicals cared mainly about unfettered opportunity not only to worship in their own way but to proselytize within society—a difference in motivation that would place the two groups on opposite sides in many future political battles. At the time, though, the interests of the evangelicals and the Enlightenment rationalists coincided and coalesced in a common support for separation of church and state. During the Virginia debate, each side borrowed the other's arguments and even appropriated the other's rhetorical devices.[13]

The language of natural rights was liberally employed by religious bodies opposing the assessment bill. A petition from four hundred Quakers, wittily signed "your real Friends," called the proposed bill "an Infringement of Religious and Civil Liberty Established by the [Virginia] Bill of Rights." The petitioners noted tartly that it was not necessary for the government to make "Provisions for learned Teachers," since all knowledge of Christianity comes directly from Christ himself.[14] The evangelical reverence for freedom of conscience also allowed for a sense of humor. One Baptist petition was accompanied by a poem written by the Reverend David Thomas:

> *Tax all things; water, air, and light,*
> *If there need be; yea, tax the* night:
> *But let our brave heroick minds*
> *Move freely as celestial winds.*
> *Make vice and folly feel your rod,*
> *But leave our consciences to God.*[15]

Most secularist petitioners, well aware of the importance of religious support to their cause, took care to include passages emphasizing their respect for religion. From Montgomery County in the western part of the state—a hotbed of freethinkers—came a petition written by John Breckinridge, a good friend of Madison's, and signed by some three hundred landholders. Breckinridge argued, in terms that were somewhat disingenuous, that religion would be secure only when "full Scope" was given to "unbiased and unprejudiced Reason."[16] Only a small proportion of secularists were brave enough to acknowledge that they were as interested in freedom of conscience for deists and freethinkers as they were in freedom for conventional religious believers—though Jefferson's original 1779 bill extended equal rights to all. One petitioner from Amelia County, in a document dated November 9, 1785, expressed his views in a fashion familiar to eighteenth-century readers—by making fun of the ardent but usually futile efforts of preachers to convince unbelievers of the error of their ways. Scoffing at the notion that government support of Christian teaching would foster conversions, he asked, "Will the Deist come to hear preaching? How then are they to be Converted? . . . The Deist many miles from church [is] laughing in his Sleeve or toping at a tavern. . . . How many Deists have the Orthodox clergy Converted lately?"[17]

The two-year debate over the assessment bill produced petitions with more than 13,000 signatures in a state with fewer than 100,000 white men over twenty-one—the only segment of the population with a voice in political matters. Petitioners opposing religious assessments outnumbered supporters twelve to one.[18] In the end, the secularists and dissident evangelicals easily carried the day. Madison's "Memorial," and the attendant publicity in newspapers throughout the state, had alerted every possible opponent of religious tax assessments. By the time Virginia lawmakers arrived in Richmond for the beginning of the 1785–86 General Assembly, the assessment bill, which once seemed certain of passage, had been relegated to the dustbin of history. Instead, Jefferson's plan to establish complete separation of church and state was taken up by the legislature. The bill did not make it through the assembly without revisions that moderated the rhetorical force of its secular arguments, but the result, unprecedented in both American and world history, achieved exactly what

Jefferson had intended—liberty for every kind of believer and unbeliever. The text of the law begins with the words "Whereas, Almighty God hath created the mind free. . . ." Jefferson's original bill had placed a salute to reason before a bow to God: "Well aware that the opinions and belief of men depend not on their own will, but follow involuntarily the evidence proposed to their minds; that Almighty God hath created the mind free. . . ." However, the lawmakers overwhelmingly defeated a move to acknowledge Jesus Christ rather than a nonsectarian deity. The rejection of any mention of Jesus, Jefferson would recall thirty years later, proved that the law was meant to protect not only Christians, and not only religious believers, but nonbelievers as well.[19] The statement that "Almighty God hath created the mind free" was a rhetorical flourish, not a legal requirement: the important point for secularists was that no Virginian—in contrast to the prevailing practices in other states—would have to affirm his belief in any god to run for public office or claim civic equality. Leaving out a reference to the primacy of human reason was, though not a meaningless concession, far less important than the unequivocal guarantee of freedom of thought at the heart of the statute:

> Be it enacted by the General Assembly of Virginia that no man shall be compelled to frequent or support any religious worship, place, or ministry whatsoever, nor shall be enforced, restrained, molested, or burthened in his body or goods, nor shall otherwise suffer on account of his religious opinions or belief; but that all men shall be free to profess, and by argument to maintain, their opinion in matters of religion, and that the same shall in no wise diminish, enlarge, or affect their civil capacities.

> And though we will know that this Assembly, elected by the people for the ordinary purposes of legislation only, have no power to restrain the acts of succeeding Assemblies, constituted with powers equal to our own, and that therefore to declare this act irrevocable would be of no effect in law; yet we are free to declare, and do declare, that the rights hereby asserted are of the natural rights of mankind, and that if any act shall be hereafter passed to repeal

the present, or to narrow its operation, such act will be infringement of natural right.[20]

The significance of Virginia's religious freedom act was recognized
immediately in Europe. News of the law was received with great
enthusiasm—not by the governments of the Old World, with their
entrenched state-established religions, but by individuals who wished
to promote liberty of conscience in their own countries. The Virginia
law, translated into French and Italian as soon as the text made it
across the Atlantic in 1786, was disseminated throughout most of the
courts of Europe, and, as Jefferson wrote Madison, "has been the best
evidence of the falsehood of those reports which stated us to be in
anarchy." Expressing his pride in Virginia's leadership, Jefferson
observed that "it is comfortable to see the standard of reason at length
erected, after so many ages, during which the human mind has been
held in vassalage by kings, priests, and nobles, and it is honorable for
us, to have produced the first legislature who had the courage to
declare, that the reason of man may be trusted with the formation of
his own opinions."[21]

In America, where the great debate over the federal Constitution was
just beginning, Virginia's law was hailed by secularists as a model for
the new national government and denounced by those who favored
the semi-theocratic systems still prevailing in most states. As the Constitutional Convention opened in 1787, with George Washington as
its president, legally entrenched privileges for Protestant Christianity
were the rule rather than the exception in most states. The convention
could have modeled the federal Constitution after the Massachusetts
constitution of 1780, which extended equal protection of the laws,
and the right to hold office, only to Christians. And not all Christians:
Catholics were permitted to hold public office only if they took a special oath renouncing papal authority "in any matter, civil, ecclesiastical or spiritual." Even that restriction was not enough for the most
committed descendants of the Puritans; sixty-three Massachusetts

towns registered official objections to the use of "Christian" rather than "Protestant," bearing out a prediction by Adams that "a change in the solar system might be expected as soon as a change in the ecclesiastical system of Massachusetts."[22] State religious restrictions were grounded not only in old prejudices but in the relative political strength of various religious constituencies. The 1777 New York State constitution, for example, extended political equality to Jews—who, though few in number, had considerable economic influence in New York City—but not to Catholics (who were not allowed to hold public office until 1806). Maryland, the home state of Charles Carroll, the only Catholic signer of the Declaration of Independence, guaranteed full civil rights to Protestants and Catholics but not to Jews, free-thinkers, and deists. The possibility of equal rights for non-Christians had never even occurred to Carroll. In his old age, he wrote, "When I signed the Declaration of Independence, I had in view not only our independence of England, but the toleration of all sects professing the Christian religion, and communicating to them all equal rights."[23] In Delaware, officeholders were required to take an oath affirming belief in the Trinity, and in South Carolina, Protestantism was specifically recognized as the state-established religion.

But the framers of the Constitution chose Virginia, not the other states, with their crazy quilts of obeisance to a more restrictive religious past, as the model for the new nation. The Constitution is a secularist document because of what it says and what it does not say. The first of the explicit secularist provisions is article 6, section 3, which states that federal elective and appointed officials "shall be bound by Oath or Affirmation, to support this Constitution; but no religious Test shall ever be required as a Qualification to any Office or public Trust under the United States." *No religious test.* This provision, much less familiar to the public today than the First Amendment, was especially meaningful and especially sweeping in view of the fact that the necessity of religious tests and religious oaths for officeholders had been taken for granted by nearly all the governments of the American states (not to mention those of the rest of the world) at the time the Constitution was written. The addition of the word *affirma-*

tion is significant, because it meant that the framers did not intend to compel officeholders to take a religious oath on the Bible. The intent could not have been clearer to those who wanted only religious men—specifically, Protestant believers—to hold office. As a North Carolina minister put it during his state's debate on ratification of the Constitution, the abolition of religious tests for officeholders amounted to "an invitation for Jews and pagans of every kind to come among us."[24]

The debate over the secular provisions of the Constitution did not break down along predictable lines. Federalists—those who supported a more powerful central government—were, on the whole, more favorably disposed toward established churches (and established institutions of all kinds) than those, like Jefferson, who feared expansion of federal power even though they recognized the need for a national Constitution.* Yet some of the most influential Federalists, including Adams and Washington, fully shared Jefferson's views on the separation of religious and civil affairs even though they did not share his profound suspicion of all government power. The constitution's prohibition of religious tests offered the opportunity to accomplish at the national level what could not, as Adams noted, be accomplished in the near future against the forces of religious orthodoxy in many states. At the Constitutional Convention, many southern delegates in the Jeffersonian camp were from states whose politics, like Virginia's, were strongly influenced by a combination of Enlightenment rationalism and dissident evangelical Protestantism. These delegates were virtually unanimous in their support of the ban on religious tests for public offices.

The second explicit secularist constitutional provision is of course the First Amendment to the Bill of Rights, ratified in 1791, with its

---

*Distinct political parties did not take shape until George Washington assumed the presidency in 1789. Washington was of course the head of the Federalist Party and Thomas Jefferson became the leader of the Democratic Republican Party, the ancestor of today's Democratic Party. At the time, Jeffersonians called themselves "Republicans" or "Democratic Republicans." The "Republican" was dropped from the party name in 1828.

declaration that "Congress shall make no law respecting an establishment of religion, or prohibiting the free exercise thereof; or abridging the freedom of speech, or of the press; or the right of the people peaceably to assemble, and to petition the Government for a redress of grievances." The First Amendment's "establishment clause," as it is called by legal scholars, is often cited by religious conservatives as evidence that the founders wished only to protect religion from government—not government from religion. It is true that the entire Bill of Rights was written to prevent the government from infringing on individual liberties, of which freedom of religion, speech, and the press were first among equals; the establishment clause is no exception. But the First Amendment's prohibition against government interference with religious liberty cannot be detached from the body of the Constitution, with its prohibition against religious tests for public office. Furthermore, the framers of the Bill of Rights hoped that the First Amendment would encourage other states to follow Virginia's example and establish complete separation between religious and civil authority. Thus Madison proposed in 1791 that the Bill of Rights specifically prohibit states from passing any law interfering with freedom of conscience. He did not succeed in persuading Congress to go along with what would then have been an unprecedented and unacceptable expansion of federal power; the states would remain free to pass their own laws regarding relations between church and state. (The Fourteenth Amendment, passed in 1868 to extend civil rights to newly freed slaves, provides that no state shall deprive its citizens of "equal protection of the laws." Not until the 1930s was the equal protection clause invoked in an effort to force states to honor federal constitutional guarantees of religious liberty and separation of church and state—finally achieving what Madison had proposed 140 years earlier.)

Without downgrading the importance of either the establishment clause or the constitutional ban on religious tests for officeholders, one can make a strong case that the omission of one word—*God*— played an even more important role in the construction of a secularist foundation for the new government. The Constitution's silence on the

deity broke not only with culturally and historically distant precedents but with proximate and recent American precedents—most
notably the 1781 Articles of Confederation, which acknowledged the
beneficence of "the Great Governor of the World." With its refusal to
invoke any form of divine sanction, even the vague deistic "Providence," the Constitution went even farther than Virginia's religious
freedom act in separating religion from government. Perhaps surprisingly, the omission of God was not a major source of controversy at
the Constitutional Convention. In the first place, delegates from the
more religiously conservative states, like Massachusetts, knew that
whatever the federal Constitution said, most public policies toward
religion would be crafted at the state level. Furthermore, the most
serious obstacles to a federal union were slavery and the fear of less
populous states that their interests would be disregarded by a government weighted in favor of larger, more heavily populated, and more
prosperous states. Preoccupied with hammering out an apportion-
ment formula declaring a slave the equivalent of three-fifths of a free
man, the delegates had little time to concern themselves with power
emanating from the celestial regions. God, unlike enslaved humans,
was not a deal breaker.

But the secularism of the Constitution did produce substantial
controversy during the ratification debates conducted by state conventions. The framers were denounced by religious traditionalists
both for the Constitution's ban on religious tests for public office and
for its failure to acknowledge God as the ultimate governmental
authority. The opposition to article 6 frequently took an anti-Semitic
and anti-Catholic tone. At the Massachusetts convention, one speaker
warned that unless the chief executive was required to take a religious
oath, "a Turk, a Jew, a Roman Catholic, and what is worse than all, a
Universalist, may be President of the United States." In the *New York
Daily Advertiser*, a writer noted that since the president was desig-
nated commander in chief of the armed forces, "should he thereafter
be a Jew our dear posterity may be ordered to rebuild Jerusalem."[25]

But the omission of God elicited the most inflamed rhetoric. The
Reverend John M. Mason, a fiery New York Federalist who did not

share John Adams's views, declared the absence of God in the Constitution "an omission which no pretext whatever can palliate." If American citizens should prove as irreligious as the Constitution, the Reverend Mr. Mason warned, "we will have every reason to tremble, lest the Governor of the universe, who will not be treated with indignity by a people more than by individuals, overturn from its foundations the fabric we have been rearing, and crush us to atoms in the wreck."[26] In Boston, one opponent or ratification predicted that the United States would suffer the fate foretold by the prophet Samuel for King Saul—"because thou hast rejected the word of the Lord, he has also rejected thee (I Samuel 15:23)." Another correspondent argued in the *Massachusetts Gazette* of March 7, 1788, that "it is more difficult to build an elegant house without tools to work with, than it is to establish a durable government without the publick protection of religion."[27]

Support for the secularism of the Constitution came from the by-then familiar coalition of Enlightenment rationalists and dissident Protestants. The stance of evangelical Protestants, who feared that any government endorsement of religion might lead to government control of religion, was most forcefully advocated in Massachusetts by the Reverend Isaac Backus, a prominent Baptist minister who shared the views of his fellow evangelicals in Virginia. "Nothing is more evident," he emphasized, "than that religion is ever a matter between God and individuals; and therefore, no man or men can impose any religious test without invading the essential prerogatives of our Lord Jesus Christ." Reaching the same conclusion from an entirely different perspective, an Enlightenment rationalist who signed himself "Elihu" praised the founders for their refusal to "dazzle even the superstitious, by a hint about grace or ghostly knowledge." The authors of the Constitution, Elihu asserted, "come to us in the plain language of common sense, and propose to our understanding a system of government, as the invention of mere human wisdom; no deity comes down to dictate it, not even a God in a dream to propose any part of it."[28]

Although there were numerous attempts by state ratifying conventions to amend the Constitution, and subvert the intent of the preamble, by declaring that governmental power was derived from God or

Jesus Christ, the proposed religious amendments were defeated. In the end, the economic necessity for a federal union trumped all other concerns. And as Jefferson and Madison had hoped, the Constitution influenced many states, if not all, to reconsider the religious restrictions in their own constitutions. The proper relationship between church and state, like the even more volatile issue of slavery, proved a recurrent source of contention as the frontier moved westward and new states were admitted to the union. Virginia's religious freedom act remained an influential model as the various states—some much more rapidly than others—expanded their definitions of religious liberty. Nowhere was the influence of Jefferson greater than in Kentucky, which in 1792 became the fifteenth state to enter the union. As in Virginia, evangelicals and secularists combined to form a majority in favor of religious liberty and separation of church and state. Between 1789 and 1792, South Carolina and Georgia also followed the Virginia model and removed all religious barriers from their constitutions. Delaware abandoned its requirement that officeholders take an oath attesting to their belief in the Trinity, and Pennsylvania changed its constitution to allow Jews (but not atheists) to hold office. The new Pennsylvania oath of office required that a man swear to his belief both in God and in an afterlife involving rewards and punishments. The other eight of the original thirteen states took decades longer to arrive at anything approaching complete separation of church and state. When Connecticut finally disestablished the Congregationalist Church in 1818, Jefferson, in a letter to Adams, could not contain his joy at the news that "this den of the priesthood is at last broken up, and that a protestant popedom is no longer to disgrace the American history and character."[29] Adams and Jefferson shared the hope that Connecticut's religious liberalization would influence Massachusetts to follow suit. Before Connecticut's action, Jefferson had considered both states "the last retreat of Monkish darkness, bigotry, and abhorrence of those advances of the mind which had carried the other states a century ahead of them. They still seemed to be exactly where their forefathers were . . . and to consider, as dangerous heresies, all innovations good or bad."[30] However, Jefferson's and

Adams's hopes for greater liberalization in the New England states would not be realized in their lifetimes. Massachusetts would not strike all religious restrictions from its laws until 1833—seven years after Adams's death—and Connecticut would withhold equal rights from Jews for another ten years after that.

Although the pace of change in customary religious arrangements seemed glacial to those members of the revolutionary generation most committed to Enlightenment values, what is striking from a twenty-first-century perspective is the speed with which many Americans came to support a freedom of thought and religious practice that overturned millennia of religious authoritarianism. Even when legal barriers to full civic equality remained, as they did for Jews in most states, the first eight years of the American republic were characterized by a de facto expansion of liberty for nonbelievers as well as for dissident religious believers, for non-Christians and Christians alike. As President Washington noted in his extraordinary 1790 letter to the Jewish community of Newport, Rhode Island, this liberty was seen by representatives of the American Enlightenment not as a grudging concession or even as a generous gift from the American government but as a right. "All possess alike liberty of conscience and immunity of citizenship," Washington wrote. "It is now no more that toleration is spoken of, as if it was by the indulgence of one class of people, that another enjoyed the exercise of their inherent natural rights. For happily the Government of the United States, which gives to bigotry no sanction, to persecution no assistance requires only that they who live under its protection should demean themselves as good citizens. . . . May the children of the Stock of Abraham, who dwell in this land, continue to merit and enjoy the good will of the other inhabitants, while every one shall sit in safety under his own vine and fig tree, and there shall be none to make him afraid."[31]

It is a remarkable demonstration of the framers' faith in their secularist constitution that Washington could speak with such assurance only a year after ratification—and a year before the Bill of Rights was adopted. The president's encouraging and egalitarian response to the Jews of Newport also offers powerful evidence against the religious right's contention that the founders intended to establish a Christian nation. The absurdity of the claim that the framers somehow over-looked, or misunderstood, the political and religious implications of leaving God out of the nation's founding document is borne out not only by Washington's matter-of-fact assumption of the distinction between religious affiliation and citizenship but by the intensity and clarity of the public debate that preceded ratification of the Constitu-tion. The founders knew exactly what they were doing, and so did their fellow citizens on both sides of the issue. Conservative clergymen like Mason denounced the godlessness of the Constitution precisely because they understood that it did indeed pose an obstacle not only to government interference with religion but to religious interference with government. The assertion that America was founded as a Chris-tian nation would have some validity if—*if only*, in the view of some right-wing extremists—the nation had remained a group of loosely linked states, forever free to continue the theocratic arrangements of the past. The religiously correct are forced to explain away the Consti-tution's omission of God by portraying the framers as so godly that any mention of the Supreme Being in the Constitution would have been as superfluous as acknowledging the sky overhead. In this tor-tured and anachronistic argument, the mere mention of a divinity—as in "the Laws of Nature and of Nature's God"—proves that Jefferson and the other signers of the Declaration of Independence were not only believers in religious liberty but Believers with a capital *B*. The image of the founders as devoutly religious men is an integral and nec-essary element of modern religious correctness: if rationalism and humanism permeated the character and thought of the iconic revolu-tionary figures, it becomes much more difficult to construct a modern scenario in which secularism is portrayed as un-American.

What is undeniable is that the seeds of America's continuing discord over whether this is a secularist or a religious nation were planted dur-ing the period when the legal foundation for the world's first secular government was laid. The fruitful but philosophically uneasy alliance between Enlightenment rationalists and evangelical Christians ensured continuing controversy over the proper degree and precise meaning of separation between church and state. In the late eighteenth century, evangelicals were still a minority—albeit an influential one—among Americans of faith, and they recognized that any laws favoring an established church would impede their own ability to gain converts and impress their values on the larger society. Many evangelicals did cherish a deep and sincere belief that any government involvement with religion was an insult to God and to the supremacy of individual conscience. But they were also acting out of realpolitik, biding their time until their growing numbers would translate into greater political influence and the ability to convince legislators that particular religious views—theirs—ought to be enshrined in general law. They soon joined more conservative religious forces in backing state laws like those compelling Sabbath observance. Nor did the evangelicals agree with the Enlightenment rationalists on the fundamental importance of secular public education—a debate, still in its infancy at the end of the revolutionary century, that has never ended.

In 1791, with the Constitution and the Bill of Rights in place, America's revolutionary secularists looked forward to a future in which the spread of literacy, knowledge, and individual liberty would prove more powerful than reactionary, long-entrenched political and religious institutions. They did not anticipate the tenacity of religious orthodoxy, or what would today be called religious fundamentalism, in American life. What they had accomplished was the establishment of a government that respected, and in many ways mirrored, the balance between Enlightenment rationalism and religion in the larger society. Americans lived no longer in an age of faith but in an age of faiths and an age of reason.

The Age of Reason and Unreason

Talking against Religion is unchaining a Tyger;
The Beast let loose may worry his Deliverer.
—BENJAMIN FRANKLIN,
Poor Richard's Almanack, 1751

In his preface to *The Age of Reason,* addressed from Paris in 1794 "to my fellow citizens of the United States of America," Thomas Paine recalled that even before America declared its independence from Britain, he had envisioned "the exceeding probability that a revolution in the system of government would be followed by a revolution in the system of religion." It was not to be—not, at any rate, in the sense Paine intended. America's revolution did separate church and state, but it did not replace conventional religion, based on belief in the supernatural, with a humanism rooted in rationality and the laws of nature. By the turn of the century, America entered its first cycle of reaction against the nation's recent secularist heritage—even as the freethought movement expanded and exerted a secularizing and liberalizing influence on a growing number of citizens. This combination of religious reaction with continuing assaults on religious orthodoxy became one of the defining cultural characteristics of the new republic.

In the early 1800s, the author of "Common Sense"—which had sold some 500,000 copies in the mid-1770s—would be castigated as a

Judas, reptile, hog, mad dog, souse, louse, archbeast, brute, liar, and of course infidel. The archbeast had earned not a penny from his most famous revolutionary pamphlet, because he allowed his words to be published freely in order to further the cause of independence—a sacrifice that made no difference to his detractors. In 1797, a scurrilous "biography," published by the Englishman William Cobbett, attested to the transformation of Paine from revered patriot into devil's spawn in little more than twenty years. "How Tom gets a living now, or what brothel he inhabits," the author exulted, "I know not, nor does it much signify. He has done all the mischief he can do in this world; and whether his carcass is at last to be suffered to rot on the earth, or to be dried in the air, is of very little consequence. . . . Like Judas, he will be remembered by posterity; men will learn to express all that is base, malignant, treacherous, unnatural, and blasphemous by the single monosyllable of Paine."[1] Cobbett, who arrived in the United States in 1792 and stayed for some years before returning to England as a social reformer, eventually changed his mind about Paine after actually reading his books—something he had neglected to do before publishing the biography.

Although Paine's economic and political ideas were too radical for some of his contemporaries, his jaundiced view of religion proved the primary cause of his fall from American grace. The shunning of Paine, who was still revered by small groups of freethinkers in pre–Civil War America but whose reputation was not truly revived until the "golden age of freethought" in the last three decades of the nineteenth century, offers what is in many respects a paradigm of America's periodic and powerful impulse to deny the importance of the secularist contribution to the building of the nation.

Born in Norfolk, England, in 1737, Paine was the son of a Quaker father and an Anglican mother—a mixed religious background, unusual among his contemporaries, that could well have contributed to his lifelong hatred of state-established churches. He left school at age thirteen to work in his father's corset-making establishment, then ran away at sixteen to go to sea. As a young man patching together a livelihood from a variety of poorly paid jobs, which included making stays for corsets, part-time teaching, and collecting excise taxes for the Crown, Paine somehow managed to buy the books he needed to improve on his rudimentary formal education. (His lifelong indebtedness was often attributed to his fondness for drink, but perhaps a fondness for books was the real culprit.) As a tax collector, Paine had ample opportunity to observe economic and social injustice in England, and he involved himself in a cause that foreshadowed his later preoccupations as a writer and radical thinker. Indignant that English Jews were obliged to pay taxes but not allowed to vote, Paine forcefully and publicly articulated his views in coffeehouse debates. Depriving Jews of legal rights, he declared in what was then a novel argument, violated the natural rights of man. Word of this troublemaking on behalf of Jews reached Paine's superiors in the tax administration, who ordered him "to cease all religious and political controversy" or face the consequences. Shortly thereafter, Paine took on another battle when he lobbied Parliament on behalf of salary increases for the poorly paid "excisemen." Having ignored the order to avoid controversy, he was, predictably, fired.

Benjamin Franklin, then representing the interests of the colony of Pennsylvania in London, was introduced to Paine by the only excise commissioner who had been sympathetic to his arguments before Parliament. Franklin convinced Paine that a man of his talents and distaste for authority would be better off in America. Jobless and penniless, His Majesty's former tax collector arrived in Philadelphia in 1774 with just two assets—his pen and a letter of recommendation from Franklin. Within a matter of months, Paine would find both his public voice and a receptive American audience. His first article, published in March 1775 in the *Pennsylvania Journal and Weekly Advertiser*, was a denunciation of slavery. Paine regarded it as particularly ironic that Americans should complain with increasing vociferousness of injustices done them by Britain while the colonists themselves enslaved other men. Six weeks after the article was published, the first antislavery society in America was established in Philadelphia, with Paine as a founding member. Certain that American independence would lead as inevitably to the abolition of slavery as to a revolution in religion, the English immigrant soon became one of the most ardent and articulate advocates of rebellion against England.

By December 1776, after the publication of Paine's legendary call to arms in "Common Sense," the thirty-nine-year-old patriotic propagandist, determined to bear firsthand witness to the struggle for independence, was immersed in the wartime travails of his adopted country. As legend has it, Paine was shivering by a New Jersey campfire with the beleaguered troops under George Washington's command when he placed a sheet of paper on top of a drumhead and wrote the sentence "These are the times that try men's souls." As soon as he finished writing, Paine rushed the first installment of "The American Crisis" to a publisher in Philadelphia. It is fact, not legend, that the stirring words were first read aloud on Christmas Eve, upon orders from General Washington, to the apprehensive young men preparing to cross the Delaware River and mount a surprise attack on the Hessians at Trenton.

Contemporary accounts agree that Paine's rallying cry had a galvanizing effect on soldiers who, in retreat after being routed by the British in the Battle of Long Island, feared that the revolutionary cause was lost. As familiar as the words have become today, it is nonetheless easy to imagine how heartening it must have been for Americans to hear, for the first time, that "tyranny, like hell, is not easily conquered; yet we have this consolation with us, that the harder the conflict, the more glorious the triumph." What would have been hard to imagine in 1776 was the reversal of fortune that awaited the much-acclaimed author.

Paine's reputation in America slowly began to change with the publication in 1791 of *The Rights of Man*, a defense of the French Revolution and a scathing critique of hereditary privilege and all forms of monarchy. Only two years earlier, many Americans had celebrated the news of the storming of the Bastille and the publication of the French Declaration of the Rights of Man, which so closely resembled the Declaration of Independence in its Enlightenment sentiments. The public remembered, and was grateful to, those Frenchmen who had provided military and diplomatic assistance to the revolutionary cause. The Marquis de Lafayette, who served as a general under Washington, was wounded at the Battle of Brandywine, and shared the hardships of the American troops during the bitter winter at Valley Forge, was an American hero. The secularists among the founders acknowledged their debt to French Enlightenment thought, and the French reciprocated by lionizing American luminaries, especially the Francophiles Franklin and Jefferson, who had represented American interests in Paris during and after the war. The near feudalism of France's ancien régime, dominated by the monarchy and the Catholic Church, reinforced the initially positive American response to the French Revolution. Many Americans also applauded the new French National Assembly's nationalization of church properties—not only because separation of church and state was enshrined in the U.S. Constitution but because many American Protestants were strongly anti-Catholic and the properties in question had belonged to the Church of Rome. But by 1791, Americans' identification with the French Revolution had begun to weaken—the first of many turnabouts in what would become a permanent love-hate relationship. Frightening firsthand accounts of mob violence and destruction of property crossed the Atlantic after French nobles began fleeing for their lives to England. King Louis XVI and Marie Antoinette, prevented from escaping across the English Channel, were prisoners of the revolutionary government. It was an inauspicious time for publication of a book defending a revolution that, in the view of at least some Americans, seemed out of control.

Paine had written *The Rights of Man* in England, where he settled in 1787 for what was intended to be a visit but turned into a stay of several years. The first part of the book, published in London in 1791, was a reply to the conservative British statesman Edmund Burke's famous indictment of the French Revolution, *Reflections on the Revolution in France* (1790). Accompanied by a letter of endorsement from Jefferson, part 1 was printed in America and France shortly after its London publication. By then, English feeling against the French Revolution—with its obvious implications for the British monarchy—was running high, and Paine soon fled, in a reversal of the journey being made by terrified French nobles, for what he thought would be the more hospitable shores of revolutionary France. Indeed, English sentiment was so against Paine that he was tried and convicted of sedition in absentia, barred from ever returning to the country of his birth, and burned in effigy. His books, too, were burned, often atop a scaffold that the incendiaries considered a fitting place for the author as well as his works. As a result of Paine's sedition conviction, part 2 of *The Rights of Man*, published in France and America in 1792, was not published in London.

In America, the reception of *The Rights of Man* was more positive—though decidedly mixed. Americans still agreed with Paine's antimonarchical arguments, having acted on them so decisively in the recent past, even if they did not approve of the violence and social disorder overtaking France. Indeed, Paine dedicated the first volume to Washington, whose personal modesty and devotion to representative government presented such a pointed contrast to the behavior of the monarchs of Europe. But most members of Washington's Federalist Party strongly objected to Paine's linkage between the American and French revolutions, considering the latter far too violent and too radical in its approach to established institutions. It was this issue that first created a breach—which developed into a chasm during the bitter presidential campaign of 1800—between Jefferson and Adams. For the most part, though, the debate over *The Rights of Man* was confined to America's governing elite; there is little evidence that the book greatly damaged Paine's reputation among the ordinary literate Americans who had been stirred only fifteen years earlier by his patriotic exhortations. What the book's mixed reception did accomplish was to knock the author down from the revolutionary pedestal he had previously occupied. Criticism of *The Rights of Man* prepared the way for the more savage and widespread attacks directed at *The Age of Reason*, which assailed organized religion in general and Christianity in particular.

Part 1 of *The Age of Reason* was written in Paris in 1793—in haste, because although Paine had originally been lionized by the French as a true ally in the cause of *liberté, égalité, fraternité*, he soon became disillusioned by the increasing violence of the revolution. When Paine declared his opposition to the execution of Louis XVI, he placed his own life in imminent danger. Arrested on Robespierre's orders, Paine was able to deliver the manuscript to his friend Joel Barlow, who was also a close friend of Jefferson's, while en route to the Luxembourg Prison on December 28, 1793. In one of the more disgraceful manifestations of ingratitude by any American administration, Paine was left for more than nine months to rot in prison—literally, because he almost died of a suppurating ulcer. Gouverneur Morris, the American minister to France from 1792 to 1794, detested Paine's views on both religion and politics and misled the French by informing them that the United States did not recognize the English-born Paine's claim to American citizenship. At the same time, Morris persuaded President Washington—who, though he, too, disagreed with Paine's economic views, recognized his debt to the man whose writings had inspired widespread popular support for the revolutionary cause—that he was doing everything possible to obtain Paine's release. Only when the freethinking James Monroe replaced Morris as minister to France did the American government exert its influence to obtain Paine's freedom. Paine wrote part 2 of *The Age of Reason* while recovering from his severe ulcerative illness in Monroe's home; at the time of Paine's release from prison, his condition was so grave that Monroe did not expect him to live. In his preface to part 2, Paine demonstrated that he belongs to the select company of political idealists who do not take refuge in illusions when they see that their ideals have been betrayed. Recalling his imprisonment and the fate of many friends who went directly from prison to the guillotine, the author declared that the "intolerant spirit of Church persecutions had transferred itself into politics; the tribunal styled revolutionary supplied the place of an inquisition; and the guillotine of the stake."

Paine was to remain in Paris until his old friend Jefferson was elected the nation's first Democratic Republican president. In 1802, Jefferson invited Paine to return home on an American ship and assured him that his abandonment by American emissaries during the Jacobin period did not reflect the true sentiments of the American people. But *The Age of Reason*, with its attacks not only on ecclesiastical hierarchies but on all religious beliefs at odds with science and rational thought, had in fact created many enemies for Paine in America. Although the text repeatedly affirms Paine's belief in some form of deity, it is nevertheless easy to understand what so enraged the defenders of institutionalized religion on both sides of the ocean:

> Every national church or religion has established itself by pretending some special mission from God, communicated to certain individuals. The Jews have their Moses; the Christians their Jesus Christ, their apostles and saints; and the Turks their Mahomet, as if the way to God were not open to every man alike.

> Each of these churches show certain books, which they call *revelation*, or the Word of God. The Jews say that their Word of God was given by God to Moses; face to face; the Christians say that their Word of God came by divine inspiration; and the Turks say that their Word of God (the Koran) was brought by an angel from heaven. Each of those churches accuses the other of unbelief; and for my own part, I disbelieve them all.[2]

Paine was surprised by the venom that awaited him when he took Jefferson up on his invitation. The revolution's greatest publicist was greeted in the press—especially the Federalist press, which seized on Paine's "infidelity" as a weapon to use against Jefferson—by admonitions to shut up, return to the Old World, or prepare to endure his just punishment in the next world. "And having spent a lengthy life in evil / Return again unto thy parent Devil" was a typical piece of advice from a New York newspaper—even though, or perhaps because, New York had become one of the centers of deist activity flourishing in the midst of the orthodox backlash.

The America Paine found when he returned in 1802 was far less hospitable to secularists in a public capacity than the America Paine had left fifteen years earlier. Had the Constitution been written in 1797 instead of 1787, it is entirely possible that God, not "we, the people," would have been credited with supreme governmental authority. Yet the revival of religious conservatism around the turn of the century, like the rise of Enlightenment liberalism in the second half of the 1700s, was an uneven process fraught with anomalies and ironies—the most obvious being the apparent contradiction between the renewal of religious conservatism and the political victory of Jefferson, the nation's best-known freethinker and deist, in the 1800 election. Throughout their presidencies, Jefferson and his successor, Madison, never ceased to uphold the separation of church and state they had conceived as a model for the new nation. But their views on orthodox religion had become a political liability, and they knew it. Jefferson, unlike Washington and Adams, refused to issue presidential proclamations of thanksgiving to God, often requested on official occasions by the evangelical churches that had played such an important role in passage of the Virginia religious freedom act and ratification of the Constitution. But Jefferson was careful to couch his refusals in terms that emphasized his opposition to government intrusion on religious prerogatives rather than to religious intrusion on government. A secular leader who made quasi-religious proclamations, Jefferson insisted, was not only violating the First Amendment but exceeding his civil authority by usurping a function that properly belonged to churches. Even so, Jefferson's undeserved reputation as an atheist and his deserved reputation as a deist were used against him by his political opponents before, during, and after the presidential campaign of

1800. Attacks on Jefferson the infidel were sharper, and more effective politically, than the rumors of his relationship with his slave and mistress, Sally Hemings.

While many prominent Federalists, including Washington and Adams, were far removed from religious orthodoxy and fully shared Jefferson's views on the separation of civil government from religion, the party had more than its share of conservative church spokesmen. All Federalists were not religious conservatives, but nearly all religious conservatives were Federalists. In 1796, when the Federalist John Adams took office as president, with the Democratic Republican Jefferson as his vice president,* the ardent Federalist minister Jedidiah Champion of Litchfield, Connecticut, offered an admiring prayer for the welfare of President-elect Adams and then added pointedly on Jefferson's behalf, "O Lord! wilt Thou bestow upon the Vice President a double portion of Thy grace, *for Thou knowest he needs it.*"[3]

In the 1800 campaign, Jefferson's own writings on the subject of religion were repeatedly used against him. One famous passage from *Notes on Virginia* (1784) was most commonly cited as proof of Jefferson's religious infidelity and unfitness for office. "The legitimate powers of government extend only to such acts as are injurious to others," Jefferson wrote. "But it does me no injury for my neighbor to say there are twenty gods, or no God. It neither picks my pocket nor breaks my leg."[4] Jefferson went on to argue:

> Difference of opinion is advantageous in religion. The several sects form a *censor morum* over each other. Is uniformity attainable?

---

*Until the Twelfth Amendment took effect in 1804, the Constitution specified that the presidential runner-up would automatically be named vice president by the electoral college. Hence, Jefferson—who lost the 1796 election to Adams—served as his vice president. Beginning in 1804, electors voted separately for the president and vice president, thereby ending a system in which political enemies might hold the nation's two top offices—and in which the death of a sitting president could nullify the voters' wishes by turning over the White House to the party defeated in the previous election. Since then, electors have voted for the vice presidential candidate of the president's party—the party ticket, as it is now known.

Millions of innocent men, women, and children, since the introduction of Christianity, have been burnt, tortured, fined, imprisoned; yet we have not advanced one inch towards uniformity. What
have been the effects of coercion? To make one half of the world
fools, and the other half hypocrites. To support roguery and terror
all over the earth. Let us reflect that it is inhabited by a thousand
millions of people. That these profess probably a thousand different systems of religion. That ours is but one of that thousand.[5]

John Mason, the New York minister who warned in 1793 of the
divine retribution awaiting America as a result of its godless constitution, turned his oratorical powers on Jefferson in 1800. He castigated Jefferson's religious views as "the morality of devils, which
would break in an instant every link in the chain of human friendship, and transform the globe into one scene of desolation and horror, where fiend would prowl with fiend for plunder and blood—yet
atheism 'neither picks my pocket nor breaks my leg.' I will not abuse
you by asking, whether the author of such an opinion can be a
Christian?"[6]

The failure of the Federalists to defeat Jefferson by linking him
with atheism is attributable in part to the high personal esteem in
which the author of the Declaration of Independence continued to be
held and in part to other political issues, among them the assault on
the First Amendment represented by the Alien and Sedition Acts.*
Another vital factor in Jefferson's election was the support of evangelical Christians, who had been his staunch allies since the debate over
Virginia's religious freedom act in the mid-1780s. Although evangelicals, many of whom believed in a literal interpretation of the Bible,

---

*The Alien and Sedition Acts were passed by the Federalist-controlled Congress,
with the support of President Adams, in 1798. The Sedition Act imposed broad
prohibitions on written and spoken criticism of the government, virtually nullify-
ing the First Amendment. Several Republican editors were tried and convicted
under the law. Ostensibly enacted in response to hostile acts by the French revolutionary government, the laws were intended to silence Jeffersonian Republicans
and destroy their party. After Jefferson's election, the new Republican-controlled
Congress allowed the Sedition Act to expire.

were far removed from Jefferson's deist views, they were nevertheless profoundly offended by the Federalist attempt to turn the candidate's private religious beliefs into a public issue. At the same time—another irony of the early 1800s—the passionate proselytizing of evangelicals was playing an important role in the reaction against freethought. Historians of American religion generally date the "Second Great Awakening" from around 1805, but popular revival movements began to crop up during and immediately after the Revolution, from New England to the Deep South.

The historian G. Adolph Koch argues convincingly in *Republican Religion* (1933) that the grassroots resurgence of theological conservatism at the turn of the century was largely the work of Baptists, Methodists, and Presbyterians, whose membership was composed primarily of Jeffersonian Republicans rather than of the wealthier, and politically more conservative, Congregationalists like Timothy Dwight. "The same uncalculating and unreasoning emotionalism which had characterized the exuberant American republicanism in the heyday of the French revolution was decorously transferred to a new channel—evangelical revivalism," Koch asserts.[7] That many Americans could embrace evangelical revivalism while voting for the deist Jefferson attests to the widespread acceptance of separation of church and state in the young republic.

The resurgence of religious conservatism in the late 1790s and early 1800s was essentially a social rather than a political phenomenon, although the ideas of that era's theological and social conservatives would have a lasting impact on American political thought. At the turn of the revolutionary century, Americans had recently lived through and were continuing to cope with extraordinary changes affecting their daily lives as well as their view of the world. Even when revolutions are welcomed by the majority, they tend to generate social instability and a longing for the anchors of former times. The American Revolution, though it did not, and was never intended to, overturn established economic arrangements and class distinctions, was no exception. As early as 1789, conservatives were issuing warnings of a deist-atheist-radical conspiracy. The prominent geographer and minister Jedidiah Morse decried freethinkers and deists—along with anti-Federalists, Freemasons, dissatisfied farmers, and debtors trying to avoid paying what they owed—as integral components of a "conspiracy against *all* Religions and Governments."[8] In many respects, the challenge to religious orthodoxy became a symbol of all the other disruptions in social order. In 1793, Lyman Beecher, who would become one of the most influential ministers of the nineteenth century, entered Yale College and found it in a most "ungodly state," characterized not only by religious skepticism but by a whole range of social vices. Beecher reported that "rowdies were plenty," wine and liquor flowed freely, and "intemperance, profanity, gambling, and licentiousness were common." All of this he blamed on the prevalence of religious heresy:

> That was the day of the infidelity of the Tom Paine school. Boys that dressed flax in the barn, as I used to, read Tom Paine and believed him; I read, and fought him all the way. Never had any propensity to infidelity. But most of the class before me were infidels, and called each other Voltaire, Rousseau, D'Alembert, etc., etc.[9]

This passage clearly demonstrates the emerging conservative linkage between private vices and public irreligion and between religious infidelity and the French Enlightenment. Infidelity, in turn, became conflated with French revolutionary terror. As Beecher's allusions to Voltaire and Rousseau indicate, French names had become a kind of shorthand for freethought and deism. The very fact of having lived in France—of having had the opportunity to be corrupted by direct contact with infidels like Voltaire—became a political accusation in the 1790s.

In reality, the religious skepticism displayed by "boys that dressed flax in the barn" could not be blamed solely on heretical notions originating on the other side of the Atlantic. The Reverend Timothy Dwight, a grandson of the severe theologian Jonathan Edwards (whose best-known sermon was titled "Sinners in the Hands of an Angry God"), assumed the presidency of Yale in 1795 and emphasized the role of peer pressure in the spread of religious infidelity. In a speech to the class of '97 he asserted that "the fashionable bias of the present time will be readily acknowledged to be unfavorable to Christianity." That fashionableness had made infidelity particularly attractive to the young, he warned:

> At home, you will see one decent or doubtful person, and another, sliding slowly down the declivity of irreligion, and many, more heedless, or more daring, leaping at once into the gulph beneath. Here, a companion will turn his back, and walk no more with Christ. There, a Parent, or Instructor, will forsake him, having loved the present world. Among these will frequently be found the gay, the pleasing, and the accomplished; and in some instances, the grave, the learned, and the honourable. On one side, the temptation will charm; on the other it will sanction. Allured, awed, supported, perhaps without a friend at hand to pluck you by the arm, or to point to you either the danger or the means of escaping it, it can scarcely be hoped, that none of you will be destroyed. Most of the Infidels, whom I have known, have fallen a sacrifice to this cause, or to the fear of ridicule.[10]

Dwight had already thrown down the gauntlet against deism, which he regarded as atheism by another name. In the widely circulated satirical poem "The Triumph of Infidelity" (1788), he declared that the eighteenth century had seen "New gates of falsehood opened on mankind, / New Paths to ruin strew'd with Flowers divine, / And other aids, and motives, gain'd to sin." As Beecher recounted in his autobiography, his Yale contemporaries thought that the college faculty would oppose free discussion of religion, but "when they handed Dr. Dwight a list of subjects for class disputation, to their surprise he selected this: 'Is the Bible the word of God?' and told them to do their best." So persuasive were Dwight's responses, according to Beecher, that the college was soon cleansed of freethought. "He heard all they had to say, answered them, and there was an end. He preached incessantly for six months on the subject, and all infidelity skulked and hid its head."[11] Skulking would seem to have been the prudent course for any heretical student at Yale during Dwight's tenure, since he personally delivered more than two hundred sermons to undergraduates on the dangers of religious infidelity. One of his most memorable perorations proclaimed the immorality of smallpox vaccination, introduced by Dr. William Jenner in 1796. An earlier form of inoculation against smallpox had been employed by progressive, educated New Englanders like the Adams family since the 1760s. In a departure from the general eighteenth-century approval of scientific advances—a predilection of many orthodox believers as well as freethinkers—Dwight argued that if God had decided from all eternity that an individual's fate was to die of smallpox, it was a sin to interfere with the divine plan through a man-made trick like vaccination.

Yet even as the defenders of orthodoxy mounted an attack on every form of Enlightenment rationalism, the secularist genie could not be stuffed back into the bottle. Many of the freethinking tempters whom Dwight described as "the grave, the learned, and the honourable" could be found within the American clergy itself. Nothing was more horrifying to those who still preached Calvinist predestination than the transformation, beginning in the late eighteenth century, of many of New England's Puritan-founded Congregationalist churches into much more liberal and rationalist Unitarian fellowships, which rejected not only predestination but a wide variety of orthodox Christian tenets, including the doctrine of the Holy Trinity. The ministers who led this transformation were American originals, men of both passion and moderation, combining a philosophical commitment to natural rights with a pragmatic reliance on empirical knowledge.

One of the most engaging (and, like so many other figures in this history, long-forgotten) leaders of the Unitarian metamorphosis was the Reverend William Bentley, pastor of the East Church in Salem, Massachusetts, from 1783 until his death in 1819. By the time Bentley took up his duties in Salem, the memory of the 1692 witch trials had receded and the mercantile, seafaring town had become one of the more cosmopolitan, intellectually open communities in America—a striking example of the evolution of secularism in the revolutionary century. Even at the height of the witch hysteria, Salem was not a backward-looking Puritan stronghold but the Massachusetts Bay Colony's version of sin city. Indeed, the accusations of witchcraft originated not in Salem itself—even though that is where tourist monuments memorialize the events—but in what was once called Salem Village, a farming community a two-hour walk from the alluring and, by Puritan standards, bawdy town. The village had been settled west of Salem in order to supply the growing port's need for food, and the family feuds involved in the witchcraft trials stemmed, at least in part, from the envy of poorer farmers on the western edge of the settlement of their eastern neighbors, who had closer and more lucrative connections with the booming town.[12]

Bentley, a Jeffersonian Democratic Republican, held religious views closely resembling those articulated in Jefferson's *Philosophy of Jesus of Nazareth*, written during his first presidential term and motivated to some extent by his desire to deflect accusations of religious infidelity. Both Bentley and Jefferson believed in the goodness but not necessarily the divinity of Christ and in the ethics but not the authority of Christianity. A true man of the Enlightenment, Bentley had broad intellectual interests shared by his parishioners, many of whom were ship's captains and mariners whose voyages had taken them to China, Japan, India, Africa, and Persia. He was said to have mastered twenty languages, and his biographer reported that he spent approximately two hours a day reading to improve his proficiency: Monday was devoted to Greek; Tuesday to French; Wednesday to Latin; Thursday to Spanish and Italian; and Friday to German, Dutch, and Slavonic dialects. Saturday was reserved for Hebrew and Greek Scriptures, sources for his sermons. On the seventh day he rested.

The minister's remarkable diaries, which by themselves should have secured him a place in American cultural history, demonstrate his interest in literally everything: Hindu, Chinese, and Japanese art;

American Indian remains; botanical and marine specimens from around the world; coins; rare books; religions of every culture and country. Jefferson held Bentley in such high esteem that he offered him the presidency of the University of Virginia, but the minister declined the honor, explaining that he could not bear to leave his long-time parishioners in Salem.

The connection among freethinkers, Unitarians, and Universalists was such that many religious conservatives considered the liberal Protestant sects just another species of infidelity. Universalism, another dissident form of Protestantism that emerged in America in the late eighteenth century, maintained—in a reversal of the Calvinist predestination doctrine—that God intended every human being to be saved. Ministers like Bentley, by virtue of their position between orthodoxy and infidelity, did indeed play a significant role in the spread of freethought throughout their communities because they encouraged open discussion of all religious ideas. Bentley even offered his pulpit to a Catholic priest—an act of stunning iconoclasm in eighteenth-century New England—to explain the tenets of his faith to anyone who cared to listen. In a comical yet revealing 1787 diary entry headed "The danger of Loan of Books, for whose sentiments, you wish not to be accountable," Bentley described the consequences of his having loaned a copy of Ethan Allen's heretical *Reason the Only Oracle of Man* to a friend:

> *Allen's oracles o*   ⸱ given by J.W. Esq was lent to Col. C.
> under solemn p   but by him lent to a Mr. Grafton,
> who was repor   d Infidel. The book was
> found at his   ...ver, examined with horror by his
> female relati ... by them conveyed to a Mr. Williams, whose shop
> is remarkable for news, & therefore examined—reported to be
> mine from the initials W.B., viewed as an awful curiosity by hun-
> dreds, connected with a report that I encouraged infidelity in
> Grafton by my prayers with him in his dying hour, & upon the
> whole a terrible opposition to me fixed in the minds of the devout
> and ignorant multitude.[13]

The following year, when conservatives were insisting that the as yet unratified Constitution should include a religious test for public office, Bentley asked, "But what security is it to a government, that every public officer shall swear that he is a christian? . . . One man will declare that the Xtian religion is only an illumination of natural religion . . . another Christian will assert that all men must be happy thereafter in spite of themselves; a third Christian reverses the image, & declares that let a man do all he can, he will certainly be punished in another world. . . . Sir, the only evidence we can have of the sincerity and excellency of a man's religion, is a good life. . . . That man who acts an honest part toward his neighbour, will most probably conduct honorably toward the public."[14]

Between 1790 and 1830, approximately half of the tax-supported Congregationalist churches in Massachusetts were transformed into Unitarian congregations. Many historians have argued that the success of the Unitarian movement, which tended to attract the most educated members of New England communities, was an important and enduring factor in the greater acceptance of Christianity by influential Americans than by their counterparts in Europe.[15] Liberal Protestantism in America, by virtue of its opposition to state-established churches, fitted comfortably into and made a major contribution to the secularist foundations of the republic. Another way of looking at Unitarianism is that it moved religion itself into the camp of Enlightenment rationalism. Men like Bentley believed as deeply in freedom of thought and of speech as they did in freedom of conscience; at the core of their religion lay not an unquestioning faith but a deep reverence for the power of the human mind and the value of human doubt.

While Bentley and the Unitarians represented the most secular and most liberal end of the conventional religious spectrum, the American ministry in this period also produced radical freethinkers who broke with religion altogether. Elihu Palmer, an unruly deist who was even less acceptable to his contemporaries than his friend Paine, began his public career in 1787 as a Presbyterian minister in what is now the New York City borough of Queens, but he did not last long in the pulpit. A local historian with whom Palmer apparently stayed while he was recovering from a smallpox inoculation explained why. One evening, Palmer's host overheard him reciting a well-known, theologically orthodox couplet: "Lord I am vile, conceived in sin, / And born unholy and unclean." Palmer turned to a female guest and "declared that he did not believe a word, not one word.... Surprised at this announcement, she advised him not to give utterance to such sentiments in public, for people would not hear of it."[16] Palmer was dismissed from his pulpit in less than a year, moved to Philadelphia, and joined the Baptist Church in 1789. The Baptists kicked him out too, and he then announced both his allegiance to Universalism and his rejection of the divinity of Christ—even though Universalists at that time accepted the divinity of Jesus. Bentley had found a hospitable reception for unorthodox theological views among Salem's Unitarians, but Palmer and his small group of followers were soon banned in Philadelphia. Alerting and outraging the Christian citizenry, he imprudently placed a notice in a local publication of his intention to preach a sermon challenging the divinity of Jesus. His biographer later reported that "the society of Universalists were in an uproar; and being joined by people of other denominations, instigated probably by their priests, an immense mob assembled at an early hour before the Universalist Church, which Mr. Palmer was unable to enter. In fact, it is stated, that he was in personal danger, and was induced to quit the city, somewhat in the stile of the ancient apostles upon similar occasions."[17] Wisely deciding that his prospects in any ministry were nil, Palmer took up the study of law and passed the bar in 1793. Unfortunately, and mystifyingly, since his local notoriety would seem to have augured ill for the practice of law in Philadelphia, Palmer returned to the city in 1793. A few months later, the nation's first epidemic of yellow fever took more than five thousand lives. Palmer's wife was among the dead, and although he survived, his sight was destroyed. His enemies naturally saw his blindness as God's punishment for heresy, notwithstanding the thousands of fresh graves housing the corpses of pious churchgoers.

Since blindness had put an end to his hopes of a legal career, Palmer took to the road as an itinerant lecturer on deism. His first stop was

Augusta, Georgia—the state had modeled its law separating church and state on Virginia's religious freedom act—where he delivered a series of lectures from the steps of the courthouse. Palmer's reception in Georgia, in contrast to his treatment in Philadelphia, was cordial and reflected the religious liberalism that still prevailed in a region where Jefferson and Madison were revered. Then he swung north to New York City, which he would make his base for speaking tours of New England and the Middle Atlantic states. Palmer delivered his first public speech in New York on Christmas Day, which he regarded as a holiday well suited to the denunciation of both Christianity and Christ. By then, Palmer had moved far beyond any form of Protestantism: unlike Bentley, he saw little good in Christianity and had a low opinion of Jesus the man. Palmer was also far more radical in his condemnation of Christianity than Paine, who respected the ethics espoused in the New Testament and believed in the virtue, if not the divinity, of Jesus. From the text of Palmer's Christmas Day speech, it is easy to understand why he usually wore out his welcome: respect for the beliefs of others was not, to put it mildly, one of his strong points. "This, my friends, we are told is Christmas day," he began, "and while the pious and learned divines of all Christendom are extolling the beauties, the excellencies, and the divinity of the Christian religion . . . be it our task to inquire into the truth or falsehood of these declarations." Palmer went on to mock the gospel account of the Annunciation and the miraculous conception of Jesus: "This story of the virgin and the ghost, to say no more of it, does not wear the appearance of much religion; and it would not, it is presumed, be difficult in any age or country, to find a sufficient number of men, who would pretend to be ghosts, if by such pretensions they could obtain similar favours. . . ." Palmer even tried to eviscerate the sacred mystery at the heart of Christianity—Jesus's redemptive death on the cross:

In his last moments he cries out, "My God, my God, why hast thou forsaken me!" What conclusion is it natural to draw from this distressing exclamation? It appears to be this, that on the part of Jesus Christ, there was a virtual renunciation of his confidence in the Creator. . . . On the part of the Father, there is a want of attention and support in this trying hour. He forsakes his beloved Son, gives him up to the murderous fury of vindictive enemies; and neither one nor the other of the parties exhibits that spirit of fortitude and constancy which might have been expected on so interesting an occasion.[18]

Elihu Palmer was emphatically not a charming or tolerant man, and it would be easy to conclude that he deserves to be forgotten. Yet he is an important figure in the history of American secularism because, like the much better known Paine, he attempted to carry the message of deism beyond its original audience of educated upper-class intellectuals. Between 1800 and his death in 1806, Palmer published two deist newspapers in New York, the *Temple of Reason* and *Prospect, or View of the Moral World*. It is significant that both ventures failed not for lack of readers but because the readers, who came from all walks of life and economic classes, failed to pay their subscription bills on time. Palmer organized deist societies in New York City, Newburgh (New York), Philadelphia, and Baltimore, and the membership was drawn not from leading citizens but from artisans and shopkeepers. With the exception of doctors, almost no members of learned professions were recorded as members.[19] His only book, the 1801 *Principles of Nature; or, a Development of the Moral Causes of Happiness and Misery Among the Human Species*, sold out three editions before 1806. In his view, nonreligious advances in human thought began with the invention of the printing press and proceeded slowly but inevitably toward the day when philosophical assaults on church and state despotism produced both the American and French revolutions. The importance of Enlightenment philosophy, and of the consequent upheavals in religion and government, lay not in the replacement of one malevolent class of rulers by a more beneficent group but in the enfranchisement of masses of men who had never before been considered fit to govern themselves. "This philosophy," he argued, "has already destroyed innumerable errors; it has disclosed all the fundamental principles which have been employed in the construction of machines, mathematical instruments, and the arrangements of those moral and political systems which have softened the savage and ferocious heart of man, and raised the ignorant slave from the dust, into the elevated character of an enlightened citizen."[20]

The idea that religious revolutions might result in a rebellion of the downtrodden was exactly what worried many leaders of the new republic. That concern was not confined to the most conservative Federalists or the most orthodox clerics but was also expressed by moderate, or what Koch calls "respectable," deists like Franklin. In 1786, Franklin warned an acquaintance against circulating an inexpensive pamphlet setting forth his arguments against the existence of God. "He that spits against the Wind, spits in his own Face," Franklin cautioned, advising his young correspondent "not to attempt unchaining the Tyger, but to burn the Piece before it is seen by any other Person. . . . If men are so wicked as we now see them *with religion*, what would they be *if without it*."[21] Deism and freethought, in this view, were fine for privileged members of society such as Jefferson, Washington, and Franklin himself but were dangerous when exported to the lower classes, ill-educated and lacking in the putative self-discipline practiced by their social betters. A prominent minister put the case against populist deism even more bluntly:

> The effort of infidels, to diffuse the principles of infidelity among the common people, is another alarming symptom peculiar to the present time. *Hume, Bolingbroke*, and *Gibbon* addressed themselves solely to the more polished classes of the community, and would have thought their refined speculations debased by an attempt to enlist disciples from among the populace. Infidelity has lately grown condescending: bred in the speculations of a daring philosophy, immured at first in the cloisters of the learned, and afterwards nursed in the lap of voluptuousness and of courts; having at length reached its full maturity, it boldly ventures to challenge the suffrages of the people, solicits the acquaintance of

peasants and mechanics, and seeks to draw whole nations to its standard.[22]

The indictment of an infidelity that "solicits the acquaintance of peasants and mechanics" was, once again, a reflection of changing American attitudes—in any event, changing clerical attitudes— toward the French Revolution. Only the most liberal clergymen, like Bentley, insisted on distinguishing between the Jacobin terror directed at the French upper classes and the original democratic and libertarian ideals embodied in the French Declaration of the Rights of Man. To Enlightenment liberals, the enemy was not the Revolution itself but the actions of a particular group of revolutionaries who had, as Paine wrote, turned into a new species of Grand Inquisitor and taken over the role of the church whose wealth they had confiscated. But by 1800, most American Protestant clergymen had chosen to forget their initial tolerance, bordering on gleeful enthusiasm, for the French rev- olutionary government's early actions abolishing the secular power of the Catholic Church. The French assault on the privileged position of Catholicism now looked like an assault on all religion: to Protestant conservatives, any church—even one as misguided as the Church of Rome—was better than no church at all. In a 1798 Fourth of July ser- mon, Dwight declared that "where religion prevails . . . a French directory cannot govern, a nation cannot be made slaves, nor villains, nor atheists, nor beasts. To destroy us, therefore, in this dreadful sense, our enemies must first destroy our Sabbath, and seduce us from the house of God."[23] The view of France as the source of America's original secularist sin would prevail among orthodox clerics through- out the nineteenth century. William Meade, the Episcopal archbishop of Virginia from 1841 to 1862, lamented that "the successful termina- tion of the [revolutionary] war, and all the rich blessings attending it, did not produce the gratitude to the Giver which was promised by the hearts of our people in the day of danger and supplication. The inti- macy produced between infidel France and our own country, by the union of our arms against the common foe, was most baneful in its influence with our citizens generally, and on none more so than those of Virginia."[24] Meade must have been regretfully contemplating the Virginia religious freedom act of 1786, which permanently expelled his church from its former state-supported Eden.

Both before and after his death, Paine was the perfect target for social and religious conservatives because his life and his writings combined associations with religious heresy, economic radicalism, and the French Revolution. Paine's books, by virtue of their greater lucidity as well as his reputation as a revolutionary, were far more widely known—certainly outside the urban centers of deist activity—than works by his like-minded American contemporaries Ethan Allen and Elihu Palmer. Mainstream twentieth-century historians have tended to dismiss the idea that Paine's deist arguments had any real impact on the general public; *The Age of Reason*, it is often said, was more often denounced by anxious clerics than read by ordinary people. That viewpoint is suspect because it reflects the customary denigration of secularists and their role in American history. *The Age of Reason* was reprinted eighteen times in five American cities between 1794 and 1796. It is impossible to determine exactly how many people read the book, but the total number of readers was surely many times more than the 25,000 printed copies. On this point, the testimony of Paine's contemporaries, including scholars working in the early years of the American republic, is persuasive. John W. Francis, a physician and historian born in 1789—and no admirer of Paine's religious philosophy—declared flatly that "no work had a demand for readers comparable to that of Paine. The 'Age of Reason,' on its first appearance in New York, was printed as an orthodox book by orthodox publishers—doubtless deceived by the vast renown which the author of 'Common Sense' had obtained, and *by the prospects of sale*."[25] A chronicler of the early American Methodist Church regretted that "the minds of many people were corrupted by the deistical writings of Thomas Paine." Paine's arguments against the truth of the Bible, the Methodist historian wrote, "were received with greater avidity by Americans on account of the eminent services he had rendered to his country during the war of the revolution. But Thomas Paine as a politician and Thomas Paine as a theologian were very different men. His book, however, against the Bible, ... together with others of a kindred character, were widely circulated, and they were exerting a most deleterious influence on the minds of many citizens, and threatened to poison the fountains of knowledge with their pestiferous contents."[26]

But Paine the theologian and Paine the politician were not different men—even though many historians, wishing to credit the author of "Common Sense" but not the author of *The Age of Reason*, have tried to make the case that they were. The antimonarchical and antiecclesiastical Paines were united in the belief that there could be no legitimacy in forms of government or forms of religion that defied reason and nature. Hence, in "Common Sense," Paine argues that "one of the strongest natural proofs of the folly of hereditary right in kings is that nature disapproves it, otherwise she would not so frequently turn it into ridicule, by giving mankind an *ass for a lion*."[27] And in *The Age of Reason*, Paine envisions a god who reveals himself not through miracles and mysteries but in a manner consistent with the laws of nature. The word *mystery*, he argues, "cannot be applied to *moral truth*, any more than obscurity can be applied to light. The God in whom we believe is a God of moral truth, and not a God of mystery or obscurity. Mystery ... is a fog of human invention, that ... represents itself in distortion. Truth never envelops *itself* in mystery, and the mystery in which it is at any time enveloped is the work of its antagonist."[28]

To this day, the received opinion about Paine—except among scholars specializing in the history of American radicalism—is that he was an important revolutionary propagandist but an unimportant thinker. The *Atlantic Monthly*, from its lofty perch in mid-nineteenth-century Boston, described *The Age of Reason* as a "shallow deistical essay," while nevertheless calling for a restoration of

Paine to the canon of revolutionary heroes.[29] However, the idea that spiritual truth can be sought and found only in accordance with reason is not "shallow" but merely controversial—no less so today than yesterday.

The story of Paine's last years in America is a painful one. Most of Paine's old friends, embarrassed by his anti-Christian writings, deserted him—Jefferson once again being a notable exception. After his ship landed in Baltimore, Paine stopped in Washington to pay his respects to the president, who had endured the no-holds-barred invective characteristic of eighteenth-century political commentary after it became known that he had played a role in Paine's return to America. In 1859, the *Atlantic* looked back on Jefferson's invitation as an act of political courage. "He [Jefferson] knew that he strengthened the hands of his enemies by inviting home the Arch-Infidel," the article acknowledged. "We are and were then a religious people. . . . Mr. Jefferson . . . was well aware that the old man was broken, that the fire had gone out of him, and that his presence in the United States could be of no use whatsoever to the party. But he thought that Paine's services to the revolution had earned him asylum, and their old acquaintance made him hasten to offer it. We think that the invitation to Paine was one of the manliest acts of Jefferson's life."[30]

In 1802, though, the American press reaction was scathing, and the commentary revived the campaign invective portraying Jefferson himself as an enemy of religion. One Federalist journal, the Philadelphia *Port Folio*, epitomized the tone of the attacks:

> If, during the present season of national abasement, infatuation, folly, and vice, any portent could surprise, sober men would be utterly confounded by an article current in all our newspapers, that the loathsome Thomas Paine, a drunken atheist and the scavenger of faction, is invited to return in a national ship to America by the first magistrate of a free people. A measure so enormously preposterous we cannot yet believe has been adopted, and it would

demand firmer nerves than those possessed by Mr. Jefferson to hazard such an insult to the moral sense of the nation. If that rebel rascal should come to preach from his Bible to our populace, it would be time for every honest and insulted man of dignity to flee to some Zoar as from another Sodom, to shake off the very dust of his feet and to abandon America.[31]

After Paine's short stay in Washington, he headed north. In Trenton, New Jersey, the stagecoach driver, moved to indignation by press commentary on *The Age of Reason*, refused Paine a seat for the trip to New York City. In New York, an admirer was suspended from church membership for shaking hands with Paine. As Paine sat in his house in New Rochelle on Christmas Eve, a bullet fired by an unknown assailant narrowly missed his head. The temper of the times with regard to religious unorthodoxy is captured in an exchange of letters in early 1803 between Paine and an old friend from the 1770s, the revolutionary firebrand Samuel Adams. Writing more in sorrow than in anger, Adams reminds Paine that he has always viewed him, as a result of his writings on behalf of independence, as "a warm friend to the liberty and lasting welfare of the human race." But he goes on to condemn Paine's defense of "infidelity" with locutions—such as having "heard" of the book—suggesting that he has not actually read *The Age of Reason*. Even so, he chides Paine for publishing views "so repugnant to the true interest of so great a part" of the citizenry:

Do you think that your pen or the pen of any other man can unchristianize the mass of our citizens, or have you hopes of converting a few of them to assist you in so bad a cause? We ought to think ourselves happy in the enjoyment of opinion without the danger of persecution by civil or ecclesiastical law.

Our friend, the President of the United States, has been calumniated for his liberal sentiments, by men who have attributed that liberality to a latent design to promote the cause of infidelity. This and all other slanders have been made without a shadow of proof.

Neither religion nor liberty can long subsist in the tumult of alter-
cation, and amidst the noise and violence of faction.[32]

Paine's reply was also written in sorrow, in temperate tones that
show an author bearing no resemblance to the coarse ruffian depicted
by the Federalist press. He informs Adams that his belief in God is
spelled out in the preface to *The Age of Reason*:

> When then (my much esteemed friend, for I do not respect you the
> less because we differ, and that perhaps not too much in religious
> sentiments), what, I ask, is this thing called *infidelity*? If we go back
> to your ancestors and mine three or four hundred years ago, for we
> must have had fathers and grandfathers or we should not be here,
> we shall find them praying to Saints and Virgins, and believing in
> purgatory and Transsubstatiation; and therefore all of us are infi-
> dels according to our forefathers' belief. . . .
>
> The case, my friend is that the world has been over-run with fable
> and creeds of human invention, with sectaries of whole nations
> against all other nations, and sectaries of those sectaries in each of
> them against the other. Every sectary, except the Quakers, had
> been a persecutor. Those who fled from persecution persecuted in
> their turn, and it is this that has filled the world with persecution
> and deluged it with blood.

A particularly important passage in this letter, in view of the constant efforts of Federalists to tar Paine with the violence of the French
Revolution, is his reminder to Adams that he wrote *The Age of Reason* when he had good reason to believe that he, too, would lose his
life in the Jacobin terror—and when he was daily appalled by the
inhumanity of the revolutionary terrorism that surrounded him. "My
friends were falling as fast as the guillotine could cut their heads off,"
he recalls, "and as I every day expected the same fate, I resolved to
begin my work. I appeared to myself to be on my death-bed, for
death was on every side of me, and I had no time to lose." Paine tells
Adams that he wrote *The Age of Reason* in great haste because he
hoped that the book would be speedily translated into French and

serve as an argument against violence. Finally, Paine reiterates his belief in the God of nature—a God who is served by helping others in this life rather than by obeisance to churches that promise eternal life. Humans "can add nothing to eternity," Paine asserts, but it is within the power of men to render a service to their God "not by praying, but by endeavoring to make his creatures happy."³³

There is no doubt that the constant Federalist attacks on Paine, and his abandonment by many old friends, took a considerable emotional toll in his final years. Many of his writings in the press during this period were saturated with a bitterness and personal venom that he had once reserved for George III. In particular, he never got over the failure of the American government to make vigorous early attempts to gain his release from prison in France, and he blamed not only Gouverneur Morris but also George Washington. The younger Paine, the practical and visionary man of the Enlightenment, reemerged in occasional essays on such topics as the causes of yellow fever, the benefits of constructing more bridges, and the importance of harbor fortifications. Although his financial situation had deteriorated, Paine remained a man of personal charity. When Elihu Palmer died in 1806, leaving no property or money, his widow—he had remarried after his first wife's death—would have been destitute without Paine's support.

Paine died on June 8, 1809, at age seventy-two. Like so many other famous freethinkers, he would be pursued beyond the grave by false reports that he had asked for a minister and recanted his antireligious views on his deathbed. In fact, he died in his sleep. He had expressed a wish to be buried in a Quaker cemetery—the Quakers being the one religious sect of which he had always approved—but the local elders decided that they did not wish to be associated with such a notorious character. One of the few charitable reactions from the clergy was voiced by the Unitarian pastor William Bentley, who praised Paine for his devotion to rationalism. "He was indeed a wonderful man," Bentley said, "& he was the first to see in what part every System was most vulnerable. Even in his attacks on Christianity he felt without knowing it, the greatest difficulties which rational Christians have felt. Without their prejudices he found what was simple, powerful, &

direct, & what might be renounced without injury to morality, to the reverence of God & the peace of the mind."[34]

Paine was buried on his farm in New Rochelle, his interment witnessed by less than a dozen friends. Among them were Marguerite de Bonneville and her two sons, Thomas and Benjamin, all refugees from Napoleonic France. Years later, Madame de Bonneville described the unceremonious burial as "a scene to wound any sensible heart." Looking around at the small group of spectators—who included none of Paine's old friends from the revolutionary years—she said, as the clods of earth were shoveled onto the coffin, "Oh! Mr. Paine! My son stands here as testimony of the gratitude of America, and I, for France!"[35]

In a final indignity, Paine's bones were spirited away in 1819 by William Cobbett—the same Cobbett who had published the slanderous biography in 1797 but who changed his mind after actually reading Paine's books. Cobbett, who had returned to England many years earlier, intended to bury Paine in his native land but, for no apparent reason, kept the bones in a box in his house. His heirs failed to keep track of the remains, so they are lost to posterity—something that probably would not have struck the author of *The Age of Reason* as a catastrophe.

In the 1820s and 1830s, Paine's memory was kept alive only by small, marginalized groups of freethinkers. In the early nineteenth century, Americans who cherished similar political, social, and religious views affirmed their common values by celebrating the birthdays of their heroes. Jacksonian Democrats observed Jefferson's birthday, freethinkers honored both Paine and Jefferson, and everyone celebrated Washington's birthday. That Washington's birthday became a national holiday while Jefferson's did not might well be related to the divisiveness engendered by Jefferson's image as a religious heretic. The British-born freethinker Benjamin Offen organized the first Paine birthday celebration in 1825 in New York City, and the practice of annual commemorations—including dancing, singing, eating, and drinking as well as serious speeches—soon spread to other eastern and midwestern communities with nests of freethinkers. When Offen had arrived in New York from England—

where Paine's writings were, ironically, much better known in the 1820s than they were in America—he was surprised at the general denigration of Paine and attributed it to "sheer religious bigotry, together with thousands of falsehoods uttered from the pulpits respecting his moral character."[36]

It was not until the eve of the Civil War that the irreproachable *Atlantic Monthly* would decry the lack of historical respect accorded Paine's contributions to the cause of independence. Another forty-three years would pass before a biographer, the minister turned free-thinker Moncure Daniel Conway, gave both the revolutionary and the religious skeptic his due. Conway's magisterial two-volume *The Life of Thomas Paine* was published in 1892, at the height of the golden age of freethought. "There is a legend that Paine's little finger was left in America," Conway recounts, "a fable, perhaps, of his once small movement, now stronger than the loins of the bigotry that refused him a vote or a grave in the land he so greatly served. As to his bones, no man knows the place of their rest to this day. His principles rest not."[37]

3

Lost Connections:
Anticlericalism, Abolitionism,
and Feminism

Adams and Jefferson, who both died on July 4, 1826—the fiftieth anniversary of the signing of the Declaration of Independence— had lived long enough to be disturbed by the resurgence of reactionary religion in the young American republic. "Oh! Lord!" Adams lamented to Jefferson in 1817. "Do you think that a Protestant Popedom is annihilated in America? Do you recollect, or have you ever attended to the ecclesiastical Strifes in Maryland, Pensilvania, New York, and every part of New England? What a mercy it is that these People cannot whip and crop, and pillory and roast, *as yet* in the U.S.! If they could they would."[1]

During the last decade of his life, Jefferson was living at Monticello and devoting most of his energy to the founding of the University of Virginia, an institution that would become an outpost of Enlightenment rationalism in an increasingly ossified South. As a result of his immersion in the demanding enterprise of creating a university, he may have been less attuned than Adams to the social implications of a conservative religious revival already far more influential in his own region than in the North. By the early 1830s, with the exception of a limited number of southern academic communities, the heritage of revolutionary secularism—and the intellectual successors of the eighteenth-century American freethinkers—had moved north. As orthodox southern religion became a pillar of slavery (and vice versa), the rich array of freethinkers so prominent in the revolutionary South—virtually all of whom, regardless of the degree of their personal belief in or skepticism about the existence of God, had subscribed to Paine's creed that "my own mind is my own church"—simply lost their place in their own society.

The great nineteenth-century American freethinkers would be nourished not in the soil that had given birth to Virginia's landmark religious freedom act but in the Northeast and in the new states joining the union as the frontier moved westward. Those dissenters would shape, and be shaped by, two movements—abolitionism and women's rights—that could not exist in a southern society based on the ownership of men by other men and on the infantilization of women by the same owners. In their degree of tolerance for religious and social dissent, New England and the Deep South traded places during the first half of the nineteenth century. This is, of course, an oversimplification, since New England, as Adams noted, certainly produced its share of infidel-bashers, while the South produced home-grown dissidents like Angelina and Sarah Grimké, the Charleston-born sisters who broke a social taboo—and contributed to a split in the abolitionist movement—by insisting on the right of women to full participation in the campaign against slavery. The difference is that the southern dissenters had no choice but to leave their native region in order to bear witness to their convictions, but New England—while continuing to produce the most prominent northern voices of religious and social conservatism—became an incubator for all types of religious and social protest. It is not an oversimplification to view this early-nineteenth-century reversal of southern and New England patterns of religious tolerance as one of the most important sources of America's modern religion-based culture wars, which, as demonstrated by the electoral map of the 2000 presidential election, retain a strong geographical as well as political dimension.

No one has described the ironic nineteenth-century shift in values, and its relation to slavery, with greater precision and insight than W. J. Cash in *The Mind of the South* (1941). The triumph of southern evangelism, Cash asserts, "also naturally involved the establishment of the Puritan ideal. From the first great revivals onward, the official moral philosophy of the South moved steadily toward the position of that of the Massachusetts Bay Colony."[2] The expanding white southern homogeneity and hegemony of faith in an infallible God led inevitably to a moral and a utilitarian justification for slavery: "Every man was in his place because He had set him there. Everything was as it was because He had ordained it so. Hence slavery, and, indeed, everything that was, was His responsibility, not the South's. So far from being evil, it was the very essence of Right. Wrong could consist only in rebellion against it. And change could come only as He Himself produced it through His own direct acts, or—there was always room here for this—as He commanded it through the instruments of His will, the ministers."[3]

Thus, southern clerics who delivered sermons enjoining slaves to regard their masters as "God's overseers" could see themselves, and be seen by others in the South, as instruments of divine benevolence.[4] Were they not conferring the gift of Christianity on heathens—and even advising masters to practice a form of slavery leavened with Christian love? As for northern churches, there is no piece of conventional historical wisdom more generally accepted and promulgated today than the idea that religion deserves the lion's share of the credit for the eventual emergence of a moral consensus against slavery among white Americans north of the Mason-Dixon Line. This false image of religion as a staunch foe of slavery is a basic tenet of modern religious correctness, a notion embraced with equal fervor by Democrats and Republicans, by the heirs of Puritans as well as by the descendants of immigrant rabbis who arrived in America too late to weigh in on the slavery question. In the nation's historical memory, the undeniable moral basis of the antislavery movement has been conflated with religion, in a mirror image of the long-established American propensity for equating irreligion with immorality. This view of the antislavery movement conveniently ignores the good Christian rioters and hecklers who frequently disrupted abolitionist lectures in Boston and New York throughout the 1830s and 1840s. That the more conservative clergymen and established churches in the North were slow to condemn slavery outright, and even slower to endorse any economic or political action that might bring about the end of the "peculiar institution," is also conveniently forgotten. The ubiquitous and influential Lyman Beecher, a stalwart foe of religious infidelity since the mighty battle against Tom Paine's pernicious influence at Yale in the 1790s, was still inveighing against the French Revolution in the 1830s. During the same period, he advised all Presbyterian churches to prohibit discussions of slavery that might break the "silken ties" between northern and southern Presbyterians. "Those *silken ties*," the great abolitionist editor William Lloyd Garrison pointedly observed, "are literally *the chains of slaves*."⁵ Now that slavery is a dead issue, Beecher's moral and political heirs are happy to claim the abolitionist movement as one of the achievements of their religious ancestors—and they have no wish to look into the question of whether some of those same ancestors made their fortunes from the products of slave labor.

By contrast with abolitionism, women's rights movements in all of their American incarnations have generally been seen, and rightly so, as a threat to religious orthodoxy. Politically astute feminists have therefore expended a good deal of energy countering Paul's dictum that wives must be subject to their husbands—and silent in church. The connection between the nineteenth-century women's movement and the abolitionist movement is well known, but the relation between both movements and anticlericalism has received much less attention from historians. Yet, the moral authority of churches—their claim to preeminence in determining the proper approach to the great moral question of the day—was challenged both by radical abolitionists and by the early advocates of women's rights. Although many of the radical abolitionists, most notably Garrison, the editor of the *Liberator*, were deeply religious—as were early proponents of women's rights such as the Grimké sisters and Lucretia Mott—they were also deeply anticlerical. "Truth for authority, not authority for truth" was the motto of Mott, a Nantucket-born Quaker lay minister, abolitionist, and feminist. What made radical abolitionists radical was their demand for an immediate rather than a gradual end to slavery. Beecher once argued that if everyone would only stop arousing public passions on the slavery question, white Christian benevolence would ensure that the system would disappear of its own accord—in another two centuries. This "solution" to the problem of slavery was seen as not only immoral but ludicrous by abolitionists, who were repelled by the contention that one group—whites—deserved the power to restrict the natural human rights of others. In parallel fashion, the nation's first generation of feminists rejected the received opinion that male authority should determine the extent of women's rights. The conjunction of radical abolitionism with early feminism is an important chapter in the history of American secularism because those who came of age in the 1820s and 1830s were the first generation of American social reformers to make the connection between reactionary religion and reactionary domestic social institutions. Unlike the grievances of the eighteenth-century colonists, nineteenth-century injustices could not be blamed on a tyrannical English king but were indisputably made in America.

The religiously correct version of American history has never given proper credit to the central importance of the Enlightenment concept of natural rights—or to the anticlerical abolitionists who advanced that concept before the public—in building the case against slavery. Throughout the three decades preceding the Civil War, the anticlerical ethos of the radical abolitionists was used against them by religious opponents of emancipation, who frequently trotted out the specter of the French Revolution and even described abolitionism itself as an atheist plot. In 1850, the slavery-exalting Presbyterian J. H. Thornwell, who was about to be named president of the College of South Carolina, declared that "the parties in this conflict are not merely abolitionists and slaveholders—they are atheists, socialists, communists, red republicans, jacobins on the one side, and the friends of order and regulated freedom on the other. In one word, the world is the battleground—Christianity and atheism the combatants; and the progress of humanity the stake."[6] The battle over religious orthodoxy at the College of South Carolina, founded as an Enlightenment stronghold, bears out Cash's observations about the shifting theology of the South in the first half of the nineteenth century. From 1820 to 1832, the institution's president was Thomas Cooper, one of the most distinguished American scientists and a critic, as a result of contemporary discoveries in geology, of any literal interpretation of the biblical creation story. Cooper was expelled from the faculty for heresy, and men of Thornwell's views took charge. While most abolitionists were neither atheists nor Jacobins, the defenders of slavery were right to make the connection between the revolutionary freethought of Paine and the radical wing of the antislavery movement. Religious conservatives today are the ones who are mistaken in their insistence that the antislavery movement had nothing to do with Enlightenment values—values that would, in turn, be adopted and adapted by abolitionist women who wished no less for themselves than they wished for slaves.

The connections between radical reform, freethought, and anticlerical religious belief are embodied in the tempestuous life of Garrison. The historian Henry Mayer, whose *All on Fire* (1998) was the first biography of Garrison published in thirty-five years, was discouraged by many academic colleagues and publishers from embarking on the project. In their view, Garrison was a cranky "Johnny one-note" and, in any case, they accepted the idea that abolitionist agitation played only a minor role in the political crisis that led to the Civil War and the emancipation of the slaves. But Mayer decided that "to write of the Civil War without Garrison . . . is to write of the American Revolution without Tom Paine, the labor movement without Eugene Debs, the civil rights movement without Bob Moses, or feminism without Elizabeth Cady Stanton."[7] That is exactly what a fair number of American scholars and journalistic commentators have done over the past 150 years. The marginalization of the unconventional is a staple of idealized history, but unconventional religious views, particularly if they can be labeled antireligious—as were those of Paine, Stanton, and Garrison—are a guarantee of ostracism. Garrison's contemporaries within the abolitionist movement had many reasons to disagree with him, from his commitment to nonviolent resistance to his overall disdain for conventional politics (to the point of refusing to vote). Nevertheless, he shares with Paine the distinction of having incurred the deepest and most enduring enmity, from social conservatives of his own generation and subsequent ones, for his savage attacks on orthodox churches and their leaders.

The future founder and editor of the *Liberator*—which, beginning in 1831, would crusade relentlessly for the immediate abolition of slavery and, even more controversially, on behalf of social equality for blacks—was born in 1805 in Newburyport, Massachusetts. He was brought up by his mother, Maria, a devout Baptist caught up in the early-nineteenth-century wave of religious revivalism. Maria seems to have been a religious fanatic even by the ardent evangelical standards of her time and place. She either kicked her less devout and often drunk husband out of the house or was abandoned by him; at any rate, she then left the seven-year-old William Lloyd in the care of the Baptist brethren in Newburyport while she moved away with his elder brother to look for work. Maria never returned to Newburyport, although she did support her son and wrote letters with such admonitions as, "Don't go near the water, for should you be drowned your soul must go to God to be judged."[8] Years later, after young Garrison had taken his first newspaper job on the *Newburyport Herald*, written his earliest pieces of journalism, and begun to display a growing concern with the political and social issues of the day, Maria warned him against the spiritual danger posed by his literary and political interests. "Had you been searching the Scriptures for truth, and praying for the direction of the holy spirit to lead your mind into the path of holiness," she advised, "your time would have been more wisely spent, and your advance to the heavenly world more rapid."[9]

Since Garrison grew up and came of age among intense evangelical believers, in a period when every brand of American religion—from the stuffiest established churches to freewheeling revivalism—was displaying resurgent strength, it is not surprising that he was unacquainted as a youth with the works of Paine. A Baptist upbringing did not prevent Garrison from falling under the spell of Byron—even though the poet's "lewd" influence on young men was deplored by ministers of every persuasion—but Paine had been too thoroughly demonized. Garrison would reach middle age before he actually read the words of the eighteenth-century thinker and social agitator with whom he had so much in common. In the November 21, 1845, issue of the *Liberator*, Garrison confessed to his readers that until a few days earlier, he had never read so much as a paragraph by Paine because he had been raised to regard the author of *The Age of Reason* as "a monster of iniquity."[10] Garrison found that he agreed with much of Paine's reasoning about both institutionalized religion and the truth of the Bible. This realization crystallized his rejection of a literal interpretation of the Scriptures, which often were used to justify slavery. Like everything else, Garrison wrote, the Bible was to be judged "by its reasonableness and utility, by the probabilities of the case, by historical confirmation, by human experience and observation, by the facts of science, by the intuition of the spirit. Truth is older than any parchment."[11] Garrison's mature religious beliefs resembled the evangelicalism of his youth only in their passion. He embraced the "natural religion" of Paine—one rejecting miracles, mysteries, and ecclesiastical hierarchies and insisting on total separation of church and state. It was also a faith based on the premise that not only all men but all men and women are created equal. The trinity of Garrison's uncompromising, nongradualist approach to abolitionism, advocacy of women's rights, and unconventional religious views would render him anathema to his more conservative contemporaries in the antislavery movement in precisely the same fashion as Paine's antireligious views had set him apart fifty years earlier from the more conservative members of the revolutionary generation.

Garrison's views on religion were undoubtedly informed by his contact with women who, through their insistence on full participation in the antislavery movement, were challenging conventional religious ideology in ways never envisaged by even the most radical men of the American revolutionary generation. The participation of women in the antislavery movement beginning in the 1830s released women's energies from domesticity into the public realm, in an irreversible process that would also give rise to the first wave of American feminism.

Before the 1830s, women almost never delivered speeches in public. On the rare occasions when women did appear in open forums, they generally spoke only about religion and only in unorthodox religious settings—given that orthodox ministers opposed any role for women in the pulpit. Thus, the first female public speakers—including Mott and the Grimké sisters—could hardly have been anything but anticlerical. The Grimkés, born and raised on a lush plantation outside Charleston, South Carolina, had left their home, family, and inheritance after they reached the conclusion that slavery was immoral. Angelina, an exact contemporary of Garrison's, drew her sister, who was twelve years older, into antislavery writing and speaking. Both sisters were Hicksite Quakers, who adhered to a more strongly anticlerical, antiritualistic, and antislavery philosophy than that of the larger and more traditional Society of Friends. The equality of women and men as moral beings was a general tenet of Quakerism, but the Hicksites believed in it more devoutly—and put their beliefs into practice more aggressively—than their mainstream Quaker brethren. Nevertheless, Sarah and Angelina shocked even some of their most radical coreligionists when they took the extraordinary step of speaking out against slavery before audiences that included both women and men—and blacks as well as whites. For a woman to speak before mixed audiences was even more shocking than for a woman to speak in public, but the Grimkés had something to say that no one else could. Because they had been raised to take their appointed places as mistresses of a slave plantation, they could testify from firsthand experience not only to the degradation of slaves but to the corruption of masters. Told from a unique perspective, their accounts drew large audiences of both sexes; from mid-May until mid-June of 1837, the sisters delivered seventeen lectures, in ten Massachusetts towns, before more than eight thousand people. Fifty years later, the impact was memorably described by their close friend the suffragist Catherine H. Birney.

The sisters attracted one of their largest audiences in the town of Lynn, where they spoke before more than a thousand men and women. The men, Birney recalled in 1885, "were spellbound and impatient of the slightest noise which might cause the loss of a word from the speakers. Another meeting was called for, and held the next evening. This was crowded to excess, many going away unable to get even standing-room." Angelina reported in her diary that at least one hundred men, their heads poking over the lowered window sashes, crowded around outside the meeting hall to hear what they could. According to those who heard her speak, Angelina was a mesmerizing orator whose commanding presence not only promoted the abolitionist cause but also changed many minds about the capabilities of women. One man wrote that he would "never forget the wonderful manifestation of this power during six successive evenings, in what was then called the Odeon, . . . the four galleries rising above the auditorium all crowded with a silent audience carried away with the calm, simple eloquence which narrated what she and her sister had seen from their earliest days. And yet this Odeon scene, the audience so quiet and intensely absorbed, occured at the most enflamed period of the anti-slavery contest. The effective agent in this phenomenon was Angelina's . . . wonderful gift, which enchained attention, disarmed prejudice, and carried her hearers with her."[12]

Initially, conservatives dismissed the Grimkés as a circus act of no importance to the established social order. In one patronizing gem of newspaper commentary, an editor maintained that there was no real reason to worry that "two fanatical women, forgetful of the obligations of a respected name, and indifferent to the feelings of their most worthy kinsmen, the Barnwells and the Rhetts, should, by the novelty of their course, draw to their meetings idle and curious women."[13] But it was a different matter once men started filling the halls to hear the women speak—once it became apparent that a great many anti-slavery New Englanders, of both sexes, did not subscribe to Dr. Johnson's proposition that "a woman preaching is like a dog's walking on his hind legs. It is not done well, but you are surprised to find it done at all."

The clergy was particularly outraged by Angelina's frequent references to the fact that many northern as well as southern ministers and church members supported slavery and believed in the innate inferiority of blacks. By the middle of June 1837, the sisters' popularity with audiences had galled the state's Congregationalist ministers so deeply that they issued a public condemnation, to be read as a pastoral letter from every pulpit in Massachusetts. "Your *minister* is ordained of God to be your teacher," the letter intoned, adding that even if topics such as slavery were not discussed in church in a way that satisfied lay members of the congregation, it was a violation of church discipline to invite outside agitators to speak on the same subjects. If those agitators were women, the violation was even more serious. "We appreciate the unostentatious prayers and efforts of woman in advancing the cause of religion at home and abroad; in Sabbath-schools; in leading religious inquirers to the pastors for instruction; and in all such associated effort as becomes the modesty of her sex," the ministers conceded, "but when she assumes the place and tone of man as a public reformer . . . her character becomes unnatural." In a clear reference to the Grimkés' descriptions of the rapes of slave women by their masters, the ministers huffed and puffed against "the intimate acquaintance and promiscuous conversation of females with regard to things which ought not to be named; by which that modesty and delicacy which is the charm of domestic life, and which constitutes the true influence of woman in society, is consumed, and the way opened . . . for degeneracy and ruin."[14]

Garrison printed these clerical effusions in the *Liberator*—he opened his pages to all points of view—while dismissing them as "popery." Angelina's and Sarah's replies to the ministers were also published, and Sarah predicted that the orthodox religious view of women's capabilities would one day seem as nonsensical as Cotton

Mather's belief in witchcraft did to the educated population—or most of it, at any rate—of New England in 1837. One of the wittiest responses to this "Clerical Bull," as Garrison called it, was written by the feminist and abolitionist Maria Weston Chapman. The satirical poem was titled "The Times That Try Men's Souls":

> They've taken a notion to speak for themselves,
>   And are wielding the tongue and the pen;
> They've mounted the rostrum; the termagant elves,
>   And—oh horrid!—are talking to men!
> With faces unblanched in our presence they come
> To harangue us, they say, in behalf of the dumb . . . [15]

The "woman question" was no side issue for Garrison, because it was inseparable from the larger issue of the validity of religious and civil authority. What obligations did one owe to a government that tolerated slavery? To a church that not only tolerated but also encouraged its members to keep silent about the most important moral issue of the day? For Garrison, the only moral answer, the only moral obligation, was nonviolent resistance to any authority that had made a pact with the devil. Individual conscience was the only arbiter, and Garrison's conscience had enough room for Paine, Voltaire, and the authority-challenging Jesus, as well as for the first stirrings of American feminism.

Although Garrison had not yet read Paine in the 1830s, one of the fullest and most fascinating expositions of his growing religious and social radicalism was published in the *Liberator* during the summer of 1836, in response to a widely reported address delivered by Beecher to the Presbyterian General Assembly in Pittsburgh. Garrison had once admired Beecher, in part because he agreed with the rock-ribbed Presbyterian's relentless attacks on drunkenness and dueling. But that admiration turned to disdain as Beecher raised his voice against antislavery agitation and all social reform movements—especially those promoting women's and labor rights—and in favor of strengthening the authority of churches and their leaders. For Beecher, the most important moral issue confronting America was not slavery, or anything to do with wages and working conditions, but the shocking American disregard for observance of the Sabbath. The Sabbath, he told the ministers assembled in Pittsburgh, was nothing less than "the great sun of the moral world, . . . the cord by which heaven holds up nations from the yawning gulf of corruption and ruin."[16]

Sunday mail was a painful thorn in the side of religious conservatives, because—in spite of their growing social influence—they had failed repeatedly in their political attempts to persuade Congress to repeal an 1810 law mandating seven-day-a-week postal service. In the debate over ratification of the Constitution, the need for efficient, inexpensive mail service controlled by the federal government was never questioned by even the most ardent advocates of states' rights, and efficient mail delivery in the eighteenth and early nineteenth centuries meant moving the mails seven days a week. In the pretelegraph era, the crucial importance of mail to long-distance business outweighed fear of God's wrath—at least as far as national politicians were concerned. The 1810 law not only required that the mails be kept moving on Sunday but that all post offices remain open for at least one hour. Indeed, this was a great service to the many rural church members who came to town only once a week—for Sunday services—and were able to pick up their mail afterward. But the convenience of the faithful carried no weight with clergymen like Beecher, who, along with that longtime foe of infidels Yale's President Dwight, led unceasing campaigns for repeal of the law. In 1828, Beecher had taken yet another unsuccessful run at the secularist postal system by founding, in New York City, a nationwide organization known as the General Union for the Promotion of the Christian Sabbath (GUPCS). Among its other activities, which included circulating 100,000 copies of one of Beecher's talks denouncing the Sabbath-breaking postal authorities, GUPCS encouraged its members to boycott any private companies that helped transport mail on Sunday. The Washington establishment could not ignore the thousands of petitions on both sides of the issue from individuals, businesses, civic groups, and even state legislatures. But Congress, then as now, could delay action on a controversial matter by referring it to a committee—

and the lawmakers referred this godly mess to the powerful Senate Committee on the Post Office and Post Roads. The committee chairman was Senator Richard M. Johnson of Kentucky, a general, a hero of the War of 1812, and a devout Baptist—but in the dissident evangelical tradition that had supported the framing of a federal constitution with no mention of God.

Both evangelicals and Unitarians had long suspected the Sabbatarians, led by old-line Presbyterians like Beecher, of using the campaign against Sunday mail as the first stage of a battle to prohibit all travel on the Sabbath—thereby rendering the Lord's Day as grim as it had been in the seventeenth century. In 1815, Salem's Unitarian pastor, William Bentley, had complained that local church officials were in the habit of detaining Sunday mail carriers in an "immoral and vexatious" manner. He decried "the endless litigations which every parish officer can create at pleasure, throughout a country in which the habits are as different as upon the [entire] Globe." Moreover, Bentley observed that small dissident religious sects would suffer the most from a ban on Sunday travel, because many of their members could not make it to their far-flung churches or open-air meetings without the use of a forbidden horse or carriage. The older established churches had claimed the prime locations in town centers in colonial times, and their congregants could generally walk—the one form of locomotion permitted by strict Sabbatarians—to services.[17]

What Congress received from Johnson in 1828 was a report declaring, in uncompromising terms, that any federal attempt to give preference to the Christian Sabbath would be a clear violation of the Constitution. The senator, who was no scholar, had considerable help in the preparation of his report from his friend Obadiah Brown, a Baptist minister and, conveniently, a postal clerk thoroughly familiar with the exigencies of mail delivery. In spite of bearing the drab title *Senate Report on the Subject of Mails on the Sabbath*, Johnson's brief—filled with Enlightenment language and concepts—proved to be hot news and was reprinted in newspapers in every state. Making an argument that strongly resembled Jefferson's rationale for refusing to issue proclamations of thanksgiving, Johnson deemed it unconstitutional for the federal government to promote Sabbath observance by ending Sunday mail delivery. Congress was merely "a civil institution, wholly destitute of religious authority." He went on to remind legislators of the religious intolerance and persecutions that had impelled their predecessors to draw a firm line—"the line cannot be too strongly drawn"—between church and state.[18] The report also noted that many Americans, Christian and non-Christian, observed the Sabbath not on Sunday but on Saturday—and that the Constitution and its Bill of Rights were designed to prevent the majority from dictating to minorities. "The Constitution regards the conscience of the Jew as sacred as that of the Christian," Johnson emphasized, "and gives no more authority to adopt a measure affecting the conscience of a solitary individual than that of the whole community."[19] The document aroused such intense public interest that, according to one New York congressman, everyone who could read at all had read newspaper excerpts from Johnson's report.[20]

Johnson used his senatorial franking privileges (some things never change) to mail free reprints to his Kentucky constituents, and printers issued inexpensive pamphlet editions in which key passages were set off in large type. Hezekiah Niles, editor of the popular Baltimore-based *Niles' Weekly Register*, recommended the report to his readers as an antidote to the anticonstitutional "religious clamor" raised by opponents of Sunday mail.[21] In any event, the Sabbatarians did not get their way, although Sunday mail service would be cut back, for nonreligious reasons, after the 1844 invention of the telegraph provided a more efficient form of business communication. But when Beecher made his "Sabbath the sun of the moral world" speech in 1836, conservative clergymen were still smarting from their most recent defeat on the Sunday mail issue. Who or what was responsible? Why, that pesky secular Constitution, which could not be gotten around even if the vast majority of Americans had no objection to imposing Christian religious rituals on dissenters.

Garrison was repelled by Beecher's moral priorities, so much so that he devoted a large portion of three issues of the *Liberator*, in July and August 1836, to answering the famous clergyman's attacks not only on Sabbath breakers but on antislavery, women's rights, and labor reform advocates. In a polemical passage worthy of Paine, Garrison mocked Beecher's assertion that the United States would "be undone" unless there was a concerted effort to restore mandatory Sabbath observance of the sort practiced in the seventeenth-century Massachusetts Bay Colony. "Yet he is giving his protecting influence to a system of slavery," Garrison thundered, "which, at a single blow, annihilates not only the fourth commandment, but THE Whole DECALOGUE! and which effectively excludes from the benefits of the Sabbath, two millions and a half of his fellow-countrymen!!" Garrison went on to use Beecher's own words against him:

> He oracularly asserts, in the style of our Fourth-of-July orators, that 'a great experiment is now in the making. It is the experiment of human liberty; and if it fails here, all hope will be taken from the earth. If we cannot succeed, no nation will try it again.'

> This wonderful 'experiment' that we are now making is precisely this—to see how long we can plunder, with impunity, two millions and a half of our population; how much labor we can extort with the cart-whip, how near to a level with the brute creation we can reduce every sixth man, woman, and child in the land . . . '*If* it fails here,' says Dr. B.; but IT HAS FAILED—we are not, we have never been, and while slavery exists we can never be, a free people . . . and we are rushing down to destruction as fast as time will allow us.[22]

Beecher had not only denounced Americans who failed to share his view of Sabbath observance, but used his speech to attack atheists, supporters of Jacobin terror (presumably running rampant in the streets of American cities nearly five decades after the French Revolution), and advocates of women's rights, racial equality, and industrial and agrarian reform. Special opprobrium was reserved for the Scottish-born freethinkers Robert Dale Owen and Frances Wright, who actually were atheists and who, moreover, had questioned the desirability and sanctity of the institution of marriage. Poor Beecher! After reading the works of Owen and Wright, he told the ministers assembled in Pittsburgh, "I felt ashamed, even though I was alone. I believe I blushed, although no human eye was upon me." Garrison shot back: "It is marvellous to behold the anxiety and alarm of Dr. B. as he contemplates the possibility of the overthrow of the marriage institution . . . among our *white* population; while he is unmoved, and as tranquil as a summer's twilight" at the systematic destruction of slave families. "Why should there be a monopoly of lewdness and incest among church-going members and slaveholding believers, to the exclusion of those who deny the existence of a God, and the authenticity of the Bible?" Garrison asked tartly.[23] Finally, in a passage that demonstrates how closely his own thinking was aligned with eighteenth-century freethought, Garrison assailed those who denigrated contemporary demands for social reform by pointing to the excesses of the French Revolution:

> So, whenever the workingmen strive to effect a just reform, they are made hideous, and driven back, by a fresh delineation of the horrors of the 'French revolution.' What has that dire tragedy to do with justice between man and man, or with equality between the employer and the employed? And were there no causes which produced it? It is popular to speak of the Goddess of Reason, of Robespierre and his vindictive associates, of the guillotine, and of the reign of atheism. But who dwells upon the fact, that a despotic government, a false religion, and a wicked priesthood, had conspired to crush, ruin and enslave the people, so that human endurance could bear no more. . . . Yet the French revolution has been a fine windfall for the priesthood and the aristocracy in all countries. The causes of it are almost wholly forgotten—its terrible effects only are remembered. Both the aristocracy and the priesthood, need to be instructed by it more than the people.[24]

Garrison's blast against Beecher encompassed most of the issues that were already creating considerable tension within the abolitionist movement—gradualism versus "immediatism"; political compromise versus moral absolutism; a traditional, behind-the-scenes role for women versus an active, nontraditional female presence; and religious orthodoxy versus religious individualism. The tension came to a head in New York City in May 1840, at the annual meeting of the American Anti-Slavery Society (of which Garrison had been a founding member in 1833). In a Machiavellian parliamentary maneuver, Garrison forced a vote on the "woman question" by appointing Abby Kelley, a Quaker and a great admirer of the Grimké sisters, to a post on the organization's powerful business committee. Kelley's appointment was confirmed by a close vote, but several hundred members—a minority, but a highly influential one—pronounced it a violation of the Scriptures to serve on a committee with a woman, walked out, and announced plans to form a breakaway antislavery organization. One of the schismatics, ironically, was the longtime abolitionist organizer Henry Stanton, whose new bride, the former Elizabeth Cady, was destined to become the most radical leader of the nineteenth-century women's rights movement. Henry then made haste across the Atlantic, ahead of Garrison, to attend the first convention of the newly formed British and Foreign Anti-Slavery Society; he was in a hurry because he intended to make common cause with British delegates against the seating of the American women already dispatched as delegates by Garrison's group.

The first "world" antislavery convention—really a British and American venture—is chiefly remembered today not for any actions regarding slavery but for its refusal to enfranchise women. Because the battle over the representation of women was rooted in the larger struggle between reactionary authoritarian religion and an individualistic concept of moral duty, the conflict within the American delegation belongs as much to the history of American freethought as it does to the history of abolitionism. The Grimké sisters were not there (Angelina, at thirty-five, was going through a difficult first pregnancy), but nearly everyone else who was anyone in American abolitionism made the trip to London. Among them were Lucretia Mott and her husband, James, both selected by the Massachusetts

Anti-Slavery Society as delegates to the international convention; Wendell Phillips and his wife, Ann, also delegates; the Stantons; and Garrison himself. Henry Stanton opposed a public role for women because he considered the women's demands so controversial, and so antipathetic to conventional religious belief, that they would antagonize Americans who would otherwise support the antislavery cause. He was a slippery character, making a speech on the floor of the convention supporting a proposal to seat women (perhaps in an effort to placate the new Mrs. Stanton) but then voting against the measure. It apparently came as a surprise to the bridegroom that his wife, who shared his abolitionist convictions, did not follow his lead on the feminist issue but instead sided with Mott, one of the American delegates being denied her seat. The Stantons' honeymoon must have included some interesting pillow talk, although their political disagreements apparently did not overwhelm their newly wed passion. The union was to produce seven children, but husband and wife grew apart over the years and eventually wound up leading largely separate lives. Nevertheless, Stanton always wrote warmly of her husband's accomplishments and said little about their disagreements. As she aged, Stanton would become much more radical in her thinking about all questions affecting women's rights, and in the 1890s, her *Woman's Bible* would create a rift in the suffragist movement that was as intellectually and morally serious as the issue that split the abolitionist movement in 1840.

The seeds of Stanton's religious iconoclasm were planted in London, where she met Mott for the first time and found her "an entirely new revelation of womanhood." The two women, appalled by the vote to exclude women delegates, walked out of the hall arm-in-arm and resolved to form a new organization, as soon as they returned to America, to promote equal rights for women. Another eight years would pass before they put their plans into action at the 1848 Seneca Falls convention—the first public gathering in America organized specifically for the purpose of discussing the rights of women. Mott's journal of those eventful weeks is filled with praise for Elizabeth but makes only a cursory mention of Henry. During a group visit to the British Museum, the two women sat together on a bench and talked earnestly about theology and politics while everyone else was touring the exhibitions. "She had told me of the doctrines and divisions among 'Friends' "; Stanton wrote in her diary, "of the inward light, of Mary Wollstonecraft, her social theories, and her demands of equality for women. I had been reading [Samuel] Combe's 'Constitution of Man,' and 'Moral Philosophy,' [William Ellery] Channing's works, and Mary Wollstonecraft, though all tabooed by orthodox teachers; but I had never heard a woman talk what, as a Scotch Presbyterian, I had scarcely dared to think." Stanton found in Mott "a woman emancipated from all faith in man-made creeds, from all fear of denunciations. Nothing was too sacred for her to question, as to its rightfulness in principle and practice. 'Truth for authority, not authority for truth,' was not only the motto of her life but it was a fixed mental habit." The devout Quaker also had a sense of humor. When Stanton confessed that she greatly enjoyed reading fiction, attending the theater, and dancing, she feared that Mott, because of her austere Quaker convictions, would disapprove. But her friend only smiled and replied, "I regard dancing as a very harmless amusement," adding that "the Evangelical Alliance, that so readily passed a resolution declaring dancing a sin for a church member, tabled a resolution declaring slavery a sin for a bishop."[25]

Born in 1793 into the well-known Coffin family of Nantucket— her father was a ship's captain—Mott, like nearly all other Quaker women, was better educated than the average woman of her generation. Both her schooling and the active religious role assumed by and permitted to Quaker women—especially the more radical Hicksite group embraced by Mott and her husband—had prepared her for her activities as an abolitionist and an advocate of women's rights. Because her personal and unorthodox faith was the center of her being and informed all of her social convictions, Mott exemplified the bonds linking Enlightenment rationalism and liberal religion. Twelve years older than Garrison and twenty-two years older than Stanton, she was a living link to eighteenth-century values—a role that, because she lived to age eighty-seven, she would be able to fill for several generations of reformers. For Garrison, whose childhood was unusually turbulent because of his parents' marital separation and his mother's absence, Lucretia and James Mott were parental figures as well as philosophical mentors. Mr. Mott was a successful textile merchant who, at a time when many of his fellow Quakers condemned slavery without renouncing its profits, gave up all his interests in the cotton trade.

By the time Garrison arrived at the London antislavery convention on June 17—he had stayed behind in New York to help clean up the mess left behind by the organizational schism—the international convention had already ruled against the seating of female delegates. Phillips, whose wife had also been selected as a delegate from Massachusetts, moved at the opening session to admit all *persons* selected as delegates, but his motion was defeated by a large margin. Unlike Henry Stanton, the other delegates did not care enough about women's reactions to bother making two-faced speeches. The British organizing committee had graciously consented to rope off a side chamber so that the ladies might listen to the proceedings while, of course, keeping silent. The refusal to seat Mott, so widely respected for her learning, moral probity, and tireless work on behalf of the abolitionist cause, was never forgotten or forgiven by those who witnessed the insult. Thirty-three years later, after Mott's death, Elizabeth Stanton alluded to the incident in a eulogy delivered at a memorial service sponsored by the National Woman Suffrage Association. "The vote by which this injustice was perpetrated," Stanton declared, "was due to the overwhelming majority . . . who, with Bible in hand, swept all before them. No man can fathom the depths of rebellion in woman's soul when insult is heaped upon her sex, and this is intensified when done under the hypocritical assumption of divine authority."[26]

After the closing session of the London convention, Mott summed up her view of reactionary religion in a conversation with Richard D. Webb, an Irish writer who became a lifelong friend. Webb had literally bumped into Mott in the British Museum's Egyptian Room, filled with mummies and sarcophagi. "We heard her remark on that occasion," he recalled, "that it was hardly reasonable to wonder so much at the idolatry of the Egyptians, seeing that the prostration of mind which prevails in the present day, if not so revolting in its manifestations, is at least as profound."[27]

Although he had arrived in London too late for the infamous vote, Garrison decided to register his objection to the exclusion of women by refusing to take his own seat on the convention floor, as did his friends Nathaniel Rogers, an abolitionist newspaper editor from New Hampshire, and Charles Lenox Redmond, a black delegate from Salem, Massachusetts. The three sat in the balcony, their nonvoting presence registering an eloquent and silent protest. Redmond expressed his sense of the indivisibility of human rights by noting that it would be especially reprehensible for him to participate in a convention that barred women in view of the fact that women in several New England towns had worked tirelessly to raise money for his travel expenses.[28]

When the Americans returned from London—news of their stand on the woman question having preceded them—a group of free Boston men and women of color gave Garrison a reception, attended by more than 2,500 people, to demonstrate their support. Garrison and Rogers were the only whites on the platform. Of Redmond's stand in London, Garrison observed that "though a warmer welcome than ordinarily awaits the white man was extended to him, as a man of color, he nobly refused to enter, where any of the advocates of human rights were thrust out. And, in thus deciding, he did more for our cause than he could possibly have done by neglecting to bear so emphatic a testimony.... I rejoice that it must be so, as it rouses a powerful influence, hitherto dormant, for the slave's cause—the cause of liberty and humanity."[29]

Eight years after the Anti-Slavery Society split over the woman question, the Seneca Falls women's rights convention would create an even closer bond between radical abolitionists and feminists. Mott and Stanton were slow to follow through on the idea of a meeting specifically devoted to the cause of equality for women, in part because both led extremely busy, obligation-packed lives. Mott, who turned fifty in 1843, remained a tireless speaker and organizer for all human rights causes and had become one of the most influential abolitionists in the nation. Stanton, who turned thirty in 1845, was occupied in the more traditional women's sphere; between 1842 and 1846, she gave birth to three children. Then Henry Stanton made a decision that may well have changed the course of women's history in America: in 1847, he insisted on moving his family from the lively intellectual atmosphere of Boston to the small New York manufacturing town of Seneca Falls, set in the Finger Lakes region of upstate New York. Henry had political ambitions less likely to be satisfied in Massachusetts, where his break with the Garrisonian abolitionists had impaired his prospects. His wife, however, preferred to live in Boston, where the ordinary cares of a young mother were eased by the proximity of friends who shared her intellectual interests and by the surplus of cheap household help provided by immigrants. Had Elizabeth Cady Stanton not been so bored, frustrated, and isolated in Seneca Falls, the start of the organized women's rights movement might well have been delayed until after the Civil War.

In the 1840s, Seneca Falls was a town of about four thousand, with twenty-five small factories producing everything from water pumps to cotton cloth. Located at the northern tip of Lake Seneca, the town was linked to the Erie Canal by a smaller canal that ran by the Stantons' house. But there was no intellectual community of the sort that had defined and enriched the Stantons' life in Boston; while Henry traveled frequently on business and political missions, Elizabeth was stuck at home, near a glorious view of factories and a commercial canal, with three children under age six. In her autobiography, she later recalled that "up to this time life had glided by with comparative ease, but now the real struggle was upon me. My duties were too numerous and varied, and not sufficiently exhilarating or intellectual to bring into play my higher faculties. I suffered with mental hunger, which, like an empty stomach, is very depressing. . . . Cleanliness, order, the love of the beautiful and artistic, all faded away in the struggle to accomplish what was absolutely necessary from hour to hour."[30] Had she not been so overwhelmed by motherhood, Stanton might have found a good deal to interest her in the Finger Lakes region, an area of striking natural beauty that was also a hotbed of dissident social and religious movements throughout the first half of the nineteenth century. The list of prominent freethinkers, abolitionists, and feminists with significant links to the area around Seneca Falls includes Susan B. Anthony; Amelia Jencks Bloomer, editor of the first feminist newspaper in America and inventor of the eponymous pantaloons; Harriet Tubman, the escaped slave who led hundreds of her people to freedom across the nearby Canadian border; Elizabeth Blackwell, the first woman to receive a medical degree in the United States; William Seward, Abraham Lincoln's secretary of state; and Robert Ingersoll. During her years in Seneca Falls, Stanton was largely dependent for intellectual sustenance on her correspondence with friends—especially Mott—and in 1848, Mott came to her rescue. She and her husband were in the area for an annual meeting of Hicksite Quakers, and Mott invited Stanton to spend the day with her at the home of friends who lived a few miles from Seneca Falls. Three other women were also present for what turned, *avant la lettre*, into a serious consciousness-raising session, because by the end of the day, the group had decided to sponsor the women's rights convention that Mott and Stanton had first envisioned when they met in London. Stanton's determination to act was fueled both by her memories of the exclusion of women from the 1840 antislavery convention and also by her more recent experiences as a mother cut off from intellectual and political life. "I poured out, during that day, the torrent of my long-accumulating discontent," she recalled, "with such vehemence and indignation that I stirred myself, as well as the rest of the party, to dare and do anything."[31]

"Anything" was a retrospective exaggeration. Of the five women who organized the convention, only Mott had extensive experience of public speaking or organizing on behalf of a cause. "Bold as they thought themselves," one twentieth-century feminist historian notes, "they did not dare preside over the meeting."[32] Mott's husband, James, called the convention to order on July 19 in the town's Wesleyan Memorial Chapel. Although an unsigned notice of a convention "to discuss the social, civil, and religious condition and rights of women" had appeared in the local newspaper only four days earlier, the roads leading to the chapel on the morning of the nineteenth were clogged with carts and carriages. Approximately one hundred women and men, including the ex-slave and prominent abolitionist editor Frederick Douglass, filled the pews when debate began on the contents of *A Declaration of Rights and Sentiments*, written on a parlor table by Stanton, in consultation with Mott and the other three women organizers. The Seneca Falls declaration stands squarely in the Enlightenment tradition, modeled after both the Declaration of Independence and the American Anti-Slavery Society's founding document, also titled *Declaration of Sentiments*, written by Garrison in 1833.

A comparison of the three declarations clearly demonstrates the powerful ties binding the nineteenth-century abolitionist and feminist rationalists to the eighteenth-century generation of American revolutionary rationalists. Garrison's 1833 text, rejecting the political compromise that had written slavery into the Constitution—referred instead to the Declaration of Independence's assertion that *all* men— not only white men—are created equal. The Seneca Falls declaration extended the assertion of equality to women:

> When, in the course of human events, it becomes necessary for one portion of the family of man to assume among the people of the earth a position different from that which they have hitherto occupied, but one to which the laws of nature and of nature's God entitle them, a decent respect to the opinions of mankind requires that they should declare the causes that impel them to such a course. We hold these truths to be self-evident: that all men and women are created equal; that they are endowed by their Creator with certain inalienable rights; . . . that to secure these rights governments are instituted, deriving their just powers from the consent of the governed. . . . But when a long train of abuses and usurpations, pursuing invariably the same object evinces a design to reduce them under absolute despotism, it is their duty to throw off such

government. . . . Such has been the patient sufferance of the women under this government, and such is now the necessity which constrains them to demand the equal station to which they are entitled.[33]

Just as the Declaration of Independence detailed the grievances of the colonists under the government of George III, the Seneca Falls declaration enumerated the economic, legal, and social injustices inflicted on women by the governance of men. The phrase "abuses and usurpations" elicited particular derision from newspaper commentators, who viewed the women's borrowing of Jefferson's language as more comical than sacrilegious. The Seneca Falls declaration also took up the subject of religious injustice, albeit with a caution befitting women who had been called infidels and atheists simply for wanting to speak in public. In church as well as state, the document noted, men had allowed women "but a subordinate position, claiming apostolic authority for her exclusion from the ministry, and, with some exceptions, from any public participation in the affairs of the church." More boldly, the convention raised an issue that would not be seriously addressed again until the second wave of feminism, in the 1970s—the religion-endorsed double standard of sexual morality. Men were indicted for having "created a false public sentiment by giving to the world a different code of morals for men and women, by which moral delinquencies which exclude women from society, are not only tolerated, but deemed of little account in man." Finally, the convention declared that man had "usurped the prerogative of Jehovah himself, claiming it as his right to assign for her [woman] a sphere of action, when that belongs to her conscience and her God." These were hardly the sentiments of atheists, although that did not stop conservative newspapers and clerics from calling the Seneca Falls declaration an "atheistic" and "infidel" document. But the religious liberals who dominated the proceedings at Seneca Falls did in fact reject a literal interpretation of the Scriptures.

After adopting the *Declaration of Rights and Sentiments*, the convention proceeded to debate more controversial resolutions—

described by the *Seneca Country Courier* as "spirited and spicey"—calling for reform of religion as well as for social action to right women's specific wrongs.[34] One resolution, considered especially important by Stanton, declared "that woman has too long rested satisfied in the circumscribed limits which corrupt customs and a perverted application of the Scriptures have marked out for her, and that it is time that she should move in the enlarged sphere for which her great Creator has assigned her."[35] The acknowledgment of a "great Creator," coupled with an indictment of traditional religion as "corrupt" and "perverted," is typical of early feminist argument: the women were attempting to attack conservative religious restrictions on their sex without seeming to criticize all religion. The balancing act was largely successful at Seneca Falls, given the iconoclastic opinions of the participants. Even so, there were objections to such phrases as the "perverted application of the Scriptures," regarded as sure to offend most Americans. The resolution was adopted, but the dissidents were undeniably right about the political inadvisability of what the public would correctly perceive as an attempt to meddle with the Bible.

The most controversial issue was whether the convention should demand that women receive the right to vote. Woman suffrage was regarded as such a radical idea, and so offensive to the majority of Americans, that many convention participants—including Stanton's husband—feared that the resolution would erase any public sympathy for what were then considered less radical demands, including expansion of educational opportunity and married women's property rights. True to form, Henry Stanton left town before the vote that passed the resolution: a vote for woman suffrage would not look good on the record of a politically ambitious man, but a vote against suffrage would deeply offend his wife. Lucretia Mott offered an additional resolution that was unanimously adopted by the convention: "*Resolved*, That the speedy success of our cause depends upon the zealous and untiring efforts of both men and women, for the overthrow of the monopoly of the pulpit, and for the securing to woman an equal participation with men in the various trades, professions, and commerce."[36] Of the five female organizers of the convention, three were joined by their husbands in signing the *Declaration*. James Mott was among the signers. Henry Stanton was not. Fifty years later, Stanton fudged the issue in her autobiography by implying that all the husbands of the organizers had signed the declaration. Whatever quarrels she had with Henry in the course of their long marriage, she belonged to a generation of women who would not have dreamed of publicly attacking, or even mildly criticizing, their husbands.

Garrisonian abolitionists became the staunchest supporters of the fledgling women's movement and of woman suffrage, at a time when the idea of equal rights for women inspired nothing but contemptuous jokes. In 1849, the *Liberator* promoted the first petition campaign on behalf of woman suffrage, and in 1850, Garrison and his wife, Helen, signed the call for the first national women's rights convention. The Seneca Falls gathering had been convened on such short notice that its participants came only from the immediate area. The 1850 convention, held in Worcester, Massachusetts, attracted delegates from across the nation and drew broader and even more negative attention from the national press than the earlier meeting in Seneca Falls. James Gordon Bennett's *New York Herald*, for example, characterized the assembly as a combination of "socialism, abolitionism, and infidelity." BIBLE AND CONSTITUTION REPUDIATED was the attention-grabbing headline over one article.[37] Garrison, who abstained from voting as part of his general opposition to a slavery-tolerating government, was understandably ridiculed for his support of woman suffrage. His response was that every American, regardless of color or sex, was entitled to equal rights under the law and "whether one chose to exercise them on grounds of conscience was immaterial to the tyranny manifested by their denial."[38]

The radical abolitionists and feminists would have a bitter falling-out after the Civil War in the debate over enfranchisement of former slaves. The most important suffragist leaders, Anthony and Stanton, felt betrayed when Garrison endorsed the Fifteenth Amendment, which gave the vote to freed male slaves but not to any woman of any color. Garrison, who supported women's suffrage as strongly as ever, nevertheless believed that there was no chance that Congress would enfranchise women in the 1860s and that it would be foolhardy to jeopardize the civil rights of former slaves by demanding a then-unattainable civic equality for women.

But the radical abolitionists and feminists never disagreed on issues involving separation of church and state or on the pernicious influence of conservative religious thought. Neither the abolitionists nor the early feminists set out to take on organized religion; they did so only when they concluded that the conservative religious institutions of their day were a positive obstacle to social reform. Garrison moved from religious orthodoxy to religious iconoclasm precisely because of the moral failure of so many religious leaders to confront the greatest moral issue of the age. Mott, acting on her inward light, was ahead of virtually all her contemporaries, male and female, on both slavery and women's rights. She never hesitated to speak out in ways that, even though they revealed her deep religious feelings, earned her the ludicrous "infidel" label from those in charge of mainstream churches. At an anti-Sabbath convention held in 1848 in Boston and attended by those who did not fear divine retribution for opening their mail on Sundays, Mott outlined a creed that would still be quoted by freethinkers of many kinds—including those who considered themselves agnostics or atheists—in the last decade of the nineteenth century:

> There are signs of progress in the movements of the age. The superstitions and idols in our midst are held up to the view of the people. Inquiring minds are asking, "Who shall show us any good?" These are dissatisfied with the existing forms and institutions of religious sects, and are demanding a higher righteousness—uprightness in everyday life. The standards of creeds and forms must be lowered, while that of justice, peace, and love of one another must be raised higher and higher. "The earth shall be filled with the knowledge of the glory of the Lord." We wait for no imagined millennium—no speculation or arithmetical calcula-

tion—no Bible research—to ascertain when this shall be. It only needs that the people examine for themselves—not pin their faith on ministers' sleeves, but do their own thinking, obey the truth, and be made free.[39]

When Mott died in 1880, she was widely judged by her contemporaries—even many who had opposed her brand of abolitionism and who continued to oppose equal rights for women—as the greatest American woman of the nineteenth century. Stanton, who did not possess her mentor's talent for maintaining cordial relations with disagreeing, and often disagreeable, personalities in various reform movements, eulogized her friend and summed up the reason for the widespread outpouring of affection and respect. "It is because Lucretia Mott was a philanthropist," Stanton said simply. "Her life was dedicated to the rights of humanity."[40]

Mott has received even less attention than Garrison from modern historians. One of the most mystifying aspects of her historical reputation is that nearly all biographies of the woman who so deeply impressed her contemporaries are saccharine children's books, emphasizing Mott's deep personal faith and goodness while largely ignoring her tough-minded side—the side that did not hesitate to take on representatives of her own religious tradition, along with slave owners and misogynist lawmakers and judges. Her impact on her contemporaries may best be judged by the attacks of her enemies, who never failed to charge her with religious as well as political heresy. A typical example, signed "Slave-Holder," was published in a local newspaper in 1853, after Mott, exposing herself to personal danger, delivered an antislavery speech in Maysville, Kentucky:

This bad woman, whose infamous calling is a war against the Constitution of the United States, a sacrilegious condemnation of the Holy Bible, preaching disobedience and rebellion to our slaves, was allowed the use of our Court House for the propagation of her infernal doctrines. . . . What will be the result of a visit from this female fanatic is not yet known; we should not be surprised, however, if it were the prelude to a heavy loss on the part of the slaveholders of the county, as a score or two of blacks were present to behold and hear this brazen infidel in her treason against God and her country.[41]

The neglect and misrepresentation of Mott is one more example of the fragmented historical record of Enlightenment-rooted American dissent. But for all their past and present cultural marginalization, dissidents who retained some connection to a recognizable religious (and Protestant) heritage—however anticlerical they may have been—are much better known today than the smaller number of emphatically and unabashedly antireligious dissidents from the first half of the nineteenth century. Unlike Mott and Garrison, antireligious freethinkers did not turn against churches because so many conventional clerics were the enemies of social reform. Instead, they identified religion itself as one of society's most important social problems, as a major contributor to and defender of evils that included, but were not limited to, slavery, poverty, and the subordinate status of women. Garrison was no atheist or infidel, but a number of his more radical near contemporaries—including Robert Dale Owen, Frances Wright, and the Polish Jewish Ernestine L. Rose, who immigrated to the United States via England in 1836—fully deserved those labels and gloried in them. Historians of American radicalism have paid more attention to Owen than to either Wright or Rose—for a variety of reasons that include his association with the utopian socialist communities inspired by his father, Robert Owen; his role, as a congressman in the 1840s, in the founding of the Smithsonian Institution; the prolific and provocative nature of his writings; and, last but not least, his maleness. In his widely circulated 1830 pamphlet, *Moral Physiology*, Owen became the first person in the United States to openly advocate birth control. This was probably the work that made Beecher blush; of some 50,000 copies printed in the United States and Europe between 1830 and 1835, approximately 10,000 were circulated in America. Wright, who was also associated with Owenite utopian communities and was an early agitator for labor reform and equal rights for women, also receives some notice in accounts of early

American radicalism. Rose, however, is virtually forgotten today, neglected or omitted altogether from histories of the women's movement even though she occupies a unique position in the history of American Jews, feminism, and freethought.

A dozen years before the failed European democratic revolutions of 1848 led to an unprecedented migration of German-speaking Jews to America, and fifty years ahead of the much larger influx of East European Jews, Rose became the first Jewish immigrant to campaign aggressively for social reform in her adopted country. She was the Emma Goldman of the 1840s and 1850s, her speeches on behalf of abolitionism, women's rights, and atheism attracting widespread attention and opprobrium at a time when American audiences were totally unaccustomed to hearing anyone with a foreign accent lay claim to a stake in America's future. She frequently shared platforms with the best-known figures in the abolitionist and women's movements, including Garrison, Stanton, and Anthony, her closest friend among the feminists. When Garrison, determined to thumb his nose at Boston's most socially prominent and conservative churches, scheduled a series of Sunday lectures at the same time as weekly religious services, Rose, with, among others, Ralph Waldo Emerson, was one of the featured speakers. It is a measure of the broad democratic and internationalist spirit of the radical abolitionists that they did not hesitate to be publicly identified with a speaker who was so obviously a foreigner and a Jew. Yet in many important ways, Rose remained, as her biographer Carol Kolmerten notes, "an 'other' in a movement of others."[42] During a joint speaking tour in 1854, she poured out her anguish to Anthony after hearing that some of the most prominent abolitionists and feminists opposed citizenship for new immigrants. In her diary, Anthony astutely observed that "Mrs. Rose is not appreciated, nor cannot be by this age—she is too much in advance of the extreme ultraists [the most radical abolitionists and reformers] even to be understood by them."[43]

What Anthony did not say was that Rose's outspoken atheism was the most significant component of her "ultraism" and her unacceptability to many of the Christian participants in both the abolitionist and the women's movements. At an 1853 convention organized by Garrison to challenge literal interpretations of the Bible, Rose made it clear that she regarded all religious belief not as a natural human impulse but as the product of indoctrination. She argued that

> a child may be made to believe a falsehood and die in support of it, and therefore there can be no merit in a [mere] belief. We find in the various sects in Christendom, among the Jews, Mohammedans, Hindoos, in fact, throughout the entire world, that children are made to believe in the creed in which they are brought up. . . . Bibles are always written so obscure as to require priestly inter-preters . . . [whose] means of salvation is to strangle every one they come in contact with who does not believe as they do; and the more Infidels and heretics they strangle the surer their reward in heaven, and the most pious and conscientious among them try to bring out the most human sacrifices.[44]

It is also a measure of the character of reformers like Garrison and Mott, whose lives were untainted by personal scandal and whose rep-utation for moral probity was an important asset in their work, that they never gave the slightest credence to the gross personal attacks regularly directed at Rose. Garrison, who enjoyed a long and famously happy marriage, as did Rose herself, was put off neither by Rose's atheism nor by the many accusations that she was an advocate of "free love." Conservatives had linked religious unorthodoxy with sexual libertinism since the eighteenth century, and the support of feminists for divorce reform and married women's property rights, which the defenders of orthodox religion viewed as an undermining of the entire institution of marriage, reinforced the association. One minister, expressing himself in decidedly un-Christlike language in a Maine newspaper, summed up the conventional religious view of Rose: "We know of no object more deserving of contempt, loathing, and abhorrence than a female atheist. We hold the vilest strumpet from the stews to be by comparison respectable."[45] With her curly black hair, olive skin, and fashionable wardrobe, Rose was more attractive, albeit in an unconventional, foreign way, than many of her contemporaries in the women's movement. In newspaper commentary on Rose's speeches, "foreign" was a code word for "Jewish," and frequent references to her gloved hands provide a comical (to the modern reader) variation on the persistent stereotype of Jews who "talk with their hands." One example of this type of commentary, from the *Albany Register* of March 7, 1854, was reprinted thirty-three years later in the massive *History of Woman Suffrage* edited by Stanton, Anthony, and Matilda Joslyn Gage. Stanton and Rose, among others, had addressed the New York state legislature on behalf of married women's property rights, and Rose's fiery speeches received the most attention in the press. The importance of Rose's Jewishness—though the word is never used—and the linkage between women's rights and religious infidelity, is made clear in the long account published under the headline WOMAN'S RIGHTS IN THE LEGISLATURE:

It is a melancholy reflection, that among our American women who have been educated to better things, there should be found any who are willing to follow the lead of such foreign propagandists as the ringleted, glove-handed exotic, Ernestine L. Rose.... [T]hat one educated American woman should become her disciple and follow her infidel and insane teachings, is a marvel.

Ernestine L. Rose came to this country, as she says, from Poland, where she was compelled to fly in pursuit of freedom. Seeing her course here, we can well imagine this to be true. In no other country in the world, save possibly one, would her infidel propagandism and preachings in regard to the social relations of life be tolerated. She would be prohibited by the powers of government from her efforts to obliterate from the world the religion of the Cross—to banish the Bible as a text-book of faith, and to overturn social institutions that have existed through all political and governmental institutions from the remotest time.... But in this country, such is the freedom of our institutions, and we rejoice that it should be so, that she, and such as she, can give their genius for intrigue full sway. They can exhibit their flowing ringlets and beautiful hands, their winning smiles and charming stage attitudes to admiring audiences, who, while they are willing to be amused, are in the main safe from their corrupting theories and demoralizing propagandism.[46]

The singling out of Rose, even though other well-known American-born feminist activists, including Stanton and Antoinette Brown, had been equally vocal in their lobbying before the New York legislature (the campaign bore fruit in 1860 with a thoroughgoing reform bill expanding married women's property rights), attests both to her power as a speaker and to her image as an exotic outsider. Another local paper, though also in disagreement with Rose's views, nevertheless gave the "native of what was once Poland" her due. "This woman . . . is a remarkable one," the article conceded. "She possesses an intellect that lifts her a 'head and shoulders' above the mass of her sex. . . . Though we dissented from much—very much—that she said, yet we did admire her eloquence, her pathos, her elocution. She spoke wonderfully well. Her arguments were strong, and well put, and her wit and sarcasm 'told' unmistakably upon the large audience that listened to her."[47]

Thoroughly internationalist in outlook, Rose adamantly insisted that all human rights were equally important and refused to make tactical concessions to the exigencies of the moment. Thus, she opposed the suspension of women's rights conventions in deference to the demands of the Civil War, as she would later oppose the constitutional amendment that gave the vote to freed male slaves but not to women. But she would also disagree sharply with Stanton's and Anthony's racism-tainted argument against the Fifteenth Amendment—that it was particularly egregious to deny the vote to educated white women while granting it to uneducated black men. Suffrage, for Rose, was a basic right owed all men and women—not a privilege to be denied on the basis of educational, economic, and class-based disadvantages. Rose's uncompromising nature goes a long way toward explaining why she was seen as an outsider, and an abrasive one at that, even by those who, like Anthony, agreed with most of her principles and respected her dedication to social reform. But Rose's personality by itself cannot account for her virtual nonexistence in the now voluminous history of the women's movement. The real explanation lies in the combination of Rose's atheism, her Jewishness, and the early timing of her immigration—a threefold "outsiderness."

The immigrant Jew as atheist and social radical has been a recognizable figure—both as a pejorative stereotype and, for fellow radicals, as an exemplar—since the end of the nineteenth century. That was not so for American Jews during the thirty-year period when Rose was most active in American social reform movements. When Rose arrived in 1836, the Jewish establishment in America was largely Sephardic, with roots dating from the seventeenth century (though German Jews were beginning to make their presence felt). Like the rabbis who had written letters of gratitude to George Washington, early-nineteenth-century American Jews were rightly convinced that the legal equality granted by the Constitution, while not prohibiting social and economic discrimination, offered them a freedom from persecution and a degree of personal liberty only dreamed of by most of their European Jewish contemporaries. The wall of separation between church and state was seen by American Jews as the guarantor of their safety, and the organized Jewish community protested against obvious attempts, like the attack on Sunday mail service, to breach that wall. Otherwise, Jews in the antebellum era, whether in the North or the South, rarely made fundamental criticisms of a society that, in their view, had been extremely good to them. Jews did not play a significant role in either the abolitionist or the early women's movement and were even more reluctant to associate themselves publicly with freethinkers. Communal leaders were mindful that Jews had, since American Enlightenment-bashing began in the 1790s, often been lumped with other religious "infidels" as well as with the French revolutionary brand of atheism. They wished to present themselves to Christian Americans as morally upright believers who just happened—a small point!—not to believe that Jesus was the Messiah. Apart from that, Jews asked only for the civic and legal equality guaranteed by the Constitution. The Jews who began arriving in larger numbers in the 1840s from Germany and from culturally German areas of eastern Europe had essentially the same attitude toward America. Someone who made herself as conspicuous as Rose, in movements that antagonized the majority of Americans, was certainly not seen by Jews as a credit to her people or, as most Americans would have put it then, "a credit to the Hebrew race."

For Jewish women, the ideal of American Jewish womanhood at midcentury was embodied by Philadelphia's Rebecca Gratz— wealthy, well-educated, pious, and the founder of the Female Hebrew Benevolent Society, the first Jewish charitable organization independent of a synagogue. Like most upper-class whites, Jewish and gentile alike, Gratz opposed the radical abolitionists and was even more horrified by the activities of women's rights advocates. She considered it "monstrous" that women should "step out of the sphere god designed [them] to fill."[48] The archival material on Gratz, maintained by many Jewish libraries, museums, and historical associations, is extensive and well-organized; the material on Rose, by contrast, is scattered among the papers of other radical reformers and in the surviving files of little-known freethought newspapers and the *Liberator*. The issue is not whether Gratz or Rose is the more important historical figure but that the memory of a pious founder of charities is much more likely to be preserved than that of an atheist who challenged the norms of her own generation and subsequent ones. Sara A. Underwood, one of the most prominent women freethinkers of the nineteenth century, anticipated quite a different outcome. Writing in 1876, Underwood recalled her disappointment at the omission of Rose from an 1870 volume titled *Eminent Women of the Age*. In spite of the "services for liberty of all kinds Mrs. Rose had performed," Underwood noted, "I turned over page after page of that book, confidently expecting to find her name given the honorable mention it deserved. But I turned over the leaves in vain. She was, doubtless, too radical for any of those who contributed to that volume to venture to seem to countenance. But I have no doubt that another book of the same kind, compiled within the next ten years, will not be likely to make the same omission."[49]

Like most other nineteenth-century freethinkers, Underwood

underestimated the durability of conservative religion and overestimated the likelihood that an avowed atheist would ever be recognized as one of the most eminent figures of any American era. Values are handed down more easily and thoroughly by permanent institutions than by marginalized radicals who, even if they change minds in their own generation—as the abolitionists did—are often subject to remarginalization in the next. Every brand of religion maintains and *is* a permanent mechanism for transmitting ideas and values—whether one regards those values as admirable or repugnant. Secularist movements, with their generally loose, nonhierarchical organization, lack the power to hand down and disseminate their heritage in a systematic way.

Garrison was the exception that proves the rule: he lived to see the end of legal slavery, though conventional wisdom would soon rewrite the story and assert that the uncouth pressure of radical abolitionists had nothing to do with the freeing of America's slaves. Garrison has recently been rediscovered, but his name was unknown, as I can attest to from personal experience as a newspaper reporter in the sixties, to most civil rights volunteers of that generation. Moreover, Garrison's reputation might never have been revived had he not published his own newspaper, which was not only a history of radical abolitionism and early feminism but a rich autobiography. The most regrettable consequence of the discontinuity in the record of American rationalist dissent is that its moral lessons must be relearned in every generation. It is telling that even so voracious a reader as Garrison was beyond the midpoint of his life when he discovered his spiritual ancestor Thomas Paine. When your own mind is your own church, it can take a very long time for future generations to make their way to the sanctuary.

4

THE BELIEF AND UNBELIEF
OF ABRAHAM LINCOLN

The Civil War, like most wars, was a bad time for religious skeptics. It was also a crucible in which Americans were forced to question their moral values as never before. On April 10, 1861—two days before the attack on Fort Sumter ushered in the war—the indefatigable Ernestine Rose delivered a lecture titled "A Defense of Atheism" at Boston's Mercantile Hall. Arguing against the idea that religious belief is a precondition for moral behavior, Rose reminded her audience that America's "present crisis" had been created by a system of slavery long upheld by many religious leaders in the North as well as the South.

As soon as the first shots were fired, the issue of northern churchmen's waffling response to slavery disappeared from public discourse and was replaced by the overpowering conviction that God was on the side of the Union army. As far as the South was concerned, He was of course on the side of the Confederacy. There was no more talk from ministers of "silken ties" between northern and southern Christians. The real cause of America's fratricidal conflict, many religious leaders asserted, was the failure of the founders to enshrine God in the Constitution. The war was nothing more—or less—than the fulfillment of the Reverend John Mason's 1793 prediction that the godless document would one day impel the Divinity to "crush us to atoms in the wreck." The only way to stop the destruction was to amend the Constitution's preamble and finally acknowledge not only God but Jesus Christ as the source of all just governmental power. In 1863, the "nondenominational," albeit entirely Protestant, National Reform Association was founded for the specific purpose of lobbying Congress to put God into the Constitution. Today's Christian conservatives frequently use the slogan "Let's put God *back* into the Constitution," thereby implying that "secular humanists" have managed to overturn what was originally intended to be a marriage of church and state. Nineteenth-century clerics knew better and were honest about their desire to reverse what they regarded as the founders' erroneous decision to separate church and state. At an 1864 convention in Pittsburgh, the National Reform delegates were in a dither about how to word the proposed amendment before presenting it to President Lincoln and the Congress, so as not to offend any orthodox Protestant denomination. They were not worried about offending Jews, Catholics, or dissident Protestant sects like Hicksite Quakers, who were appalled by the idea of tampering with the Constitution in order to blur the distinction between church and state. After rejecting acknowledgment of "Almighty God" and "His revealed will" as too imprecise, the ministers finally agreed on a rewording of the preamble that would replace "We, the People of the United States, in order to form a more perfect union . . ." with "Recognizing Almighty God as the source of all authority and power in civil government, and acknowledging the Lord Jesus Christ as the Governor among the nations, His revealed will as the supreme law of the land, in order to constitute a Christian government . . ."

The religious stalwarts who founded the National Reform Association met with Lincoln in February 1864 and presented him with their forthright petition for a Christian government:

> You . . . as no other of our Chief Magistrates ever did, have
> solemnly reminded us of the redeeming grace of our blessed Savior,

and of the authority of the Holy Scriptures over us as a people. By such acts as these you have awakened a hope in the Christian people of this land that you represent them in feeling the want of a distinct and plain recognition of the divine authority in the Constitution of the United States.[1]

The ministers had some reason to hope that Lincoln would respond to them favorably. In 1862, he had issued an order, unprecedented in American history, that military commanders observe Sunday as a day of rest in deference to the religious sensibilities of Christian soldiers. But Lincoln was also one of the canniest politicians ever to occupy the White House, and he had no intention of using his authority on behalf of a measure as potentially divisive as the Christian amendment in the midst of a war that had already pitted brother against brother and neighbor against neighbor. Observing that "the work of amending the Constitution should never be done hastily," he promised to "take such action upon it as my responsibility to my Maker and our country demands."[2] Lincoln's action was to take no action at all. Congress also ducked the proposal to Christianize the Constitution and continued to table similar resolutions year after year.

The ministers may have derived some consolation from the fact that Congress, though unwilling to become embroiled in debate over a substantive constitutional amendment, was easily persuaded to take the symbolic action of acknowledging the deity on American coins. The union of God and Mammon came about as the result of a suggestion by a Pennsylvania minister to Secretary of the Treasury Salmon P. Chase, who was known to be the most religiously orthodox member of Lincoln's cabinet and who took credit for Lincoln's invocation of God at the end of the Emancipation Proclamation. Originally, the president had planned to end the historic decree freeing the slaves with the sentence "And upon this, sincerely believed to be an act of justice, warranted by the Constitution, upon military necessity, I invoke the considerate judgment of mankind."[3] Supposedly acting on Chase's recommendation, Lincoln added "and the gracious favor of Almighty God" to the "considerate judgment of mankind."[4] Scholars have also suggested, on the basis of less evidence, that Chase was responsible for the addition of "under God" to the famous closing sentence of the Gettysburg Address: "It is rather for us to be here dedicated to the great task remaining before us—that from these honored dead we take increased devotion to that cause for which they here gave the last full measure of devotion; that we here highly resolve that these dead shall not have died in vain; that this nation, under God, shall have a new birth of freedom; and that government of the people, by the people, for the people shall not perish from the earth." The words "under God" do not appear in Lincoln's first or second handwritten draft of his address, so he may have added the phrase as he spoke. Lincoln did write "under God" in three subsequent copies he made of the speech.

But Chase was definitely responsible for the push to add a religious motto to American coins. After receiving the Pennsylvania clergyman's proposal for a more devout currency, the secretary of the treasury promptly ordered the director of the mint to change the format of coins to reflect "the trust of our people in God." To Chase's dismay, he soon discovered that only Congress could authorize any alteration of the currency. After considerable deliberation about the exact wording of the motto—should it be "Our country; our God" or "God, our Trust"?—Congress settled on "In God we trust" for a new two-cent coin issued in 1864. By the end of 1865, the original permission had been extended to engrave the motto on coins of nearly all denominations.⁵ (This wording naturally provided endless opportunities for the pun "In gold we trust." A later variation, during the period of controversy over the gold standard, was "in God we trust—for the short weight." Theodore Roosevelt, one of the most devout Christians ever to be elected president, attempted in 1907 to dispense with the motto precisely because of those sacrilegious puns. He succeeded only in arousing a storm of criticism from ministers who had previously been among his strongest supporters. Roosevelt, who had dubbed Paine a "filthy little atheist," was himself called an infidel for his attempt to remove God from American money.)

However, no displays of symbolic piety during the Civil War could completely rewrite the miserable record of organized religion's response to what most northern Christians were finally prepared to call the sin of slavery. Only the small minority of freethinkers, many of them longtime abolitionists, could lay aside the question of how a just God could allow their nation to engage in a war instigated by the desire of men to own other men. The nonbeliever was free to view slavery as the work—the evil work—of man alone. For many believers, the war was a crisis of faith, if not in God, then in the earthly institutions that purported to speak for God. Religious institutions responded to the crisis by expanding their proselytizing. In the first year of the war, the American Bible Society published 370,000 more Bibles than it had in 1860. From 1861 until the end of the war, more than 5.2 million Bibles were printed.[6] The intensity of the Christian imagery associated with the Union cause—never equaled before or since the war—represented an extremely successful effort to supercede the compromised and compromising religion that had consented to the existence of slavery for so long. "The Battle Hymn of the Republic," one of the most powerful calls to arms ever set to music, was not only religious but Christian to the core. The last verse of Julia Ward Howe's anthem, as well known during the war as the famous first verse is today, explicitly articulates the song's Christian doctrinal basis and emotional appeal: "In the beauty of the lilies Christ was born across the sea, / With a glory in His bosom that transfigures you and me; / As he died to make men holy, let us die to make men free, / While God is marching on." But what was a devout Christian from the North, fighting under instructions from his God, to make of an equally devout southern cousin whose God—ostensibly the same God—had handed down a contradictory set of instructions? While the Civil War ushered in a revival of religious devotion for many, it also raised fundamental questions about whether religion was really a force for good in the world.

During the war years, no one agonized over these moral and ethical issues more profoundly, or articulated them more clearly for the American public, than Abraham Lincoln. A discussion of Lincoln is central to the history of American freethought, because he grappled with and exemplified so many of the complicated, often dissonant forces that have shaped American attitudes toward religion. So large does Lincoln loom in the American pantheon that every religious and antireligious group wants to claim him as a member; over the years, he has been described in print as an agnostic, unbeliever, freethinker, spiritualist, every sort of Protestant, and as a Roman Catholic. The weird claim of Catholicism for a man raised in an evangelical Baptist frontier environment appears to have originated in the fact that Lincoln did indeed have an aunt who was a Catholic—and she had a son named Abraham. In 1927, Cardinal George Mundelein of Chicago seems to have confused Lincoln's aunt with his stepmother—who was not a Catholic—and the aunt's son with the future president. Mundelein informed a credulous Chicago press that when a traveling priest arrived to say Mass for Lincoln's stepmother, "Mr. Lincoln would prepare the altar himself."[7] The Chicago prelate, it should be noted, was one of the foremost early-twentieth-century advocates of Americanizing a Catholic Church still strongly associated with immigrants. What better way to accomplish that than to link Catholicism with the martyred president who was considered a secular saint? The universality and durability of Lincoln's fascination to both the orthodox and the unorthodox can be gleaned even from a glancing survey of the hundreds of books devoted solely to his religious belief or nonbelief: *Abraham Lincoln, the Ideal Christian* (1913); *Lincoln the Freethinker* (1924); *Abraham Lincoln and Hillel's Golden Rule* (1929); *Abraham Lincoln: Fatalist, Skeptic, Atheist, or Christian?* (1942); *The Religion of Abraham Lincoln* (1963), and *Abraham Lincoln: Theologian of American Anguish* (1973). One of the most recent studies of Lincoln's belief is an elegant exegesis of his Second Inaugural Address, *Lincoln's Greatest Speech* (2002), by Ronald C. White, dean and professor of religious history at San Francisco State University.

Although the intensity of scholarly and popular interest in Lincoln's faith has never wavered in the 140 years since his assassination, many claims about his religious devotion amount to nothing more than the apocrypha that inevitably shrouds the real beliefs of men of mythic stature. One such story, quoted uncritically by a number of nineteenth- and early-twentieth-century biographers, appeared soon after the war in the *Western Christian Advocate*, a leading Protestant journal. The paper reported that Lincoln, after receiving the news that Lee had surrendered to Grant at Appomattox, called his cabinet into session, and, upon the president's suggestion, "all dropped on their knees, and offered in silence and in tears their humble and heartfelt acknowledgment to the Almighty for the triumph he had granted to the national cause." The article claimed that the conveniently anonymous source was "a friend intimate with the late President Lincoln."[8] In 1890, John E. Remsburg, a well-known freethinker, set out to track down the origin of the story. Only one of Lincoln's cabinet members, Hugh M. McCulloch (Lincoln's last secretary of the treasury) was still living, but he answered Remsburg's inquiry in unequivocal terms in a letter dated February 1891. "The description of what occurred at the Executive Mansion," McCulloch wrote, "when the intelligence was received of the surrender of the Confederate forces, which you quote from the *Western Christian Advocate*, is not only absolutely groundless, but absurd. After I became Secretary of the Treasury I was present at every Cabinet meeting and I never saw Mr. Lincoln or any of his ministers upon his knees or in tears."[9]

The persistence of this story, and many others like it, reveals a good deal more about conventional American religious attitudes than it does about Lincoln. It was not enough for the Great Emancipator to be seen as a deeply moral man or even a believer in God; he had to be presented as a Christian, a believer in divine revelation, and a commander in chief who, granted victory, thanked his God for having been on the side of the strongest battalion. "It was not until after Mr. Lincoln's death," wrote his friend and law partner Ward Hill Lamon in 1872, "that his alleged orthodoxy became the principal topic of his eulogists; but since then the effort on the part of some political writers and speakers to impress the public mind erroneously seems to have been general and systematic."[10] Lincoln, who had picked Lamon to escort him to Washington in 1861, amid rumors that he would be assassinated before being sworn in as president, then appointed him marshal for the District of Columbia. In that capacity, Lamon was responsible for the president's personal safety—a difficult task, since Lincoln frequently disregarded his friend's warnings. At times when political passions ran especially high—the White House not being the armed fortress it is today—Lamon slept on a cot, his weapon at the ready, to protect his president from any armed intruders. On the evening of Lincoln's assassination at Ford's Theatre, though, Lamon was in Richmond on a special presidential assignment; before leaving, he had warned Lincoln not to go out at night and especially to avoid the theater. Lamon's last task as a government official was to escort the body of his martyred friend back to Springfield for burial.

Ordinarily, books published in the first decade after the death of an important political leader—especially one who has been assassinated—are of interest primarily for their insight into the temper of the time. That generalization applies even more strongly to the literary and personal quarrels surrounding books by friends and colleagues: *I knew him better than you knew him.* No one would argue, for instance, that Kenneth O'Donnell, Theodore Sorensen, or even so distinguished a historian as Arthur Schlesinger, Jr., presented a full and evenhanded portrait of John F. Kennedy, their boss and friend, in the books they wrote about him in the sixties and early seventies. But no one would deny that the judgments of contemporaries who knew Kennedy well, and knew him long before he began running for the presidency, are an important contribution to the permanent historical record of his character. In the case of Lincoln—whose stature as the leader who preserved the Union meant that his assassination produced an even greater outpouring of memoir and biography than Kennedy's would—the tendency to place a higher value on the reminiscences of old friends than on those of more recent acquaintances and political hangers-on was reversed. Greater credence was given in the late nineteenth century to the reminiscences of people who met Lincoln after he became a major political figure, or knew him only slightly, than to those of people who knew him well and worked with him long before the Lincoln-Douglas debates catapulted the man from Illinois into the national spotlight. As a general rule, the post-presidential acquaintances emphasized Lincoln's religiosity, while those who had known the president from his young manhood emphasized his religious skepticism. The views of old friends who regarded Lincoln as a freethinker were greeted with outright disbelief and intense animosity.

The contrasting responses to two biographies titled *Life of Abraham Lincoln*—the first by Josiah Gilbert Holland in 1866, the other by Lamon in 1872—demonstrate what Americans did and did not want to hear about their recently slain president. Holland was a well-known poet, magazine writer, and editor for many years of the respected *Scribner's Magazine*. His *Life*, published only a year after the president's death, was basically a quickie book (albeit a tome of more than five hundred pages) designed to capitalize on public interest in a dramatic news event—as common a phenomenon in the nineteenth as in the twenty-first century. Holland did not know Lincoln personally, and he spoke only of Lincoln's virtues, ignored all defects of character, and, above all, emphasized his devout Christianity. He concluded that "the power of a true-hearted Christian man, in perfect sympathy with a true-hearted Christian people, was Mr. Lincoln's power.... While he took care of deeds fashioned by a purely ideal standard, God took care of results. Moderate, frank, truthful, gentle, forgiving, loving, just, Mr. Lincoln will always be remembered as eminently a Christian president; and the almost immeasurably great results which he had the privilege of achieving were due to the fact that he was a Christian president."[11] One of Holland's chief pieces of evidence for Lincoln's Christian piety was a conversation between Lincoln and one Newton Bateman, who served as Illinois superintendent of public instruction in the late 1850s and had an office in the same building as the future president; the details of the conversation of course came entirely from Bateman. During the 1860 presidential campaign, Lincoln expressed his distress over the fact that twenty out of Springfield's twenty-three Protestant ministers opposed his election. "Mr. Bateman, I am not a Christian—God knows I would be one," Lincoln reportedly told Bateman. The future president went on to say that he could not understand how ministers who believed in the New Testament, "in the light of which human bondage cannot live a moment, . . . are going to vote against me. I do not understand it at all." Later, Lincoln supposedly added, "I know there is a God, and that he hates injustice and slavery. I see the storm coming, and I know that his hand is in it. If he has a place for me—and I think he has—I believe I am ready. I am nothing, but truth is everything. I know I am right, for Christ teaches it, and Christ is God." The account of this conversation, which makes Lincoln sound both pompous and schizoid, is bizarre on several counts. Why would Lincoln say in one breath that he was not a Christian and in the next that Christ was God? In his public speeches, Lincoln almost never referred to Jesus and never described him as God. Moreover, why would Lincoln confide views to Bateman, a mere professional acquaintance (albeit a respected one), and not share them with his closest friends? In his bestselling book, Holland had an answer:

> The effect of this conversation upon the mind of Mr. Bateman, a Christian gentleman whom Mr. Lincoln profoundly respected, was to convince him that Mr. Lincoln had, in his quiet way, found a path to the Christian standpoint—that he had found God, and rested on the eternal truth of God. As the two men were about to separate, Mr. Bateman remarked: 'I had not supposed that you were accustomed to think so much upon this class of subjects. Certainly your friends generally are ignorant of the sentiments you have expressed to me.' He replied quickly: 'I know they are. I am obliged to appear different to them; but I think more upon these subjects than upon all others, and I have done so for years; and I am willing that *you* should know it.' "[12]

As evidence of the slain president's Christian orthodoxy, these passages make no sense. If Lincoln was indeed a devout believer, why would the majority of clergymen in his hometown have opposed his candidacy? And why would he have felt "obliged" to conceal his true respect for religion from his friends—not to mention all of those unfriendly ministers, who might well have changed their opinion of him had he professed his devout Christianity to them? Why should he reveal his religious orthodoxy privately to only one man, when it would surely have helped his candidacy to proclaim his belief in Jesus from the rooftops? Something else was at work in the favorable popular and critical reception of Holland's book, and that something was a desire to identify the martyred leader with every conventional definition of virtue—Christian orthodoxy being one of them.

Lamon's 1872 *Life*, like Holland's a work of more than five hundred pages, dealt only with Lincoln's experiences before he became president. A second volume was supposed to cover the presidential years, but it was never written because the first volume was a financial and critical failure. Although he loved Lincoln as a friend and admired him as a leader, Lamon avoided the hagiographical tone that had characterized nearly everything written about Lincoln since his death. He wrote of Lincoln's love for the doomed Ann Rutledge, his bouts of depression, his ambition, his knack for political compromise, and—most damningly, in the view of the critics—his long history of religious skepticism. The book was based both on Lamon's firsthand observations and on extensive material supplied by William H. Herndon, Lincoln's law partner in Springfield since 1844. Herndon had begun to gather reminiscences from those who had known the future president from his teenage years, but he decided not to write a book himself at that time and sold his collection to Lamon. He would write his own book on Lincoln in the 1890s and would outrage conservative critics with the statement "Now let it be written in history and on Mr. Lincoln's tomb: 'He died an unbeliever.' " Herndon also had a reputation for drinking, and Mary Todd Lincoln despised him—but Lincoln, as attested to by their amicable and successful sixteen-year partnership, held him in high regard. It is possible that Herndon's unsavory reputation influenced the negative reception of Lamon's biography, but the real reason for the antipathy was that Herndon and Lamon presented a side of Lincoln that no one wanted to acknowledge. Many sincere Christians, Lamon suggested, were understandably eager to believe that Lincoln shared their religious beliefs because "his great prominence in the world's history, and his identification with some of the great questions of our time, which, by their moral import, were held to be eminently religious in their character, have led many good people to trace in his motives and actions similar convictions to those held by themselves."[13]

Lamon's testimony is persuasive because—unlike Herndon—he was not a crusading agnostic but instead regarded Lincoln's religious skepticism as both a personal and a political liability. "It is very probable," he asserted, "that much of Mr. Lincoln's unhappiness, the melancholy that 'dripped from him as he walked,' was due to his want of religious faith. When the black fit was on him, he suffered as much mental misery as [John] Bunyan or [William] Cowper in the deepest anguish of their conflicts with the evil one. . . . To a man of his temperament, predisposed as it was to depression of spirits, there could be no chance of happiness, if doomed to live without hope and without God in the world."[14]

As a young man, Lincoln had read both Paine's *The Age of Reason* and the French philosopher Constantin Volney's *The Ruins*, another influential treatise on religious skepticism written in the 1790s. (The first twenty chapters of the book were translated by Thomas Jefferson for an American edition.) Lincoln apparently read these books in 1831–32, while he was a clerk in the general store at New Salem, Illinois, a town of twenty-five families but with a much larger population of transients. The self-educated store clerk probably borrowed the books from Dr. John Allen, a neighbor and Dartmouth College graduate who had moved west for health reasons and had founded a debating society of young men. Twelve years later, after Lincoln had been admitted to the bar and taken on Herndon as a law partner in Springfield, the two men discussed the "infidel" books. Herndon, who was a self-proclaimed agnostic by the 1860s, later maintained that it was Lincoln whose arguments had helped undermine his religious faith. There are good reasons to take Herndon's recollections with more than a grain of salt, since freethinkers were just as eager as religious believers to project their own beliefs onto the martyred president. However, the fact that Herndon's view of Lincoln was shared by many old friends certainly suggests that the freethinking side of Lincoln's nature should be included in any overall evaluation of his beliefs. In the 1870s, few commentators (with the exception of the critic of the *New York World*, a newspaper more favorably disposed than most toward liberalism in religious matters) saw any merit in Lamon's book or Herndon's publicly expressed views. An article in the journal *Christian Union*, which many believed to have been written by its editor, the prominent minister and orator Henry Ward Beecher, declared that Lamon was inspired by an "anti-Christian animus" and added that "he does not know what Lincoln was, nor what religion is." Beecher, a son of the Enlightenment foe Lyman Beecher, would grow much more liberal in his views as he aged. One of his funeral orations would be delivered in 1887 by Robert Ingersoll, a close personal friend in spite of their differing views of religion. When the *Christian Union* article appeared, Lamon wrote Beecher an indignant, bluntly phrased reply. "That I did not know what Mr. Lincoln was," he said, "I must take leave to contradict with some emphasis; that I do not know what religion is, in the presence of so many illustrious failures, I may be permitted to doubt." Lamon continued:

> Speaking of Mr. Lincoln in reference to this feature of his character, I express the decided opinion that he was an eminently moral man. Regarding him as a moral man, with my views upon the relations existing between the two characteristics, I have no difficulty believing him a religious man! Yet he was not a Christian. He possessed, it is true, a system of faith and worship, but it was one which Orthodox Christianity stigmatizes as a false religion.

> ... Those who would canonize Mr. Lincoln as a saint should pause and reflect a brief moment upon the incalculable injury they do to the cause which most of them profess to love. It would certainly have been pleasant to me to have closed without touching upon his religious opinions; but such an omission would have violated the fundamental principle upon which every line of the book is traced. Had it been possible to have truthfully asserted that he was a member of the Church of Christ or that he believed in the

teachings of the New Testament, the facts would have been proclaimed with a glow of earnest and unfeigned satisfaction.[15]

Whether Lincoln was or was not a devout religious believer—and a Christian—is a question that has never been answered. As the twentieth century progressed, the definition of "Christian" expanded; most modern scholars who insist on faith as the animating force in Lincoln's life do not feel obliged to claim that he believed in the divinity of Christ or the Bible as the revealed word of God. But the same scholars, like their counterparts in the nineteenth century, tend to dismiss out of hand the credibility of those who emphasized Lincoln's skeptical side. In *Abraham Lincoln: Theologian of American Anguish*, Elton Trueblood offers the characteristic argument that "no serious modern historian" accepts Herndon's characterization of Lincoln as an unbeliever. The author declares that if the freethinking Herndon was right, "we are forced to the conclusion that Lincoln was the archhypocrite. His hundreds of statements affirming the reality of God's guidance would have to be assigned to insincerity, a task too great even for the most inveterate debunker."[16]

So we are to dismiss the Lincoln who repeatedly refused to join any church and believe the ministers who claimed that he was just about to join *their* congregations before being felled by an assassin's bullet. We are to remember the Lincoln with a command of the Scriptures unusual even in an era when the Bible was the basic text for every literate person and to forget the Lincoln who observed that the Bible could be used in support of just about any cause. Hypocrisy is hardly the only explanation for the divergence between the religious references in Lincoln's speeches and the private skepticism observed by his friends. The public Lincoln, attempting to steer the nation through its greatest crisis, may well have longed for the guidance of a power greater than man and referred to that guidance in his speeches—even if he himself lacked unquestioning and wholehearted faith. Lincoln was renowned, and often criticized, for the slowness of his decision-making processes, and he repeatedly rejected the notion of a revealed truth that descends from on high in a sudden burst of clarity, sweeping away all doubts. He explicitly, and sardonically, expressed this viewpoint during the long and tortuous deliberations leading to his decision to issue the Emancipation Proclamation. Responding to a demand for immediate emancipation from a mass assemblage of Chicago Christians, Lincoln replied:

> I am approached with the most opposite opinions and advice, and that by religious men, who are equally certain that they represent the Divine will. I am sure that either the one or the other is mistaken in that belief, and perhaps in some respects both. I hope it will not be irreverent for me to say that if it is probable that God would reveal his will to others, on a point so connected with my duty, it might be supposed he would reveal it directly to me; for, unless I am more deceived in myself than I often am, it is my earnest desire to know the will of Providence in this matter. *And if I can learn what it is, I will do it!* These are not, however, the days of miracles, and I suppose it will be granted that I am not to expect a direct revelation. I must study the plain, physical facts of the case, ascertain what is possible and learn what appears to be wise and right.[17]

In the same ironic tone, Lincoln outlined a concern that he would articulate more fully in his unforgettable Second Inaugural Address. He noted that "the rebel soldiers are praying with a great deal more earnestness, I fear, than our own troops, and expecting God to favor their side; for one of our soldiers, who had been taken prisoner, [said] . . . that he met with nothing so discouraging as the evident sincerity of those he was among in their prayers." The utility of religion in support of slavery had pushed radical abolitionists like Garrison away from all established churches, but Lincoln—to the dismay of abolitionists who favored immediate emancipation—did not see either religion or its relation to slavery in such Manichean terms. Lincoln's evolution from a cautious gradualist on abolition into the Great Emancipator is of course a remarkable case study of the complementarity and conflict between morality and pragmatic politics.

What makes Lincoln a compelling figure to religious believers and nonbelievers alike is that his character was suffused with a rare combination of rationalism and prophetic faith in almost perfect equipoise. Lincoln's strong rationalist side, as well as his sardonic wit—"I hope it will not be irreverent for me to say that if it is probable that God would reveal his will to others . . . it might be supposed he would reveal it directly to me"—was evident in his response to the Chicago ministers. A man who does not expect to be the beneficiary of revealed truth, who must make a decision based on his evaluation of the "plain, physical facts of the case," should not be cast in the role of a Moses, Isaiah, or Jeremiah. At the same time, Lincoln's public statements—even those permeated by doubt—surely do not support Herndon's description of him as a convinced unbeliever. The man who wrote the Second Inaugural Address, with its majestic cadences calling on his countrymen to act "with malice toward none; with charity for all; with firmness in the right, as God gives us to see the right," cannot have been an unbeliever in the twentieth-century sense. But in both the eighteenth and the nineteenth centuries, the word *unbelief*, used in a religious context, was more likely to connote doubt than outright rejection of all religion. And if one substitutes "doubter" or "skeptic" for "unbeliever," the sixteenth president of the United States surely qualifies.

Lincoln's Second Inaugural Address, his last major speech, has frequently been called a sermon. One religious scholar, William Wolf, describes the address as "one of the most astute pieces of Christian theology ever written," adding that Lincoln "achieved a religious perspective above partisan strife that was not shared by most of the Christian theologians of his day or any day."[18] In a moving line-by-line analysis of the text, the historian Ronald White argues that "the religious cast of the Second Inaugural gave it a power and authority that were singular."[19] But that was not how the speech was perceived at the time. As contemporary newspaper commentary makes clear, many Americans found the Second Inaugural Address puzzling and pedestrian, filled with doubt and ambiguity rather than with a prophetic sense of purpose. Everyone is right—and therein lies the difficulty of classifying Lincoln's true religious outlook. In the heart of the address, Lincoln returned to the troubling issue he raised

before the Chicago ministers in 1863—the fact that both northern and
southern combatants believed God to be on their side:

> Both read the same Bible, and pray to the same God; and each
> invokes His aid against the other. It may seem strange that any men
> should dare to ask a just God's assistance in wringing their bread
> from the sweat of other men's faces; but let us judge not that we be
> not judged. The prayers of both could not be answered; that of nei-
> ther has been answered fully. The Almighty has His own purposes.
> "Woe unto the world because of offences! for it must needs be that
> offences come; but woe to that man by whom the offence
> cometh!" If we shall suppose that American Slavery is one of those
> offences, which, in the providence of God, must needs come, but
> which, having continued through His appointed time, He now
> wills to remove, and that He gives to both North and South this
> terrible war, as the woe due to those by whom the offence came,
> shall we discern therein any departure from those divine attributes
> which the believers in a Living God always ascribe to Him?
> Fondly do we hope—fervently do we pray—that this mighty
> scourge of war may speedily pass away. Yet, if God wills that it
> continue, until all the wealth piled by the bond-man's two hundred
> and fifty years of unrequited toil shall be sunk, and until every
> drop of blood drawn with the lash, shall be paid by another drawn
> with the sword, as was said three thousand years ago, so still it
> must be said, "the judgments of the Lord, are true and righteous
> altogether."

With due respect to the theologians who see Lincoln as a profound
religious thinker, it is easy to understand why many of Lincoln's contemporaries saw this section of the speech as a muddle. The president's declaration that "it may seem strange that any men should dare
to ask a just God's assistance in wringing their bread from the sweat
of other men's faces" was greeted by the audience, according to the
New York Herald, as "a satirical observation," which "caused a half
laugh."[20] But it is unlikely that Lincoln meant to convey satire or sarcasm, in view of his immediate admonition to "judge not that we be
not judged." The next sentences, so deterministic in their view of

God's relationship to slavery, can be read in several ways—as evidence of the fatalism that was another strong element in Lincoln's character, as a statement that men cannot comprehend the ways of God, and as either a rhetorical or a genuine questioning of God's ways: *shall we discern therein any departure from those divine attributes which the believers in a Living God always ascribe to Him?* If this clause was an intentional rhetorical device (and surely it was, given Lincoln's skills as an orator), it was also a real question—one that flowed from the skeptical side of Lincoln's religious persona. To the doubter, Lincoln's reassertion of belief in the goodness of God's plan—*the judgments of the Lord, are true and righteous altogether*—is in some sense profoundly undermined by his having raised the issue of whether war, not to mention slavery itself, posed a serious challenge to the conventional attribution of goodness to a Living God. If Lincoln was a theologian, his was a theology filled with inconsistencies, hesitations, and unanswerable questions.

The absence of triumphalism and religious certainty in the Second Inaugural merits particular notice in view of the political rhetoric, combining religion and the doctrine of American exceptionalism, that surrounds and attempts to sanctify America's current military actions. As White notes, Lincoln "offered little comfort for those who in every crisis or war want to chant, 'God is on our side.'" And even though the arguments of the Second Inaugural are grounded in biblical concepts, "Lincoln speaks forever against any 'God bless America' etiology that fails to come to terms with evil and hypocrisy in its own house."[21] Indeed, the impartial stewardship of Lincoln's God—*He gives both North and South this terrible war, as the woe due to those by whom the offence came*—may explain the initial coolness of the reception accorded his "greatest speech" in the North. The unmistakable implication of complicity in slavery on the part of all Americans, including Lincoln himself, was as far removed from the fervid moral righteousness of "The Battle Hymn of the Republic" as it is from George W. Bush's pious excoriation of evildoers.

Nevertheless, the theological cast of Lincoln's address elicited a fair amount of editorial criticism on grounds that it represented a departure from the American tradition of separation of church and state. The *New York World*, which rashly went so far as to compare Lincoln's views on church and state to those of the reactionary Pope Pius IX (which would have been news to the pope as well as to the president's freethinking friends), sternly declared that Lincoln had abandoned "all pretense of statesmanship" by taking "refuge in piety" in the address.[22] This reaction is notable not because it is an accurate evaluation of Lincoln's general views or of the address itself but because it demonstrates how unaccustomed nineteenth-century Americans were to hearing presidents use any religious rationales (as distinct from commonplace biblical references) in their speeches on public affairs.

It is significant that almost no one, apart from Lincoln scholars, remembers the quasi-theological portions of the Second Inaugural, while the closing paragraph is familiar to every American with a scintilla of historical knowledge: "With malice toward none; with charity for all; with firmness in the right, as God gives us to see the right, let us strive on to finish the work we are in; to bind up the nation's wounds; to care for him who shall have borne the battle, and for his widow, and his orphan—to do all which may achieve and cherish a just, and a lasting peace, among ourselves, and with all nations." Lincoln, who had less than six weeks to live, was speaking not as a theologian or a saint but as a good and merciful man (*too* merciful, in the view of many northerners who wished to see their southern compatriots punished severely for their rebellion against the Union). After Lincoln's death, his would-be canonizers would appropriate that goodness and mercy under the banner of religion. The attempt to Christianize a president who had never been a member of a Christian church was predictable, if paradoxical, after a war of extraordinary brutality fought by both sides in the name of Christian righteousness. "There was something in the hearts of good and typical Christian[s] . . . which exploded," commented a Union general who had witnessed the savage guerrilla warfare between northern and southern sympathizers in Missouri and Kansas, where thousands of civilians were tortured, mutilated, murdered, or driven from their homes.[23] If these were typical Christians, could Christianity truly be termed good? Could religion be relied on to soften the exploding hearts of men? The transformation of the martyred leader into patron saint of the new American political religion was an attempt to proclaim, in a confident affirmative, that religion was the answer. For Lincoln, poised between belief and unbelief, religion was the question.

5

EVOLUTION AND ITS DISCONTENTS

When Robert Ingersoll heard about Darwin's theory of evolution, his immediate response was to ponder "how terrible this will be upon the nobility of the Old World. Think of their being forced to trace their ancestry back to the duke Orang Outang, or the princess Chimpanzee."[1] The first American reviewer of Darwin's *The Origin of Species* (1859), the Harvard botanist Asa Gray, took a much more sober view of the subject in the March 1860 issue of the *American Journal of Science and Arts*. Gray was then America's best-known botanist, a friend of Darwin's, and a believing Protestant whose religious leanings were closer to traditional Calvinism than to the more liberal Unitarianism common among New England intellectuals on the eve of the Civil War. He was the first important American scientist to insist that there need be no conflict between religion and the theory of evolution by means of natural selection, in which organic change and the emergence of new species are explained by randomly arising variations, passed on to subsequent generations, that enable some organisms to compete more effectively than others in the struggle for existence. Creeds based on literal acceptance of the biblical creation story could not, of course, be reconciled with evolutionism, but advocates of a Christianized Darwinism, like Gray, could accept Darwin's general principles (if not all of the particulars) without denying the existence of a divine first cause. Natural selection could therefore be viewed as the mechanism by which God chose to manifest himself throughout the physical world. Although this sounds like an early version of the current argument for the teaching of "intelligent design" in schools, there is one crucial difference: Gray was suggesting not that educators give equal time to a religious and a naturalistic version of evolution but that it was possible to teach evolutionary theory in entirely naturalistic terms without addressing the nonscientific issue, best left to the realm of faith, of whether God set the process in motion. This position, most recently endorsed by the influential paleontologist Stephen Jay Gould in *Rocks of Ages* (1999), has held an enduring appeal for American scientists as well as theologians. For nineteenth-century religious liberals like the ubiquitous Henry Ward Beecher, who refused to turn their backs on either religion or the new scientific knowledge, Gray's philosophical balancing act was heavensent. For freethinkers like Ingersoll, Darwinian evolution offered an unambiguous opportunity to explain in natural terms what had, for aeons, been explained solely in supernatural terms. For men of faith, however, Darwinism represented both opportunity and danger, a powerful natural theory of the origins and development of life that must somehow be reconciled with the traditional explanations offered by religion.

Gray himself was responding to the argument of his equally well known but much more religiously orthodox colleague, the geologist Louis Agassiz, who insisted that evolutionism inevitably led to atheism. Even a God who served as first cause and as an intelligent designer was not enough for Agassiz, who maintained that all life must be viewed by scientists as the product not only of original divine intent but of constant and continuing attention from the Deity, whose eye was on the sparrow, lizard, and amoeba, as well as on His noblest creation, man. Gray's elegant summary of the basic philosophical difference between Agassiz and Darwin could just as easily be applied to the battle between creationists (though Agassiz was considerably less dogmatic than modern creationists) and evolutionists today:

> In a word, the whole relation of animals, etc., to surrounding Nature, and to each other, are regarded under the one [Agassiz's] view as ultimate facts, or in the ultimate aspect, and interpreted theologically; under the other [Darwin's] as complex facts, to be analyzed and interpreted scientifically. The one naturalist, perhaps too largely assuming the scientifically unexplained to be inexplicable, views the phenomena only in their supposed relation to the Divine mind. The other, naturally expecting many of these phenomena to be resolvable under investigation, views them in their relation to one another, and endeavors to explain them as far as he can (and perhaps farther) through natural causes.[2]

The outbreak of the Civil War did nothing to dampen the interest of American scientists and intellectuals in the new ideas about evolution, but it delayed a wider public discussion of both the scientific and the religious implications of Darwin's theories. As the subject of evolution began to engage the American public (as distinct from scientists) in the mid-1870s, debate extended beyond the relatively small intellectual community concerned with such matters in Europe. The broader scope of popular discussion in America disseminated information—and misinformation—about the new theory of how life developed. It was a debate with far-reaching implications, unforeseen at the time, for future American attitudes toward science, religion, and secularism. An 1873 editorial in the *New York Times* reflected the deep concern of social and religious conservatives about the impact of scientific rationalism on the American public. Adopting a tone similar to that of late-eighteenth-century conservatives, who feared that the French Revolution's religious and economic radicalism would contaminate American workers and farmers, the *Times* argued that if the theories of Darwin "were confined to the walls of universities or the pages of scientific reviews, it would not be a matter of so much consequence, since their audiences would be both small and discriminating; but in fact, under the guise of science and philosophy, they give only too much color to the thought of the age, especially to that of the young and immature mind." The editorial charged, with considerable justification, that scientists would "cooly rule the supernatural quite out of the universe with their dictum: 'Prove it.' " Books containing dangerous scientific theories "lie upon the bookshelves in the houses of Christians, and such doctrines are served up in diluted, but none the less dangerous, form in the lecture platforms, in the magazine and the newspaper, and are too often taught in the college or the school." Finally, the *Times* declared that it was the duty of journalists to do battle against the "prejudice against the supernatural" that science was attempting to instill in impressionable young minds. " 'The watchman on the walls of Zion' can no longer afford to confound modern doubt with old or exploded heresies, or even to ignore them," the editorial concluded. "Science should be confined to its own domain; the material should not encroach upon the spiritual, and youth should be taught that knowledge comes in other ways than by experiment."[3]

The writer of that editorial would undoubtedly be pleased, were he alive today, to know that news of the death of belief in the supernatural was greatly exaggerated—and that nineteenth-century scientists and freethinkers greatly underestimated the staying power of conservative religion in American life. At the time, there seemed ample reason for Ingersoll to predict that scientific knowledge would inevitably replace what he considered superstition—or, at the very least, that a majority of Americans would comfortably accept separate spheres of influence for science and religion. In the late 1800s, acceptance of the scientific method in general and evolutionary theory in particular was unquestionably spreading—not only among the college-educated but among those with a secondary school education. As the number of American public high schools increased rapidly between 1870 and 1900, the new ideas about evolution made their way into the secondary school science curriculum. Indeed, the Roman Catholic Church's fear that the teaching of secular science in public schools might erode the faith of Catholic children was a major factor in the establishment of the nation's first religiously based school system. Protestants outside the South, by contrast, rarely argued that it was the function of schools to teach the biblical creation story: it was the job of home and church to instill religious beliefs, to decide how to reconcile scientific evolutionism with faith, and to speculate about when or whether God had displayed his hand in the evolutionary process. That the teaching of secularist science in American public schools would surface repeatedly as an issue in the closing decades of the twentieth century, setting the United States apart from all other developed nations, would have been unimaginable to the nineteenth-century heirs of the Enlightenment.

To Darwin's contemporaries, it soon became evident that the theory of evolution by means of natural selection posed a much greater threat to orthodox religion than geological discoveries of the late eighteenth and early nineteenth centuries, which had undermined biblically based notions of the age of the earth but had not shaken humanity's view of itself as a uniquely created species, fashioned in God's own image, unrelated to and with full dominion over the birds of the air and beasts of the field. In *The Origin of Species*, Darwin had avoided any explicit discussion of human evolution—though the inferences to be drawn from his general theory were evident to his scientific colleagues—but in *The Descent of Man* (1871) he unequivocally spelled out his view of the place of homo sapiens in nature.

"We thus learn that man is descended from a hairy, tailed quadruped," he declared, "probably arboreal in its habits. . . . This creature, if its whole structure had been examined by a naturalist, would have been classed among the Quadrumana, as surely as the still more ancient progenitor of the Old and New World monkeys. . . . [A]ll the higher mammals are probably derived from an ancient marsupial animal, and this through a long series of diversified forms, either from some reptile-like, or some amphibian-like creature, and this again from some fish-like animal."[4] Moreover, man's connection with lower animals was indisputable in light of "the marvellous fact that the embryos of a man, dog, seal, bat, reptile, &c., can at first hardly be distinguished from each other." Then Darwin uncompromisingly asserted that "only our natural prejudice, and that arrogance which made our forefathers declare that they were descended from demi-gods . . . leads us to demur to this conclusion. But the time will before long come, when it will be thought wonderful that naturalists, who were well acquainted with the comparative structure and development of man, and other mammals, should have believed that each was the work of a separate act of creation."⁵

Darwin's theory of human descent, coupled with astronomical discoveries that infinitely expanded previous concepts of the universe and reduced the earth to its real status as one small planet, struck a blow not only at the religious view of man as a special creation of God but at humanity's exalted opinion of itself. "How insignificant we are, with our pigmy little world!" wrote Samuel Clemens (Mark Twain) in an 1870 letter to his fiancée, Olivia Langdon. "[W]as *our* small globe the favored one of all? Does one apple in a vast orchard think as much of itself as we do? . . . Do the pismires argue upon vexed questions of pismire theology—& do they climb a molehill & look abroad over the grand universe of an acre of ground & say, 'Great is God, who created all things for Us?' "⁶ Ingersoll, in an 1877 lecture, treated the likelihood of reptilian ancestry with a satirical equanimity that resembled Twain's:

> I read about rudimentary bones and muscles. I was told that everybody had rudimentary muscles extending from the ear into the cheek. I asked "What are they?" I was told: "They are the muscles with which your ancestors used to flap their ears." I do not now so much wonder that we once had them as that we have outgrown them.
>
> . . . I would rather belong to that race that commenced a skull-less vertebrate and produced Shakespeare, a race that has before it an infinite future, with the angel of progress beckoning forward, upward and onward forever—I had rather belong to such a race, commencing there, producing this, and with that hope, than to

have sprung from a perfect pair upon which the Lord has lost money every moment from that day to this.[7]

For conservative religious believers, the application of Darwin's theory to humans was not only blasphemous but ego-shattering. One critic noted that while the Bible "places a crown of honor and dominion on the brow of our common humanity . . . Darwinism casts us all down from this elevated platform, and herds us all with four-footed beasts and creeping things. . . . [I]t treats us as bastards and not sons, and reveals the degrading fact that man in his best estate—even Mr. Darwin—is but a civilized, dressed up, educated monkey, who has lost his tail."[8] Had that view prevailed among the leaders of mainstream Protestant sects in an era when Protestantism was the dominant American religion, educated Americans would have been forced to choose between their faith and the modern world. But since so many Protestant theologians and church leaders sought an accommodation between science and religion, many American Protestants could open themselves to new ideas and still take comfort in their faith.

For Catholics, no such compromise was possible. Between 1870 and 1900, the Catholic population of the United States rose from four million to twelve million, mainly because of immigration from Germany and southern and eastern Europe. Because most of the new American Catholics were poor and poorly educated, and because the church soon began establishing parochial schools to shelter Catholic children from secularist thought, the debate over evolution bypassed the fastest-growing segment of American religious believers. At the time, institutional Catholicism, under the leadership of Pope Pius IX, had adopted a hostile posture toward any scientific encroachment on religious authority. The pope, who had stifled rebellious modernizers within the church by foisting the new doctrine of papal infallibility upon the First Vatican Council in 1869, had also pushed an uncompromisingly antiscientific and antimodernist platform through the council. With a proclamation declaring "let him be anathema . . .

[w]ho shall say that human sciences ought to be pursued in such a spirit of freedom that one may be allowed to hold as true their assertions, even when opposed to revealed doctrine," the pontiff set the Catholic hierarchy on a retrograde intellectual course that would remain unaltered until the second half of the twentieth century.[9] Not until 1950, in the encyclical *Humani Generis,* did the church, under Pope Pius XII, arrive at the conclusion embraced by liberal Protestants as early as the 1870s—that believers might retain an open mind on the question of whether the human body evolved from lower life forms as long as they continued to regard the human soul as the direct creation of God. For American Protestants, however, it was already possible in the nineteenth century to choose the spiritually and socially easier course of embracing both some form of evolution and some form of God. Ingersoll predicted that liberal Protestantism's qualified acceptance of evolutionism would create many more agnostics and freethinkers, and that did indeed happen during the "golden age of freethought" in the 1880s and 1890s. But the accommodationism of mainstream American Protestantism also had the effect of making agnostics, atheists, and uncompromising rationalists look like crackpots and extremists—an image that endures to this day. If the dominant Protestant religion was willing to bend its tenets to accommodate as unsettling a theory as Darwinian evolution, many, arguably most, Americans felt that scientific rationalists should be equally willing to accommodate comforting faith in a divine creator: refusal to adopt a "moderate" position—always equidistant from two points— was tantamount to radicalism. Twentieth-century American scientific accommodationists like Gould—usually not religious believers themselves but fearful of the threat to science from the unreconciled Christian right—are still bending over backward to reassure the public that there need be no conflict between science and religion. While the reconciliation of science with religion is certainly possible, for individuals as well as for a society, it is a mistake, albeit a soothing one, to suggest that the process is easy or automatic. The scientific method itself, with its demand (as the *Times* editorial rightly noted in 1873) to

"prove it," discourages the leaps of faith in the unverifiable that are the essence of any religion. That so many manage to accommodate belief systems encompassing both the natural and the supernatural is a testament not to the compatibility of science and religion but to the flexibility, in both the physical and metaphysical senses, of the human brain.

In the post–Civil War era, the accommodationist response of so many Protestant leaders was only one of the social factors that shaped the nation's reception of evolutionism and gave it a distinctly American character. The appeal of evolutionary theory was reinforced by a profound American faith in progress—never stronger, at least outside the former Confederacy, than in the last three decades of the nineteenth century. The reunified (in a governmental if not a cultural sense) United States was expanding in every possible way, from its large cities, swelled by immigration, to the western states, where previously untapped natural resources were being exploited to power the nation's burgeoning economy. Between 1870 and 1900, the population nearly doubled as a result of immigration, from some thirty-eight million to more than seventy-four million. Americans were witnessing an unprecedented application of once abstract scientific principles to inventions that made the fortunes of the Gilded Age and reshaped everyday life. This was, after all, the era when man conquered the dark—at least in urban areas. Thomas Edison's patenting of the first commercially viable incandescent lamp in 1879 was followed just three years later by the opening of the world's first permanent electric-light power plant in New York City. The Centennial Exhibition of 1876, held in Philadelphia, was a spectacular celebration of American technology, featuring new inventions that included the telephone, the typewriter, and the prototype of the first galvanized cables (which would soon be used to build the Brooklyn Bridge). The main attraction was the 1,500-horsepower Corliss Steam Engine, taller than a house, which provided power for all the equipment in the fair's vast machinery hall. The widespread public fascination with the new technology was borne out by the fair's huge attendance: nine million

Americans, out of a total population of forty-eight million, visited the exhibitions during the centennial year. While the Victorian faith in progress, and technology as an instrument of progress, was hardly unique to America, ordinary Americans' view of their country as the leader of the forces of technology and invention was a powerful reinforcer of the sense of exceptionalism that had characterized the nation since its founding. It was, of course, possible to respond enthusiastically to technology while retaining grave suspicions about science—and that was the position of many religious conservatives. But the late-nineteenth-century advances in both scientific understanding and applied technology posed a particularly formidable challenge to orthodox religion because, taken together, they offered a logical explanation of processes once thought to be inexplicable curses or miracles. As understanding of natural causes expanded, the need for supernatural explanations decreased. And even if nineteenth-century medicine had little to offer in the way of treatment or cures for most of the diseases whose origins scientists were beginning to understand, there were notable exceptions. By the 1880s, some (though by no means all) American surgeons began to adopt the aseptic procedures pioneered by England's Joseph Lister, and enlightened general practitioners came to understand that many infections could be prevented simply by keeping themselves and their patients clean. The bacterial explanation of infectious disease—originally considered as unproven a theory as evolution—began to gain greater acceptance, as educated Americans became aware of the findings of Louis Pasteur and the pioneering German bacteriologist Robert Koch.

Evolution was not a theory that offered immediate practical benefits, but, like the germ theory of the origins and transmission of disease, it stripped away the myth and mysticism from fundamental questions of how—though not *why*—organisms, including humans, live and die. Darwin could not account for the original source (which, for the religiously orthodox, could only be God) of the variations that led to natural selection and human evolution. But, as one historian notes, "what really mattered was not that an agnostic had ready at hand a scientific explanation for the origin of life, the formation of the solar system, or any other specific problem; rather, it was that he had the impression that science could provide one—if not right away, then eventually."[10] Informed by lectures and new journals founded for the specific purpose of explaining science to general readers, many educated Americans were no longer disposed to accept primitive "seeing is believing" arguments like the one made by the Reverend Thomas A. Eliot, who dismissed all fossil evidence for evolution because no one had ever witnessed one live animal turning into another.[11] In the 1870s, daily mass-circulation newspapers also paid attention to discoveries supporting the theory of evolution. Among the most famous were fossil birds, with teeth and other reptile attributes, discovered in Kansas by the eminent paleontologist Othniel C. Marsh, one of the earliest and most effective popularizers of science in America. Those who attended the lectures of Marsh or of Thomas Huxley may not have witnessed the spectacle of a reptile turning into a bird, but the unearthing of a species with characteristics of both life forms powerfully suggested a common ancestry. Moreover, the spokesmen for conservative religious sects, with a faith based not only on the unseen but on phenomena that contradicted all the accepted laws of nature, were hardly in the best position to argue that only seeing justifies believing.

The extensive newspaper coverage devoted to Huxley's 1876 visit to America reflected both the internationalization of high-level science and the intense public interest in, if not necessarily acceptance of, evolution. The agnostic Huxley, the most effective popularizer of Darwin's ideas and a celebrity in his own right, was accompanied on his voyage to America by the London correspondent of the *New York Tribune*. As their ship steamed into New York Harbor, the correspondent noted that "Mr. Huxley stood on the deck of the *Germanic* . . . and he enjoyed to the full that marvelous panorama. At all times he was on intimate terms with Nature and also with the joint work of Nature and Man! . . . As we drew near the city . . . he asked what were the tall tower and tall building with a cupola, then the most conspicuous objects. I told him the Tribune and the Western Union Telegraph buildings. 'Ah,' he said, 'that is interesting; that is American. In the Old World the first things you see as you approach a great city are steeples; here you see, first, centers of intelligence.' "[12]

That America was no longer regarded as a parochial backwater of science was demonstrated by Huxley's speedy departure for New Haven and Yale College, where he was eager to see Marsh's most recent fossil discoveries. Huxley, who planned to deliver a lecture in New York on the genealogy of the horse, had only studied European fossil specimens, while Marsh's studies of fossils from the American West had led him to the conclusion that the horse originated in the New World rather than in Europe. Huxley spent several days talking with Marsh and going over his findings, and he revised his opinions— and his lecture—in the face of what he considered incontrovertible new evidence of the horse's New World genealogy. In a later memoir, Marsh observed that Huxley's willingness to "give up his own opinions in the face of new truth" indicated "the generosity of true greatness."[13] Huxley delivered three lectures before packed houses in New York, and a lengthy front-page account of his final address in the *New York Times* indicates the extent of the interest in evolution on the part of nonscientists, who only fifteen years earlier had probably never heard the name Charles Darwin:

Prof. Huxley's third and final lecture was delivered last night at Chickering Hall, in the presence of one of the largest and most brilliant audiences which has yet greeted him in this country. The subject of his discourse was the "demonstrative" evidence in favor of the evolution theory, and consisted mainly of a description of the process by which the existing horse is to be traced back, step by step, to a lower form, which, in respect to its arms, hands, and teeth very nearly resembles that division of the mammals to which man belongs. . . . The lecturer added that in all probability, when the geological formation of the great Northwest could be thoroughly examined, a still more ancient species will be found, with a fifth finger or thumb on the forehoof, which will complete the series. Enough, however, had been discovered to demonstrate the truth of the evolution hypothesis—a truth which could not be shaken by the raising of side issues. . . . As to the only other imaginable hypothesis—that all those connected forms had come into existence at different times and by special creation—it was sufficient to say that not a particle of evidence of any kind had been adduced in its favor, while on the other hand, the truth of evolution was based upon precisely the same species of evidence as the Copernican theory of the movement of the sun and planets.[14]

In yet another demonstration of the long attention span of nineteenth-century audiences and readers, the *Times* followed its glowing synopsis with the full text of the speech, running to more than three columns. The positive tone of the extensive news coverage of Huxley's speeches contrasted sharply with the disapproval voiced on newspaper editorial pages, reflecting the gap not only between controversial new scientific ideas and received opinion but between newspaper owners and reporters. The *Times*, which published five news stories and five editorial pieces on Huxley's visit in less than two weeks, was given to heavy-handed mockery of its reporters' "fanciful" enthusiasm for theories that "prove nothing" about the origins of human life. Reporters were young, injudiciously enthusiastic, and overly impressed by celebrities, the *Times* opined, and therefore readers ought not to pay too much attention to the theories reported in news columns. (The editorial page's contradiction of the paper's own news reports may have confused some readers, but it certainly attests to the separation between the news and editorial side of the nineteenth-century *Times*.) The editorial pronouncement on Huxley's final lecture reflected, as always, the fundamental concern of conservatives within the American establishment—including leaders in publishing, finance, and government as well as the orthodox clergy—about the impact of evolutionary theory, should it become widely accepted, on religious faith. The *Times* position was that Darwinian evolution by means of natural selection *must* be modified in a fashion compatible with religion, just as literal accounts of the biblical creation story had been modified to uncover "a striking general coincidence between the Mosaic narrative and modern [geological] theories, and Biblical scholars have changed many of our former interpretations of these records." The editorial writer dismissed Huxley's analogy between the structure of the horse and human anatomy, adding that "for Mr. Huxley to speak of the evidence for evolution as being on a par with Copernican theory, only shows how far [astray] theory will lead a clear brain."[15]

While most scientists, along with many other well-educated Americans, accepted some form of evolution by the early 1880s, their acceptance did not always extend to the Darwinian concept of natural selection as the primary agent of evolutionary change. Many American naturalists, especially those intent on reconciling science and religion, were drawn not to Christianized Darwinism but to the now discredited concept of evolution based on the eighteenth-century theories of Jean-Baptiste de Lamarck. Lamarck argued that environmentally acquired characteristics could be passed on to the next generation and were responsible for most evolutionary development—a theory that dovetailed neatly with the American faith in progress. Darwin himself came to believe that the environment played a more important role in evolution than he originally thought, but he never wavered in his insistence that natural selection was the most important factor. It must be recalled that the entire nineteenth-century discussion of Lamarckism versus Darwinism took place without knowledge of the true laws of genetics, first laid out in 1866 by the Austrian monk Gregor Mendel but ignored during his lifetime and rediscovered by independent researchers only in 1900. American neo-Lamarckists in the 1860s and 1870s believed in what they called the laws of "acceleration and retardation," which specified that characteristics of an adult of one species could metamorphose into embryonic characteristics in the next higher species—thus "accelerating" the development of advanced traits and facilitating the emergence of a higher organism. Lacking knowledge of genes—encoded in reproductive cells from the beginning of each organism's life—as the true bearers of heredity, the neo-Lamarckists could easily envision a form of evolution compatible with the special creation of man. By crediting the Creator with the power to actually reshape an organism during its lifetime in order to provide the biological building blocks for the next higher species, it was possible to see the direct hand of God not only as first cause but at every stage of development. Lamarck's theory of the inheritability of acquired characteristics was particularly malleable for ideological ends, whether religious or political, precisely because it rejected any notion of random variations in the universe and insisted that species could have evolved only as the result of some all-encompassing plan.*

The muddling of science with unscientific ideology was most evident in Gilded Age America's attraction to the turgid metaphysics of the British thinker Herbert Spencer, who applied Darwin's principle of natural selection to the social as well as the natural world—a mistake Darwin never made. Trained as a civil engineer, Spencer dabbled in many branches of science, philosophy, and technology before finding his true vocation, in the words of the historian Richard Hofstadter, as "the metaphysician of the homemade intellectual and the prophet of the cracker-barrel agnostic."[16] Spencer was also the favorite philosopher of religious Americans who wished to have their God and evolution too, as a result of his insistence that however much science might have to teach about the natural world, there was still a place for religious worship of "the Unknowable." Spencerian social Darwinism thus became that most suspect of all metaphysical systems—one flexible enough to be all things to all people, including

---

*In the twentieth century, Joseph Stalin's anointed biologist, Trofim D. Lysenko, would take the same incorrect theory, with disastrous consequences for Soviet science, in a political rather than a religious direction. With the ringing proclamation that "the zygote is no fool," Lysenko insisted—rejecting the Mendelian laws never known to the previous century's neo-Lamarckists—that not only could acquired characteristics be transmitted from one generation to the next but those characteristics could be modified by changes in the political and social as well as the natural environment. Pushed to an extreme by zygotes even more foolish than the one that produced Lysenko, the theory not only wrecked Soviet agriculture for generations but also was used by Communist Party hacks to promote the notion that a Soviet upbringing, free of "bourgeois individualism," could modify the genes that make up the human brain and produce a new *homo Sovieticus*. Lysenkoism was a joke to the rest of the scientific world by the 1930's, but it was no joke in Stalinist Russia and led to the imprisonment and deaths of thousands of Soviet researchers with the courage to stand up for scientific truth. (For a fuller discussion, see *The Rise and Fall of T. D. Lysenko* by Zhores Medvedev [1969] and *A Question of Madness* by Zhores and Roy Medvedev [1971].)

those who would normally have been at one another's throats. Even though Spencer himself is virtually unread today, his brand of social Darwinism, with its appeal to religious believers as well as to secularists, had a long-term impact on American culture. Hofstadter aptly defined American social Darwinism as a philosophy animated by "a kind of secular piety," expressing a "naturalistic Calvinism in which man's relationship to nature is as hard and demanding as man's relationship to God under the Calvinistic system."[17] Never as influential in his native England as he was to become in America, Spencer began publishing his ideas several years before *The Origin of Species* (a fact to which he often alluded proudly). He combined belief in the inevitability of social progress with advocacy of laissez-faire economics and a minimal role for government; in his view, governmental intervention in society could only preserve the less fit at the expense of the more fit. Darwin's concept of natural selection as the chief agent of evolutionary change fitted neatly into Spencer's metaphysics: "survival of the fittest"—a term coined by Spencer, not Darwin—applied not only to man in a state of nature but to civilized man. It was a philosophy well suited to the deeply rooted American belief in individualism, as well as to the more rapacious business interests of the Gilded Age. Among Spencer's greatest American admirers were Andrew Carnegie, Thomas Edison, and John D. Rockefeller. American sales of Spencer's *Synthetic Philosophy*, comprising more than six thousand pages written between 1860 and 1896, amounted to an astonishing 390,000 volumes by the time of his death in 1903. An example of Spencer's logic (if it can be called that) appears in his 1858 account of the moment of awakening that led to all of his later philosophical works:

During a walk one fine Sunday morning (or perhaps it may have been New Year's Day) . . . I happened to stand by the side of a pool along which a gentle breeze was bringing small waves to the shores at my feet. While watching these undulations I was led to think of other undulations—other rhythms; and probably, as my manner was, remembered extreme cases—the undulations of the ether, and the rises and falls in the prices of money, shares, and commodities. In the course of the walk arose the inquiry—Is not the rhythm of motion universal? and the answer soon reached was—Yes. . . . Of course these universal principles ranged themselves alongside the two universal principles I had been recently illustrating—the instability of the homogenous and the multiplication of effects.[18]

By "the instability of the homogenous," Spencer meant that everything progresses from homogeneity, or simplicity, to heterogeneity and complexity—nebular gases turn into planets, embryos into more biologically complex adults, and, courtesy of Darwinian theory, lower species turn into higher. And let us not forget, as Spencer's wealthy admirers never did, the progress from the simplicity of a single dollar to a diversified fortune, thanks to the "universal" rhythm of the financial markets.

Spencer translated the biological theory of natural selection into what he called "social selection," opposing all state aid to the poor, public education, health laws, government tariffs, and even government-supported postal service. Of the poor, he declared, "If they are sufficiently complete to live, they *do* live, and it is well they should live. If they are not sufficiently complete to live, they die, and it is best that they should die."[19] Or, as Scrooge put it, "If they would rather die, they had better do it, and decrease the surplus population."

Spencer's political conservatism had much more appeal for American than for British intellectuals, who, as one British historian of science notes, were already drawn in the 1870s and 1880s to the "liberal socialism which is the special characteristic of modern Britain."[20] America's more fluid class structure—of which the expansion of public education at every level was only one manifestation in the post–Civil War era—bolstered the appeal of the idea that individuals could succeed purely by their own efforts. One irony seemed lost on Spencer's American enthusiasts: the nation's expanding support for public education, which Spencer deplored, provided far more opportunities for the "fittest" of the poor to succeed than did the restrictive privately financed schools prevalent throughout so much of the Old World.

Although there is nothing mysterious about the appeal of Spencerian thought to the most reactionary American robber barons, it is more difficult to understand why he was taken so seriously by a great many Americans not identified with extreme conservatism. Many freethinkers and religious liberals were admirers of Spencer's unrestrained individualism even though, unlike Spencer, they recognized the need not only for basic government services like the post office but for social action to ameliorate the harshest aspects of industrial capitalism. Carnegie, to cite just one example, helped found a system of public libraries that became a model of partnership between the public and private sectors of the economy. Social Darwinism seemed to hold a particular fascination for erudite Americans in the humanities, who often had trouble distinguishing between physical science and metaphysical speculation. The eminent historian and philosopher John Fiske, who delivered the main address at a farewell banquet for Spencer after his widely publicized American lecture tour in 1882, offered a comparison of the significance of Darwin and Spencer that would rank high on any all-time list of historical misjudgments. In Fiske's view, Spencer's magnum opus was "so stupendous that that of Darwin is fairly dwarfed in comparison." Had Spencer never lived, Fiske added, Darwin's theory of evolution would probably have been forgotten.[21] Fiske went on to pay tribute to Spencer for helping to reconcile evolution and religion, in a revealing passage that invokes divine sanction for the application of the "survival of the fittest" principle to civilized man. He told his affluent audience that when "we see that the very same forces, subtle, and exquisite, and profound, which brought upon the scene the primal germs of life and caused them to unfold, which through countless ages of struggle and death . . . cherished the life that could live more perfectly and destroyed the life that could only live less perfectly. . . . Human responsibility is made more strict and solemn than ever, when the eternal Power that lives in every event of the universe is thus seen to be in the deepest possible sense the author of the moral law that should guide our lives, and in obedience to which lies our only guarantee of the happiness which is incorruptible—which neither inevitable misfortune nor unmerited obloquy can ever take away."[22]

In other words, the fittest men—those who will survive and prosper regardless of what natural or social misfortunes come their way—are those who "live right" as a higher power commands. The perennial appeal of this idea to Americans, in a line running from Ben Franklin through Norman Vincent Peale to more recent self-help gurus of every ilk, explains a good deal about Spencer's relatively higher status in the New World than in the Old. Darwin himself offered much less fodder for those who wished to extend his conclusions about man in a state of nature to man in a state of civilization. He was no believer in the inevitability of progress, divinely guided or otherwise, and observed that history provides little support for such generalizations. "Ancients did not even entertain the idea," he noted, "nor do the Oriental nations at the present day." Progress, Darwin observed, "seems to depend on many concurrent favorable conditions, too complex to be followed out."[23] One of those conditions, he added, was a cool or temperate climate. Furthermore, Darwin stated explicitly that natural selection becomes subordinate to environmental factors—and man's own moral evolution—as soon as humans enter into a state of civilization. Civilized societies, he said, care for both the physically and the mentally deficient and allow them to reproduce. "The aid which we feel impelled to give to the helpless is mainly an incidental result of the instinct of sympathy," he observed, "which was originally acquired as part of the social instincts, but subsequently rendered, in the manner previously indicated, more tender and widely diffused. Nor could we check our sympathy, even at the urging of hard reason, without deterioration in the noblest part of our nature. . . . [I]f we were intentionally to neglect the weak and helpless, it could only be for a contingent benefit, with an overwhelming present evil."[24] The real difference between Darwin and Spencer lay in the former's devotion to the scientific method—an empirically based search for truth grounded in awareness that new evidence may always pose a challenge to previous conclusions. Darwin was not reluctant to reevaluate his ideas, as he did in crediting environmental influences with a greater role than he had in *The Origin of Species*, and he carefully noted exceptions along with general rules. Spencer, by contrast, tied up everything—from the discovery of new planets to improved plumbing—in a grand metaphysical scheme that did not allow for new and contrary pieces of evidence.

The public debate over evolution—whether conducted in small-town lecture halls or in the elegant urban clubs where businessmen gathered to assure themselves that their fortunes were evidence that they were indeed the fittest—was largely a northern affair. So, too, was the attempt by theologians and church leaders to reconcile evolutionism and religion. No such *geographical* split existed in the intellectual life of any other Western nation. In the postbellum era, the religious divide between North and South, rooted in the relationship between southern churches and slavery, widened and hardened. New ideas were identified with the hated Yankees—and evolution was certainly a new idea. Just as abolitionists and women's rights advocates left the South in the 1820s and 1830s, so did intellectual dissenters and scientists head North in the 1870s. The 1832 expulsion of Thomas Cooper for heresy from the faculty of the College of South Carolina was a preview of the thoroughgoing postwar southern spurning of anything, and anyone, identified with racial, political, and religious change, and that continuing rejection would retard southern economic progress for nearly a century. In 1878, two years after Huxley's triumphant series of lectures in the Northeast, the geologist Alexander Winchell was dismissed from the faculty of Vanderbilt University in Nashville for publishing his opinion that human life had existed on earth long before the biblical time frame for the creation of Adam. Winchell's firing was enthusiastically endorsed by Methodists in the region, who pointed out that Vanderbilt was a school founded by Methodists and dedicated to the goals of the church, and that contemporary scientific theories could only lead students astray from the path of true faith. Northern scientists and theologians scoffed at the southern Methodists, noting that mainstream Protestant thinkers had long accepted geological findings on the antiquity of the earth. "The stupid Southern Methodists that control the university, it seems, can learn nothing," wrote *Popular Science Monthly* editor E. M. Youmans, setting the tone for a century of patronizing commentary by northern intellectuals on the South.[25] While religious opposition to evolutionism did surface periodically in the North, it never occupied the dominant position that it almost effortlessly achieved within the southern religious establishment. The lasting consequences of this old cultural division remain apparent today; it is no accident that the South and the Southwest formed the geographical and ideological center of the Christian right in late-twentieth-century America. Jerry Falwell, Pat Robertson, and Bob Jones, to name only a few stalwarts of right-wing fundamentalism, are the religious and political heirs of the nineteenth-century ministers and politicians who were determined to purge scientific rationalists from southern churches and educational institutions.

The growing knowledge and acceptance of evolutionism—even though it bypassed important segments of American society—contributed significantly to a major expansion of the freethought movement in the United States in the 1870s and 1880s. Darwin's theory of evolution through natural selection was particularly persuasive to those who moved during this period from liberal Protestantism to outright agnosticism—a list that included such prominent personalities as Charles Eliot Norton—the future president of Harvard—and the feminists Elizabeth Cady Stanton, Susan B. Anthony, and Matilda Joslyn Gage. Nineteenth-century agnostics and freethinkers were even more sensitive than their twentieth-century heirs to the charge that there could be no morality in the absence of religion, and they felt an urgent need to articulate a humanistic code of behavior that did not depend on belief in a system of divine rewards and punishments. Science made an important contribution to this secularized morality not because it had answers for perennial metaphysical questions but because it placed high value on the pursuit of truth through observation, experimentation, and constant questioning.

In the absence of the Christian faith in immortality, there was no question of greater importance to agnostics than the manner in which they proposed to face suffering and death. Freethinkers could find no evidence in nature of a God who took any active interest in human affairs, nor could they believe in the miraculous resurrection of the body that lay at the heart of Christian faith. For those who accepted Darwinian evolution by means of natural selection, the philosophical problem was particularly acute. It was impossible to reconcile natural selection—which involved competition, suffering, death, and the extinction of entire species—with the concept of an intelligent, omnipotent, and benevolent deity. Why would a kind God choose such a cruel way of determining who would live and who would die? Moreover, the Victorians confronted the harshest exigencies of natural selection, in the form of deaths in infancy and childhood, far more frequently than their twentieth-century descendants. Science might one day provide an antidote to the common diseases that, in 1870, took the lives of half of all urban infants before their first birthday, but that time had not yet come. The agnostic must bear his losses, and find a way to carry on, without the faith and hope that sustained his Christian neighbor— "For now we see through a glass, darkly; but then face to face: now I know in part; but then I shall know, even as also I am known." Yet many freethinkers, not surprisingly, found themselves unable to face those losses without the hope that some form of consciousness might continue after death. Some believers in a nonhierarchical, personal religion, among them William Lloyd Garrison, turned to spiritualism—strongly opposed by conventional churches—after the death of a beloved family member. Even the tough-minded Anthony, who considered herself an agnostic, mused that "if it be true that we die like the flower, leaving behind only the fragrance . . . what a delusion has the race ever been in—what a dream is the life of man."[26] There is a special place in the pantheon of rationalist heroes for the short list of freethinkers, including Ingersoll and

Ernestine Rose, who unflinchingly and unfailingly rejected the idea
that it was possible to communicate with the spirits of the dead. Stalwarts of the freethought press and lecture circuit like B. F. Underwood turned to spiritualism in their later years even as they continued
to reject the miracles of the Bible as pure superstition. To George E.
Macdonald, a staff member of the *Truth Seeker*, America's best-
known freethought newspaper, beginning in 1875, and its editor from
1909 to his death in 1937, there was no mystery about why so many
aging warriors were swept up in the spiritualist enthusiasms of
post–Civil War America. In a charming memoir published in 1932,
Macdonald spoke of numerous friends who had turned to spiritualism or some other form of mysticism in their old age. "I have known
men, once Freethinkers, to lean toward Christian Science, even
Bahaism," he recalled. "And I have ceased to wonder thereat, not
because I can explain their action, but because I have seen so many of
them and they are no longer novelties—not even an individualist
turning authoritarian. Doubtless their state of reaction may be called a
spiritual second childhood, matching that of the body and mind. Like
children, the aged must play it safe."[27] Any agnostic who did not play
it safe faced the stringent task of constructing an ethical system that
dealt with suffering and extinction—one's own as well as that of the
human species—as a part of nature rather than as a cog in the machinery of divine justice. Nature could be modified not through the supernatural intervention of one God or many spirits but only through
greater medical and scientific understanding.

When Huxley's beloved three-year-old son died unexpectedly in
1860, a close friend, the pious but open-minded Episcopal clergyman
and author Charles Kingsley, suggested that the grieving father would
derive spiritual comfort if he could only bring himself to believe in
some form of life beyond the grave. Huxley's reply is a poignant classic of uncompromising secular humanism:

> As I stood behind the coffin of my little son the other day, with
> my mind bent on anything but disputation, the officiating minis-
> ter read, as part of his duty, the words, "If the dead rise not again,
> let us eat and drink, for to-morrow we die." I cannot tell you

how inexpressibly they shocked me.... I could have laughed
with scorn. What! Because I am face to face with death and
irreparable loss, because I have given back to the same source
from whence it came, the cause of a great happiness ... I am to
renounce my manhood, and howling, grovel in bestiality? Why,
the very apes know better, and if you shoot their young, the poor
brutes grief [*sic*] out and do not immediately seek distraction in a
gorge. . . .

If at this moment I am not a worn-out, debauched, useless carcass
of a man, if it has been or will be my fate to advance the cause of
science, if I feel that I have a shadow of a claim on the love of those
around me, if in the supreme moment when I looked down into
my boy's grave my sorrow was full of submission and without bitterness, it is ... not because I have ever cared whether my poor
personality shall remain distinct for ever from the All from whence
it came and whither it goes. . . .

I know right well that 99 out of 100 of my fellows would call me
atheist, infidel, and all the other usual hard names. As our laws
stand, if the lowest thief steals my coat, my evidence (my opinions
being known) would not be received against him.*

But I cannot help it. One thing people shall not call me with justice
and that is—a liar. As you say of yourself, I too feel that I lack
courage; but if ever the occasion arises when I am bound to speak,
I will not shame my boy."²⁸

Huxley's surviving son considered this intimate letter, in an era when
respectable men and women did not broadcast their private sorrows to
the world, important enough to be included in a volume of selected
letters published in 1900, just five years after his father's death.

Because the deaths of small children were so common—and
because they produced a special agony for those who had no hope of

---

*England, like many American states (but unlike the U.S. government, with its
constitutional provision banning religious tests for any "public trust"), prohibited
those who refused to take an oath on the Bible from testifying in court.

reunion with winged holy innocents in heaven—the secular sermons delivered at funeral services for the children of freethinkers provide a moving insight into the way agnostics attempted to bear the unbearable. At an 1882 burial service for a friend's child, Ingersoll delivered what became one of his most widely reprinted speeches. "Every cradle asks us 'Whence?' " he told the grieving parents, "and every coffin 'Whither?' The poor barbarian, weeping above his dead, can answer these questions just as well as the robed priest of the most authentic creed. The tearful ignorance of the one, is as consoling as the learned and unmeaning words of the other. . . . If those we press and strain within our arms could never die, perhaps that love would wither from the earth. May be this common fate treads from out the paths between our hearts the weeds of selfishness and hate. . . . They who stand with breaking hearts around this little grave, need have no fear. The larger and nobler the faith in all that is, and is to be, tells us that death, even at its worst, is only the perfect rest."[29]

One of the glories of nineteenth-century freethought was that its most passionate adherents never laid claim to the absolute knowledge professed by congregants of orthodox faiths. Freethinkers did not hesitate to describe atheism and agnosticism as faiths like any other, often using the term *religion* in a secular sense to define an ethical and metaphysical system grounded in the search for truth rather than in the conviction of having found the truth. The scientific method, combining inductive and deductive reasoning, was very much a part of the secularist religion, but true freethinkers did not make a religion out of science itself. At a widely publicized though much-mocked national freethinkers' convention held in upstate New York in 1878, a Cornell University professor memorably summarized the secularist freethought creed. "We have or may have a religion of unselfish devotion to others and to our own highest ideals," he prophesied, "a religion of character, of abiding enthusiasm for humanity, and of complete intellectual honesty. Into our little human lives it will bring something of the grandeur of these infinite surroundings, a high purpose amid which and for which we live."[30]

6

THE GREAT AGNOSTIC AND
THE GOLDEN AGE OF FREETHOUGHT

On January 25, 1893, cultural and business leaders from New
York, Chicago, and Detroit converged on the obscure south-
western Michigan town of Dowagiac for the dedication of a theater
financed by the estate of the town's most prominent citizen, the
engagingly named Philo D. Beckwith. Set in a rich agricultural region
studded with orchards and pig farms, Dowagiac, with a population of
around seven thousand, was a company town at the time of Beckwith's death in 1889. His Round Oak Company, one of the leading
manufacturers of stoves and furnaces in the United States, employed
one man out of every four in the area. Beckwith was a paternalistic,
civic-minded businessman whose high wages and generous benefits,
including the almost unheard-of concession of sick pay, insulated
Round Oak throughout the eighties from the violent clashes between
labor and management making headlines in larger cities, including
nearby Chicago (only an hour's train ride away along the southern
shore of Lake Michigan). But Beckwith was not only a generous
employer who wanted to bring the performing arts to his hometown, he was a committed freethinker who wished, as one historian of
American freethought puts it, "to make the townsfolk aware and

appreciative of his personal pantheon of heroes and heroines whom he considered to be the true benefactors of the human race."[1] That pantheon, carved of Lake Superior red sandstone on the facade of the theater, did not reflect the predictable enthusiasms of a successful Gilded Age entrepreneur. It featured men and, even more extraordinarily, women who, as far as political and religious conservatives of the day were concerned, constituted a rogues' gallery: Ingersoll, Paine, Voltaire, Susan B. Anthony, George Eliot, Victor Hugo, George Sand, and Walt Whitman. Busts of Goethe, Shakespeare, Beethoven, and Chopin also gazed down upon Dowagiac's main shopping street. On opening night, a cast of famous actors, including William S. Hart, performed *Much Ado about Nothing* for the bejeweled black-tie audience. The evening's featured speaker was none other than Ingersoll, who had seized the once-in-a-lifetime chance to dedicate a building prominently displaying his own graven image—a distinction customarily reserved for the honored dead. Anticipating Ingersoll's arrival and the attention the presence of the Great Agnostic would bring to the town, the *Dowagiac Times* captured the mood of the local citizenry. In a burst of hyperbole, the newspaper applauded the prospect that "we shall be able to sit in the finest equipped and decorated theater in America and listen to the greatest reasoner, advocate, poet and orator the world has ever known and all at home." Adding the disclaimer that "few among us agree with him in politics, religion, and all minor points," the paper nevertheless emphasized that "every good man and woman agrees in the supreme right to disagree. We would not wish to live in a world where honest discussion was a lost art."[2]

The Beckwith Memorial Theater—or "temple of the performing arts," as it was described by civic boosters—represented more than a gesture of noblesse oblige by a quirky Gilded Age paterfamilias. The cultural ideals exemplified by the project, received locally with the mixture of pride and self-consciousness that may be inferred from the newspaper commentary, were rooted in a larger humanist and rationalist movement that reached out not only to residents of the oldest and largest centers of culture and commerce but to inhabitants of small-town America, particularly in the midwestern and Plains states.

The area around Dowagiac was certainly no hotbed of freethought; indeed, evangelical revivalist movements flourished there after the Civil War (as they would again in the twentieth century), and even today many residents call the town "the buckle on the Bible Belt." Yet there was also, as the newspaper article indicates, a considerable tolerance for irreligion and an openness toward new ideas. Part of that tolerance could be attributed to Beckwith, whose status as the town's most important businessman conferred a certain respectability on religious skepticism. But the spread of American freethought was a national rather than a local or regional phenomenon and can best be understood, whether in small towns or large cities, as one strand in the cultural fabric of a period that fostered intellectual curiosity among citizens of widely varying backgrounds and stations in life.

The period from, roughly, 1875 to 1914 represents the high-water mark of freethought as an influential movement in American society. Like other dates that attempt to pinpoint the beginning and end of a historical period, these are somewhat arbitrary; by the beginning of the twentieth century, there were already signs of a strong reaction against the spread of religious skepticism—just as there had been a century earlier in reaction to Enlightenment "infidelity" (a term that was still very much in use in 1900). Paradoxically but not surprisingly, the growing dissemination of secularist ideas in post–Civil War America was accompanied by an expansion of all religious institutions. Between 1850 and 1906, for instance, capital expenditures for construction of churches tripled. By one estimate, more than 43 percent of Americans in 1910, compared with only 5 percent in 1790, had formal ties to a church or synagogue.[3] A significant part of this growth was attributable to the establishment of new congregations by former slaves throughout the southern states. The allegiance of slaves to Christianity did not, of course, figure into any tally of church membership before the war; if one does not count, literally and figuratively, as a person, one can hardly be counted as a church member. But the deep faith that sustained so many blacks under slavery was quickly translated into a vast network of churches representing the only form of black enterprise that whites did not try to smash after the end of Reconstruction. With a few notable exceptions like W. E. B. Du Bois, the author of the brilliant and seminal *The Souls of Black Folks* (1903)—who grew up not in the South but in Massachusetts—black Americans in the nineteenth century, deeply attached to the one powerful institution not controlled by whites, had little connection with the freethought movement.

Among whites, Catholic immigration from eastern and southern Europe accounted for the largest share of the growth in church membership; most Catholic immigrants came from countries in which theirs was the dominant religion, and their priests came with them. East European Jews also brought their rabbis, but, unlike Catholics, Jewish immigrants varied widely in their degree of religious observance: secular Jews were already influential in America's established German Jewish community, but agnosticism and outright atheism, usually wedded to socialism, would prove to be much stronger intellectual currents among the new immigrants from Russia and Poland. In the postwar decades, close connections—especially in large cities—began to develop between gentile freethinkers and German Jews like Felix Adler, who founded the Ethical Culture Society in 1876. The *Truth Seeker*, for instance, had the highest regard for Adler and always covered his lectures. There were fewer connections between native American freethinkers and the poorer Jewish immigrants who began arriving after 1880—Rose and Elizabeth Cady Stanton had shared a platform, but Emma Goldman and Stanton never did. All of Ingersoll's works, however, were published in Yiddish translation: his passionate agnosticism struck a chord with secular Jews who had rejected traditional observance and who shared Ingersoll's faith in science and self-education. "Some Mistakes of Moses," a satirical deconstruction of Genesis and Exodus, was, as might be expected, the Ingersoll lecture most frequently translated into Yiddish.

To describe the last quarter of the nineteenth and the first decade of the twentieth centuries as a golden age of freethought is to suggest not

that a majority of Americans were persuaded by rationalist or antireligious arguments but that those arguments reached a much broader
public than they ever had in the past. Unlike eighteenth-century
deists, nearly all of whom identified with Jeffersonian democracy,
American freethinkers of the late nineteenth century were anything
but unified in their political views, which ran the gamut from anarchism to Spencerian conservatism. Freethinkers might be Democrats,
rock-ribbed Republicans, or, on occasion, socialists with either a capital or a small *s*. The one political concern that did unite all freethinkers was their support for absolute separation of church and state,
which translated into opposition to any tax support of religious institutions—especially parochial schools. For the most part, tax support
of religious schools had been a nonissue on a national basis before the
Civil War—although New York City's Catholic leadership had pushed
unsuccessfully in the 1840s for government subsidy, long established
in many European countries, of religious education. By the 1870s,
when the growth of the older Irish Catholic community and new
immigration from the Catholic countries of Europe began to transform the ethnic and religious makeup of most large cities, the financ-
ing of parochial school education became a divisive issue throughout
the country. Nineteenth-century opposition to tax subsidies for
parochial schools is often portrayed by modern supporters of religious school vouchers as a manifestation of singleminded anti-
Catholicism, but that was certainly not true for freethinkers. Deists of
Jefferson's generation fought tax support for religious institutions at a
time when the only influential American religious sects were Protestant. Their nineteenth-century successors were unquestionably
appalled when the Roman Catholic Church became the first large religious denomination to establish its own school system in America,
and they viewed the growth of Catholic schools as a threat to the
expansion of public education—a major goal of all social reformers
after the Civil War. In addition, Pius IX's well-publicized denunciations of religious pluralism, secular government, modernism, and science reinforced long-standing American suspicions, on the part of

devout Protestants as well as freethinkers, of "papists." But free-thinkers, secularists, rationalists, infidels, agnostics, and atheists—whatever they call themselves or are called by others—have always taken the position that the American government has no business spending any money on any institution whose purpose is the promotion of any religion.

Because Americans of different faiths were accustomed to religious liberty in practice as well as in theory, separation of church and state—however compelling as a constitutional principle—was not an issue that touched the daily lives of most citizens. Arguments over the mention of God on coins or tax exemption of church property could not provide freethinkers with a basis for appeal to the larger public. The absence of a political focus—a problem unknown to anticlerical Europeans, who formed a political opposition to governments based on monarchy, narrow economic privilege, and church authority—is generally considered a weakness of the American freethought movement. But this lack of identification with a particular political point of view or party was also a strength, in that it enabled freethinkers to exert a strong influence on other reform movements that were non-partisan in character. For if freethinkers did not have a political platform, they nevertheless agreed on a wide range of social, cultural, and artistic concerns, which generated such fierce debate in the decades after the Civil War that they would form a template for the nation's "culture wars" a century later. These included free political speech; freedom of artistic expression; expanded legal and economic rights for women that went well beyond the narrow political goal of suffrage; the necessity of ending domestic violence against women and children; dissemination of birth control information (a major target of the punitive postal laws, defining birth control information as obscene, that bore the name of Anthony Comstock); opposition to capital punishment and to inhumane conditions in prisons and insane asylums; and, above all, the expansion of public education.

American secularists were dedicated to the improvement of free cultural and educational institutions for pragmatic as well as philosophical reasons. The unprecedented postwar expansion of public schools, libraries, and museums—the latter two supported by private philanthropists as well as public funds—contributed greatly to the willingness of Americans to entertain, if not necessarily to adopt, unfamiliar ideas. Free public education for the many rather than the few was essential to the secularist vision of a society in which every individual, unhampered by gatekeepers who sought to control the spread of dangerous knowledge, could go as far as his or her intellect would permit. In the view of freethinkers, the most pernicious gate-keepers were religious authorities; thus, education must be both secular and publicly financed. Indeed, by the 1870s the word *secularist* was used not only as a general philosophical term but as a specific defini-tion, in either the affirmative or the pejorative sense, of those who advocated public schooling free of religious content.

Freethought periodicals, which proliferated after the Civil War, were important sources of communication within the freethinking community. They included the venerable *Boston Investigator*, dating from 1831; the *Truth Seeker*, founded in 1873 in Peoria, Illinois, but soon relocated to New York City; the *Blue Grass Blade* in Lexington, Kentucky; the *Free-Thought Ideal* and *Free-Thought Vindicator* in Ottawa, Kansas; the irresistibly titled *Lucifer, the Light-Bearer* in Topeka, Kansas; and the *Iconoclast* in Austin, Texas, whose editor, William Cowper Brann, was shot in the back and killed by an enraged Baptist in 1898. Brann is an unusual figure in the annals of American freethought, because he was a militant racist—a stance that made him a pariah within the national freethought movement (though many northern freethinkers, like others in the North, saw racism as a strictly southern phenomenon).

The most influential freethought publication—the only one with a truly national circulation—was the *Truth Seeker*. On the masthead of the first issue, published on September 1, 1873, editor D. M. Bennett and his wife, Mary, proclaimed that the publication would devote itself to "science, morals, free thought, free discussions, liberalism, sexual equality, labor reform, progression, free education, and what-ever tends to elevate and emancipate the human race." Its lively letters to the editor column provided a forum not only for readers in large

cities with established freethought organizations but for "village atheists" in small towns, particularly in the South, where religious
unorthodoxy could lead to social ostracism or worse (as Brann's
shooting demonstrated). The writers and editors of the nineteenth-
century *Truth Seeker* were an eclectic bunch. They included proponents of sexual abstinence and free love, urban sophisticates and
devotees of pure country air, spiritualists and uncompromising rationalists, temperance campaigners and promoters of a European appreciation of wine (the latter was perhaps an inheritance from the old
association between freethought and revolutionary France), and
health nuts of every ilk. In 1929, George Macdonald recalled that
there "has always been a considerable fringe of ascetics in the
Freethought ranks—foes of rum, tobacco, corsets, sex, meat, and
white bread. . . . Their slogan is: 'The whiter the bread the sooner
you're dead.' "[4] This quirkiness and diversity of interests was
reflected in the freethought press, with opposition to organized religion and devotion to separation of church and state as the two unify-
ing themes.

But the freethought lecture circuit—not the press—was the chief
mode of communication between committed agnostics and a larger
public that was interested in but did not define itself by religious
skepticism. Americans flocked to lectures in every area of the country—whether in great cities where well-off inhabitants could afford to
pay the munificent sum of one dollar for a ticket to a lecture by the
famous Ingersoll (scalpers in New York City, the newspapers
reported disapprovingly, got up to two dollars) or in towns like
Dowagiac, where a citizen might spend a nickel to hear a traveling lecturer at the Universalist Church, the established venue for heretical
talks. General circulation newspapers treated the talks—especially the
more controversial ones—as legitimate news events. Ingersoll, Stanton, and Anthony made headlines and sold newspapers wherever they
went. When Anthony spoke at the Dowagiac Universalists' invitation
in 1874 (two decades before she was enshrined in the Beckwith Theater's dissident pantheon), the church was packed even though the

one local newspaper described her arguments as "lengthy but not particularly convincing . . . and [eliciting] but little enthusiasm." Not little enough, the writer was forced to admit, because when Anthony asked her local audience for a show of hands on the woman suffrage issue, "the ladies" surprised the men by responding with an uppity and overwhelming "aye."⁵

It is difficult, in an era in which most Americans acquire their information from packaged sound bites that require almost no effort from audiences, to convey the excitement of a time when people were willing to expend a good deal of energy looking at evidence, and listening to opinions, that challenged the received wisdom of previous ages. Autodidacts considered it fun to sit or stand for hours and hear lecturers discuss Shakespeare's sonnets, the poetry of Byron, the philosophy of Voltaire, the new biblical criticism based on the premise that the Scriptures were written by humans, evolution, electrification, the germ theory of disease, or woman suffrage. Their faith-inspired counterparts were equally eager to listen to evangelists deliver lengthy sermons on salvation and damnation. Freethought lecturers, unable to hold out the prospect of salvation or threaten damnation in the next world, could appeal to their audiences only by holding out a different vision of how to think and live on this earth.

The most masterful articulator of the secularist vision was Robert Green Ingersoll (1833–99). Without him, the golden age of American freethought is as difficult to imagine as abolitionism without Garrison or the first wave of feminism without Stanton. Ingersoll's position as the preeminent orator of his generation enabled him to reach millions of Americans who might otherwise have refused to give a personal hearing, unmediated by a hostile press, to the case against conventional religion. One of the two most important figures in the history of American secularist dissent (the other of course being Paine), Ingersoll bridged the gap between the theoretical deism of the Enlightenment and the practical freethought, focusing on specific social problems, that defined the late-nineteenth-century movement. While he was hardly the first person to make the connection between authoritarian religion and authoritarian social values, Ingersoll was the first American to lay out a coherent secular humanist alternative, touching on everyday matters like marriage and parenthood, to life as defined by traditional religious faith—and to present the case for freethought to a broad public. Like Paine's written polemics, Ingersoll's speeches were delivered in vivid, down-to-earth language, intended for the many rather than the few, and understandable to all. With his immense passion and physical energy, he spoke in hundreds of towns each year at the height of his career in the eighties and nineties, and his influence reached far beyond nests of infidel intellectuals in the cultural centers of the northeast. The breadth of Ingersoll's influence was attested to by the depth of antagonism he aroused. He is a critical figure in the struggle for true freedom of conscience in America—meaning the freedom *not* to worship any god as well as to worship God in one's own way—not only because he fought for intellectual and spiritual liberty but because his principles required the sacrifice of his political ambitions. Ingersoll's enemies as well as his admirers acknowledged that he could have had a major political career were it not for his avowed agnosticism. And although Ingersoll commanded large lecture fees—his critics often portrayed him in cartoons as a Judas piling up coins by betraying God—there is little doubt that he would have done even better financially, as one of the nation's leading trial lawyers, had he devoted himself solely to representing wealthy robber barons.

The son of a Presbyterian minister, Ingersoll was born on August 11, 1833, in Dresden, a tiny settlement on the shore of Lake Seneca in the region of upstate New York so susceptible to religious enthusiasms that it was known as the "burned-over district"—meaning that each new wave of evangelical revivalism swept through the area like a wildfire. Religious critics of "Robert Injuresoul" had two theories about the origins of his agnosticism. On the one hand, they suggested that he was reacting to an upbringing filled with hellfire and damnation called down upon him by his father; on the other, that young

Robert had not been threatened with *enough* hellfire during his childhood. Both explanations are partly true and partly false. His father, John Ingersoll, was a minister who does not seem to have been an old-fashioned Calvinist. The elder Ingersoll repeatedly became involved in conflicts with his congregations—more than a dozen of them during Robert's childhood—over views that were too theologically liberal and too strongly abolitionist for most of his parishioners. But as a minister's son, Robert was administered a heavier than usual dose of religious observance. At a time when clerics like Lyman Beecher were lamenting Americans' increasingly lax observance of the Sabbath, no preacher's kid could escape the grim exigencies of a Christian Sunday. "When I was a boy Sunday was considered altogether too holy to be happy in," Ingersoll recalled. "[W]hen the sun fell below the horizon on Saturday evening, there was a darkness fell upon the house ten thousand times deeper than that of night. Nobody said a pleasant word; nobody laughed; nobody smiled; the child that looked the sickest was regarded as the most pious. That night you could not even crack hickory nuts. If you were caught chewing gum it was only another evidence of the total depravity of the human heart." Sunday morning was of course spent in church, and services lasted several hours. In a passage that never failed to draw laughs and groans from his audiences, Ingersoll described the rest of the holy day:

In those days, no matter how cold the weather was, there was no fire in the church. It was thought to be a kind of sin to be comfortable while you were thanking God. . . .

After the sermon we had an intermission. Then came the catechism with the chief end of man. . . . We sat in a row with our feet coming within about six inches of the floor. . . . After that we started for home, sad and solemn—overpowered with the wisdom displayed in the scheme of atonement. When we got home, if we had been good boys, and the weather was warm, sometimes they would take us out to the graveyard to cheer us up a little. It did cheer me. When I looked at the sunken tombs and the leaning stones, and read the half-effaced inscriptions through the moss of silence and forgetfulness, it was a great comfort. The reflection came to my mind that the observance of the Sabbath could not last always. Sometimes they would sing that beautiful hymn in which occurs these cheerful lines: "Where congregations ne'er break up,/And Sabbaths never end." These lines, I think prejudiced me a little against even heaven.[6]

This meditation on the dour Sabbaths of his boyhood was not so much an attack on religion as an argument against the punitive mode of child rearing advocated and practiced by the substantial number of Americans who still believed in the Calvinist depravity of newborn souls and in the absolute legal as well as moral right of parents to punish as they saw fit. The revolutionary idea that children have rights was born in the Enlightenment, but the practical application of that concept, in schools and within families, was very much a product of the progressive side of the Victorian era. John Dewey—still a bête noire of conservatives, who tend to characterize him as the apotheosis of twentieth-century "permissiveness" in education—was born in 1859, the year in which *The Origin of Species* was published. Freethinkers were strongly attracted to Dewey's educational philosophy, based on the premise that truth cannot be apprehended through revelation but only through observation and experience. Although these ideas would become more widely accepted in the twentieth century, they were rooted in changing nineteenth-century concepts of human development. Among these was the notion—again, rooted in the Enlightenment—that children's moral well as intellectual development could best be fostered through love rather than fear. The idea that a child could grow in wisdom, age, and grace without being subjected to the rod posed a challenge to the still pervasive Victorian belief in the moral and educational value of corporal punishment—an article of faith long held by the more conservative clergy. No one detested the socially legitimized abuse of children more than Ingersoll, and he found a responsive chord among liberal Christians when he pointed out that Jesus had preached the opposite. "Do you know," he asked audiences, "that I have seen some people who acted as though they thought when the Savior said, 'Suffer the little children to come unto me, for of such is the kingdom of heaven,' he had a raw-hide under his mantle, and made that remark simply to get the children within striking distance?" If anyone planned to whip his children again, Ingersoll cautioned, "I want you to have a photograph taken of yourself when you are in the act, with your face red with vulgar anger, and the face of the little child, with eyes swimming in tears and the little chin dimpled with fear, like a piece of water struck by a sudden cold wind."[7] Ingersoll's argument against corporal punishment within the family—that it degraded the parent as much as or even more than the child—paralleled his argument against the death penalty, which he saw as a form of state-sanctioned murder that coarsened an entire society and thus did more damage to the public than to criminals.

Because the Ingersoll family rarely stayed in one place long enough for the children to finish a school year, Robert was almost entirely self-educated—no disadvantage for a nineteenth-century lawyer or politician. He had only two years of formal elementary schooling, and the turning point in his intellectual life seems to have been the discovery of Shakespeare in his teens—a moment of illumination he often recalled in his speeches:

[O]ne night I stopped at a little hotel in Illinois, many years ago, when we were not quite civilized. . . . While I was waiting for supper an old man was reading from a book, and among others who were listening was myself. I was filled with wonder. I had never heard anything like it. I was ashamed to ask him what he was reading; I supposed that an intelligent boy ought to know. So I waited, and when the little bell rang for supper I hung back. . . . I picked up the book; it was Sam Johnson's edition of Shakespeare. The next day I bought a copy for four dollars. My God! More than the national debt. . . . For days, for nights, for months, for years, I read those books, two volumes, and I commenced with the introduction. . . . That book has been a perpetual joy to me from that day to this; and whenever I read Shakespeare—if it ever happens that I fail to find some new beauty, some new presentation of some wonderful truth, or another word that bursts into blossom, I shall make up my mind that my mental faculties are failing, that it is not the fault of the book.[8]

Ingersoll and his elder brother, Ebon Clark—who shared Robert's antireligious views—came of age in southern Illinois, one of the many areas of the country in which the family briefly resided during the peripatetic ministerial career of its paterfamilias. After a brief and unsatisfying career as a schoolteacher, Ingersoll read law in the offices of a prominent attorney in Marion, Illinois, and, like Lincoln, passed the Illinois bar on the basis of knowledge acquired from his independent study. Ingersoll was admitted to the bar in 1854, at age twenty-one, and he and his brother soon opened a law practice in Shawneetown, which called itself the "Metropolis of Southern Illinois." In 1857, the two moved their practice north to Peoria, in part because they were staunch abolitionists and the political and social climate in the southern part of the state was strongly influenced by proslavery settlers who had migrated north from Tennessee, Kentucky, and Mississippi. In 1860, on the eve of the Civil War, Ingersoll ran as a Democrat for Congress—his first and only campaign for office—but soon switched to the Republicans because of their stronger antislavery stance. His outspoken opposition to laws mandating the return of fugitive slaves to their owners—laws defended by most Democrats at the time—doomed his campaign from the start.[9]

In December 1861, Ingersoll helped organize the Eleventh Illinois Cavalry Regiment and was placed in command with the rank of colonel. (In the first year of the war, many young men with no military background were commissioned as officers.) At the Battle of Shiloh in 1862, which claimed ten thousand lives, the main responsibility of his regiment was to hold the rear and "stop successive stampedes of deserters from the front line."[10] In December 1862, the young officer was captured by the guerrilla forces of Nathan Bedford Forrest in Tennessee. He was not held as a prisoner of war but was paroled—a curious custom by today's military standards—in an agreement that allowed officers to be released on the condition that they promise not to return to battle.

After his release, Ingersoll returned to his wife, Eva, whom he had married just nine days before leaving for the front. Eva Parker Ingersoll was the daughter of parents who revered Paine, and she thoroughly shared her husband's rationalist views—as indicated by his dedication of the first volume of his collected works: "To Eva A. Ingersoll, My Wife, A Woman Without Superstition." By all accounts, the marriage was an extraordinarily happy one, a fortuitous state of affairs in that it insulated Ingersoll from the attacks directed at free-thinkers, beginning with Tom Paine, who were tarred with rumors—some even substantiated—of libertinism. The historian Samuel Porter Putnam, author of *400 Years of Freethought* (1894), was only one of the prominent freethinkers whose personal life would embarrass the movement. Putnam died in 1896 under mysterious circumstances in Boston, where he and a female companion, a twenty-year-old freethought speaker from Kentucky named May Collins, were said to have been asphyxiated by the gas lamps in Miss Collins's room. The *Truth Seeker* reported that the bodies of both were found fully clothed, since Putnam had called in order to accompany the lady to the theater. Needless to say, there was considerable speculation about how two people, fully awake and fully dressed, could have been overcome before smelling the gas. An even greater embarrassment to liberal religious believers was Henry Ward Beecher, who, in his later years, was as close to being a freethinker as a man could get and still be a member of the clergy. In 1875, Beecher's one-time friend and parishioner Theodore Tilton sued the eminent minister for having allegedly committed adultery with Tilton's wife, Elizabeth. Although the jury could not reach a verdict, the accusation itself provided ammunition for religious conservatives, who hated liberal Protestantism almost as much as they did agnosticism. The response of conservatives to the Beecher affair was complicated by the involvement of the radical feminist and spiritualist Victoria Woodhull, who published the alleged details of Beecher's adultery with Elizabeth Tilton in her own newspaper, *Woodhull and Claflin's Weekly*. Attacking the hypocrisy of a

society that inveighed against free love but tolerated sexual miscon-
duct by powerful men, Woodhull was prosecuted under the Comstock
laws. Conservatives who wanted to see the liberal Beecher punished
for his sins were placed in the uncomfortable position of being on the
same side as one of the most notorious women in America. In any
case, Beecher was not punished for his sins—not in this world, at any
rate—and went on to resume his career as a cleric and orator after his
trial ended in a hung jury.

Ingersoll's spotless reputation as a husband and father was a source
of considerable frustration to those who would have loved to catch
him in bed, dead or alive, with a young woman. One conservative
critic, miffed by the many references in Ingersoll's obituaries to his
happy family life, grumbled that it was "not easy to perceive just why
his private virtues have been so breathlessly brought forward and
detailed with so much strenuous insistence; for surely husbands who
are faithful, fathers who are loving, and friends who are generous and
sympathetic, are not so rare in this our world as to make of them phenomena to be noted in the annals of the age."[11] Ingersoll's attitude
toward women was unusual, in that he combined a bedrock belief in
the intellectual equality of the sexes with old-fashioned chivalry and
idealization of romantic love. In his last court appearance, in which he
represented a widow attempting to overturn a prenuptial agreement
on grounds that her husband had underrepresented his true worth,
Ingersoll took umbrage at the opposing attorney's argument that the
wife must have known how rich her husband was because she could
not possibly have married him for love. Furthermore, the lawyer
argued, since the man was already seventy-five when he met his future
wife, he could not possibly have been in love with her but must have
entered a marriage of convenience to obtain a caretaker for his declin-
ing years. Ingersoll remarked tartly that if it was truly impossible for
a seventy-five-year-old to be in love, "I hope no fate like that will ever
overtake me." He then spun a tale of a 125-year-old woman who,
when asked how old a woman had to be before ceasing to have
thoughts about love, replied, "I don't know, honey; you will have to
ask somebody older than I."[12]

In the years immediately after the Civil War, long before Ingersoll became the Great Agnostic, it seemed that he was on the way to fulfilling his political as well as his personal hopes. A much sought-after orator on behalf of Republican candidates (including his brother, who was elected to Congress three times), Ingersoll was appointed state attorney general by the Republican governor of Illinois in 1867. He would never hold another appointive or elective public office. By the late 1860s, after an unsuccessful try for the Republican gubernatorial nomination in Illinois, Ingersoll's antireligious views—already well known to his friends, family, and close professional associates—were becoming equally well known to those who heard him speak throughout the Midwest. Ingersoll could not have entertained any illusions about the compatibility of his religious views and his political ambitions: Lincoln and Ulysses S. Grant might have been elected without becoming church members, but no one who uncompromisingly denounced churches and many of their leaders could hope to attain high or even low public office. As the *New York Times* would observe in an editorial after his death, Ingersoll's irreligion meant that he "never took that place in the social, the professional, or the public life of his country to which by his talents he would otherwise have been eminently entitled." Ingersoll lacked proper reverence, the editors intoned—and what was worse, "he gloried in it, gloried in having a hollow where the bump of veneration ought to be. It has justly been said that he was 'no respecter of parsons,' but that was only part of his radiating and centrifugal disrespect. Geniality, courage, frankness without scruple and without deference: these are the qualities which were so completely summed up in Ingersoll as in any man we can recall." Thus, it was no more than a "stroke of justice" that Ingersoll had been barred from serving his country in any official public position.[13]

Although Ingersoll could never have hoped to become a successful political candidate after revealing his agnosticism to the world, he could and did achieve national renown as a political orator in 1876, when, before delegates to the Republican National Convention in Cincinnati, he placed the name of James G. Blaine in nomination for the presidency. Before a spellbound hall of delegates, Ingersoll compared Blaine to an "armed warrior" and "plumed knight," but Blaine's connection with an 1860s corruption scandal led the convention to choose Rutherford B. Hayes.

Ingersoll's Republicanism was rooted both in his abolitionist attachment to the party of Lincoln and in his support for the gold standard—an issue on which he differed from many of his fellow freethinkers, who were in favor of free silver as well as freethought. However, Ingersoll's support for both Grant and Blaine also derived from their stance on behalf of separation of church and state. Grant wanted to strengthen the barrier between church and state and even suggested that it might be a good idea to tax church property, a proposal that went nowhere. But in 1875, Blaine, then a congressman from Maine, introduced a constitutional amendment, along lines first suggested by Madison during the debate over ratification of the Bill of Rights, that did go somewhere. The amendment would have extended the federal Constitution's secularist provisions to the states:

> No state shall make any law respecting an establishment of religion, or prohibiting the free exercise thereof; and no money raised by school taxation in any State, for the support of public schools, or derived from any public fund thereto, shall ever be raised under the control of any religious sect; nor shall any money so raised, or lands so devoted, be divided between religious sects or denominations.

Blaine's amendment passed the House by an overwhelming vote of 180 to 7 and fell just two votes short in the Senate of receiving the two-thirds majority necessary for presentation to the states for ratification. Nevertheless, sixteen state legislatures passed similar amendments in the years after the defeat of Blaine's proposal at the federal level, and those state laws stand today as a powerful barrier to vouchers for religious schools.

From the "plumed knight" speech in 1876 until his death in 1899, Ingersoll's oratory helped elect a good many Republican candidates. Yet his political speeches, even though they rarely touched on religion, often elicited scathing commentary on his religious views. "The party which employs such agents to sustain its falling vitality had better die a quiet death," the Democratic *New York Sun* said of Ingersoll's participation in the 1876 campaign. "To give him praise, to circulate his worthless wit, is an outrage. The only office which the press ought to perform is to help exterminate such a moral pestilence or hang the mortal carrion in chains upon a cross beam."[14] Such criticism did not deter Republican candidates from wanting the nation's most famous orator to take to the stump on their behalf, but it did deter them from appointing Ingersoll to a cabinet post that would have required Senate confirmation. Nevertheless, it says something about the degree of tolerance for the unconventional in nineteenth-century America that so many Republican candidates— some devoutly religious themselves—were eager to enlist the oratorical talents of the nation's most prominent agnostic. There is no twenty-first-century version of Ingersoll—indeed, there was no twentieth-century version of him—but it is impossible to imagine any recent presidential candidate soliciting or accepting an endorsement from a public figure defined chiefly by his opposition to religion. The ungrateful Blaine, who finally received the Republican presidential nomination in 1884, was the one Republican candidate who, in an effort to distance himself from his old supporter's irreligious reputation, failed to enlist Ingersoll's oratorical assistance. As it turned out, Blaine might have been better advised to distance himself from his supporters among the Protestant clergy. He is generally believed to have lost New York State, and the close election, to Grover Cleveland because one of his Presbyterian backers, the Reverend Samuel D. Buchard, described the Democrats as the party of "rum, Romanism, and rebellion." Blaine, who was present at the speech, did not disavow the remarks and lost New York by only one thousand votes—a margin surely attributable to the outrage of Irish Catholic voters. The vast majority of Irish Catholics would have voted for the Democrats anyway, but it was generally agreed that there must have been at least a thousand second- or third-generation New Yorkers rich enough and distant enough from their Irish roots to vote for the party of the gold standard—if a Protestant had not insulted them. Ingersoll later told reporters that he had stayed out of the campaign because he did not want to scare off the preachers but added, in a letter to his brother-in-law and publisher, C. P. Farrell, that he felt sorry for the six hundred ministers who had called on Blaine and "assured him of the support of Jehovah and Co.—I hate to have the old firm disappointed."[15]

Because freethinkers were not of one political mind, Ingersoll's role in the Republican Party was of no particular importance to them. But, as the philologist Harry Thurston Peck observed in 1899, Ingersoll's renown as a political orator was the Trojan horse that gained a hearing for his secularist views among those who did *not* consider themselves agnostics or freethinkers. Had Ingersoll originally become nationally known as a militant agnostic rather than as a political orator, Peck argued with considerable justification, he would probably have been ignored by respectable citizens. "Had he in the first place sought for widespread recognition as an opponent of Christianity, and of revealed religion, he would no doubt have gathered audiences; yet they would not have been precisely the same kind of audiences. . . . Hence it came about that instead of declaiming to the sort of audiences that usually gather to applaud the wonted peripatetic infidel—a crowd of illiterate or half-educated men, of long-haired agitators and obscene fanatics—Colonel Ingersoll delivered his attacks on Christianity before audiences made up in part, at least, of intelligent, serious-minded, influential men and women. The political partisan had won a hearing for the professional atheist."[16] Needless to say, Peck did not intend his observations as a compliment.

It is all but impossible to re-create the dramatic impact of an orator who lived before the age of sound recording. Shortly before his death, Ingersoll visited the Menlo Park, New Jersey, laboratory of his friend Thomas Edison and made several recordings of excerpts from his most famous speeches. At the Ingersoll Birthplace Museum in Dresden, maintained by the Council for Secular Humanism (an indefatigable, chronically underfinanced organization based in Buffalo, New York), visitors can pick up a headset and hear a tinny voice declare: "While I am opposed to all orthodox creeds, I have a creed myself; and my creed is this. Happiness is the only good. The time to be happy is now. The place to be happy is here. The way to be happy is to make others so. This creed is somewhat short, but it is long enough for this life, strong enough for this world. If there is another world, when we get there we can make another creed." But that faint sound, digitally restored from some of the oldest cylinders in the RCA historical vaults, cannot convey what impelled people in the West to travel hundreds of miles, and those in eastern cities to stand in line for hours, to hear Ingersoll speak.

He was a rotund, unimposing figure, described by one of his twentieth-century biographers, C. H. Cramer, as "the George Herman Ruth of the platform." Ingersoll's girth impelled the *Oakland Evening Tribune* to observe that in another century the amount of fat and oil in the Great Agnostic's body would have produced a spectacular auto-da-fé.[17] He had one physical characteristic—a sensuous, protruding lower lip—that particularly appealed to women. Eva Ingersoll, who often accompanied her husband on his lecture tours, took a sanguine view of the women she called "Robert's sweethearts," who waited outside lecture halls for a glimpse of or a handshake from their idol. They were probably less enamored of Ingersoll's appearance than of his views on women. In "The Liberty of Man, Woman, and Child," he would follow up a passionate plea for equal rights for women with a meditation on love and marriage that expressed his romantic side and his enduring love for his wife. "And do you know," he told his audiences, "it is a splendid thing to think that the woman you really love will never grow old to you. Through the wrinkles of time, through the mask of years, if you really love her, you will always see the face you love and won. And a woman who really loves a man does not see that he grows old; he is not decrepit to her; she always sees the same gallant gentleman who won her hand and heart."[18]

Ingersoll generally spoke without notes, always proceeding immediately to the center of the stage and beginning without benefit of any fulsome introduction. His delivery was both logical and bitingly witty, and he deliberately avoided the extravagant rhetorical style—one of the best examples being William Jennings Bryan's famous "cross of gold" speech accepting the Democratic presidential nomination in 1896—favored by many politicians as well as the best-known clerical preachers of the era. Even the most orthodox religious members of Ingersoll's audiences were often charmed by his cheerful manner and obvious enjoyment of his own jokes. A newspaper in Des Moines, Iowa, reported that a majority of those attending Ingersoll's lecture "were strictly orthodox; and how they did roar. Foreordination laughs jostled freewill smiles; Baptist cachinations floated out to join apostolic roars, and there was a grand unison of orthodox cheers for the most unorthodox jokes."[19] Nothing travels less well over time than humor, but it is easy to see why nineteenth-century audiences would have laughed at Ingersoll's combination of merriment and sarcasm. In "Some Mistakes of Moses," he wooed his listeners with the theories of a well-known theologian who suggested, having half assimilated Darwin, that the serpent who persuaded Eve to eat of the forbidden fruit was probably a humanoid ape with the gift of speech. To the innocent Eve, the devilish ape resembled a man. The ape had then been punished for his role in the Fall, the theologian surmised, by being deprived of his original gift of speech and reduced to the chattering of monkeys. Ingersoll commented: "Here then is the 'connecting link' between man and the lower creation. The serpent was simply an orang-outang that spoke Hebrew with the greatest ease, and had the outward appearance of a perfect gentleman, seductive in manner, plausible, polite, and the most admirably calculated to deceive. It never did seem reasonable to me that a long, cold, and disgusting snake with an apple in its mouth, could deceive anybody; and I am glad, even at this late date to know that the something that persuaded Eve to taste the forbidden fruit was, at least, in the shape of a man."[20]

In 1880, when Ingersoll delivered lectures on two successive May Sundays at Booth's Theater on Twenty-third Street in Manhattan, newspapers still followed the journalistic custom of reporting applause and laughter in their accounts of speeches. This posed something of a dilemma for the *Times*, which placed a disapproving three-tier headline over its account of Ingersoll's May 23 speech:

COL. INGERSOLL AT BOOTH'S
THE GREAT INFIDEL PREACHER
ROUNDLY HISSED

———

Some Things Which Even Sunday Evening Amusement Seekers would not stand–the God of the Bible ridiculed and denounced–the lecturer's views about the coming Convention

Public interest in Ingersoll was so intense that no one who had a ticket was willing to sell it to a scalper at any price. The audience was eminently respectable, consisting "half of ladies," but the *Times* noted a "remarkable absence of persons of prominence" (presumably persons like the newspaper's owners). The hissing mentioned in the misleading headline seemed to be confined to representatives of the American Bible Society, who were handing out free copies of the King James Version outside the theater. The *Times* went on to chronicle a two-and-a-quarter-hour lecture titled "The Gods" that seems to have been interrupted every few minutes by peals of laughter:

Col. Ingersoll... turned his attention to the teachings of the Churches on the subject of salvation. "The Catholics," he said, "will give you a through ticket to heaven, and they will attend to your baggage, and keep it too. [Great laughter] The Protestants, on the other hand, won't even tell you what train to get on." He read and ridiculed the Catholic creed. One thing he liked about this Church was purgatory. It was a place where a man could make a motion for a new trial. [Laughter] ... Protestantism was next handled without gloves. The Episcopalian religion, he said, was founded by Henry VIII, now in heaven, [Laughter] at the same moment that he put off his wife Catherine and took up Anne Boleyn. For awhile the new religion was regulated by law, and

God was compelled to study acts of Parliament to find out whether a man might be saved or not. [Laughter][21]

The newspaper reports of Ingersoll's speeches, even when accompanied by slanted headlines and negative editorial commentary, demonstrate that the challenge to orthodox religion was considered important enough to merit extensive coverage—regardless of what "persons of prominence" might think. They also indicate a considerable latitude in public discourse on the subject of religion. In the nineteenth century, freedom of religion meant just that—the freedom to believe in and practice one's creed. It did not mean that particular religious beliefs were exempt from public criticism or even from public ridicule.

But the journalistic emphasis on Ingersoll's jibes at religion and the Bible—the infidel preacher would say anything for a laugh!—was almost never balanced by a fair exposition of the humanistic philosophical and ethical system with which he proposed to replace orthodox faith. In a final pronouncement two days after Ingersoll's death, the *Times* summed up the conventional wisdom on the importance of religion. "If we believe, what every sane man must believe," the paper declared, "that religion is upon the whole a help to good behavior, then it must be owned that whoever sets out to deprive people of their religion without pretending to offer them anything in its stead is a public malefactor. Not that Bob Ingersoll took anything like so serious a view of himself as that. He went about denying or ridiculing for the joy it gave him to agitate dignitaries and bigwigs. The effect upon the public could not have been otherwise than bad."[22]

Then as now, the idea that an atheist or agnostic believes in nothing was a cornerstone of the orthodox mindset. It did give Ingersoll joy to agitate bigwigs, but he took his humanist creed very seriously and in all his speeches addressed the accusation that freethinkers had nothing to offer in place of religion. Nearly every newspaper account of "The Gods" omitted the passages in which Ingersoll responded to that accusation:

Notwithstanding the fact that infidels in all ages have battled for the rights of man, and have at all times been the fearless advocates of liberty and justice, we are constantly charged by the church with tearing down without building again. . . .

We are not endeavoring to chain the future, but to free the present. We are not forging fetters for our children, but we are breaking those our fathers made for us. We are the advocates of inquiry, of investigation, and thought. This of itself, is an admission that we are not perfectly satisfied with our conclusions. Philosophy has not the egotism of faith. . . .

We are laying the foundations of the grand temple of the future— not the temple of all the gods, but of all the people—wherein, with appropriate rites, will be celebrated the religion of Humanity. We are doing what little we can to hasten the coming of the day when society shall cease producing millionaires and mendicants— gorged indolence and famished industry—truth in rags, and super-stition robed and crowned. We are looking for the time when the useful shall be the honorable; and when REASON, throned upon the world's brain, shall be the King of Kings, and God of Gods.[23]

These are not the words of a cynic who goes about "ridiculing for the joy it gave him to agitate dignitaries and bigwigs." Ingersoll's vision may have been overly optimistic, but it was hardly lacking in idealism.

One reason for Ingersoll's fame was that he traveled the length and breadth of the country at a time when most Americans did not. He was unique in that he appealed equally to freethinkers weaned on intellec-tual and philosophical debates in comfortable Manhattan and Boston parlors and to those compelled to ride fifty miles across the prairie for a talk with an infidel neighbor. The Ingersolls had moved to New York in 1885 and lived in a Gramercy Park town house (on the site of the pres-ent Gramercy Park Hotel) until his death. Their Sunday-evening recep-tions soon became an institution for cultural, artistic, and business luminaries representing many professions and shades of opinion. The guest list read like a Who's Who of fin du siècle New York: Andrew Carnegie; Henry Ward Beecher; the actors Maurice Barrymore, Edwin Booth (brother of John Wilkes Booth), and Julia Marlowe; Samuel J. Tilden, the losing Democratic presidential candidate in 1876; the famous Hungarian violinist Eduard Reményi; Elizabeth Cady Stanton; and even the young Harry Houdini who, like most professional magicians, disdained belief in the supernatural. Thus, Ingersoll's audiences in the South, Middle West, and Far West received him not only as the leading voice of American freethought but as an emissary from cosmopolitan culture. His lectures drew on a combination of self-education and erudition, experience representing beleaguered small farmers in Peoria and major corporate and political clients in Washington and New York, early poverty and self-made wealth, rural roots and urban sophistication.

Indeed, Ingersoll's Illinois background attested to the geographical diversity of American freethought, which had deep roots not only in the East but in the Middle West and the West—especially in Illinois, Iowa, Kansas, Missouri, and Texas, where anticlerical refugees from central Europe began settling as early as the 1820s. Those refugees arrived in even greater numbers after the failed European democratic revolutions of 1848, creating vibrant outposts of freethought from St. Louis to Austin, Texas. A majority of the "Forty-Eighters" were Germans (including German Jews); twenty thousand settled in Texas alone. But, as Fred Whitehead and Verle Muhrer point out in one of the few books on the subject, religious iconoclasm on the frontier—a mental location that, for much of the nineteenth century, included not only the Southwest and the Rocky Mountain states but a good deal of what is now thought of as the Middle West—has been overlooked by most American intellectual historians.[24]

One ironic reason for the blind spot may be the success of rebellious midwestern sons, most notably Sinclair Lewis (born in Sauk Centre, Minnesota, in 1885 but educated at Yale), in making their native region a twentieth-century symbol, particularly to intellectuals on the East and West Coasts, of American smugness and conformity. *Main Street,*

Babbitt, and *Elmer Gantry,* with their bored and repressed housewives, hypocritical preachers, and boosterish businessmen, are familiar to anyone who has a passing acquaintance with American realist literature. But few readers have any image of the freethinking, populist Middle West of the 1890s described in *North Star Country* (1945), a regional history by the radical activist and Iowa-born writer Meridel Le Sueur:

> So the questions flew back and forth over the jug, the harvest, in the corn row; thinking came with hunger and drought; despite the poverty, books were selling like hotcakes: Henry George, Bellamy's *Looking Backward . . .* and pamphlets on co-operation, socialism. Thoughts sprang up after them like dragon's teeth, and talk arose like a storm. . . . Literature tables were piled high. The Populist movement had become a vast university of the common people, a debating society. There was a renascence of culture. Everyone could write to the papers, which were supported by his own pennies. All could speak out their minds, write speeches; songs and words came to the silent throat . . . from the suffering that flowed like the mighty inland rivers from each inward self to that of others.[25]

There was a brashness, a rough-hewn character to freethought on the ever-shifting frontier that did not always sit well with freethinkers who had carved out an intellectual niche for themselves in the more settled communities of the Northeast. The irreverent cartoons of Watson Heston, who was born in 1846 in Ohio and spent much of his adult life in Missouri, personified the abrasive frontier style; his drawings were sometimes considered too blasphemous even for the pages of the *Truth Seeker.* In *The Bible Comically Illustrated,* Heston's best-known work, he settled on the straightforward technique of depicting literally scenes from the Bible. In one drawing, an enraged God pours every sort of offal, including a dead cat, upon his rebellious people: "And I will cast abominable filth upon thee, and make thee vile, and will set thee as a gazingstock" (Nahum 3:6). In another cartoon, a balding Elijah sits contentedly while bears, conveniently supplied by the Lord, feast upon little children who have mocked the prophet. In this charming tale from the Second Book of Kings, Elijah curses the children in the name of the Lord for calling him a "bald head," and swift physical retribution is dispensed by God's beasts: "And there came forth two she bears out of the wood, and tare forty and two children of them" (2 Kings 2:24). The cartoonist lived in Carthage, Missouri, and in the last years before his death in 1905, contributed illustrations to the *Free-Thought Ideal* of Ottawa, Kansas.

Heston published in the *Truth Seeker* as well as in regional papers, but, as the *Truth Seeker* acknowledged in its obituary, he frequently battled with the editors and resisted their efforts to send him to art school in New York so he could learn to modify the "coarseness" of his style. Heston's *Bible*, published by the Truth Seeker Company in 1900, nevertheless sold at least ten thousand copies. Yet few copies of the book—or of his earlier, separately published volumes of illustrations for the Old and New Testaments—have survived. It seems likely that many of Heston's works, with their graphic (in both the literal and metaphoric senses) hostility toward religion, were destroyed by embarrassed descendants of the original purchasers. Emulating the proper Victorians who deleted bawdy references from their eighteenth-century parents' love letters, the children and grandchildren of many nineteenth-century freethinkers must have been intent on ridding their homes of the evidence of their forebears' shameful unorthodoxy.*

---

*In Dowagiac, the site of Philo D. Beckwith's grand theater adorned with busts of famous freethinkers, many residents are still embarrassed by the town's old connection with irreligion. The Beckwith Theater was razed in 1968 to make way for an undistinguished commercial building; some of the busts were preserved but others were destroyed by the wrecking ball. When I asked numerous civic leaders what had happened to Ingersoll's head, they assured me that it had been pulverized. Only by accident did I discover that Ingersoll's sculpted remains had been rescued by Joseph Spadefore and Jack Ruple, two local freethinkers. The bust resided in Ruple's driveway until 2001, when it was salvaged by Roger E. Greeley, who has written extensively on Ingersoll, and transported to its present home at the Ingersoll Birthplace Museum in Dresden, New York. Spadefore, an outspoken ninety-one-year-old when I interviewed him in 2000, hooted at the town burghers' story about the Ingersoll bust having been smashed. "They've all known exactly where it is since 1968," he said, "because I tried often enough to get the bust preserved and displayed by the town. I guess a lot of people around here still think that old Bob deserved to be reduced to smithereens in vengeance by an angry God. I'm sure those secular humanists in New York will take good care of Bob, but as for me, I'd have liked to walk past a statue of him right here in Dowagiac."

Both the illustrations and the texts of freethought newspapers on the frontier were geared toward the "university of the common people" described by Le Sueur. American freethought in the West was largely a product of the kind of self-education that shaped Ingersoll's early life. Agnostics on the frontier also displayed much less deference than easterners did to liberal religious sensibilities, mainly because fundamentalist Bible-thumping evangelists—not the more accommodating Unitarians or Universalists—were the most influential representatives of Protestantism west of the Mississippi. Since fundamentalists did not hesitate to condemn freethinkers to hell, freethinkers on the frontier were equally blunt in their ridicule of religion. Like Heston's cartoons, Ingersoll's satire went over well with frontier settlers accustomed to speaking their minds in an environment in which religious disputes were often viewed as "fighting words."

St. Louis, Topeka, Kansas City, Des Moines, and Austin had well-established freethought groups by the mid-1880s, but Ingersoll also made a point of appearing in smaller towns and cities. In 1896, on a ten-city swing through Texas, he attracted such large crowds, drawing from a hundred-mile radius for each appearance, that his manager announced plans to commandeer a portable four-acre tent to handle the audiences for his next tour. Mrs. Anna M. Brooks, who rode more than thirty miles on horseback to hear Ingersoll's speech on "The Liberty of Man, Woman, and Child" in Sherman (pop. circa 9,000) typified the Texans who rode dozens, and even hundreds, of miles to hear the Great Agnostic. Arriving several hours early in the hope of meeting Ingersoll personally, she headed straight for the town's best hotel, where she was sure he would be dining before his lecture, and introduced herself to Mrs. Ingersoll—who promptly invited her up to their room. "We went in," Mrs. Brooks recalled in a starstruck letter to the editor of the *Truth Seeker*, "and she said: 'Robert, here is one of your sweethearts.' We shook hands, and when I told him how far I rode through the mud to see him and hear him he said he would give me a pass to the lecture. I thanked him but told him I thought myself fortunate that I had already bought my seat in a good place. He said he was sorry I had been in such a hurry to pay out my money.... I gave

Mrs. Ingersoll my recipe for biscuit." George Macdonald, who noticed that a copy editor had cut out the last line of Mrs. Brooks's letter, restored it and added a commentary on its significance to the freethought community:

> At first the words may be incongruous or mere gossip, but the more you look at them the more significant they become. Colonel Ingersoll and his family have had a good deal of mouth praise, much of which they are obliged to be grateful for when they know it is formal, perfunctory, and not straight from the liver. We can vision the honest Texas woman, living on a ranch, perhaps travel-ing miles on horseback and by rail to meet them; knowing that they were surrounded by people who would give them more flat-tery than they would enjoy, . . . feeling that words were cheap, and that everything costing money was at their disposal; and yet, wish-ing in some signal way to attest her friendship and admiration, she bestows—not for what it is worth to them but for what it is valued at by herself, . . . the unbelieving woman of the Lone Star State. . . . She gave Mrs. Ingersoll her recipe for biscuit![26]

Another element of Ingersoll's character was his ability to maintain warm relations with many of those who disagreed with his antireli-gious views, his Republican politics, or both. In spite of his distaste for socialist and populist economic theories, Ingersoll was on close terms with Eugene V. Debs, and he exerted a strong influence on Debs's contemporaries Robert M. LaFollette and Clarence Darrow. Decades after Ingersoll's death, all three men spoke of their great admiration for him and the ways in which his speeches had helped shape their social consciousness.

The forty-two-year-old Ingersoll met the twenty-year-old Debs in 1875, when Debs, as president of the Occidental Literary Club of Terre Haute, Indiana, invited the Peoria lawyer—who was just begin-ning to "come out" as an agnostic—to speak before the group. The future Socialist candidate for the U.S. presidency (he received more than 919,000 votes in the 1920 election even though he was in prison for sedition as a result of his outspoken antiwar views) was so enthralled by Ingersoll that he not only accompanied him to the train station but bought himself a ticket and rode all the way to Cincinnati so that they could continue talking. In a letter of condolence to his old friend's widow, Debs described Ingersoll as "an older brother" who "with the rarest genius, in beautiful alliance with his heroism, his kindness, and his boundless love ... made the name of Ingersoll immortal."[27] "Fighting Bob" LaFollette, the Wisconsin governor and senator who, from 1901 until his death in 1925, fought for the kind of progressive social legislation that would later become the basis of the New Deal, regarded his entire generation as having been influenced by Ingersoll—not because Ingersoll was right on every issue but because of his insistence on intellectual freedom. "He wanted men to think boldly about all things," LaFollette wrote in 1911. "He demanded intellectual and moral courage. He wanted men to follow wherever truth might lead them. He was a rare, bold, heroic figure."[28]

It is significant, given Ingersoll's long identification with the Republican Party, that his greatest admirers were those who went on to support progressive and liberal causes in the first three decades of the new century. His early-twentieth-century champions were not the "business of America is business" Republicans; there could have been no better evidence of Ingersoll's true worth than to have been revered in the next generation by its LaFollettes and ignored by its Coolidges and Hardings. Had Ingersoll lived longer, his economic views would likely have been modified by the upheavals of the twentieth century, for he was never as thoroughgoing a fiscal conservative (as the term was understood both in his own time and in ours) as his unwavering support for the gold standard suggested. He argued in favor of estate taxes that would require the rich to pay a larger percentage than the poor, even while he generally opposed the idea of a tax on *earned* income.

Like his hero Paine, Ingersoll generally subscribed to the proposition that government was, at best, a necessary evil, but he also believed that some evils could be corrected only by government.

Ingersoll was most prescient in his insistence that government step in to defend the civil rights of black Americans. In 1883, when a conservative Supreme Court struck down the Civil Rights Act of 1875, which had outlawed racial discrimination in public accommodations, Ingersoll issued a withering blast at the justices. Describing the decision as "a disgrace to the age in which we live," he declared that the high court's opinion "puts the best people of the colored race at the mercy of the meanest portion of the white race. It allows a contemptible white man to trample upon a good colored man."[29] It would take eighty years for Congress to pass another law forbidding discrimination not only in public accommodations but in employment and education.

What Darrow, Debs, and Ingersoll had in common, apart from their agnosticism, was a deep commitment to the liberties enumerated in the Bill of Rights. There is no doubt about where Ingersoll would have stood had he lived to see the post–World War I Red Scare, the Palmer raids, the imprisonment of his friend Debs for opposing America's entry into the war, and the wave of nativism that shut off most immigration from southern and eastern Europe after 1924. In 1886 and 1887, his stand on the Haymarket Square affair foreshadowed the crucial role that religious skeptics would play in the organized civil liberties movement of the twentieth century. Just as the Dreyfus Affair forced every politically aware French person to choose sides, the murder convictions of the anarchists charged in the Haymarket case, four of whom were hanged in 1887, proved to be a defining issue for politically conscious Americans of the Gilded Age. Emma Goldman, who had arrived in the United States as a sixteen-year-old immigrant from Russia in 1885, would describe the executions of the Haymarket defendants as "the decisive influence in my life: that made me an Anarchist, a revolutionist."[30] As one historian notes, Haymarket was the first "Red Scare" in American history, leading to "a campaign of radical-baiting and repression that has rarely if ever been surpassed."[31]

The famous Haymarket "riot" of May 4, 1886, began not as a riot but as a peaceful assembly in Chicago's Haymarket Square to protest police shootings of strikers the previous day at the McCormick Reaper Works. The main issue in the strike was labor's demand for an eight-hour workday. At Haymarket, the speakers—who were indeed anarchists—called for an eight-hour day and criticized the police, but the assembly of several thousand remained peaceful until police entered the square and ordered the workers to disperse. Someone— the person was never found or identified—threw a bomb, killing seven policemen and an unknown number of onlookers and injuring more than sixty. Eight anarchists, including the immigrant editors of the anarchist newspaper *Arbeiter Zeitung*, were indicted for murder. In newspapers across the country, the defendants were presumed guilty. *The Chicago Times* described the anarchists as the "rag-tag and bob-tail cutthroats of Beelzebub from the Rhine, the Danube, the Vistula and the Elbe." The *New York Times* declared that "no disturbance of the peace that has occurred in the United States since the war of rebellion has excited public sentiment throughout the Union as it is excited by the Anarchists' murder of policemen in Chicago on Tuesday night. We say murder with the fullest consciousness of what that word means. It is silly to speak of the crime as a riot. All the evidence goes to show that it was a concerted, deliberately planned, and coolly executed murder." The *St. Louis Globe-Democrat* said flatly, "There are no good anarchists except dead anarchists."[32] In a forerunner of the anti-immigrant measures that would be imposed after the First World War, the deportation of all anarchists was urged by many government officials as well as the press. As the trial unfolded, the prosecution never presented any evidence that any of the defendants had thrown the bomb or even talked about throwing a bomb; the case was based entirely on alleged statements and writings that might be construed as a general incitement to violence. The trial judge instructed the jury that it was not necessary for the prosecution to prove that the defendants had urged a specific criminal act: the jury need only conclude that the commission of a crime *might* be the result of such talk. Three days before the executions, urging commutation of the death sentence to life imprisonment, Ingersoll remarked that "there is neither law nor sense in an instruction like this. . . . Any man who had been arrested with the . . . Anarchists and of whom it could be proved that he ever said a word in favor of any change in government, or of other peculiar ideas, no matter whether he knew of the meeting at the Haymarket or not, would have been convicted."[33]

For Ingersoll, the case was another reminder of the limitations that his antireligious views had placed on his public sphere of action. The chief counsel for the Haymarket defendants, William Black, had wanted to hire Ingersoll as cocounsel and dispatched an assistant, George Schilling, to ask for his help. Schilling, originally a cooper (a maker of casks for dry or liquid goods), was a socialist in his youth and later, as a left-wing Democrat, became secretary of the Illinois State Board of Labor Statistics. He knew Ingersoll well and sought his advice several times during the trial and subsequent unsuccessful appeals on the defendants' behalf. In a letter to Ingersoll's granddaughter, Eva, after her grandfather's death, Schilling explained why Ingersoll had offered his assistance privately rather than publicly. Ingersoll had told Schilling that "the tocsin has already been sounded by the press and the pulpit that Anarchism is the logical fruit of Ingersollism, and that the doctrine of no God, no accountability to a Supreme Power, must inevitably lead to no government, no authority on earth." He advised the defense team to "get a lawyer of national reputation who is a pillar of the church and who can cover these men with his conservative life and character."[34] Ingersoll also shared Schilling's concern about the makeup of the jury, which included factory foremen and superintendents who might identify with their employers enough to be swayed by their negative opinion not only of anarchists but of all labor organizers. "Never get tried by the other fellow's hired hand," Ingersoll said. "If you do, you will get left every time. When I die and appear before the bar of Heaven for judgment, if God will come forward Himself and listen to my story, I'll stand a show. But if He will turn me over to one of His clerks, I'm gone."[35]

After appeals were exhausted, Ingersoll also wrote a letter, at Schilling's suggestion, urging his friend Governor Richard Oglesby to commute all of the death sentences to life imprisonment. Still fearing that association with atheism could do the defendants no good and might lead the governor to reject the plea for commutation, Ingersoll asked Schilling not to mention the letter publicly until Oglesby had made his decision. Although Ingersoll had the greatest respect for Oglesby, he feared that the governor would "be overawed by the general feeling—by the demands of the upper classes." His fear proved well-founded. Following the recommendation of the judge and the prosecutor, Oglesby commuted three of the sentences to life imprisonment but refused to interfere in the other five cases. (Only four of the defendants were executed because one committed suicide in jail.) Six years later, Oglesby's successor as governor, John Peter Altgeld, defied public opinion and ended a bright political career by pardoning the remaining defendants whose sentences had been commuted to life imprisonment. Altgeld, who denounced the trial judge for conducting the proceedings with "malicious ferocity," concluded that there had been no evidence to show that any of the defendants had been involved in the bombing.

Schilling felt obliged to set the record straight after Ingersoll's death because old allegations that the Great Agnostic had refused to join the defense team for financial reasons were still being bandied about by left- and right-wing critics. Religious conservatives, who strongly supported capital punishment, had of course been in favor of the hangings—but they were eager to seize one more chance to portray Ingersoll as an economic opportunist rather than as a sincere opponent of religion. On the left, some who had detested Ingersoll's Republican politics were eager to credit the notion that he had failed to join the defense team because the proferred fee was too small.

Given Ingersoll's passionate commitment to First Amendment rights, his publicity-seeking tendencies, and his hatred of capital punishment, it seems unimaginable that he would have stood on the sidelines during this supremely important test of the American justice system had he not been utterly convinced that his participation would do irreparable harm to the defendants. Large and small decisions of this nature were constantly faced by agnostics who were active in other reform movements, and many chose to downplay their religious skepticism in order to pursue their other social goals. To Ingersoll, the battle against orthodox religion was more important than his other political ambitions. He chose to be an outside agitator, and that is often cited as the reason why he has been forgotten. Yet his memory was not erased quickly or easily. A quarter of a century after his death, his collected works still in print, Ingersoll continued to be treated as a serious antagonist by representatives of the more conservative religious denominations. In 1925, the Reverend James M. Gillis, editor of the *Catholic World*, delivered a lecture on Ingersoll—one of a series that included Voltaire, Edward Gibbon, and Paine—lamenting the fact that the Great Agnostic had *not* been forgotten. "His fame, good or evil, persists as a tradition to the young, as a memory to those in middle age," Gillis said. "He is the nearest approach we Americans have had to Voltaire."[36]

Only a small proportion of Americans were moved to reject religion altogether in response to the proselytizing freethinkers of the nineteenth century, but many more turned away from the more rigid and unquestioning forms of faith. Even more important, freethinkers made a powerful case for a secularist approach to public affairs rooted in an Enlightenment heritage unfamiliar to many in late-nineteenth-century America. Ingersoll did more than anyone to restore Americans' memory of their country's secular and rationalist tradition. In one of his most frequently delivered lectures, he declared of the founders:

> They knew that to put God in the Constitution was to put man out. They knew that the recognition of a Deity would be seized upon by fanatics and zealots as a pretext for destroying the liberty of thought. They knew the terrible history of the church too well to place in her keeping, or in the keeping of her God, the sacred rights of man. They intended that all should have the right to worship, or not to worship; that our laws should make no distinction on account of creed. They intended to found and frame a government for man, and for man alone. They wished to preserve the

individuality of all; to prevent the few from governing the many, and the many from persecuting and destroying the few.[37]

This vision of America as a republic founded "for man, and for man alone"—as opposed to a society singularly blessed by and answerable to God—was as controversial a century ago as it remains today. It lies at the heart of the culture wars that began not in the late twentieth century but in the impassioned debate during the golden age of freethought.

7

DAWN OF THE CULTURE WARS

Once upon a time, and not so very long ago, there was a world in which everyone knew who he was and what God expected him to do. In this kingdom, religion defined and enforced virtuous moral behavior, creating a social consensus that embraced both private and public life. As the conservative historian Gertrude Himmelfarb puts it: "Responsibility, respectability, sobriety, independence were the common values of everyday life. And it was because they were commonplace that they could naturally and confidently be applied to public affairs."[1] This fable forms the foundation of the modern conservative contention that nearly everything wrong in American culture today can be traced to the breakdown of a once seamless social consensus that only a century ago dealt comfortably in moral absolutes but has now abandoned the sea of faith for the swamp of moral relativism. There is no place in this tidy vision for dissenters whose definition of respectability was neither commonplace nor confidently applicable to public affairs—for such diverse nonconformists, in different walks of life, as Ingersoll, Mott, Stanton, Anthony, Goldman, Darrow, Debs, Whitman, Twain, and Du Bois. There is certainly no place for agnostics and atheists—or, for that matter, for unorthodox believers who fought for reform of religious institutions—in a historical narrative based on the idea that nearly everyone in late-nineteenth-century America had the same idea of what constituted personal and civic virtue.

A crucial element in this prelapsarian image is the belief that secularist and antireligious movements never enjoyed any real success among Americans before cultural anarchy enveloped the nation in the 1960s. In this view, Ingersoll is justly forgotten because he was both unimportant and wrong. Stanton and Anthony? They receive lip service for their role in the long struggle to obtain the vote for women, but their unconventional religious views are never acknowledged. Since time has stripped all radicalism from the idea of women's suffrage, it is important—particularly for the Christian right, whose spiritual ancestors once equated "giving" women the vote with promoting atheism and free love—to deny that old-fashioned feminism had anything to do with opposition to traditional religion.

Far from presenting an example of a comfortable and comforting alliance between secular and religious values, the years between 1870 and the First World War constituted an era in which the historic American tension between secularizing and religious impulses flared into open warfare. Post–Civil War America was an extraordinarily dynamic society, coping with challenges that included the arrival of more immigrants than any country had ever absorbed in a comparable period, the unfinished work of Negro emancipation, the fight for labor rights, rapid urbanization, the growing gap between rich and poor in an era of expanding industrial capitalism, the changing status of women, and the struggle for free expression in the press and the arts. In the cultural and political debate over these issues, there was always a strong undercurrent of conflict over the proper role of religion and the limits of religious influence in civil society—a conflict not only between secularism and religion but within religion itself. Those who fought for more humane treatment of prisoners, for instance, made an essentially moral argument on behalf on their proposed reforms—that a society could not call itself decent if it employed criminal brutality to punish criminals. But while freethinkers and liberal religious believers agreed on a definition of decency, religious conservatives emphatically disagreed and cited select passages from the Bible in support of a harsh standard of punishment—including starvation rations, beatings by guards, and prison chain gangs.* Religious liberals could and did cite their own favorite biblical passages in support of social reform, but the greater their degree of religious liberalism, the greater their reliance on secular rather than sacred rationales. Ingersoll felt that the secularization of liberal Protestantism was one of the most important achievements of the American freethought movement. Turn-of-the-century fundamentalism (a term that was not used until around 1910, when a religious publishing house issued the first of a twelve-part series of mass-market booklets titled *The Fundamentals*) was a response to what was perceived as the penetration of much of American Protestantism by infidel ideas.[2]

The nineteenth-century accommodation between religion and secularist freethought included non-Orthodox Jews as well as Protestants but not Roman Catholics, who were constantly warned by church leaders of the dangers of secularization. Since Protestantism remained America's dominant faith throughout the nineteenth century, Ingersoll was probably right in his belief that secularizing tendencies within Protestant churches could only contribute to the legitimization of freethought. It was left to conservative Protestants and the Catholic hierarchy to take up the battle against both freethought and liberal Christianity.

Orthodox religion played both an overt and a covert role in the conflicts over two independent but intimately related issues—the rights of women, including not only the vote but deeper social ques-

---

*Since the mid-1990s, chain gangs have been revived by several southern states. In Texas, chain gangs are considered a particularly effective punishment for juvenile offenders because they subject the teenagers to public humiliation within their communities.

tions such as the inferior legal status of women within marriage, and the first systematic attempts, led by conservative Protestants, to set up a formal censorship mechanism in the face of obstacles posed by the First Amendment. The nineteenth-century confrontation over censorship ranged from semicomical attempts to put fig leaves on statues of nudes to serious attempts to impose an early frost on the literature and art that were irrevocably altering the once provincial American cultural landscape, and broadening the limits of public discourse with unprecedented candor about everything from the human body to religion. The writers who led the way, most notably Whitman and Twain, were freethinkers—and it is no accident that the former ran afoul of the Comstock laws and the latter became a target of local censors as soon as they caught on to what Huck Finn had to say. In these embryonic culture wars, not everyone who took a consistently liberal and libertarian stand was a freethinker, but nearly all freethinkers strongly supported both the expansion of women's rights and freedom of artistic expression. The "woman question" and the battle against censorship were identifiable causes that transcended the political disunity of freethinkers and created a more geographically, socially, and ethnically diverse freethought movement than the one that had existed before the Civil War.

Only one group—black America—was notably absent from the expanding postwar freethought coalition. There were several explanations for the lack of an influential freethought presence within the black community. Christianity, melded with elements of African spiritual beliefs and customs that had somehow survived among the enslaved in America, had been a profound source of strength for blacks under slavery. Early eighteenth-century planters, who quite rightly feared the implications for a slaveholding society of Jesus's teaching that all men are brothers, were persuaded by Anglican authorities that it was possible to teach slaves a form of Christianity, portraying masters as God's overseers on earth, that upheld rather than undermined the "peculiar institution." But slaves drew their own conclusions from both the Old and the New Testaments, as suggested by the pervasive imagery in Negro spirituals referring to the captivity and liberation of the Hebrews from Egyptian bondage. With Emancipation, the African-American church was one institution that did not have to be created from scratch, that stood ready to offer its members old solace and a new sense of purpose appropriate to free men and women. An intellectual movement that emphasized individualism over community, as freethought did, and that challenged faith in any personal God, could not have been expected to hold much appeal for a people whose adoption and adaptation of Christianity was by then inseparable from its fight for personal and communal dignity.

Moreover, former slaves in the 1870s and 1880s were dealing with new threats not only to their modest post-Emancipation gains but to their very existence as a free community. As Congress and the Supreme Court nullified Reconstruction-era guarantees and turned their backs on the de facto reenslavement of "free" citizens of color in the South, freethought concerns such as Darwinian evolution and literary censorship would have seemed ludicrously trivial to most black leaders. And if freethought issues were not of great moment to blacks, neither were black issues a priority for most white freethinkers—even though many had been ardent abolitionists. Ingersoll's forthright condemnation of the 1883 Supreme Court decision permitting racial discrimination in public accommodations was the exception rather than the rule, within society as a whole as well as among freethinkers. In the *National Republican*, Ingersoll used the highly respected Frederick Douglass, a devout but unorthodox religious believer and one of the few well-known blacks with strong ties to freethinkers, to illustrate his point about the absurdity and immorality of the decision. Describing the ruling as a violation "of freedom, of human rights, of the sacredness of humanity," Ingersoll expressed amazement that "a man like Frederick Douglass can be denied entrance to a [railroad] car, ... prevented from entering a theatre," and thrown into "some ignominious corner ... by a decision of the Supreme Court!"[3] For the most part, though, white freethinkers invested much more energy in their fight against repressive religion than in the struggle against repressive American racism. During the Gilded Age, the vast majority of northern whites—and freethinkers were no exception—were unconcerned about racial discrimination in the North. Northern free-thinkers disowned the maverick racist editor William Cowper Brann, but Brann's southernness only reinforced the mindset that viewed bigotry as a strictly southern characteristic.

Another reason for the gap between freethought and black America was that only a minuscule proportion of blacks—Douglass being one of them—had been exposed to the cosmopolitan educational and cultural influences that shaped the freethought movement. Du Bois, whose place in American and black intellectual history would be secure had he never done anything after writing *The Souls of Black Folks* in 1903—though his work as editor of the provocative NAACP magazine the *Crisis*, from 1910 to 1934, would be equally influen-tial—was one of the few influential African Americans strongly affected by freethought. Not only was his education atypical for blacks of his generation, it would remain so for many generations to come. Born in Great Barrington, Massachusetts, in 1868, Du Bois entered Harvard College in 1888 after attending all-black Fisk Uni-versity. The brilliant young scholar became a protégé of William James and, after receiving his bachelor's degree from Harvard in 1890, went on to graduate study in Germany. Du Bois emerged from his schooling both as an intellectual whose chief concern was the future of his race and as an internationally minded, culturally sophisticated offspring of the golden age of freethought. In his eighties, Du Bois would describe his early religious development as "slow and uncer-tain." Raised as a liberal New England Congregationalist (again, in contrast to the majority of blacks, who were brought up in the Baptist evangelical tradition), Du Bois was sent at age seventeen to an ortho-dox missionary college. "My 'morals' were sound, even a bit puri-tanic," he recalled, "but when a hidebound old deacon inveighed against dancing I rebelled. By the time of graduation I was still a 'believer' in orthodox religion, but had strong questions which were encouraged at Harvard."[4] Du Bois finally became a self-described freethinker in Europe, where, like so many African Americans of so many generations, he had his first opportunity "of looking at the world as a man and not simply from a narrow racial and provincial outlook."[5] In a passage that marks him as a man of both the nineteenth and the twentieth centuries, Du Bois wrote of the paradox inherent in the coupling of his love of religious music and painting with his rejection of religion—and of the contrast between his attraction to Christian art and his hatred of the reactionary political activities of many Christian churches:

> Religion helped and hindered my artistic sense. I know the old English and German hymns by heart. I loved their music but ignored their silly words with studied inattention. Grand music came at last in the religious oratorios which we learned at Fisk University but it burst on me in Berlin with the Ninth Symphony and its Hymn of Joy. I worshipped Cathedral and ceremony which I saw in Europe but I knew what I was looking at when in New York a Cardinal became a strike-breaker and the Church of Christ fought the Communism of Christianity.[6]

In his later life, Du Bois developed strong socialist and communist sympathies and would even, in 1961 at age ninety-three, join the moribund American Communist Party as a protest against McCarthyism. However, his antireligious views long antedated his left-wing politics and had begun to complicate his relations with less radical black intellectuals and educators by the 1890s. Being a protégé of William James did not mean that an outstanding black graduate had any chance of being hired to teach at Harvard in the last decade of the nineteenth century, so Du Bois could only look for work within the struggling network of Negro colleges when he returned home from his studies in Europe. In 1894, he took a job teaching at Wilberforce University, a school in Xenia, Ohio, run by the odd couple of Ohio's state government and the African Methodist Episcopal Church. At Wilberforce, Du Bois immediately irked his superiors by refusing to lead students in public prayer. While such a gesture would certainly not have improved Du Bois's prospects had he been a white teacher at a white church college in 1894, the centrality of religion to the black community magnified the impact of such religious insubordination on a black campus. By the second half of the 1890s, Du Bois would write, he "increasingly regarded the church as an institution which defended such evils as slavery, color caste, exploitation of labor and war."[7] He was saying no more than Ingersoll had been saying since the 1870s, but attacking the church was far more problematic for a member of a race that necessarily attached great importance to its image of moral and religious rectitude, both as a matter of internal discipline and as a way of placating hostile whites. In 1895, Booker T. Washington made a famous speech in which he cautioned Negroes against demanding full social equality before they had achieved economic equality, and Du Bois replied with an equally vehement argument—one that would resonate throughout the twentieth century—that Negroes were entitled to pursue both their full rights as citizens and their personal ambitions in every area of American life. This argument was closely connected to religion—though it is not usually portrayed that way—because on a deep level it was a dispute over just how humble blacks had to be to survive in white America. The Christianity preached by slave owners had glorified the humility of slaves as an intrinsic moral virtue. Du Bois had as little regard for humility, as a virtue or as a tactic, as he eventually came to have for Christianity. Without overstating the case—for Washington certainly wished to see his people prosper in the material world—the fissure between the two men represented a conflict between an essentially religious and an essentially secularist ethic, and it was a debate that would resurface powerfully three-quarters of a century later within the civil rights movement. That the tension between secularism and religion affected every group within late-nineteenth-century American society is underlined by the parallel unfolding of a culture war within the women's movement of the 1890s. Like Du Bois and Washington, the fin du siècle feminists were quarreling about just how much humility women should be required to display, before God and white men, in order to attain recognition as full human beings.

* * *

From the 1848 Seneca Falls convention to the current battle over abortion, no cause has better demonstrated the conflict between America's religious and secular values than the drive for women's rights. As soon as news of the Seneca Falls convention began to circulate, feminism began to be portrayed by its opponents as a threat to religion. The conservatives' accusation was quite accurate: to say that a woman's voice should count equally with a man's in public decisions was to assault centuries of theological teachings and social assumptions about the innate inferiority of women. Most of the first-generation feminists were women who adhered to some form of personal faith, but they were also deeply dissatisfied with being relegated to the status of followers—in their churches no less than in society as a whole. In the second half of the nineteenth century, women like Lucretia Mott, who retained her deep but idiosyncratic belief in the "inward light," moved so far from orthodoxy that they were cast out by denominations to which they had given much of their lives. Stanton and Anthony, especially as they became familiar with Darwin's theories, moved more decisively into the agnostic camp.

Only after the Civil War did the depth and intractability of opposition to women's suffrage become fully apparent to the first generation of American feminists. The Fifteenth Amendment, ratified in 1870, gave the right to vote to emancipated male slaves, but women of all colors were still excluded. It is impossible to exaggerate the bitterness of feminists when it became clear that most of the men who had fought so hard to obtain the vote for ex-slaves were unwilling to expend any of their political capital on obtaining the franchise for women. Old allies in the feminist-abolitionist coalition like Garrison and Stanton became political enemies. It is a blot on Stanton's moral record, and a measure of the bitterness of feminists at what they saw as a betrayal by male abolitionists, that she expressed her anger in racist and nativist terms at the first meeting of the National Woman Suffrage Association in 1869. "Think of Patrick and Sambo . . . and

Yung Tung, who do not know the difference between a monarchy and a republic," Stanton indignantly told the delegates, "who can not read the Declaration of Independence or Webster's spelling book, making laws for Lucretia Mott, Ernestine L. Rose, and Anna E. Dickinson."[8] Stanton might have had the grace to mention Harriet Tubman and Sojourner Truth, who had spoken so passionately for so many years on behalf of women's rights as well as against slavery. In fairness to Stanton, she was also indignant about the denial of the vote to black women; the political problem for men like Garrison was that suffrage for women of any color was considered so outlandish an idea that it would have doomed the amendment enfranchising black men.

Regarding men as unreliable allies, Stanton and Anthony founded their National Woman Suffrage Association as an all-female organization. More conservative suffragists, led by Lucy Stone (a near contemporary of Stanton's and a longtime rival for leadership within the movement), countered with the American Woman Suffrage Association, which admitted male members. The split between the two wings of the movement, which would last until the 1890s, may have delayed the attainment of women's suffrage by a full generation. But there was much more to the 1870 split than disagreement over tactics and personal rivalry. Stanton and Anthony did not believe that the wrongs of women could be remedied solely by the vote; they saw women's inequality in employment, education, and legal rights, especially within marriage, as much deeper issues, rooted in a religiously based tradition that led women to see themselves as inferior. Lucy Stone's American Association, by contrast, maintained that all of women's wrongs would be speedily remedied once suffrage was attained. The organization's narrow goal was much more appealing to men—even liberal men—than a broadly based attack on the fundamental assumptions governing relations between the sexes. The parallel between the feminist split and the Du Bois–Washington dispute is most obvious here; Du Bois's broad attack on racism, like Stanton's indictment of male domination, was more threatening to those in power than the less sweeping goals of suffrage for women or economic progress for blacks. As one feminist historian puts it, "The leaders of the American [Association] were afraid to associate suffrage with any extraneous or radical ideas or individuals."[9]

One of those radical ideas—arguably the most important—was the belief, articulated in the 1848 Seneca Falls *Declaration of Rights and Sentiments*, that religion lay at the heart of women's second-class status. Feminist leaders—contrary to Himmelfarb's notion of a Victorian consensus on the definition of virtue—emphatically disagreed with one another over general ideas of virtue as well as over the specific meaning of virtue in women. The women who founded the movement in 1848 argued that they deserved the vote because they were the equal of men (twenty-one years before John Stuart Mill made the same case in his famous essay *On the Subjection of Women*), but those who joined the suffragists after the Civil War based their case on the idea that women were morally superior to men. Many of these second-generation suffragists were conventionally religious, wished to purge the movement of any association with atheism, and saw the vote for women as a way to raise the moral tone of American society. In his history of the *Truth Seeker*, Macdonald observed that free-thinking suffragists demanded the vote "in the name of right and justice," while the Christian suffragists fought for the franchise "in the name of Christ in order that God might be voted into the Constitution, the Bible into the schools, and Christian doctrine generally into civil law."[10] The Women's Christian Temperance Union, founded in 1874, soon had a much larger membership than either Stanton's or Stone's suffrage organization. Focusing as much on the need to protect American families from obscene literature and popular entertainment as on the drive to criminalize drinking—the WCTU established a Department of Impure Literature in 1883—the Christian women's organizations could not have been farther in their general social beliefs from the first-generation feminists. Nevertheless, by the mid-1880s, Anthony became convinced that the movement could never hope to achieve its legislative goals if conventional Christians could not be persuaded that the vote for women was a respectable cause.

Stanton disagreed, but her old friend took on the task of negotiating a merger with the more conservative "Lucy Stoners" and a lobbying alliance with the much larger WCTU. Although Anthony thoroughly shared Stanton's views on religion, she had not publicized her opinions and was therefore a considerably less controversial figure. During the same period, Stanton was beginning work on her *Woman's Bible*, which Anthony viewed as a mischief-making project with endless potential to alienate not only conservatives but all religious believers. A preview of the differences between Stanton and the Christian suffragists came at the 1885 meeting of the National Association in Washington. Stanton supported a resolution that would have condemned all religions "teaching that woman was an afterthought in creation, her sex a misfortune, marriage a condition of subordination, and maternity a curse"—in other words, every religion with a significant following in the United States. In a powerful speech, she went on to extend her condemnation to all of the world's major religions:

You may go over the world and you will find that every form of religion which has breathed upon this earth has degraded woman. . . . I have been traveling over the old world during the last few years and have found new food for thought. What power is it that makes the Hindoo woman burn herself upon the funeral pyre of her husband? Her religion. What holds the Turkish woman in the harem? Her religion. By what power do the Mormons perpetuate their system of polygamy? By their religion. Man, of himself, could not do this; but when he declares, 'Thus saith the Lord,' of course he can do it. So long as ministers stand up and tell us Christ is the head of the church, so is man the head of woman, how are we to break the chains which have held women down through the ages? You Christian women look at the Hindoo, the Turkish, the Mormon women, and wonder how they can be held in such bondage. . . .

Now I ask you if our religion teaches the dignity of woman? It teaches us the abominable idea of the sixth century—Augustine's idea—that motherhood is a curse; that woman is the author of sin, and is most corrupt. Can we ever cultivate any proper sense of self-respect as long as women take such sentiments from the mouths of the priesthood?"[11]

One can understand why the politically adroit Anthony, mindful of what the dissemination of such statements would mean for her efforts to effect an alliance with Christian women's organizations, maneuvered to table the resolution. The delegates were convinced by her argument that "for us to begin a discussion here as to who established these dogmas would be anything but profitable. Let those who wish go back into the history of the past, but I beg it shall not be done on our platform."[12]

Two years later, in 1887, the tactical importance of an alliance with Christian suffragists became clear when the U.S. Senate took its first vote on a women's suffrage amendment. The measure was resoundingly defeated by a 34–16 margin—with 24 abstentions, mostly from men who supported the amendment in theory but who feared the wrath of their constituents if they actually voted for it. Nevertheless, the WCTU had joined forces with suffragist organizations for the first time, marshaling the signatures of more than 200,000 women on petitions to Congress. The lopsidedness of the Senate vote confirmed Anthony in her conviction that it would be impossible to overcome male opposition without support from women who defined themselves as Christians first, suffragists second. In return for the powerful lobbying assistance of the WCTU, suffragist organizations gave their support to, or at least did not oppose, Sunday closing laws and proposals for nationwide prohibition. And in return for the American Association's agreement to merge with Stanton and Anthony's National Association, Stanton's views about the need for a radical restructuring of the role of women in society were denigrated or simply ignored. When the merger became a fait accompli in 1890, the day-to-day operations of the new National American Woman Suffrage Association were placed in the hands of Anthony, who, because of her willingness to relegate larger social goals to the back burner, was more acceptable than Stanton to the younger, more conservative suffragists. Stanton was formally elected the association's first president, but it was understood that the more "moderate" Anthony would really be in charge as executive vice president. In an almost wistful voice, Anthony expressed her hope that the organization's platform "be kept broad enough for the infidel, the atheist."[13] That was not to be—as Anthony, ever the astute politician, knew perfectly well. By 1892, Stanton had retired from active involvement in the suffrage movement to concentrate on preparation of *The Woman's Bible*, an enormous undertaking with Stanton as its primary writer and editor but also including essays by other female biblical scholars.

It was not surprising that the women's movement, on the cusp of a new century, would turn to younger leadership. The seventy-year-old Anthony was essentially a transitional figure, soon to give way to her assistant, the thirty-something Carrie Chapman Catt. Catt would live to witness the signing of the Nineteenth Amendment, which, after more than seventy years of struggle, gave women the right to vote in 1920. And Anthony, who died in 1906, would receive all the lagniappes—including her name on the amendment—customarily accorded monumental founders. Stanton might have been enshrined too—had she only shut up about religion. Instead, she published the first volume of *The Woman's Bible* in 1895, the year she turned eighty and Anthony turned seventy-five. The National Council of Women sponsored a lavish birthday tribute for Anthony, but no sponsor could be found for a similar ceremony honoring Stanton. Anthony, who never wavered in her loyalty to Stanton (and vice versa) in spite of their disagreements, insisted that a tribute be organized and wrote more than a hundred fund-raising letters to make the event happen.

On November 12, 1895, more than six thousand people packed the Metropolitan Opera House in New York to honor Stanton. In a display worthy of Busby Berkeley, the eminent old woman sat on the stage on a red velvet chair under a canopy of evergreens, with red carnations spelling out her name against a background of white chrysanthemums. The tributes, from women's groups throughout the country and around the world, lasted more than three hours before Stanton began to talk. As Elisabeth Griffith notes in her landmark biography, *In Her Own Right* (1984), Stanton spoke with an "unfamiliar modesty," attributing the outpouring of tributes not to her own popularity but to "the great idea I represent—the enfranchisement of women."[14] But then, true to form, Stanton could not resist taking a swipe at religion, branding church leaders as especially recalcitrant in their views on the rights of women. Poor Anthony! When Stanton had showed her an advance draft of the speech, Anthony had tried to persuade her to leave out the inflammatory subject of religion. "My only criticism," Anthony said mournfully, "was that she did not rest her case after describing the wonderful advance made in state, church, society, and home, instead of going on to single out the church and to declare it especially slow in accepting the doctrine of the equality of women. I tried to make her see that it had advanced as rapidly as the other departments but I did not succeed, and it is right that she should express her ideas, not mine."[15]

Anthony also tried to persuade Stanton not to publish her *Woman's Bible*—with a similar result. The *Bible* examines many of the most important events of the Old and New Testaments, beginning with the creation of Eve from Adam's rib, as literary fictions of men. Griffith suggests that Stanton's effort "seems less impressive today, now that many of her conclusions about Biblical interpretations and sources are widely accepted."[16] In fact, Stanton's effort seems *more* impressive today precisely because none of her feminist conclusions regarding the Scriptures were accepted in her own time. In the last quarter of the twentieth century, her *Bible* was superceded by innumerable learned studies, written by women who had access to the full range of higher educational institutions, including theological seminaries, whose doors were open only to men in Stanton's lifetime. Many of these scholars, much more interested than Stanton was in reconciling feminism and religion, insist that Stanton did not deny the greatness of the Bible or of Christianity but only claimed that men had misinterpreted the Scriptures. But that interpretation is not supported by Stanton's witty dissection of the New Testament—especially of that first Christian misogynist, Paul. Her style, which combined biblical scholarship with matter-of-fact observations about past and present everyday life, is embodied in her analysis of a well-known passage from the First Epistle to Timothy, in which Paul insists that women must "adorn themselves in modest apparel, with shamefacedness and sobriety; not with braided hair, or gold, or pearls, or costly array; But (which becometh women professing godliness) with good works. Let the woman learn in silence with all subjection" (1 Timothy 2: 9–11). Stanton observed drily that the apostles "all appeared to be much exercised by the ornaments and the braided hair of the women." She continued:

> While they insisted that women should wear long hair, they objected to having it braided lest the beautiful coils be too attractive to men. But women had other reasons for braiding their hair beside attracting men. A compact braid was much more comfortable than individual hairs free to be blown about with every breeze.
>
> It appears very trifling for men, commissioned to do so great a work on earth, to give so much thought to the toilets of women. Ordering the men to have their heads shaved and hair cropped, while the women were to have their locks hanging around their shoulders, looks as if they feared that the sexes were not distinguishable and that they must finish Nature's work.[17]

Stanton's introduction to the New Testament section of her *Bible* undercuts any concept of her as a believer whose only quarrel with Christianity was that men had misread the Scriptures. "Does the New Testament bring promises of new dignity and of larger liberties for woman?" she asked rhetorically. "When thinking women make any criticisms of their degraded position in the Bible, Christians point to her exaltation in the New Testament, as if, under their religion, woman really does occupy a higher position than under the Jewish dispensation. While there are grand types of women presented under both religions, there is no difference in the general estimate of the sex.

In fact, her inferior position is more clearly and emphatically set forth by the Apostles than by the Prophets and the Patriarchs. There are no such specific directions for woman's subordination in the Pentateuch as there are in the Epistles." Nor was Stanton impressed by the argument that the traditional Christian veneration of Mary (whom Protestants had downgraded anyway) was a compliment to women. She derided the notion that the entire female sex should feel honored because Mary was the mother of Jesus. "Surely a wise and virtuous son is more indebted to his mother than she is to him," she noted acerbically.[18] Stanton's jaundiced view of Christianity in no way implied a high regard for Judaism's treatment of women, and observant Jews were no more impressed by Stanton's comments on their sacred writings than Christians were by her analysis of the Gospels and Epistles. The *Jewish Messenger* declared that no Jewish woman in America would be persuaded by Stanton's *Bible*. In a letter to a friend, Stanton gave her account of a visit from an irate delegation of observant Jewish women:

> They said Jewish women were reverenced in their religion, that the wife and mother was considered the most exalted position a human being could fill; that their men thought it would be a desecration to their holy office to tax them with public affairs, they worship their women. Why, then, if they really do consider them so exalted, do they say in their synagogues every Sunday, "I thank thee, O Lord, that I was not born a woman!" "That," they say, "is an interpolation in our service and was not originally there."

Stanton's reference to Sunday synagogue-going reveals her ignorance of Jewish observance, and she does not record the women's reaction to her next salvo, in which she remarked that Jewish men would be much better advised to say, "I thank thee O Lord, that I was not born a jackass."[19]

Although Stanton's *Bible* is filled with scholarship, it was intended not primarily as a scholarly work but as a call to battle—a battle that had been rejected by the Christian women who had taken over the old freethinking suffragist movement. As Maureen Fitzgerald notes in her perceptive introduction to a 1993 facsimile edition, Stanton chose to publish the book for precisely the reason that conservatives wanted to stifle it—because it was a "scandalous, radical act" that challenged the widely accepted religious foundations of the subordination of women. To those suffragists, including Anthony, who told her it was politically unwise to arouse religious opposition, Stanton said flatly that this "much-lauded policy is but another word for *cowardice.* . . . Reformers who are always compromising, have not yet grasped the idea that truth is the only safe ground to stand on."[20]

The Woman's Bible created all the commotion Stanton could have hoped for. It became a bestseller, going through seven printings in six months and appearing in several foreign-language translations. But the compromising reformers in charge of the suffrage association were furious with their former leader, who was being branded as a heretic in sermons and newspaper editorials. Less than a year after the celebration honoring Stanton on her eightieth birthday, delegates to the annual convention of the Suffrage Association passed a resolution disavowing *The Woman's Bible* and, in effect, the founder of the entire suffrage movement. The fight in favor of the resolution was led by none other than Anthony's protégée Catt. Finally rising to the defense of her closest friend and of her own secularist principles, Anthony made an impassioned plea to the convention:

Are you going to cater to the whims and prejudices of people who have no intelligent knowledge of what they condemn? If we do not inspire in woman a broad and catholic spirit, they will fail, when enfranchised, to constitute that power for better government which we have always claimed for them. You would better educate ten women into the practice of liberal principles than to organize ten thousand on a platform of intolerance and bigotry. I pray you, vote for religious liberty, without censorship or inquisition. This resolution, if adopted, will be a vote of censure upon a woman who is without peer in intellectual and statesmanlike ability; one who has stood for half a century the acknowledged leader of progressive thought and demand in regard to all matters pertaining to the absolute freedom of women.[21]

Anthony's entreaty failed to win over the delegates, yet the presence of agnostics and freethinkers within the movement would remain disproportionate in spite of the alliance with groups like the WCTU. That reality only reinforced the determination of younger leaders like Catt—many of whom were secret agnostics themselves—to cover up the anticlerical origins of the suffragist movement. The measure of Carrie Chapman Catt's true views can be gleaned from her participation, in 1921, at the dedication of the Ingersoll Birthplace Museum in Dresden. Yet even after passage of the Nineteenth Amendment, the generation of suffragists that had censured Stanton continued to deny her role in the movement. The suffrage amendment was named after Anthony, though Stanton was the first to propose it. In 1923, a ceremony to commemorate the seventy-fifth anniversary of the Seneca Falls convention was planned with endless tributes to Anthony and no mention of Stanton—either in the formal program or in the printed brochure. Stanton's daughter, Harriet Blatch, was the only speaker to mention the founding mother of the suffragist movement. As recently as 1977, when female runners carried a torch from Seneca Falls to a meeting in observance of International Women's Year in Houston, Stanton was still treated as an unperson. Anthony's grandniece was sitting on the dais in Houston, but no descendant of Stanton's had been invited.[22] Only in the 1980s did Americans, beyond a small circle of feminist intellectuals, begin to rediscover Stanton. By then, the second wave of feminism had refocused attention on the issue Stanton was among the first to raise in America—the need for women to change their view of themselves. And time has borne out the truth of Stanton's belief that the vote alone would not correct injustices rooted in an ancient and pervasive perception of women as inferior beings. While Stanton has been restored to history, the essential role of agnostics in the women's rights movement has never been acknowledged. Even Stanton's children contributed to the long obfuscation of their mother's antireligious beliefs. After their mother's death in 1902, Blatch and her brother, Theodore Stanton, began to collect their mother's papers for eventual publication. "In an effort to whitewash her into respectability," Griffith reports, "they had rewritten her letters, destroyed her diary, and altered her autobiography. Having wreaked havoc with the primary sources, they then destroyed some of the documents."[23] Exercising filial censorship on *Eighty Years and More*, they deleted Stanton's entire chapter on women and theology. Fortunately for future historians, the children could not destroy the original edition of their mother's autobiography—or the public records of her many speeches, so repellent to conservative suffragists, declaring that no woman could be free as long as she let her minister, priest, rabbi, or imam tell her what to do.

If many agnostics attempted to conceal the extent of their participation in the women's movement, they were entirely open about their role in the battle against late-nineteenth-century censorship. There was no point to secrecy since there was no possibility that upstanding Christians would associate themselves with opposition to the obscenity laws that will always be associated with the name of Anthony Comstock. The nineteenth-century battle over censorship pitted secularist against religious values in an even more clear-cut fashion than the controversy over woman's place in society. Freethinkers were the only consistent opponents of censorship from the 1870s until the First World War; nearly a half century before there was an American Civil Liberties Union, without a body of judicial precedent to bolster their argument, freethinkers spoke out in defense of those accused of obscenity and blasphemy (which was prosecuted as obscenity in many Comstock-era cases). The National Liberal League, founded in 1876 and later renamed the American Secular Union, managed to gather fifty to seventy thousand signatures (contemporary sources disagree about the number) on a petition asking Congress to repeal the 1873 Comstock laws. Congress ignored the petition, but the willingness of so many people to associate themselves publicly with such an unpopular position indicates that the secularist challenge to religious dominance came not from a tiny fringe but from a substantial and respectable—though not in Comstockian terms—minority. Ingersoll's was the best-known individual voice against censorship, and when legal defenses failed—as they usually did—he used his Republican connections, which went all the way to the White House, to intervene behind the scenes on behalf of freethinkers sentenced to prison. As a devoted family man, Ingersoll disagreed strongly with the views expressed in many of the publications that surfaced most frequently in Comstock cases (*Cupid's Yokes*, an antimarriage polemic described by Ingersoll as merely silly, was a typical example), but he did not consider them obscene and, most important, did not believe that government officials should be in the business of defining obscenity. The ambiguities in the law prompted Ingersoll to make the tongue-in-cheek suggestion that censors take a close look at the Bible, which "contains hundreds of grossly obscene passages not fit to be read by any decent man; thousands of passages, in my judgment, calculated to corrupt the minds of youth."[24] In Ingersoll's view, the Comstock laws were also being used to intimidate editors, publishers, and writers of antireligious works—which might also be defined as obscene.

In one sense, it would be a mistake to overemphasize the importance of Comstock, who, as the crusading liberal columnist Heywood Broun pointed out in 1927, had been transformed into a larger-than-life symbol long before his death in 1915. Even though Comstock was personally responsible for jailing editors who published everything from diatribes against marriage to advertisements for venereal disease remedies, Broun argued that the self-appointed censor's "actual interference with books, plays and paintings of sincere intent was slight."[25] It is tempting to dismiss as a comic anachronism a man who did not even finish high school but described George Bernard Shaw as "an Irish smut dealer," who saw lust everywhere he went and chastised boys for lying on the beach and looking up women's bathing dresses. (The miscreants could not have seen much, since respectable women in the late nineteenth century always wore both pantalets and opaque stockings under their bathing dresses.) Comstock's public statements and his preoccupation with the female form began to sound archaic within his own lifetime. "No one reveres the female form more than I do," he once told an interviewer for the *New York Evening World.*

"But the place for a woman's body to be—denuded—is in the privacy of her own apartments with the blinds down."[26]

Comstock's real importance, and one of the keys to his success, lay in his embodiment of an iconographic American story—the rise of a man who, lacking conventional assets of money, social standing, even education, manages by virtue of the strength and singlemindedness of his passions to gain the support of the powerful. Comstock was only twenty-four in 1868 when, having sniffed out lewdness on the streets of New York as a volunteer for the Young Men's Christian Association, he drafted an antiobscenity statute and persuaded the New York state legislature to pass it. Until then, his main achievement had been to hold down a job as a shipping clerk in a dry goods store, where he annoyed his coworkers by expressing his disapproval of their dirty jokes. Comstock became the head of the YMCA's Society for the Suppression of Vice, which widened its activities with financial support from some of the wealthiest men in New York, including J. P. Morgan and the soap manufacturer Samuel Colgate. In 1873, Comstock worked his magic on the U.S. Congress, although it is not clear how, even with the backing of organized religion, such an inexperienced and obsessed young man managed to sway hard-bitten legislators. Judging from diary entries in which Comstock recorded his endless lobbying in Washington, some congressmen may have voted in favor of the obscenity statute for the sole purpose of getting rid of the angry and intrusive Puritan ghost haunting their offices.

For the first time in American history, a federal law set criminal penalties for those who sent obscene material through the mails—but the definition of obscenity was highly subjective. Postal authorities—Comstock himself was deployed as a special postal agent—had discretion to determine what did and did not violate the intent of the law. Devices and information on the prevention of conception or birth (the term *birth control* did not then exist) were explicitly deemed obscene, but postal officials nevertheless enjoyed a good deal of discretion about which cases to prosecute. Depending on the mood and sophistication of a particular postal inspector, anatomical drawings using medical terms might—or might not—be defined as obscene. "French postcards" of nude women, freethought attacks on the Bible, and, for that matter, any novel or poem that attracted the attention of a local Comstock—all might land either the sender or the receiver in jail. Colgate, who served as president of New York's antivice society (soon elevated to the status of committee), could well have run afoul of the law himself when his company published and mailed a pamphlet advertising the benefits of one of his new products—Vaseline— and touting its value as a contraceptive. An embarrassed Colgate scrapped plans to publish more copies of the advertising pamphlet when the *Truth Seeker* gleefully reprinted the glowing claims for Vaseline as a method of birth control. (Unfortunately, the mistaken belief that Vaseline was an effective contraceptive would linger well into the twentieth century and lead to a good many unwanted pregnancies.) Local organizations like Comstock's New York committee had the power to sniff out criminals, using tactics that would be considered entrapment today, and to enlist the aid of the police in making arrests. All of this represented a fundamental hardening—a difference in degree that became a difference in kind—of the policy articulated by Congress in 1865, when it had passed a toothless law that gave the Postal Service the power to confiscate obscene publications but authorized no criminal penalties. The 1865 law had been a response to complaints—it is not entirely clear from whom—about Union soldiers collecting and exchanging postcards of nude women. Comstock received the ultimate cultural tribute in 1905 when the Irish "smut dealer" Shaw coined the term *comstockery*, which then entered English as a common noun. Comstock bore approximately the same relation to the popular censorship crusade of the Gilded Age as Senator Joseph McCarthy did to grassroots American anticommunism in the 1950s, although Comstock never wielded as much national influence as McCarthy and did not damage nearly as many lives and careers. When Comstock targeted unpopular dissenters, like the editors of freethought publications, the public was either approving or indifferent. But whenever Comstock drew attention to himself by attacking popular amusements that most people considered harmless—such as Egyptian belly dancers at the 1893 Chicago World's Fair and female trapeze artists in circuses—he became a figure of ridicule.

Comstock's three-year pursuit of D. M. Bennett, editor of the *Truth Seeker*, illustrates the modus operandi of the nineteenth-century thought police. Typically, one of Comstock's confederates would write a letter to a target like Bennett and order a publication that had already been deemed obscene by postal officials. In 1877, Bennett was tricked into mailing a copy of the ubiquitous *Cupid's Yokes* and a treatise titled *How Do Marsupials Propagate?* to a Pennsylvania clergyman. Ingersoll looked into the case and wrote the U.S. postmaster general on Bennett's behalf, arguing that the two publications might be silly and tasteless but that postal authorities had been mistaken to find them obscene. Ingersoll had campaigned for Rutherford B. Hayes in the 1876 election (even though James Blaine, not Hayes, had been his first choice), and Hayes's postmaster general dropped the case against Bennett as a personal favor to the Great Agnostic. The obscenity issue, however, had been a red herring in Bennett's case: Comstock's real target was the *Truth Seeker* itself. To close the nation's most influential freethought newspaper under the Comstock law would have been a difficult proposition, because its editorial columns dealt mainly with politics and religion—subjects that, unlike obscenity, were generally recognized as falling within the protection of the First Amendment. It was much easier for Comstock to go after the newspaper by arresting its editor for being involved in the circulation of a racy pamphlet. Indeed, Comstock personally visited Bennett's printers after the arrest and threatened them with jail if they continued to print the *Truth Seeker*. He also attempted to intimidate the news distribution company that delivered the paper in the New York area. It was this threat to the *Truth Seeker*, rather than interest in the obscenity issue, that prompted Ingersoll's intervention in the case.

Unfortunately, Comstock went after Bennett a second time, and the cooperative Bennett fell for the same trick twice. In 1878, Comstock himself wrote Bennett a letter, signed with a pseudonym, requesting a copy of "Cupid's something or other." The too trusting or too careless Bennett promptly mailed the pamphlet and was arrested. The sixty-year-old editor was convicted and sentenced to thirteen months of hard labor in a federal penitentiary. Ingersoll tried to obtain a presidential pardon for Bennett, but this time the strategy failed. Religious groups, irked by Hayes's pardons of other Comstock defendants, were putting pressure on the president with writing campaigns. Bennett, whose reputation as an unfaithful husband did not help his cause with Hayes—or with Mrs. Hayes, who had heard gossip about the editor from her own friends in New York—would serve out his full sentence.

As freethought publications proliferated in the 1880s and 1890s, prosecutions of their editors became more frequent—lending additional support to Ingersoll's contention that the antiobscenity statutes were being used to target atheists, agnostics, and freethinkers. Bennett was not the only white-haired editor targeted by Comstock. Another rogue journalist was Charles C. Moore, a former minister, who in 1884 in Lexington, Kentucky, founded the *Blue Grass Blade*, a newspaper advocating both freethought and prohibition. Freethinkers were as divided in their views on temperance as on many other political issues. There was, however, a strong prohibitionist strain among freethinkers who regarded male drunkenness as the main cause of marital violence against women. The difference between freethought prohibitionists and Christian prohibitionists was that the freethinkers wanted to make drunkenness grounds for divorce—and to make it possible for a woman to leave a violent husband without incurring social stigma—whereas the Christians, while viewing drunkenness as a vice, did not consider either drinking or violent abuse grounds for leaving a marriage. The *Blade*, at any rate, was widely read in Lexington, the state capital, by friend and foe alike; when a new issue was about to come out, the printer had to bar the door and windows not only to keep Christian vigilantes away but to prevent eager readers from grabbing free copies. In addition to a closely guarded subscription list that, according to Moore, included many state officials, the paper sold some 750 copies of each issue on the streets of Lexington. In 1899, after many narrow escapes from the postal posse, the sixty-two-year-old Moore was arrested and sentenced to two years in jail for publishing obscenity in his alleged "free love" paper. It is impossible to figure out the precise nature of Moore's comments on "free love" from contemporary newspaper accounts because, whatever the exact words, they were considered too racy to print in a family paper. Moore occupied himself in prison with a project not envisioned by Comstock—an autobiography, written under the benevolent supervision of a warden who was delighted to find a heretical newspaper editor occupying a cell customarily reserved for thieves, con men, arsonists, and an assortment of violent criminals. *Behind the Bars: 31498*, published in late 1899, after Moore's sentence was commuted to six months, may be one of the few pieces of jailhouse literature ever to include letters of congratulation from the author's fellow prisoners and the prison warden. The book is a picaresque tale of an incorrigible dissident, from his youthful abandonment of the ministry, through his attempts to support himself as a coffee salesman and writer of advertising jingles for Levering's Coffee, to his struggle to keep publishing the *Blade*. Like so many other freethinkers, Moore originally turned against orthodox religion because of its support for slavery. When he presented himself for ordination as a Baptist minister at Bethany College in West Virginia, he told the presiding clergyman that he would never teach the doctrine of slavery "as our Southern preachers do." In response, the minister picked up a copy of the Bible and began reading from the favorite epistle of reactionary clerics: "Let as many servants as are under the yoke count their own masters worthy of all honour, that the name of God and his doctrine be not blasphemed" (1 Timothy 6:1). Moore concluded that the passage "plainly sustained the Southern view of slavery. . . . I was ordained to the ministry . . . but those five verses [6:1–5] from the New Testament . . . planted the first seeds of Infidelity in my brain and heart—first as an intellectual conviction, and next as a moral repugnance."[27] Moore's autobiography also provides evidence of the growing public curiosity about freethought as the nineteenth century drew to a close. When he returned home after his sentence was commuted, he was greeted by a crowd of some five hundred at the Lexington train station and made a speech that was reported with careful objectivity by the local press.

Making a dubious comparison between his own relatively comfortable six-month incarceration and the long and arduous solitary confinement of Alfred Dreyfus, Moore declared that "we were both persecuted for religion's sake, he by Catholics. . . ." At that point, the *Lexington Leader* reported, a female voice from the crowd cried out, "That's a lie." After the yelling died away, an undeterred Moore finished, "And I by Protestants."[28]

By the turn of the century, the most important reinforcement of censorship came not from formal prosecutions but from the informal cultural controls promoted not only by churches but also by members of the rapidly expanding Christian women's organizations established after the Civil War, most notably the Women's Christian Temperance Union. Grassroots censors, unlike Comstock and his wealthy backers, exercised their influence from the bottom up rather than from the top down. The WCTU had been founded in an effort to coordinate the spontaneous, and frequently mocked, efforts of groups of women to close down small-town saloons by praying in front of them. Under the presidency of Frances Willard, the WCTU would soon become the largest American women's organization, boasting more than 200,000 members by 1890. Although the organization had been established to fight for restrictions on alcohol, its members branched out into a wide range of activities designed to uplift the moral tone of an increasingly cosmopolitan, increasingly urban America whose polyglot population and diverse cultural proclivities were seen as a threat to traditional small-town values. It was this aspect of the WCTU agenda that inspired such grave doubts in Stanton about an alliance with Christian suffragists. In *Purifying America* (1998), a history of women's procensorship activism, Alison M. Parker notes that the WCTU worked closely with Protestant ministers right from the start. In addition to providing ministers with descriptions of various immoral publications that might be used as the basis for sermons, WCTU representatives spoke from the pulpits of Protestant churches

Thomas Paine, c. 1788, the author of *The Age of Reason*, was the first American freethinker stigmatized as an atheist.

1792 cartoon, titled "'Mad Tom,' or 'the Man of Rights,'" attacks Paine's *The Rights of Man*. The broken crown and scepter in the bottom right foreground allude to the French Revolution.

Ernestine L. Rose, c. 1845, the first Jewish immigrant activist in the freethought, abolitionist, and feminist movements, was one of the few nineteenth-century religious iconoclasts to describe herself as an atheist.

Truth for authority,
not
authority for truth,

Lucretia Mott.

Lucretia Mott, c. 1870, a devout Quaker, was also an ardent feminist, abolitionist, and—as her personal motto, inscribed in her own handwriting,
suggests—an opponent of ecclesiastical authority.

Robert Ingersoll, the Great Agnostic, 1877.

Ingersoll delivers an oration in celebration of Thomas Paine's birthday in New Rochelle, New York, in May 1894.

And they heard the voice of the Lord God walking in the Garden in the cool of the day; and Adam and his wife hid themselves from the presence of the Lord God amongst the trees of the Garden.—Gen. iii, 8.

Watson Heston, a freethinking cartoonist, sketched literal depictions of biblical stories in *The Bible Comically Illustrated* (1892). Here is his image of the moment just after Adam and Eve commit the original sin.

And Noah went in, and his sons, and his wife, and his sons' wives with him, into the ark.—Gen. vii, 7.

Heston envisions the entry of God's chosen into Noah's ark, as Mrs. Noah threatens the nonchosen with a broom.

HOW TO SELL BIBLES—A SUGGESTION TO THE AMERICAN BIBLE SOCIETY.

This cartoon, c. 1890, is a commentary on the Comstock antiobscenity laws. The policeman chases the salesman because the biblical story of King David's son Amnon, who raped his half sister Tamar, might well have been defined as obscene under the law—had the tale not appeared in the Bible.

Elizabeth Cady Stanton, founding mother of the nineteenth-century women's rights movement, c. 1885.

George E. Macdonald, pictured here at age thirty-one in 1888, was the editor of the *Truth Seeker*, the nation's best-known freethought publication, from 1909 until 1937.

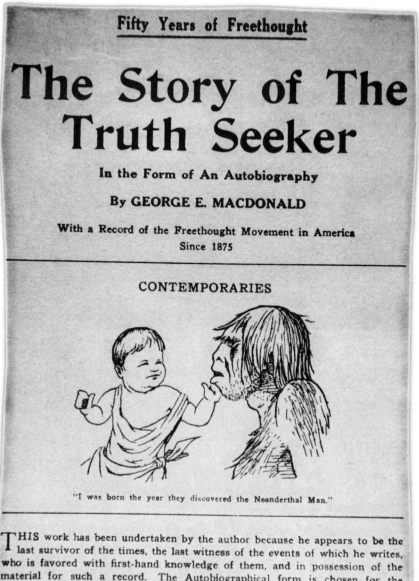

The Story of The Truth Seeker

In the Form of An Autobiography

By GEORGE E. MACDONALD

**With a Record of the Freethought Movement in America
Since 1875**

CONTEMPORARIES

"I was born the year they discovered the Neanderthal Man."

THIS work has been undertaken by the author because he appears to be the last survivor of the times, the last witness of the events of which he writes, who is favored with first-hand knowledge of them, and in possession of the material for such a record. The Autobiographical form is chosen for the reason that having been associated for more than half a century with the weekly paper in which these events were originally chronicled, he can speak as observer and participator. The History would not be quite complete, as the reader will discover, with his name and his part omitted, for the events recorded are his Life. Whatever the quality of the work, it is the only one of the kind.

On the frontispiece of the first volume of *Fifty Years of Freethought* (1929), Macdonald noted that the year of his birth, 1857, coincided with the discovery of the remains of Neanderthal man—an event of great importance to freethinkers, who welcomed evidence of the natural origins of the human race as a refutation of the biblical creation story.

Clarence Darrow, c. 1925—
the year he served as defense
counsel in the Scopes "monkey
trial."

President George W. Bush bows his head in prayer—a regular practice at the
beginning of cabinet meetings in the Bush White House. The president is
flanked by Secretary of State Colin Powell (background) and Secretary of
Defense Donald Rumsfeld.

in every city hosting their annual national conventions. The WCTU also sponsored "Mother's Meetings" in which women read and discussed books certified as pure by the organization. A 1900 recommended reading list for mothers included the works of Louisa May Alcott (*Little Women* for grown women), Charles Dickens, and Walter Scott.[29] The group even went so far as to recommend selections from Shakespeare, in an expurgated edition, for children. Contemporary authors omitted from the WCTU recommended list included, not surprisingly, Twain, Theodore Dreiser, and Whitman, all of whose works ran afoul of the Comstock laws at some point.

On one level, both the Comstock laws and the censorship activities of women's groups were a response to the post–Civil War proliferation of sensationalist mass-circulation newspapers and magazines, including "penny dreadfuls" concentrating on horrendous crime stories. These publications were perceived by the guardians of middle-class virtue as appealing mainly to the urban poor, including native migrants from rural America as well as immigrants from abroad. Nevertheless, women's groups were particularly alarmed by the possibility that tales of gore, gambling, drinking, and loose women would insinuate themselves—were already insinuating themselves—into middle-class homes. On a deeper level, the cultural censorship of the Gilded Age was a response to the emergence of an American literature that celebrated nature and the body, reveled in the spoken American language as well as the written English language, dealt more candidly with disturbing subjects such as prostitution and racial attitudes, and, above all, portrayed a world in which the certitudes of faith no longer applied. Prosecutions of small-time pornographers could not hold back this flowering—or, from the standpoint of religious conservatives, putrefaction—of American culture. The more pervasive "from the ground up" cultural censorship, aimed at high as well as low culture, attempted to impose the piety and propriety of an idealized past on new cultural institutions from public high schools to newly established public libraries. Against this informal cultural censorship, the secularist response would prove much more effective than it had against the Comstock laws; the public's appetite for the poetry of Whitman and the novels of Twain created a popular base that did not exist for the defense of freethought publications whose raison d'être was proselytizing against religion. In 1884, the year in which *The Adventures of Huckleberry Finn* was published, the Watch and Ward Society (a close ally of the New England branch of Comstock's Committee for the Suppression of Vice) was among the first in what would become a long line of those who have tried to censor one of the greatest American novels ever written. Louisa May Alcott, among the first in an equally long line of those who have mistaken *Huckleberry Finn* for a children's book, joined the fray by declaring, "If Mr. Clemens cannot think of something better to tell our pure-minded lads and lassies, he had better stop writing for them."[30] The book sold a then-extraordinary total of more than fifty thousand copies in its first two months of publication.

There is no better example of the synergy between late-nineteenth-century freethought and the new voices of American literature than the changing fortunes in the 1880s of an already familiar voice, the much-maligned Walt Whitman. Born in 1819, he belonged to the dissident American minority that never forgot and never ceased to revere the nation's heritage of Enlightenment secularism. His father, an ardent admirer of Paine, was born on July 14, 1789, the day the Bastille was stormed, but, unlike many other members of his generation, he never repudiated the Enlightenment ideals that had given birth to both the American and the French revolutions. Whitman was his father's son; like Ingersoll, he used his prominence to fight the stereotype of Paine as a "filthy little atheist." Whitman's preface to the first edition of *Leaves of Grass* is the work of an unreconstructed descendant of Paine:

> There will soon be no more priests. Their work is done. They may wait awhile ... perhaps a generation or two ... dropping off by degrees. .... A new order shall arise and they shall be the

priests of man, and every man shall be his own priest. The churches built under their umbrage shall be the churches of men and women. Through the divinity of themselves shall the kosmos and the new breed of poets be interpreters of men and women and of all events and things. They shall find their inspiration in real objects today, symptoms of the past and future. . . . They shall not deign to defend immortality or God or the perfection of things or liberty or the exquisite beauty and reality of the soul. They shall arise in America and be responded to from the remainder of the earth.[31]

The scandalous debut of *Leaves of Grass* in 1855, and the ensuing interval of nearly three decades before a commercial publisher would agree to issue an unexpurgated edition, is a well-known chapter in American literary history. Whitman himself paid most of the publishing costs of the four editions that followed the initial one. Ralph Waldo Emerson, to his everlasting credit, was one of only two universally respected American writers of the day (the other was Henry David Thoreau) to praise *Leaves of Grass*. When the second edition appeared in 1856, a line from Emerson's letter to Whitman was embossed on the cover: "I greet you at the beginning of a great career." Whitman demonstrated his commitment to freedom of speech by ending the volume with an excerpt from a Boston newspaper review expressing a decidedly contrary opinion: "This book should find no place where humanity urges any claim to respect, and the author should be kicked from all decent society as below the level of a brute. There is neither wit nor method in his disjointed babbling, and it seems to us he must be some escaped lunatic, raving in political delirium."[32]

In 1881, nearly three decades after the publication of the first edition of *Leaves of Grass*, the Boston publisher Osgood & Company finally offered to meet Whitman's demand that his poems be published without expurgations. At first glance, it seems strange that a publisher would have taken on such a controversial work, replete with explicit sexual references and imbued with a view of the world that contradicted orthodox religion at every turn, at a time when a legal mechanism for banning books from the mails was well established. In 1855, there had been no Comstock laws—yet no publisher dared to take on the unexpurgated Whitman. What had changed by the second decade of the golden age of freethought, as both the WCTU and the Comstock agents knew, was the willingness of American readers to trust their own judgment rather than the fulminations of orthodox ministers or orthodox literary critics. There is a tendency to dismiss the censorship of the past, whether recent or distant, as an archaic and somewhat comical phenomenon, the work of those who would shroud table legs with ruffled skirts in order to protect pure-minded lads and lassies. In this view—frequently held by cultural liberals as well as cultural conservatives—no one could possibly be shocked today by words that shocked Americans in 1855, 1885, or 1905. Indeed, no one is shocked today by the familiar Whitman lines considered suitable for high school anthologies and textbooks: I hear America singing, the varied carols I hear . . . O Captain! my Captain! our fearful trip is done . . . I loaf and invite my soul. But pity the poor high school teacher who makes the mistake of using an unexpurgated version (yes, there still are expurgated versions) of "I Sing the Body Electric" for an English assignment:

> Hair, bosom, hips, bend of legs, negligent falling
>   hands, all diffused—mine too diffused . . .
>   love-flesh swelling and deliciously aching,
> Limitless limpid jets of love hot and enormous,
>   Quivery jelly of love, white-blow and delirious juice,
> Bridegroom-night of love, working surely and softly
>   into the prostrate dawn.

Lines such as these are still shocking, in the sense that all great poetry shocks by baring the essence of the familiar. Moreover, the explicitness of the sexual imagery startles even though the proliferation of hard- and soft-core pornography has undoubtedly deadened the responses of modern readers, as well as audiences for movies, television, and pop music, to any artistic descriptions of the erotic. That

Whitman retains the capacity to startle is a measure of his greatness as a poet, and it is certainly easy to understand the depth of the shock that his verse elicited in nineteenth-century readers—including even those, like Emerson, of the greatest literary sophistication. The hostility of most contemporary critics to Whitman's poetry was generated not only by what he had to say but by the way he said it. The first edition of *Leaves of Grass* fell upon the eyes and ears of readers accustomed to the rhyme and meter of Emerson, Henry Wadsworth Longfellow, and John Greenleaf Whittier. These readers were hardly prepared for Whitman's unconventional layout of words on the page, much less for his abandonment of traditional rhyme. But the religious censors' objections to Whitman derived not from his style but from his substance—especially the explicit sexual references that served to indict the poet as a freethinker and a free lover. The pejorative association between free love and religious infidelity was even stronger in the late nineteenth than it had been in the late eighteenth century, in part because many social activists in the late Victorian era were calling for a change in relations between men and women that really did have radical implications for the future of the religiously mandated patriarchal family. Stanton, one of the few public figures who refused to be cowed by the free-love accusation—quite possibly because her position as a married mother of seven placed her above reproach—tartly remarked that she was wholly in favor of free love if the phrase meant that no woman should ever feel obligated to have sex without desire. But only Emma Goldman had the courage to turn the notorious phrase from a negative into a positive and fling it at the Comstocks of the world. "Free love?" she asked memorably. "As if love is anything but free!"[33] Whitman, in spite of, and quite possibly because of, the unconventionality of his own sex life, did not want to be publicly identified with anyone who openly favored free love; his poems nevertheless provided all the ammunition his opponents needed.

The thirty-year controversy over Whitman's poems drew an unmistakable line between secularists and guardians of orthodox religion. The battle was fully joined in 1881, with the Osgood firm's attempt to publish an unexpurgated *Leaves of Grass* as a commercially viable book. During what became a two-year furor, Whitman's leading advocate was William Douglas O'Connor, a freethinker, minor poet, short story writer, and novelist whose friendship with Whitman dated from the 1860s. Not until Jerome Loving's *Walt Whitman's Champion* (1976) was O'Connor's importance as an early defender of First Amendment rights recognized. Whitman himself once remarked that he wondered what the fate of his writing would have been "if I had been born of some other mother and had never met William O'Connor."[34] Like Emerson, O'Connor immediately recognized the genius of *Leaves of Grass*; he and Whitman became close friends while both were working for the government in Washington during the Civil War. In June 1865, O'Connor rose to Whitman's defense for the first time when the poet was fired from his job as a clerk in the Bureau of Indian Affairs by Secretary of the Interior James Harlan, a devout Methodist. A month earlier, Harlan had sent a memo to all bureau chiefs in the department asking for the names of those civil servants who had ignored "in their conduct, habits and associations the rules of decorum and propriety prescribed by a Christian Civilization"—a description that certainly fitted Whitman.[35] Harlan decided that *Leaves of Grass* was indecent after inspecting a copy that Whitman kept in his office desk. An outraged O'Connor wrote, and invested his own money in the publication of, an essay in defense of Whitman titled "The Good Gray Poet." It is an important document in the history of American free speech, because it questions whether a government agency ought to be able to fire an employee simply for expressing unpopular opinions. It was one thing for critics to denounce Whitman's works as obscene and un-Christian, O'Connor argued, and quite another for a government official to determine that he would do everything within his power to carry out the judgment of the critics and insure that "this author, for having written his book, shall starve."[36] In 1865, Americans were much more interested in the end of a war that had killed 2 percent of the U.S. population than in the dismissal of a controversial poet from a minor government job. Thus, O'Connor's pamphlet accomplished little on behalf of Whitman at the time, apart from eliciting more condemnation of the poet and praise for the boss who sacked him. But "The Good Gray Poet" laid the groundwork for anticensorship arguments that would be made on Whitman's behalf with much greater success in 1881.

Although Whitman's enemies in the literary and religious establishment were as numerous and as vitriolic in 1881 as they had been for decades, new dissenting voices were beginning to be heard. In 1880, *Scribner's Monthly* had published an essay praising the originality of Whitman's poems—though the author, E. C. Stedman, also took care to express his disapproval of the poet's sexual imagery. Nevertheless, the essay was the first public acknowledgment of Whitman as a poet of the highest rank by a critic outside his immediate circle of friends. With its 1881 contract offer to Whitman, the Osgood publishing firm ratified the newly favorable evaluations of the poet's literary worth. But this broadening of taste within the literary community was also accompanied by a broadening of censorship activities intended to prevent readers from exploring and indulging their changing tastes.

In November 1881, Osgood published the sixth edition of *Leaves of Grass*, which was sold in bookstores and by mail order for the next three months. But on March 1, 1882, the firm received a letter from the Boston district attorney, Oliver Stevens, who threatened to ban the book from the mails and demanded its "voluntary" withdrawal from circulation as an alternative to prosecution under the Comstock laws. Stevens met privately with the publisher and presented a list of expurgations that would satisfy his office as well as the Comstock-inspired New England Committee for the Suppression of Vice. The proposed cuts included many of the explicit sexual allusions in "I Sing the Body Electric" and "Song of Myself," as well as an entire poem, which soon gained the fame that only persecution can bring, titled "To a Common Prostitute." Whitman's defenders always pointed out that the poem begins with a stanza expressing the same compassion that Jesus manifested toward the woman taken in adultery:

> *Be composed—be at ease with me—I am Walt,*
> *Whitman, liberal and lusty as Nature;*

Not till the sun excludes you, do I exclude you;
Not till the waters refuse to glisten for you, and the
leaves to rustle for you, shall my words refuse to
glisten and rustle for you.

On April 10, 1882, six weeks after the district attorney's demand, Whitman's publisher withdrew the book from circulation. The next stage of the battle began when O'Connor published a three-thousand-word essay, "Suppressing Walt Whitman," in the *New York Tribune*. The piece made public what had theretofore been a private matter between the poet and his publisher, and the entire freethought and literary communities became aware of the political pressure that, without any formal legal action, had impelled the publisher to abandon *Leaves of Grass*. O'Connor described the threats made by the district attorney and indicted the publisher for caving in at Whitman's expense. "They might have gathered grit by trying to imagine John Murray flinching from the publication of Byron," O'Connor wrote scathingly. "On the contrary, shaking in abject cowardice at the empty threat of this legal bully, they meanly break their contract with the author, abandon the book they had volunteered to issue, and drop from the ranks of the great publishers into the category of hucksters whose business cannot afford a conscience."[37]

One of the freethinkers galvanized by the article was George Chainey, a Baptist minister turned freethinker who regularly preached his new gospel of humanism in Boston's Paine Memorial Hall. His oratorical defense of Whitman, titled "Keep Off the Grass," included a recitation of "To a Common Prostitute." When Chainey reprinted the lecture, as he always did, in his weekly *This World*, the vice hounds were off and running. Boston's postmaster, a man named Tobey whose first name seems lost to history, refused to mail the periodicals without the approval of District Attorney Stevens. At that point, O'Connor turned to Ingersoll—a great admirer of Whitman—and Ingersoll protested to the acting U.S. postmaster general. The unfortunate Tobey soon received an order from Washington to mail the controversial periodicals.

A new Whitman champion now entered the scene—Ezra H. Heywood, a socialist and famously devoted husband and father who was nevertheless president of the New England Free Love League. Comstock had already managed to send Heywood to prison for six months for distributing the ubiquitous *Cupid's Yokes* and a textbook with explicit anatomical drawings. Undeterred by the memory of his jailing five years earlier, Heywood once more threw down the gauntlet before Comstock, by publishing a special edition of his paper, the *Word*, that included both the evil poem with "prostitute" in the title and "A Woman Waits for Me," an explicit description of the importance of sex to both women and men. An enraged Comstock sprang into action, arresting Heywood for a second time and extending the legal threat to Whitman beyond the Boston area by declaring that if he found *Leaves of Grass* on sale anywhere in New York he would take firm steps to suppress the book. As was his custom when the burden of his duties permitted, Comstock took it upon him to personally arrest Heywood at his home in Princeton, Massachusetts. Like many other bullies, Comstock seems to have been fond of dogs and small children, and when Heywood's daughter toddled into the parlor, the commissioner tried to coax the little girl onto his knee. "Don't pollute her by your caresses," the recalcitrant Heywood told his adversary.[38] It is a measure of how much had changed in American society since publication of the first edition of *Leaves of Grass* that the judge at Heywood's trial summarily dismissed the count in the indictment charging that the printing of Whitman's poems violated the Comstock obscenity laws. Modernists and freethinkers were proving themselves effective foes of religious reactionaries, and what might have been seen as an issue of nothing more than obscenity in the 1850s was seen three decades later as an issue of artistic freedom. Meanwhile, in the midst of the brouhaha, Whitman had found another publisher (Rees, Welsh and Company of Philadelphia) who agreed to his demand for publication of an unexpurgated edition. By the end of 1882, the book had sold 3,118 copies and Whitman had earned $1,091.30 in royalties. For the first time, Whitman was able to count on a regular income from his writing.[39]

Whitman's problems with his earlier publisher, Osgood, gave rise to the enduring expression "banned in Boston," but *Leaves of Grass* was not banned there for long. By 1883, both the Boston and the Cambridge public libraries had removed the book from restricted circulation and placed it on the open shelves. The publicity engineered by O'Connor also brought Whitman to the attention of many who had overlooked *Leaves of Grass* in its earlier editions. Whitman's poetry became a touchstone for, and a connection among, many kinds of American freethinkers before the First World War. For Goldman, Whitman was one of three American writers—the others being Emerson and Thoreau—who bridged the gap between her Russian-bred radicalism and the libertarian side of the American intellectual and political tradition. She read Whitman for the first time in 1893, while serving a ten-month sentence at a penitentiary on Blackwell's Island (now Roosevelt Island) in New York's East River for incitement to riot. There had been no riot, but Goldman was charged and convicted for having delivered a speech in Union Square urging the unemployed to ask the rich for work, then for bread—and, if they received neither work nor bread, to just take the bread. Initially ostracized by the other prisoners because of her reputation as an anarchist and her refusal to attend chapel on Sundays, Goldman had been placed in charge of the prison sewing room, which provided garments for an insane asylum, poorhouse, and smallpox hospital also situated on the island. The prisoners' attitude changed when Goldman talked back to a supervisor who had insisted that she force the inmates to meet larger work quotas. Eventually Goldman was reassigned to the prison hospital as an orderly—a less demanding job that gave her a great deal of time to discover America through its literature. Out of her reading was born a deep love for what she would call "the other America"— the America of Whitman, Thoreau, and Debs—as opposed to the America of the nineteenth-century robber barons. In the early 1900s,

Goldman frequently published excerpts from Whitman and Thoreau in her journal, *Mother Earth*. Whitman's may have been the only patriotic vision of America that could have appealed to as thorough-going an internationalist as Goldman, because his love of country never romanticized or sentimentalized the nation's virtues. In "By Blue Ontario's Shore," reflecting on the then-recent horrors of the war and Lincoln's assassination, he had outlined a patriotism as far removed from flag-worshiping idolatry as his "natural religion" was removed from orthodox theology:

> *O I see flashing that this America is only you and me,*
> *Its power, weapons, testimony are you and me,*
> *Its crimes, lies, thefts, defections, are you and me. . . .*
> *The war (that war so bloody and grim, the war I will*
> *   henceforth forget) was you and me. . . .*
> *I am for those that have never been master'd,*
> *For men and women whose tempers have*
> *   never been master'd,*
> *For those whom laws, theories, conventions,*
> *   can never master.*
> *I am for those who walk abreast with the whole earth,*
> *Who inaugurate one to inaugurate all.*
> *I will not be outfaced by irrational things,*
> *I will penetrate what it is in them that is sarcastic upon me. . . .*

Whitman's poetry had a profound effect on women as well as men, though conservative literary critics invariably declared his verses unfit for discussion or reading in mixed company; Stanton was one of many readers who discovered Whitman only when the 1881–82 editions of *Leaves of Grass* were published. She greatly admired Whitman's poetry in general—especially his emphasis on individual liberty—but thought him ignorant of woman's capacity for active pleasure in the sex act. Observing that Whitman "seems to understand everything in nature but woman," Stanton criticized "A Woman Waits for Me" on grounds that it "speaks as if the female must be forced to the creative act, apparently ignorant of the great natural fact that a healthy woman has as much passion as a man, that she needs nothing stronger than the law of attraction to draw her to the male."[40] She was undoubtedly thinking of lines such as "I pour the stuff to start sons and daughters fit for these States, I press with slow rude muscle." Needless to say, Stanton's was a very different viewpoint from that of the critics who lambasted Whitman for making any explicit mention of women's sexuality. What mainstream critics never discussed was the desire for the bodies of men that prevented Whitman from fully appreciating the sexuality of women—particularly in the act itself.

Whitman's abstract view of heterosexual intercourse notwithstanding, his general vision of woman spoke powerfully to the secularist, freethinking wing of the feminist movement. He was the first great poet to state explicitly, "I am the poet of the woman the same as the man, / And I say it is as great to be a woman as to be a man." One of the most striking aspects of his verse, even to a twenty-first-century reader, is his use of "men and women" where other writers simply use "man" to stand for the whole of humanity. This is not the self-consciousness of politically correct language policepersons attempting to produce "gender-free" literature but a matter-of-fact acknowledgment of woman's right to an active role in every aspect of life. If Whitman was unable to imagine a fully sexual woman, he had no problem presenting women as the heroes of their own lives. In the controversial "A Woman Waits for Me," he presented an image of the women feminists were fighting to become:

> They are not one jot less than I am,
> They are tann'd in the face by shining suns
>   and blowing winds,
> Their flesh has the old divine suppleness and strength,
> They know how to swim, row, ride, wrestle, shoot, run,
>   strike, retreat, advance, resist, defend themselves,
> They are ultimate in their own right—they are calm,
>   clear, well-possess'd of themselves.

The strong appeal Whitman held for the "new woman" of the late nineteenth century is captured in eloquent letters quoted by Sherry

Ceniza in *Walt Whitman and 19th-Century Women Reformers* (1998). Helen Wilmans, a Chicago journalist and freethinker—like so many other freethinkers, she was largely self-educated—discovered Whitman in 1881 and then founded a small newspaper titled *Woman's World*. In her first issue, she discussed Whitman and told her readers, "It is the 'I' that I like in Walt Whitman's works. The honesty of the self-assertion; the frank confession of egotism. Doubt of one's self begets chronic distrust of one's own manhood or womanhood."[41] In a letter to Whitman, she told the poet that *Leaves of Grass* had given her "new conceptions of the dignity and beauty of my own body and of the bodies of other people, . . . has educated me . . . [and] done more to raise me from a poor working woman to a splendid position on one of the best papers ever published, than all of the influences of my life."[42]

Ingersoll the proselytizer and Whitman the poet were the two defining voices of the golden age of freethought, so it is not surprising that the two were friends (although they did not meet face-to-face until 1890, two years before Whitman died of pneumonia). They did not agree on everything: unlike Ingersoll, Whitman was willing to concede the existence of some form of pantheistic deity. But Ingersoll regarded Whitman as the supreme poet of the age—a judgment that went a long way with Whitman—and he lectured on Whitman as frequently as he did on Shakespeare. Ingersoll was on a speaking tour of western Canada when the news of Whitman's death reached him on March 26, 1892, and, having already promised his friend that he would speak at the funeral, he set out by train for Camden, New Jersey. Ingersoll almost missed the March 30 ceremony because his train was delayed by severe weather, but the burial, too, was delayed by the crush of mourners who filed past Whitman's casket in the parlor of his small house. As the *New York Herald* reported, mourners "came by hundreds and thousands—the 'common folk' whom he loved. They gathered about the tiny, shabby little cottage in Mickle Street, in Camden, until the street was blocked and the policemen began to look anxious. They had been bidden to come at eleven; at ten there was a throng, and it was deemed wise to open the door and let the people in. From that time until after one the line was never broken, and though it was hurried along as fast as possible, still the waiting throng grew larger. If it had been some great general instead of a simple singer one might have understood the rush."[43] When the doors to the parlor were finally shut, the oak casket was covered with sprigs of violets left by the mourners.

Ingersoll arrived at Whitman's house just as the casket was being moved to the cemetery. In his oration at the graveside, he quoted from the poem that so many censors had tried to banish from the public prints (see Appendix):

He came into our generation a free, untrammeled spirit, with sympathy for all. His arm was beneath the form of the sick. He sympathized with the imprisoned and despised, and even on the brow of crime he was great enough to place the kiss of human sympathy. One of the greatest lines in our literature is his, and the line is great enough to do honor to the greatest genius that has ever lived. He said, speaking of an outcast: "Not till the sun excludes you do I exclude you."

Ingersoll then described Whitman as one who "wrote a liturgy for mankind; he wrote a great and splendid psalm of life, and he gave to us the gospel of humanity—the greatest gospel that can be preached."[44] This eulogy, an instant classic reprinted in newspapers throughout the nation, offers the definitive answer, resonating from America's golden age of freethought, to those who would shun the nation's freethinkers and secularists as believers in nothing.

8

UNHOLY TRINITY: ATHEISTS,
REDS, DARWINISTS

In 1924, a year before he squared off against Clarence Darrow in the
Scopes "monkey trial," William Jennings Bryan warned that a "scientific soviet is attempting to dictate what shall be taught in our
schools, and, in doing so, is attempting to mold the religion of the
nation."[1] Bryan was of course referring to the growing acceptance of
Darwin's theory of evolution by American educators outside the
South. The image of a "scientific soviet" intent on destroying American religion conjured up the conspiracy of atheism, political radicalism, and heretical science envisioned by the demonizers of American
secularism since the 1790s. With the Bolshevik Revolution, which
established a Soviet leadership that unabashedly proclaimed its atheism and devotion to "scientific communism," American antisecularist
crusaders could point to a Moscow address as headquarters of the
conspiracy against American religious values. The powerful antisecularist reaction that began with the First World War and continued
throughout the twenties would confound the expectations of religious liberals, agnostics, and scientists. All three groups viewed the
Scopes trial, with its prosecution of a high school biology teacher for
violating a Tennessee law prohibiting the teaching of evolution, as the

last gasp of an archaic and embattled American fundamentalism. The secular humanists were not merely premature but definitively wrong in announcing the death of American fundamentalism, although the proportions of their historic misjudgment would not become fully apparent until the rise of the Christian right as a national political power in the late 1970s.

In the history of American secularism, the fundamentalist counter-attack of the twenties represented not the last gasp but the first blast of renewed opposition by religious conservatives to the modernist ideas that had been widely disseminated during the golden age of freethought. Antievolutionism and opposition to "atheistic communism" (the latter rendered obsolete only when the Soviet empire imploded in 1991) would become lasting pillars of the twentieth-century conservative religious agenda. On the secularist side, a new alliance emerged between freethinkers—a term that had not yet become an anachronism in the twenties—and the political left. Their bond was forged not by common economic or social views, since many freethinkers regarded both socialism and communism as religions like any other, but by a shared commitment to separation of church and state and freedom of speech. That sometimes uneasy coalition gave birth to the modern concept of civil liberties and the organized American civil liberties movement.

Although the comeback of "old-time religion" in the twenties has often been attributed to the horror engendered by the brutality and destructive use of science and technology in the First World War, both the resurgence of religious fundamentalism and the secularist counterattack were responses to the increasingly visible secularization of American society evident since the turn of the century. Long before 1914, American fundamentalists were alarmed by the spread of secularist science and its influence on American thought and social institutions. There may have been no scientific soviet, but evolutionism—bolstered by a new understanding of genetics—did indeed gain widespread acceptance among educated Americans in the first decade of the twentieth century. From the fundamentalist point of view, nothing was more significant and more threatening than the endorsement of evolution by those responsible for educating American children. When Thomas Huxley delivered his lectures in 1876, America's best universities were just beginning to incorporate evolution into their teaching of physical sciences. Only thirty years later, most high school biology and zoology texts supported the concept of organic evolution, if not necessarily Darwin's theory of natural selection. The unprecedented expansion of public secondary schooling during the pre–World War I Progressive Era meant that with every passing year more and more students, including the children of fundamentalists themselves, were exposed to scientific ideas that contradicted any literal interpretation of the Bible. The historian of science George E. Webb, in a comprehensive 1994 account of the century-long controversy over the teaching of evolution in American schools, quotes passages from early-twentieth-century textbooks that, because they are phrased in a fashion that seems to challenge religion, might well be stricken from biology texts today. A 1912 high school botany text, for instance, states unequivocally that evolution "has been accepted because it appeals to the mind of man as being more reasonable that species should be created according to natural laws rather than by an arbitrary and special creation."[2] The increasing American deference to science was clearly the work not of freethinkers alone but, as Ingersoll had anticipated, of the ever-expanding group of liberal Protestants who were able to reconcile contemporary science with their brand of faith. But advocacy of the scientific method as the key to learning was very much the work of secularizers, if not necessarily of agnostics and atheists. In a 1904 textbook, Maynard M. Metcalf, a biology professor and a Christian himself, nevertheless praised the movement to exclude religious speculation from the teaching of life sciences—which he dismissively called "the last stronghold of the supernaturalist" because many orthodox believers felt that biology, unlike geology or chemistry, required a theological approach compatible with the doctrine that man was directly created by God.[3] (Two decades later, Darrow would try to call Metcalf as a witness for the defense in the Scopes trial but would be stymied by the judge's refusal to hear any expert scientific testimony.)

In the first fifteen years of the century, the secularizing influence of science was closely linked with Progressive Era politics, which in turn had an enormous impact on the freethought movement. Progressive causes and campaigns offered a political outlet that had not existed in the 1870s and 1880s for the social values of many (though not all) freethinkers. Until the 1880s political party allegiance (as Ingersoll's Republicanism illustrated) was heavily influenced by the two major parties' stances on slavery, the Civil War, and Reconstruction. As the end of the century approached, other social issues gained greater political importance, especially for those who came of age after the Civil War. A basic tenet shared by turn-of-the-century progressives, including those who, like Teddy Roosevelt, were deeply religious, was that society could be improved through rational planning, including intervention by government—whether that meant building more schools or passing laws to clean up the meatpacking industry. Such policies, and many of the freethinking progressives who espoused them, would find a new home in the liberal wing of the Democratic Party when Franklin D. Roosevelt was elected in 1932.

Evolutionism, with its vision of an organic progression from lower to higher species, provided a handy and influential, if intellectually dubious, scientific rationale for social progressivism. As Darwin himself had pointed out, the willingness of humans in society to help preserve the weakest of their species ran counter to the "tooth and claw" process of natural selection that established the species in the first place. Americans who espoused both freethought and progressivism, and who wished to help the more defenseless members of society, followed Darwin rather than Spencer in rejecting the extension of "survival of the fittest" to man in a state of civilization. A minority of freethinkers, however, were social conservatives strongly influenced by Spencerian social Darwinism. Their antireligious views were coupled with a strong element of contempt for the poor and uneducated. The social Darwinists were often anti-Semitic, anti-Catholic nativists who espoused birth control not only as a means of liberating women but as a way to reduce the number of children produced by the lower, "unfit" classes of society.

* * *

Freethinkers also held diverse positions regarding early twentieth-century socialism. Most were extremely suspicious of both doctrinaire socialism and communism—although atheists and agnostics were frequently called socialists, communists, or anarchists by conservatives who prefaced every group they disliked with the adjective *atheistic*. Occasionally they would reverse the word order and preface *atheist* with the adjectives *socialistic* or *communistic*. It is true that nearly all socialists were atheists or agnostics, although the 1890s saw the emergence of a small Christian socialist movement advocating the social gospel of a Christ who drove the moneylenders out of the temple and befriended the poor and outcast. But the majority of American freethinkers, however attracted they might be to political programs espoused by both progressives and American socialists, regarded European-style socialist ideology as a creed based on faith rather than reason. In 1904, the *Truth Seeker* explicitly indicted socialism as just another form of blind faith:

> A religion cannot be built upon the known, it must place its heaven far off, beyond the ken of man, and beyond the possibility of its being brought within his ken. So with socialism. When one says to a socialist that the conditions here are all awry, that our officials are nearly all tyrants, that our courts do not do justice, that a man elevated to office imagines himself a tin god set up to rule over those who delegate power to him, the socialist says, Oh, that will all be regulated when socialism comes. He says this just as a Christian says to a sufferer, be patient, resign yourself to the will of God, and in his good time all will be well. The how, why or wherefore of these things is left to the imagination. The Christians have implicit faith in their God, the socialists the same faith in the state.[4]

If this was an unfair characterization of pragmatic American socialists like Debs, who did not persuade nearly a million of his countrymen to vote for him by advising them to wait for a socialist nirvana, the *Truth Seeker* was nevertheless articulating a viewpoint held by large numbers of freethinkers. Political radicals regarded religion as merely one pillar of an unjust society, and they fully expected the pillar to collapse with the overturning of an economic order that favored the rich and oppressed the poor. Committed freethinkers, by contrast, regarded orthodox religion as the foundation of most other social evils. Because religion imprisoned the mind with visions of eternal rewards and punishments in the afterlife, it prevented men and women from devising rational solutions to finite earthly problems. Goldman was one of the few political radicals whose views on the fundamentally oppressive role of religion in society dovetailed with the freethought position.

What American freethinkers and socialists did share was a view of entanglements between religion and government as inimical to democracy. Both groups were particularly disturbed by the enduring strength of fundamentalism in the South and by the growing influence of the Roman Catholic Church on state and municipal governments in other regions of the country. The nineteenth-century attacks on modernism and science by Pius IX, and on socialism and communism by his successor, Leo XIII, had struck at the heart of both socialism and freethought. In one of his best-known encyclicals, Leo had declared, in a tone of outraged astonishment, that it "has even been contended that public authority with its dignity and power of ruling, originates not from God but from the mass of the people, which considering itself unfettered by all divine sanction, refuses to submit to any laws that it has not passed of its own free will."[5] The pope's blast against socialism and communism might just as easily have been aimed at the U.S. Constitution, and this sent a shudder through the ranks of American freethinkers and political progressives. Ironically, prominent nonbelievers like Darrow would become the staunchest defenders of Al Smith, the first Catholic presidential candidate, when his 1928 presidential candidacy set off a vicious wave of nativism and anti-Catholicism. Freethinkers were consistent in upholding the constitutional prohibition against any religious test for high office.

In the decade and a half leading up to the First World War, the new association between freethinkers and the political left was reinforced by the interaction of foreign-born Jewish reformers and radicals and native American, non-Jewish social and religious dissenters. The conservative attempt to label freethought as un-American, and ungentile, was as old as the debate over the godless Constitution, so eloquently described by one minister as "an invitation for Jews and pagans of every kind to come among us." By 1914, there really *was* a connection between immigrant Jews and American-born heretics—a link that had been nonexistent when the early-nineteenth-century freethought movement was born out of nonconformist Protestantism and Enlightenment philosophy. The Scottish-born radicals Frances Wright and Robert Dale Owen were virtually the only "foreign" ambassadors to American freethinkers before the Civil War. From the 1830s through the 1850s, the Polish-born Ernestine Rose was the only Jew—immigrant or American-born—who played a visible role in the freethought, feminist, and abolitionist movements. By the end of the Civil War, American Jews—their numbers swelled by immigration from Germany and central Europe after the failed European democratic revolutions of 1848—had a higher profile in community affairs and respectable social reform efforts such as the promotion of public education. But Jews still avoided taking an active role in any political or social movement, including freethought, that might have presented them in an unfavorable light to their gentile neighbors. This was true even of someone as prominent as Felix Adler, the founder of the Society for Ethical Culture, who certainly qualified as a kissing cousin of native freethinkers like Ingersoll.

Popular anti-Semitism had lain largely dormant during the period of German Jewish immigration, but after 1880, which marked the beginning of a huge influx of Russian and East European Jews, anti-Semitism began to feed on the visible and growing presence of identifiably Jewish Jews in the nation's large cities. The Haymarket affair, even though none of the defendants were Jews (though some Americans thought they were), fueled nativist sentiments that equated immigration with anarchist violence. For those who opposed attempts to organize workers, the image of the Jew as anarchist was conflated with the image of the Jew as labor agitator—and Jews did indeed play an important role in what would eventually become the mainstream American labor movement. The new generation of Jewish immigrants scandalized their thoroughly assimilated predecessors by attracting attention from gentile America in two distinct but not always mutually exclusive ways. Many of the new arrivals simply acted more openly Jewish—more religiously observant, more insistent on traditional customs that marked them as outsiders—than the German Jews. At the same time, there was a politically radical agnostic minority strongly influenced by European Marxist, socialist, and anarchist thought and quite willing to challenge American institutions. "Red Emma" Goldman was the most fiery, persuasive, and visible representative of that minority, an outspoken atheist and feminist as well as an anarchist who would come to occupy a unique position in the history of both American political radicalism and secularism. Her love for "the other America," nurtured in a prison library on Emerson, Thoreau, and Whitman, enabled her to bridge the gap—in ways that most of her immigrant contemporaries could not—between the native American individualist and rationalist traditions and the European radical sentiment so alien to mainstream American sensibilities.

One of Goldman's most important protégés was Roger Nash Baldwin, who founded the American Civil Liberties Union in 1920 and served as its director until 1948. Baldwin fell under Goldman's spell in 1909, at age twenty-five, when he was working in a settlement house in St. Louis and a friend persuaded him to attend a lecture by the infamous anarchist. Raised as an "agnostic Unitarian" in Wellesley, Massachusetts, by parents who could trace their lineage to the *Mayflower*, the descendant of America's founding immigrants had not expected to be impressed by the words of a more recent—and notorious—immigrant. "I was indignant at the suggestion that I could be interested in a woman firebrand reputed to be in favor of assassination, free love, revolution and atheism," Baldwin would recall in his forties, "but curiosity got me there. It was the eye-opener of my life. Never before had I heard such social passion, such courageous exposure of basic evils, such electric power behind words, such a sweeping challenge to all the values I had been taught to hold highest."[6] That first encounter would become the basis of an unlikely friendship between the self-educated Russian-born Jewish anarchist and the scion of one of New England's most prominent families. Baldwin was infected with the anti-Semitism endemic to the American aristocracy of his generation; his letters as a young man contain offhand references to pushy Jewish parvenus whose sly aggressiveness was taken for granted by upper-class Protestants. In her relationship with Baldwin and other privileged members of his generation, Goldman managed to span not only the gap between European and American radicalism but between Jew and gentile. Not the least of Goldman's assets was immense personal charm, attested to by contemporaries of both sexes, that does not come across in snapshots of a dumpy woman with a generally severe expression. The young Baldwin, who had probably never met a Jew socially while he was growing up in Wellesley, soon began inviting Goldman to lunch with friends and arranging for her to lecture in such respectable venues as the St. Louis Women's Wednesday Club, where she spoke on Henrik Ibsen. Baldwin found Goldman, who was fifteen years his senior, "charming, witty, warm, and intellectual in fields unknown to me."[7] Goldman was eager to educate Baldwin, and she never stopped recommending books to him—even after she was deported in 1919 during the Red Scare and their friendship could continue only on an epistolary basis.

Around the time she met Baldwin, Goldman also became acquainted with the future birth control crusader Margaret Sanger, one of eleven children from a working-class Catholic family (though her father was a freethinker) in upstate New York. The two women traveled in intersecting bohemian radical circles in Greenwich Village, although Goldman was already famous and Sanger, though she had begun her proselytizing on behalf of contraception, was largely occupied with her responsibilities as a wife and the mother of two young children. Goldman had a strong influence on Sanger, although the complicated and competitive relationship between the two passionate women would prevent Sanger, after she became a public figure in her own right, from ever acknowledging her intellectual debt to Red Emma. By June 1914, Sanger had started a publication titled the *Woman Rebel;* she also invented the term *birth control,* which appeared in print for the first time in the paper's debut issue. Goldman contributed an essay summarizing her philosophy, which linked woman's emancipation with control over her reproductive faculties and freedom from domination by God and men. Like Stanton before her, Goldman emphasized the importance of internal psychological constraints, influenced by religious beliefs, in forming woman's image of herself as an inferior being. Full human development for any woman, Goldman argued, "must come from and through herself. First, by asserting herself as a personality, and not as a sex commodity. Second, by refusing to bear children, unless she wants them, by refusing to be a servant to God, the State, society, the husband, the family, etc., by making her life simpler, but deeper and richer."[8]

Before the First World War, Sanger received support from Goldman that was not yet forthcoming from the kind of upper-middle-class women who by then dominated the suffragist movement. In 1914, any identification with the subject of contraception would have called the respectability of the suffragists into question in even more damaging fashion than their association with Stanton's *Woman's Bible* had in the 1890s. Even though the *Woman Rebel* provided no specific information on birth control but merely advocated the right of women to limit the size of their families, Sanger was arrested under the Comstock law in August 1914. Comstock, who had pushed hard during his 1873 stint as God's lobbyist in Washington for a postal obscenity law encompassing information about the prevention of conception, declared his pleasure at having lived long enough to see the arrest of a female virago who had dared to defy the statute. He died of pneumonia only a year later, after an arduous journey to San Francisco, where he represented the United States at a convention of the

International Purity Congress. Meanwhile, Goldman was distributing the *Woman Rebel* at every opportunity on her nationwide lecture tours and encouraging Sanger to embark on a tour of her own. Speaking out in favor of the right to practice contraception was nothing new for Goldman; her first public declarations on the subject preceded Sanger's by several years. By 1914, Goldman was offering practical advice, in Yiddish and English lectures, about the uses of condoms, pessaries, and douches. Two years later, she was arrested in New York not under the Comstock statute but under a state law that made it a crime to advertise, loan, or distribute any recipe, drug, or medicine for the prevention of conception. At her trial in New York City, which attracted hundreds more people than could be accommodated in a small room in the city's Criminal Court Building, Goldman told the presiding judge and the spectators that she viewed birth control as one element in the larger struggle "towards the betterment of the human race, towards a finer quality, children who should have a joyous and glorious childhood, and women who shall have a healthy motherhood, if that is a crime, your Honor, I am glad and proud to be a Criminal."[9] Given the choice of paying a hundred-dollar fine or spending fifteen days in jail, Goldman—an old hand at attracting attention to her causes through incarceration—cheerfully went off to jail.

The charges against Sanger, like those in many other Comstock-law cases brought in the more secular climate after 1900, had been dismissed well before Goldman's trial. Goldman had spoken out forcefully in protest against Sanger's arrest, but Sanger did not return the favor—evidence of a widening rift between the two allies in the cause of women's reproductive freedom. One reason for Sanger's silence was undoubtedly her sense that being identified with Goldman might destroy any hope of obtaining financial support for family planning from wealthy upper-class Protestant and Jewish women, who would not wish to be associated with either anarchism or atheism. Sanger biographer Ellen Chesler notes that as birth control became more respectable (except to Catholics) in the twenties and thirties, Sanger became even more determined to cover up her early connection not only with Goldman but with other political radicals. "Margaret continued to popularize Goldman's claim for the revolutionary potential of women's control over their own bodies," Chesler writes, "but never admitted any debt to her. She would deliberately disparage Goldman in her own memoirs and lie outright about their association in a 1935 letter to a new supporter of birth control."[10] In a particularly stark gesture of ingratitude, Sanger would refuse to support the ailing Goldman's attempts in 1934 to regain her American citizenship. The personal rivalry between Goldman and Sanger notwithstanding, the larger issue from Sanger's standpoint was the tactical importance of downplaying the connection between immigrant radicals and American progressives. Sanger's effort to distance herself from the socially radical and antireligious origins of the birth control movement paralleled the determination of suffragists to distance themselves from the religious unorthodoxy that gave birth to nineteenth-century feminism. It is easy to forget, since the Catholic Church is now the only large American religious denomination whose ecclesiastical hierarchy continues to oppose birth control, that only a century ago the leaders of nearly all churches were united in their resistance to any public discussion of the subject.

None of the distinctions so important to secularists themselves in the early 1900s—between atheists and "agnostic Unitarians," communists and socialists, those who saw science as the servant of man and those who worshiped science as a god, or, for that matter, a Jewish radical and an ex-Catholic birth control advocate—were given any credence by conservatives who emerged from the First World War convinced that secularism itself was the villain threatening everything Americans held holy. As always, war had lowered the level of American tolerance for any kind of dissent; the difference between the First World War and previous conflicts was the presence of an immensely larger and more powerful federal apparatus to seek out and punish dissidents. Darrow later described the Red Scare as "an era of tyranny, brutality, and despotism, that, for the time at least, undermined the foundations upon which our republic was laid."[11] Pacifists and socialists, including some, like Debs, who had merely spoken out against the war and others, like Baldwin, who had actually resisted the draft, went to jail under the Espionage Act of 1917. A sedition clause added in 1918, modeled after the notorious Sedition Act of 1798, prohibited "any disloyal, . . . scurrilous, or abusive language about the form of government of the United States." The scope of the law was so broad that the Justice Department brought more than two thousand prosecutions, which sent nine hundred people to jail, during the nineteen months of America's participation in the war. The combination of fanaticism and foolishness that informed so many of the prosecutions is exemplified by the hilariously titled *United States v. Spirit of '76*, a case brought against Robert Goldstein, a movie producer who had made a short film about the American Revolution. In imposing a ten-year sentence on Goldstein, the judge declared that the film's depiction of atrocities committed by the British against the American colonists was a violation of the Espionage Act because it might lead the public "to question the good faith of our ally, Great Britain."[12] Meanwhile, a diligent young Justice Department employee named J. Edgar Hoover was preparing for the next battle against suspected traitors by compiling lists, complete with names, addresses, and places of business, of "Reds," anarchists, socialists, and other suspected radicals. From a civil liberties perspective, a large job clearly lay ahead.

The ACLU, with Baldwin as its first director, officially came into being on January 20, 1920, six months after Baldwin's release from jail. The organization's first national committee consisted of men and women from across the political spectrum, including the future Supreme Court justice Felix Frankfurter, then a professor at Harvard Law School; Elizabeth Gurley Flynn, a dyed-in-the-wool Communist; Jane Addams, the founder of Hull House; Norman Thomas, a dedicated socialist; U.S. Representative Jeanette Rankin, the only member of Congress to vote against America's entry into the war; and Mary Wooley, president of Mt. Holyoke College and a conservative

Republican. With the founding of the ACLU, the heirs of Paine and Ingersoll would turn to the courts to defend the Bill of Rights. In the nineteenth century, Ingersoll had called on his friends in high office to intercede on behalf of freethinkers and political radicals jailed for acting on their belief that the First Amendment means what it says. When the Boston post office head tried to suppress Whitman's *Leaves of Grass* in 1881, it had been a relatively simple matter for Ingersoll to intervene on the poet's behalf by contacting the U.S. postmaster general, who owed his job to the newly elected President Hayes, who owed a large favor to Ingersoll for campaigning on behalf of the lackluster Republican ticket. In the more complex and compartmentalized society that emerged out of World War I, such personal appeals were harder to manage and less likely to bear fruit (although they did not always succeed in the Gilded Age either). Only an organized, focused citizen movement could effectively take on the burden of defending civil liberties in the new American century, with its larger, more powerful, more impersonal federal government.

In contrast to many of his contemporaries, Baldwin always possessed a broad vision, as opposed to a single-cause mentality, concerning the constitutional issues that might fall within the scope of the ACLU's mission. Separation of church and state was a vital concern, but the ACLU's small staff was fully engaged during the first two years of the organization's existence with the unprecedented civil liberties issues raised by the actions of the federal government during the Red Scare. The Bolshevik Revolution and the execution of Tsar Nicholas II and his family had engendered shock and fear in the American public not unlike the horror of eighteenth-century Americans at the executions of Louis XVI and Marie Antoinette. The First World War should have taught Americans that an ocean could no longer isolate them from the troubles of Europe, but America's refusal to join the League of Nations demonstrated a national unwillingness to accept the lesson. Getting rid of dangerous immigrants who were already here and battening down the hatches against those who still wanted to come were seen as the means to protect Americans from the unrest and uncertainty of a rapidly changing world.

Moreover, twentieth-century America, unlike the eighteenth-century republic, did harbor a significant visible minority, including home-grown radicals as well as immigrants, that sympathized not only with the Russian Bolsheviks but with those who advocated violent political tactics at home. As soon as the war ended and labor abandoned its moratorium on salary demands, violent strikes broke out from coast to coast—at a time when the right of workers to organize was regarded as a "communistic" notion not only by the bosses of indus-try but by many Americans who were workers themselves. Although many strikers were influenced by communist ideology, few were members of the Communist Party—and the majority were far more likely to be homegrown American socialists or supporters of prewar Progressive Era reforms. Nevertheless, violent labor unrest became firmly associated with Russian Bolsheviks—Reds—in the American popular mind. Only a week after the armistice was signed on Novem-ber 11, 1918, the mayor of New York felt it imperative to forbid any display of red flags in the streets of the nation's largest, most cosmo-politan, and most Jewish city. The same month, a large and peaceful rally of socialists in Madison Square Garden was broken up when sev-eral hundred soldiers and sailors stormed the doors and had to be sub-dued by mounted police. That most of the socialists detested Bolsheviks meant nothing to the rioters. The wartime prosecutions of pacifists and socialists under sedition laws that made it a crime even to speak against the war had prepared the public for the blurring of dis-tinctions between different kinds of left-wing political dissenters—between socialists who believed in working through the American constitutional system and violent radicals who truly did want to destroy American and capitalist institutions.

The radical minority on the political left showed its hand in 1919, in a series of bomb threats and explosions that terrified the public. The violence gave Attorney General A. Mitchell Palmer, who called himself "the Fighting Quaker," an excuse to launch a series of raids unprecedented in their scope and disregard for both the First Amend-ment's guarantee of freedom of speech and assembly and the Fourth Amendment's protection from unreasonable search and seizure. In

April, a bomb mailed to the home of the Senate Immigration Committee chairman, who had proposed restricting immigration as a way to keep out communists, blew up in the hands of a servant who opened the door for the postman. During the same month, bombs in brown paper wrapping, addressed to prominent business leaders and government officials, were intercepted in post offices around the country. The addressees included Palmer, Supreme Court Associate Justice Oliver Wendell Holmes, Jr., J. P. Morgan, and John D. Rockefeller. With the threat of a coal strike looming in September, Palmer obtained an injunction from a federal court and prepared, with the aid of the industrious Hoover, to launch a wholesale hunt for communist and anarchist agitators. Goldman, whose citizenship had been revoked, was in the first group of deported aliens. On December 20, 1919, she was marched onto the ship *Buford*—dubbed the "Red Ark" by the press—and deported, along with her friend and former lover Alexander Berkman and 247 other Jewish immigrant radicals, to Soviet Russia. For Goldman, who would later write that she had come to consider herself American "spiritually rather than by the grace of a mere scrap of paper," there was a heartrending irony in being forced to return to Russia by the government of the country whose liberties, however imperfect she found them, she had come to cherish.* It was an irony lost on most Americans. The *New York Times* spoke for the political center in its news account and editorial commentary on the deportations of Goldman and Berkman. "The goal of the Federal agents," the *Times* observed, "was the capture of the leaders, the 'intellectuals' of agitation, and on the *Buford*, in the opinion of Chief

---

*The irony only deepened when the intellectually fearless Goldman turned her critical gaze on the new Bolshevik state. The result was *My Disillusionment in Russia*, published in 1923 after Goldman, repelled by the repression she saw in Lenin's Soviet Union, left to live in Berlin. Her biting critique of Soviet communism set her apart not only from many of her European radical contemporaries but from many American leftists like Baldwin, who told Goldman that she was being too hard on the Bolshevik government. Like many other American liberals of his generation, Baldwin made excuses in the twenties and thirties for Soviet human rights violations far greater than the ones he had devoted his life to fighting at home. With the 1939 Nazi-Soviet Pact, he began—again, like many other Americans on the political left—to revise his view of the Soviet state.

Flynn [William J. Flynn of the Justice Department's Bureau of Investigation, later the FBI], went the brains of the radical movement."[13] In its editorial, the *Times* went on to describe both Goldman and Berkman as "among the most virulent and dangerous preachers and practicers of the doctrines of destruction."[14] That one of the country's most respected newspapers would resoundingly endorse the deportation of immigrants solely because of the unpopularity of their opinions is a telling measure of the lack of any generally accepted concept of First Amendment free speech rights at the time—and of the formidable task facing the fledgling civil liberties movement. It is true that Berkman had committed an act of political violence in 1892, when he attempted unsuccessfully to assassinate Henry Clay Frick. Goldman, who was living with Berkman then, certainly knew of his plans, though she was never charged as a coconspirator. While Berkman was spending fourteen years in prison for his crime, Goldman came to believe—and stated publicly—that individual acts of violence, such as those committed by anarchists in Russia, were useless in the American context. In any case, the 1919 deportations were based solely on the views and political associations of the deportees, not on any specific actions. Had government authorities considered Berkman a continuing danger to society, they would surely not have released him on parole in 1906, six years before the end of his twenty-year sentence— or allowed him to remain in the country.

In the two months after Goldman's deportation, more than six thousand Communists, suspected Communists, and unlucky fellow travelers were arrested in their homes and places of employment. On January 1, 1920, Palmer's agents fanned out across the country and raided halls where American Communists were meeting, as was their custom, to celebrate New Year's Day. Those in attendance were immediately taken to jail, and the agents seized membership lists in order to arrest the absentees. In *Only Yesterday* (1931), Frederick Lewis Allen captured the fear-filled public mood, and the equation of religious with political unorthodoxy, as seen not by cautious centrists but by contemporary liberals:

Politicians were . . . proclaiming, "My motto for the Reds is
S.O.S.—ship or shoot. I believe we should place them all on a ship
of stone, with sails of lead, and that their first stopping-place
should be hell." College graduates were calling for the dismissal of
professors suspected of radicalism; schoolteachers were being
made to sign oaths of allegiance; business men with unorthodox
political or economic ideas were learning to hold their tongues if
they wanted to hold their jobs.

. . . Innumerable other gentlemen now discovered that they could
defeat whatever they wanted to defeat by tarring it conspicuously
with the Bolshevist brush. Big-navy men, believers in compulsory
military service, drys, anti-cigarette campaigners, anti-evolution
Fundamentalists, defenders of the moral order, book censors, Jew-
haters, Negro-haters, landlords, manufacturers, utility executives,
upholders of every sort of cause, good, bad, and indifferent, all
wrapped themselves in Old Glory and the mantle of the Founding
Fathers and allied their opponents with Lenin.[15]

The obvious link between the Red Scare and the founding of the
ACLU, and the prominent place of political leftists on the first
ACLU board, ensured that radical political dissenters would receive
both the credit (from liberals) and the opprobrium (from cultural
conservatives) for their role in defining the modern American concept of civil liberties. But the equally significant role of those who
posed a radical challenge to religion has too often been slighted and
conflated with political radicalism. The twentieth-century civil liberties movement owes as much to the heritage of Ingersoll as it does to
Baldwin and Goldman; in its early years, it represented a logical
legalistic progression from the nineteenth-century practice of asking
for mercy from the powerful to protect the rights of minorities. The
consistent message of freethinkers in the late nineteenth century—
that human beings must seek solutions to their problems not in
heaven but on earth—was a necessary precursor of the collective
defense of individual liberties envisioned by the secularists who
wrote the Constitution.

* * *

The Red Scare abated after 1920, but its conflation of atheism and bolshevism continued to influence social discourse on a wide variety of issues. In no instance was this more powerfully dramatized than in the prosecution of twenty-four-year-old John T. Scopes, arrested in May 1925 in Dayton, Tennessee, for violating a recently passed state law forbidding any mention of evolution in public school classes. Shortly after the Tennessee statute went into effect, the ACLU notified newspapers throughout the state that it stood ready to provide legal and financial assistance to any teacher who would challenge the law. George Rappelyea, a mining engineer in Dayton, read about the offer and persuaded Scopes (who was understandably worried about losing his job as a high school biology teacher) that it was his duty as an educator to offer himself as a test case. The Scopes trial is a notable episode in the history of American secularism on two grounds. First, it marked the beginning of the ACLU's consistent defense of the constitutional principle of separation between church and state, its front-and-center stance for the rest of the century in cases raising issues of either religious intrusion on government or government encroachment on religious liberty. Second, the outcome of the Scopes case, and the publicity surrounding it, led many—arguably most—American secularists to underestimate the vitality of fundamentalism.

The participation of two high-profile lawyers—Bryan for the prosecution and Darrow for the defense—guaranteed that Scopes would be tried in a national spotlight. Hundreds of national and international newspaper correspondents, as well as representatives of the new medium of radio, converged on the small town (pop. 1,100) of Dayton to cover what was billed as an epic battle between science and religion; Western Union set up a temporary telegraph office in the back room of the town's general store. Dayton, with its holy rollers holding camp meetings in the evening and vendors hawking plastic monkeys as well as statues of Jesus suitable for attaching to windshield mirrors, provided endless fodder for ridicule by northern newspaper columnists—including the celebrated H. L. Mencken, who covered the entire trial. Throughout the proceedings, fundamentalists were portrayed by most of the northern press as a doltish, near-extinct species destined for the fate of the dinosaurs and Neanderthal man (whom the fundamentalists did not recognize as a relative).

Bryan, the three-time Democratic presidential candidate and Woodrow Wilson's secretary of state, was the hero of fundamentalist rural America. Since the end of the Wilson administration, he had devoted himself to campaigning around the nation on behalf of state laws banning the teaching of evolution. He famously declared that "it is better to trust in the Rock of Ages than to know the ages of the rocks; it is better for one to know that he is close to the Heavenly Father than to know how far the stars in the heavens are apart."[16] But Bryan's views on evolution should not have been reduced to the cartoon fundamentalism that could be, and often was, inferred from some of his statements. As a populist, he had long been appalled when Spencerian social Darwinists parroted "survival of the fittest" as a slogan against social reforms designed to redistribute some of the immense wealth accumulated by the richest Americans during the Gilded Age. During the war, he became increasingly convinced that Darwin's ideas had produced philosophers—most damningly, Nietzsche—whose ideas had led Germans to believe that they had a right to dominate the world. The violent Bolshevik Revolution, with its self-proclaimed basis of materialism and atheism, solidified Bryan's convictions. His primary objection to the theory of evolution was inseparable from his populism: if the human species was, as evolutionists suggested, incapable of completely rising above its lower animal instincts, then all ideas of modifying the human condition through social reforms—necessarily instigated by the same brutish human animals—were doomed. This view of evolution makes Bryan a genuinely tragic historical figure, for he did not grasp the truth that social reforms are rendered more, not less, necessary for a human species forever struggling to control the worst aspects of its animal nature.

Darrow was the most famous agnostic and the most famous trial lawyer in America. An advocate of free silver who shared many of Bryan's beliefs on economic policy, Darrow had supported him in two of his three presidential campaigns. But Bryan's increasingly aggressive fundamentalism, as well as his refusal to disavow the Ku Klux Klan, estranged the two men long before their confrontation in Dayton. Throughout the trial, the sixty-eight-year-old Darrow was portrayed as a man of the present, while the sixty-five-year-old Bryan was portrayed as a man of the past. It would have been more accurate to say that Bryan and Darrow interpreted the past in irreconcilable ways. Darrow grew up in Kinsman, Ohio, where his father was "the village infidel" and the village coffin maker. The elder Darrow was deeply interested in science and bought Darwin's and Huxley's books as soon as they became available by mail order. "I had little respect for the opinion of the crowd," Darrow would recall. "My instinct was to doubt the majority view. My father had directed my thought and reading. He had taught me to question rather than accept. He never thought that the fear of God was the beginning of wisdom. I have always felt that doubt was the beginning of wisdom, and the fear of God was the end of wisdom."[17] For Bryan, faith was the sine qua non. Speaking from the pulpit of a Dayton church on the Sunday after the trial began, Bryan declared that while "God does not despise the learned, he does not give them a monopoly of his attention. The unlearned in this country are much more numerous than the learned.... Thank God I am going to spend the latter years of my life ... in a civilization to be based on salvation through blood [of Jesus]."[18]

Scopes's conviction was a foregone conclusion at a trial in a courtroom festooned with large signs admonishing jurors and spectators, "Read Your Bible Daily." Darrow had hoped to introduce expert scientific testimony that would not only explain the theory of evolution but point out that many church leaders—even if not in Dayton—believed that both science and evolutionism were compatible with religion. At every turn, the judge refused to admit scientific evidence and asserted that the only question was whether Scopes had violated existing Tennessee law. The trial should logically have ended with the judge's rejection of scientific evidence, but then Bryan recklessly agreed to take the stand himself, at the defense's request, as an expert witness on the Bible. Bryan's vainglorious eagerness to appear as a witness was manna in the wilderness to an experienced courtroom dramatist like Darrow. After eliciting Bryan's profession of belief in every biblical miracle—the creation of the earth in seven days, the swallowing and regurgitation of Jonah by the whale (in the Bible, a "great fish," as Bryan pointed out), God commanding the sun to stand still so that Joshua and the Israelites would have enough time to slaughter their enemies—Darrow closed in for the kill. How was it possible for the sun to stand still, he asked Bryan, since it had long been known that the sun does not move. Or did Bryan believe that the sun moved around the earth because that was what people believed in biblical times? Bryan was naturally forced to concede that the earth moves around the sun, which led to his acknowledgment that the Bible is filled with metaphors appropriate to the limited knowledge of man in the biblical era. He also conceded that each of the six days of creation might stand for millions of years. Bryan's exhausted admission that even he did not interpret the Bible literally made him appear pathetic or traitorous to his adherents and ridiculous to his detractors, and the case went to the jury. Predictably, Scopes was convicted of violating the Tennessee law (which he had) and ordered to pay a hundred-dollar fine. The conviction was eventually reversed by the Tennessee State Supreme Court, but on the narrowest of technicalities—that the judge, not a jury, had decided the terms of the sentence. Consequently, Darrow and the ACLU failed to achieve what they wanted out of the appeal—a decision that would have opened the way for a further appeal questioning the constitutional validity of the law itself. The lawyers did not have the chance to argue that a prohibition of the teaching of evolution violates the First Amendment's establishment clause by making religious doctrine the standard for a public school curriculum. In the wake of the Scopes trial, liberal Protestant and Reform Jewish leaders argued that the Tennessee law amounted to nothing less than the establishment of a state church. The Reverend Alfred C. Dieffenbach, editor of the *Christian Register*, an influential

Unitarian publication, warned that the adoption of antievolution laws by other states would establish fundamentalist Protestantism as the state religion in many areas of the country.[19]

Nevertheless, the Scopes trial was widely perceived in the North, largely as a result of coverage that focused not on the tragic but on the farcical aspects of the case, as proof positive that "backwoods fundamentalism" had suffered a stunning blow. Even Dieffenbach believed that the conflict between modernism and fundamentalism would inevitably result in a decisive defeat for the fundamentalists and a near-universal rejection of any literal interpretation of the Bible. The usually astute Frederick Lewis Allen was convinced that the prosecution of Scopes, and Bryan's wilting under Darrow's questioning, had forever discredited fundamentalist religion in the minds of most Americans. In his view, fundamentalism had won in theory because the antievolution law remained on the books, but it had lost in practice. "Legislators might go on passing anti-evolution laws," he observed, "and in the hinterlands the pious might still keep their religion locked in a science-proof compartment of their minds; but civilized opinion everywhere had regarded the Dayton trial with amazement and amusement, and the slow drift away from Fundamentalist certainty continued."[20] Bryan's death (probably of complications from diabetes, which had only recently become treatable with insulin—too late for older diabetics whose organs had already been severely damaged by the disease) came only a week after the trial and was frequently used as a metaphor for the death of the ideas he represented. That was the way things looked from Harvard Square and Greenwich Village.

But fundamentalist ideas were far from dead in much of the country, and the Scopes trial actually energized religious antievolutionists. Of particular importance was the success of Texas officials in persuading eminent New York publishers to rewrite passages of their biology texts to comply with the state's demand that passages on evolution be omitted. The Texas drive was led by Governor Miriam Ferguson, who declared, "I am a Christian mother . . . and I am not going to let that kind of rot go into Texas textbooks."[21] The reason the South

exerted such a disproportionate influence on textbook content was
that the states south of the Mason-Dixon Line tended to have uni-
form policies regarding the purchase of schoolbooks, while northern
states generally gave local school officials more latitude. Thus, the
South provided the largest single market for texts, and publishers
understood that they would have to bow to the demands of southern
censors or lose their business. As the century progressed, many
southern states would relax their textbook censorship policies—only
to reinstate them when the Christian right revived evolution as an
issue in the 1980s. Texas, with a huge school system and a powerful
religious right, exercises especially tight control over textbook content to this day.

One telling example of the growing success of religious censors in
the twenties is the contrast between two editions, the first published
in 1921 and the second in 1926, of a widely used text, *Biology for
Beginners*, by Truman Moon. The frontspiece of the 1921 edition featured a portrait of Charles Darwin. By 1926, Darwin had been
removed and replaced with a drawing of the human digestive system.
The publisher, Henry Holt, also issued a separate edition for Texas
schools—one that, at the insistence of the state's textbook commission, omitted three chapters dealing with the descent of man. (Holt's
texts for other states were unaltered.) Another major publisher, Allyn
& Bacon of Boston, admitted that every contract for the purchase of
schoolbooks in Texas required the publisher and the author to submit
to censorship by the state commission. But no alterations were
required, a representative of the publishing firm assured the *New
York Times*, because the books had been "tactfully" written in the
first place. In other words, the writer and the publisher censored
themselves, thereby relieving Texas censors of that burden.[22] The very
word *evolution* disappeared from most textbooks written after 1925:
even when evolutionary concepts were introduced, the word *development* was substituted. While the "development" of plant and lower
animal species was discussed, *human* descent—a subject too hot to
handle—was usually omitted. Many school systems responded to the
demands of antievolutionists by downgrading biology itself—with or

without evolution—in the science curriculum. In 1936, Oscar Riddle, a leading biologist with the Station for Experimental Evolution at Cold Spring Harbor, New York, told the American Association for the Advancement of Science that high schools were teaching less biology than they had in the first decade of the twentieth century.[23] Antievolutionists were suspicious of any curriculum that attempted to instill an appreciation of the scientific method of forming hypotheses and reaching conclusions, and they insisted that high school science courses focus on the "practical" uses of science, such as hygiene and plant breeding, rather than on speculation that might raise spiritually dangerous questions. The emphasis in American public education on practical as opposed to theoretical science was one result of the antievolutionist successes of the twenties, and it had a lasting deleterious impact on American scientific literacy. In the long run, grassroots censorship had a much greater effect on popular thought than did northern journalists' ridicule of the hard-line fundamentalism displayed during the Scopes "monkey trial."

In the decade after the trial, secularist civil libertarians were largely asleep at the switch while fundamentalists were extending their influence over public education. In part, this somnolence was a testament to the capacity of fundamentalists to learn from their mistakes. From the ridicule that greeted Bryan's anachronistic histrionics, his successors as defenders of the faith learned that there was much more to be gained from exercising the power of the purse through backdoor negotiations with publishers than from putting idealistic young teachers on trial. Moreover, covert financial power was much less susceptible to challenges on First Amendment grounds than overt displays of state power over individual teachers and schools. Another factor contributing to a certain complacency on the part of secularists during the twenties was the widespread illusion that science had already won the day and that it was only a matter of time—and not very much time, at that—before the enemies of rationalism simply gave up. Secularists mistook the consumerist enthusiasm for the technological fruits of science that proliferated throughout the twenties—radio, talking motion pictures, automatic traffic lights, to name only a few—for a

genuine understanding and acceptance of science as a way of inter-
preting nature in general and human behavior in particular.

Indeed, mainstream denominations as well as fundamentalists soon
learned how to use the new communications media to spread their
religious messages. One of the most powerful and appealing messages
in an era of expanding prosperity was that faith would not only guarantee the believer a place in heaven but also help him earn a fortune on
earth. The association of virtue with financial success was as old as
American Puritanism, but the unabashed marketing of religion as a
product that might guarantee success was, if not altogether new, so
grossly expanded as to constitute a difference in kind rather than
merely in degree. The most famous clerical orators of the nineteenth
century, whether they spoke for conservative or liberal faiths, offered
an image of man's relationship with God that was, if anything, a brake
on American consumerism. The long clerical campaign to shut down
the post office on Sunday, for example, was successfully resisted for
decades by business leaders who wanted to keep their products moving. Lyman Beecher and his son Henry may have been at the
antipodes of establishment Protestantism in the nineteenth century,
but both would have objected to the conflation of religion and bank-
ing described by Sinclair Lewis in his novel *Babbitt* (1921). As George
W. Babbitt dresses for work, he gazes out his bedroom window at a
bank tower rising above the skyline of the fast-growing city of Zenith:

> Its shining walls rose against April sky to a simple cornice like a
> streak of white fire. Integrity was in the tower, and decision. It bore
> its strength lightly as a tall soldier. As Babbitt stared, the nervousness
> was soothed from his face, his slack chin lifted in reverence. All he
> articulated was "That's one lovely sight!" but he was inspired by
> the rhythm of the city; his love of it renewed. He beheld the tower
> as a temple-spire of the religion of business, a faith passionate,
> exalted, surpassing common men; and as he clumped down to
> breakfast, he whistled the ballad "Oh, by gee, by gosh, by jingo"
> as though it were a hymn melancholy and noble.[24]

If business was embraced as a religion by the Babbitts of the new American century, religion was also seen as a business. This philosophy was most fully articulated by Bruce Barton, one of the creators of the industry already dubbed "Madison Avenue," in *The Man Nobody Knows* (1924). This nonfiction best seller offered a portrait of Jesus as the greatest salesman, advertising copywriter, and executive of all time. Barton, the son of a minister, was one of the founders in 1919 of what would become the premier New York advertising agency Barton Batten Durstine Osborn, located, naturally, on Madison Avenue. He is credited with coining the corporate names General Electric and General Motors, and he also came up with one of the best-known slogans of all time for the Salvation Army: "A man may be down, but he is never out." Barton's presentation of Jesus merits close examination because it bears a strong resemblance to the image of the aggressive Messiah championed by American fundamentalists today (though Barton himself, who served as chairman of BBDO until 1961, was not a fundamentalist).

The main premise of *The Man Nobody Knows* was that Jesus had been burdened with an overly meek image that needed to be remedied to appeal to red-blooded Americans in the Roaring Twenties. The book opened with the author's memory (not unlike that of Ingersoll, another preacher's kid) of having been bored witless in Sunday school. Young Bruce was not captivated by a Jesus who was called the lamb of God. "The little boy did not know what that meant," Barton recalled, "but it sounded like Mary's little lamb. Something for girls— sissified. Jesus was also 'meek and lowly,' a 'man of sorrows and acquainted with grief.' " In other words, little Bruce saw Jesus as a wimp. But when he grew up to found his own advertising agency, he realized that the Sunday school teachers must all have been wrong about Jesus because only "strong magnetic men inspire great enthusiasm and build great organizations." Barton saw a Christ who had "picked up twelve men from the bottom ranks of business and forged them into an organization that conquered the world."[25] The book went on to applaud Jesus's capacities as an executive (molding the disparate apostles into a well-oiled staff—with the exception of Judas), a great outdoorsman (fishing on the Sea of Galilee and climbing all those hills), a garrulous socializer ("the most popular dinner guest in Jerusalem"), and, of course, the greatest success at advertising the world has ever known. Jesus's parables were his personal advertisements and—most important—he specialized in attention-grabbing miracles and declarations of his powers, such as making the crippled walk and claiming that he had the power to forgive sins. Barton asked, "Can you imagine the next day's issue of the *Capernaum News*—if there had been one?"

PALSIED MAN HEALED
JESUS OF NAZARETH CLAIMS RIGHT TO
FORGIVE SINS
PROMINENT SCRIBES OBJECT
"BLASPHEMOUS," SAYS LEADING CITIZEN.
"BUT ANYWAY I CAN WALK," HEALED MAN
RETORTS.[26]

Finally, Barton pointed out, Jesus's entire ministry exemplified the secret of business success in any era—service. Whether a man was the owner of a small car-repair business or the president of General Motors, he could learn how to better himself and serve his customers by following the example of the businessman from Nazareth. "Great progress will be made in the world when we rid ourselves of the idea that there is a difference between *work* and *religious work*," Barton argued. "The race must be fed and clothed and housed and transported, as well as preached to, and taught and healed. Thus *all* business is his Father's business."[27]

The boosterish melding of religion with business, backed up by new communications and advertising media, was a cultural shift that encouraged the public display of spiritual allegiances that had once belonged to the realm of private life. To pursue God and Mammon with equal vigor, and to trumpet one's commitment and devotion, had become an American virtue—one at odds not only with freethought but with the "inward light" that had infused the dissenting eighteenth- and nineteenth-century American Protestantism of Lucretia Mott and

William Lloyd Garrison. The Jazz Age spirit of religious display did not express itself directly in politics in the fashion that has become so familiar to Americans during the past twenty-five years, but it marked the beginning of the long and slow encroachment on the zone of privacy that had enabled previous American presidents to seek election and govern without being obliged to share their religious beliefs with the public.

Most secularist civil libertarians in the twenties saw the new civil religion of boosterism—Protestant boosterism, to be precise—as a target for satire rather than as a threat to libertarian values. Unlike Ingersoll, they did not view organized religion per se as an enemy of progress and intellectual liberty but instead attacked specific religious sects when they attempted to impose their beliefs, in a manner viewed by civil libertarians as unconstitutional, on society as a whole. Since the beginning of the modern civil liberties movement, religious conservatives have attempted to portray those who believe in absolute separation of church and state as opponents of all religion. Nothing could be further from the truth. In a tradition rooted in Jeffersonian liberalism, the ACLU has defended religious minorities—Jews, Jehovah's Witnesses, Seventh-Day Adventists—as vigorously as it has opposed public school prayer and expenditure of tax money on religious schools.

But one minority—Catholics—posed a special problem for American secularists in the twenties and thirties. On the one hand, American Catholics of that generation were an insecure and, as far as many Protestants were concerned, suspect minority. On the other, the Catholic hierarchy—unlike Jewish leaders, who were extremely circumspect about advancing anything that might be seen as a parochial ethnic or religious agenda—behaved more like a majority religion in its aggressive attempts to impose its dogmas on other Americans. This seeming paradox reflected the increasing sophistication of American bishops in regions of the country where the Catholic population was large enough to possess political clout. The American hierarchy had learned how to use the tools of democracy—a democracy viewed with deepest suspicion by the Vatican in Rome—not only to fight anti-Catholic prejudice but to promote specifically Catholic social and religious interests.

In many areas, especially the South, Catholics elicited emotions ranging from suspicion to hatred and were depicted as a religious fifth column with a dual allegiance to the American government and the Vatican. Al Smith's 1928 presidential campaign, met throughout much of the South and West with Klan demonstrations and death threats, was a grueling experience from which the candidate himself never fully recovered emotionally. Smith, a native New Yorker and a streetwise New York politician accustomed to working with Protestants and Jews of every conceivable background and belief, had simply not imagined the depth of the bigotry that awaited him west of the Hudson River and south of the Mason-Dixon Line.

In the early days of the republic, Protestant suspicion of Catholics was rooted in the knowledge that in every country where Catholicism was the state-established religion, the church had persecuted adherents of other faiths. Protestants had behaved similarly into the 1600s, but with the Enlightenment, Protestant states of the Old World began accommodating themselves to other religions in ways that Catholic states did not. At the time the Constitution was written, the Inquisition was still functioning throughout Catholic Europe. The godless American Constitution protected all religions, but what would Catholics do if they ever obtained a majority through immigration? That question, based on the history of the church in Europe—and in regions of the New World colonized by Catholic Europe—underlay much of the anti-Catholic sentiment of the nineteenth and early twentieth centuries. Of course, anti-Catholic nativism was directed not only at the Catholic religion but at poor immigrants who happened to be Catholic—first the Irish, then the Slavs and Italians who poured into the country between 1880 and 1924. In similar fashion, anti-Semitic nativism—which flourished not during the period of German Jewish immigration before 1860 but when poorer Russian and eastern European Jews began arriving in the post–Civil War era—was an expression of economic and class prejudice as well as religiously motivated bigotry. But in late-nineteenth-century America—for the first time in Western history since the Christianization of the Roman Empire—distrust of the Catholic Church's intentions was far more widespread than distaste for religious Judaism. Catholicism was seen by many Americans not merely as another form of Christianity but also as an enemy of non-Catholic Christianity. Moreover, in contrast to the Catholic hierarchy, Jewish religious and community leaders took a uniformly laudatory and grateful view of the American secular government. While Catholic leaders were attacking America's "godless" public schools, Jewish leaders viewed those same schools as a blessing unimaginable in lands where their educational aspirations had been legally circumscribed by church (usually Catholic or Russian Orthodox) and state acting as one. The fear that Catholic demands might undermine not only American secular institutions but the very idea of America as a government deriving its power from the consent of the governed had been memorably articulated in an 1888 speech before the National Education Association by Thomas J. Morgan, a prominent Baptist minister. Morgan derided Catholic charges that public schools failed to inculcate morality as simply resentment because "the public schools of this country are not Roman Catholic":

> To say that the common schools are godless ... and therefore must be set aside, stirs up a deep sentiment within us. We will be asked at no distant day to recognize that there is no religion except Catholicism; that there is no worship except that of the Cathedral; that the state has no right to exist except as a servant of the church. In other words ... if you accept that criticism [of public schools] as just, you yield everything that we prize in the civilization of the nineteenth century, represented by Martin Luther, and represented in its outflowering by American ideas; you recognize that all that is a sham and a pretense, that it is to be thrown aside, and that we are to go back to medievalism, with all that condition implies.[28]

Such apocalyptic predictions must be viewed against the background of equally immoderate attacks on America's public schools by nineteenth-century Catholic leaders. John Hughes, bishop of New York from 1842 until 1864, regarded as "the father of Catholic education" in America, described the public schools as a "dragon ...

devouring the hope of the country as well as religion." Secular public education, he said, was the dispenser of "Socialism, Red Republicanism, Universalism, Infidelity, Deism, Atheism, and Pantheism—anything, everything, except religion and patriotism."[29]

Despite such views and the Vatican's fervid defense of theocracies, it is unlikely that the church's leaders ever entertained any illusions about the possibility, or even the desirability, of turning America into a Catholic state. (By the end of the nineteenth century, the American bishops' main demand on the public schools—which enrolled many Catholic children whose parents could not afford parochial school tuition—was that they refrain from reading excerpts from the Protestant King James Bible at the start of the school day. In fact, many school systems with large numbers of Jewish and Catholic immigrant students had already abandoned the practice.) But the image of Catholics as a state within a state, biding their time for the chance to overturn America's secular government, persisted. It was revived during Smith's campaign and reappeared, in a still powerful form ultimately rejected by voters, during John F. Kennedy's 1960 campaign. In retrospect, the virulence of the anti-Catholic attack on Smith must be seen as the beginning of the end for socially respectable antiCatholicism in America. The Klan reaction to Smith's campaign in the South and Southwest had a good deal of educational value for the rest of the country; obscene and violent threats directed at a national presidential candidate—the "Happy Warrior," as Franklin D. Roosevelt called Smith—merited press coverage that the daily violence against and intimidation of southern blacks did not. Secularists like Darrow, with their devotion to the Enlightenment ideal of complete freedom of conscience, were repelled by the bigotry directed toward Smith, and so it was that the nation's best-known agnostic since Ingersoll became one of Smith's most vocal defenders.

The "Catholic problem" for secularists in the twenties and thirties was not the rights of individual Catholics but the church hierarchy, which no longer hesitated to use its power, whenever possible, to impose its moral tenets on other Americans. That power was most obvious, and most effective, in the church's all-out battle against birth control—which placed the hierarchy in absolute opposition to the secularist view of individual rights. The American church had opposed evolutionism even before the First World War, but not with the same energy and financial resources that it would bring to bear on the birth control issue in the twenties.

Catholic leaders believed in the twenties that they had a chance to use the law and political pressure, through formal and informal means, to stifle public debate concerning contraception. By then, the church had come to regard Sanger as its archenemy because she was beginning to succeed in making birth control a respectable subject for discussion—the first step toward legitimizing the actual use of contraceptives. Sanger returned the hatred, not only because of the church's obstruction of her activities but because she was driven by the memory of a pious Catholic mother who died of tuberculosis at age fifty, having given birth eleven times.

In November 1921, the hierarchy overplayed its hand in New York City: police, acting at the suggestion of Archbishop (soon to be Cardinal) Patrick Hayes, waded into a crowd of more than one thousand at Town Hall and broke up a mass meeting that was to have been the culmination of an educational conference on birth control. Sanger and another speaker, a British former member of Parliament, were arrested, dragged off the stage in full view of the audience, and booked on disorderly conduct charges by police who said openly that they were following the archbishop's recommendations. A blue-ribbon panel, including representatives of the ACLU and such prominent citizens as the attorney Paul D. Cravath (of the prestigious and still flourishing Manhattan law firm Cravath, Swaine & Moore) and Henry Morgenthau (who would become Franklin Roosevelt's secretary of the treasury), found no evidence to formally link the church to the incident. Nevertheless, a spokesman for Hayes declared that "decent and clean-minded people would not discuss a subject such as birth control in public." But decent people *were* discussing the subject in public; Sanger had reached upper-middle-class women and men who would never have paid attention to Goldman. Nearly every newspaper in New York denounced the police action as a violation of free speech.[30]

Before the First World War, freethinkers and socialists were the only groups that unequivocally condemned the Comstock law's definition of contraceptive information as obscene and unequivocally defended the right of a woman to determine how many children she would have. Ingersoll, speaking before there were any reliable methods of contraception, nevertheless envisioned the day when science would "make woman the owner, the mistress of herself" by enabling her "to decide for herself whether she will or will not become a mother." Effective means of contraception, Ingersoll said, would put an end to the poverty of families with more children than parents could support. "This frees woman," he declared. "The babes that are then born will be welcome. They will be clasped with glad hands to happy breasts. They will fill homes with light and joy."[31] Only the most liberal religious leaders before the war, most notably the Reform Jewish leader Rabbi Stephen Wise, had anything remotely favorable to say about birth control. But that was no longer true by the twenties, when mainstream Protestant leaders as well as Jews were changing both their theology and their attitudes about the practical benefits of contraception. Thus, the Catholic hierarchy was taking on not only freethinkers in its battle against birth control but other religious denominations as well. Ironically, the Catholic Church would become the chief defender of nineteenth-century obscenity and anti-contraception laws written by right-wing Protestants who truly despised Catholics.

The church's opposition to birth control, like the fundamentalist attack on evolution, was an expression of an overarching hostility to secularism and all its works. Birth control belonged to a world in which human beings—and human beings of the female sex, at that— were in charge of themselves insofar as nature itself allowed. Birth control, like evolutionism and bolshevism, was identified with atheism in the conservative religious universe. In 1925, Archbishop Hayes, in an annual appeal on behalf of Catholic Charities, blasted contraception on grounds that it represented "not what the God of nature and grace, in his Divine wisdom, ordained marriage to be; but the lustful indulgence of man and woman. . . . Religion shudders at the wild orgy of atheism and immorality the situation forebodes."[32]

The ACLU was involved from its inception in the birth control dispute: attempts to ban discussion of the subject and break up public meetings violated First Amendment guarantees of free speech and free assembly. The argument that laws forbidding the distribution of contraceptives were attempts to impose religious doctrine—first conservative Protestant, then Catholic—on a pluralistic society was rarely raised at the time; approaching the crusade against birth control as a form of censorship struck a much more positive note with the American public in the twenties, especially since each attempt to break up a public meeting, particularly if Sanger was involved, generated widespread publicity and tended to cast the authorities in a foolish, if not a repressive, light. In 1929, the Catholic mayor of Boston—America's most Catholic city—issued a permit for a lecture on birth control but then banned Sanger from speaking. Sanger stood dramatically on the stage with a piece of tape covering her mouth, while Arthur Schlesinger, Sr., the prominent historian and Harvard professor, read her prepared statement. Baldwin promptly declared that "a square issue of discrimination" had been raised by the mayor's attempt to dictate who might speak and who might not. The ACLU then published a booklet, *Censorship in Boston,* denouncing any type of prior restraint on speech—although it left open the question of subsequent criminal proceedings against "indecent" books and plays—a much narrower construction of First Amendment rights than the ACLU applied to political speech at the time. The organization's early skittishness about obscenity cases reflected Baldwin's Puritan streak. His own private life was unorthodox; when he married shortly after his release from prison, he and his bride recited wedding vows describing monogamy as tyranny and declaring their openness to "many loves." But Baldwin viewed the growing public frankness about sex as vulgar and did not believe that sexual speech merited the same level of constitutional protection as political speech.

The long Catholic onslaught against birth control would ultimately prove to be a losing battle (though the effort succeeded in keeping some Comstock-era laws on the books until the 1960s), but it marked a turning point in the church's relationship to secular American society. Before the First World War, the American hierarchy generally confined its pronouncements on secular issues to matters directly affecting Catholics. Public education was a pernicious institution because it might weaken the faith of Catholics; if Protestants and Jews wished their children to attend schools infected with the germ of modernism, that was their business. With the crusade against birth control, the church set out on a radically different course, intended to prevent non-Catholics from gaining access to something deemed immoral by the church not merely for its own members but for all. In that respect, the twenties provided a foretaste of the positions on abortion that would be adopted fifty years later not only by the Catholic Church hierarchy but by fundamentalist Protestants.

With hindsight, the twenties can best be seen as a decade that combined spreading secularization with rising religious influence, from many denominations, throughout American society. There were no legal attacks on the godless Constitution, as there are today, but religion entered the public square—the powerful new square dominated by mass communications media unimaginable before the First World War—with a vigor that belied the turn-of-the-century freethought prediction that religious faith would wither away under the glare of scientific truth. Given the persistent vitality of historically rooted denominational hatreds, it would have been impossible in the twenties for fundamentalist Protestants and the conservative American Catholic hierarchy to recognize the common ground that they would discover with the rise of the antiabortion movement in the 1970s. But the cultural foundation of that later alliance was laid in the decade after the First World War. America's most conservative religious leaders spoke out as if with one voice—though most would not, in that decidedly nonecumenical era, have agreed to attend one another's services—to condemn secularism, modernism, and any social philosophy, whether it went by the name of humanism or communism, based on belief in the right of men and women to shape their world without regard to divine authority. The one truly ecumenical phenomenon of the twenties was the proselytizing of a robust faith linked with robust capitalism.

The twenties also marked the end of the freethought movement as a distinct intellectual force in American life. The older generation of freethinkers, nourished on the impassioned rationalism embodied by Ingersoll and Stanton, was dying out. Members of the new generation invested their energies in causes—civil liberties, birth control, support of public schools, the defense of science, the fight against capital punishment—that often brought them into conflict with organized religion but did not have the undermining of institutional religion as their chief goal. The new, advertiser-financed medium of radio, which rapidly displaced lectures as a form of popular entertainment, was far less open than the old speakers' platforms to unconventional ideas about religion. The farmers who rode fifty miles across the prairie to hear Ingersoll speak in the 1890s were likely to be found in their own living rooms, listening to their own radios, in the 1920s—and radio sponsors did not spend their money to promote attacks on the God of the Bible. Freethought ideals did survive the disappearance of the freethought movement, but—unlike religious evangelism—they were ill suited, because of their emphasis on facts rather than emotion, to the new mass communications media.

It is significant that the one commercially successful attempt by a freethinker to reach a mass audience in the twenties and thirties—a series of literary classics and iconoclastic contemporary fiction and nonfiction known as the "Little Blue Books"—relied solely on the old-fashioned medium of print. The publisher of the pamphlets, sold for as little as five cents apiece during the Depression, was Emanuel

Haldeman-Julius, the Philadelphia-born son of a Russian Jewish immigrant bookbinder. Although Emanuel was born in 1889, he was a throwback to the earlier American freethought tradition of self-education embodied by Ingersoll and Darrow (who would become his closest friend in the 1920s). Like Darrow and so many earlier free-thinkers, Haldeman-Julius dated his agnosticism from his childhood reading of Paine's *The Age of Reason*. Like Goldman—though his radicalism was strictly American-made—Haldeman-Julius bridged the gap between the new left-wing Jewish immigrant milieu and the older native American tradition of freethought rooted in liberal Protestantism. He joined the Socialist Party before the First World War and would remain a democratic socialist, staunchly opposed to both communism and fascism, until his death in 1951.

Haldeman-Julius was also a publishing genius, as savvy in his own way as Bruce Barton. In 1919, thirty years before standard commercial publishers began to market inexpensive paperback books, he used the presses and subscription lists of a once-famous socialist weekly paper, *Appeal to Reason*, to bring out his own line of classics in pamphlet form. Initially considered a quixotic venture, the Little Blue Books succeeded through a combination of Enlightenment pamphleteering, Progressive populism—with its emphasis on cooperative economic endeavor—and shrewd twentieth-centry marketing. The first two pamphlets in the series were *The Rubáiyát of Omar Khayyám* and Oscar Wilde's *The Ballad of Reading Gaol*—which the fifteen-year-old boy, unable to afford clothbound books, had stumbled across in ten-cent pamphlet form in a small bookstore in Philadelphia. That first encounter with the Wilde poem was a pivotal moment for the young bookbinder's son. "It was winter, and I was cold," he would recall, "but I sat down on a bench and read that booklet straight through, without a halt, and never did I so much as notice that my hands were blue, that my wet nose was numb, and that my ears felt as hard as glass. Never until then, or since, did any piece of printed matter move me more deeply. . . . I'd been lifted out of this world—and by a 10¢ booklet. I thought, at the moment, how wonderful it would be if thousands of such booklets could be made available."33

Haldeman-Julius realized his dream in 1919, when he raised the capital to print his first pamphlets through a mailing to 175,000 *Appeal to Reason* subscribers. His idea combined populist and grass-roots capitalist simplicity—he asked readers to send him five dollars, in return for which he promised to send them fifty pamphlets as they came off the presses:

> Five thousand readers took me up, which meant I had $25,000 to work with. I hurried through the 50 titles (and they were good ones, too, for I haven't believed in trash at any time in my life) and got many letters expressing satisfaction with the venture. Encouraged, I announced a second batch of 50 titles, and called for $5 subscriptions. . . . Meanwhile, the booklets were selling well to readers who hadn't subscribed for batches of 50.34

The first pamphlets sold for twenty-five cents, but the price soon dropped to ten and then to five cents as Haldeman-Julius attracted new readers by advertising in mass-circulation newspapers. By the early twenties, Haldeman-Julius's press in Girard, Kansas, was turning out 240,000 Blue Books a day. The list included the Bible (like all other old-fashioned freethinkers, Haldeman-Julius had studied it from cover to cover), the Greek classics, Goethe, Shakespeare, Voltaire, Emile Zola, H. G. Wells, and Ingersoll. Haldeman-Julius also published the controversial writings of contemporaries, including Sanger and Havelock Ellis, who at that time had difficulty finding commercial publishers for their controversial views on sex and birth control. More than 300 million Blue Books were printed between 1919 and 1949, when commercial publishers began to enter the paperback marketplace. The writer Harry Golden notes that during the Depression students bought fifty secondhand Blue Books for a dollar and resold them after they were read—thus ensuring a huge circulation among Americans who could not afford hardcover books. "There is no way of estimating how many millions read these books,"

Golden recalls. "Other thousands upon thousands of 'little blue books' floated around hospitals, penal institutions, charitable wards, CCC [Civilian Conservation Corps] camps, and military barracks."[35] Haldeman-Julius became a wealthy man by pursuing a childhood dream that ran counter to the assertion of his near contemporary Mencken that "no one ever went broke underestimating the intelligence of the American people." Although Haldeman-Julius was a socialist, the Little Blue Books were a quintessentially individualist freethought enterprise. Based on the premise that the education and freedom of the individual mind were the highest good, Haldeman-Julius's grassroots publishing venture could not have been farther removed from the grim conformist and collectivist ideologies, whether capitalist, fascist, or communist, that were gaining strength throughout the twenties.

It is not surprising that most isms of the twentieth century proved to be just as antithetical as orthodox religion to so individualistic a movement as freethought, for Enlightenment-rooted freethought was never a philosophy that tried to explain everything. As the Columbia University historian Allan Nevins would remark in 1943, freethought was a cause "not of mere hostility to dogma, but of scientific inquiry, of fearless adherence to logic, of a strict discrimination between the known and the unknowable." Freethinkers "asserted that human intelligence is limited, that they accepted its limits realistically, and that they built upon this realism a set of practical plans for making human society better and happier."[36] And dictatorial regimes recognized evidence-based freethought as an enemy. The International Freethought Congress was scheduled to meet in Rome in 1925, but Mussolini's fascist regime refused to issue visas for the participants, marking perhaps the last time freethinkers would be considered so menacing and powerful as to merit an official government ban.

The realistic and individualistic character of the previous generation of freethinkers is beautifully conveyed in George Macdonald's *Fifty Years of Freethought*, which struck an inescapable elegiac note for the movement to which he had devoted his life. Indeed, Macdonald and Clarence Darrow were, by the 1920s, the only surviving contributors from the *Truth Seeker*'s first decade, the 1870s. The memoir ends in 1925, with a column of obituaries published in that year's *Truth Seeker*. "The conventional local eulogy of the dead Free-thinker," Macdonald explained, "states that 'his religion was the Golden Rule.' When the obituary notice contains those words, it is known that the deceased was an Infidel." One obituary reported the death of Helen H. Gardener, a feminist freethinker whose lectures on "Men, Women, and Gods" had been published by the *Truth Seeker* in 1885. Miss Gardener, the obituary informed readers, had willed her brain to Cornell University "for the purpose of a physical demonstration of her theory that the brain is immune from sex—that woman's is the same as man's. The test seemed to substantiate that thought."[37] The bequest's scrupulous dedication to fact already seemed archaic in an era when new secular religions were embarking on a quest for heaven on earth with as little regard for the distinction between the knowable and the unknowable as the old religions manifested when they preached of a heaven beyond earthly existence.

Darrow, whose life and career encompassed the individualistic freethinking intellectualism of the century into which he was born and the secularist activism of the century in which he died, sounded a cautionary note in his 1932 autobiography as new and powerful forces of unreason gathered around the world. "The number of people on the borderline of insanity in a big country is simply appalling," he said, "and these seem especially addicted to believing themselves saviors and prophets. It takes only a slight stimulus to throw them entirely off their balance."[38]

9

Onward, Christian Soldiers

Conflict between secularist and religious values is not the first, and sometimes not even the last, subject that arises when Americans reflect on the turbulent years of the Depression and the Second World War. The social changes associated with both the New Deal and the war were so far-reaching, and the national and international politics of the thirties so impassioned, that historians have tended to overlook the equally significant change that occurred in the balance of religious power, reshaping not only the American dialogue between secularism and religion but relations among representatives of differing faiths. What happened, quite simply, is that the Catholic Church—even though it represented only a minority of the American population—became the nation's most powerful denomination, exercising its spiritual and temporal clout at the confluence of morality, business, and public policy. Although Catholic involvement in public policy issues increased during the twenties, the church's influence was still largely confined to centers of Catholic population. By the end of the thirties, the Catholic hierarchy had become the single most powerful national religious voice on three major issues—censorship, birth control, and anticommunism. Not that Jewish and Protestant leaders failed to speak out on such matters, and often in opposition to the church's positions, but they did not and could not, in view of the less doctrinaire and less hierarchical nature of their religious traditions, speak with the unified voice of the American Catholic bishops.

Catholics in the thirties had come to constitute a religious minority unprecedented in American history—one that combined a past (and not a very distant past, as the hatred directed toward Al Smith had demonstrated) of minority vulnerability with a present of immense institutional power. America's eighteenth-century secularist founders, nineteenth-century freethinkers, and early-twentieth-century civil libertarians generally viewed all minority religions—Judaism, Quakerism, and Catholicism, as well as newer fringe sects—as vulnerable entities in need of protection not only from government but from fellow citizens who wished to maintain majoritarian Protestantism as the dominant civil religion. Catholics, who accounted for only 5 percent of the American population in 1800, were just such an exposed minority throughout the nineteenth century. By the 1930s, however, nearly 25 percent of Americans were Catholic—a compelling example of the flourishing religious pluralism envisioned by the framers of the godless Constitution. With its growing membership, deep financial base, and politically savvy leaders, the church no longer needed protection from outsiders; earlier generations of secularists had never envisaged a religious minority not only freed from fear of persecution but capable of institutionalizing its views in laws affecting other Americans. The men who wrote the Bill of Rights were understandably concerned not with the disproportionate power of any minority but with the tyranny of the majority.

In the fourth decade of the twentieth century, America was still an overwhelmingly Protestant nation, but Protestants were so divided that it would have been ludicrous to refer to a "Protestant" political or social position. New York Episcopalians or Congregationalists had little in common, theologically or socially, with southern Baptists—and southern Baptists were equally removed from northern Baptists. Jews did tend to share the same views on political questions—especially those involving separation of church and state—but they made up too small a minority (approximately 3.75 percent), and were still too fearful of stimulating anti-Semitism, to advance their own public policy agenda in as open and aggressive a fashion as the Catholic Church did. This was true even on the issue of highest importance to the American Jewish community—the admission of refugees from Nazi Germany. Not only did the Catholic hierarchy speak with one voice, but it did so at a time when lay Catholics treated their priests and bishops with a deference that would be unimaginable to most American Catholics today.

One of the first demonstrations of the new Catholic power, and the hierarchy's willingness to use it openly, was a 1934 boycott of Philadelphia movie theaters. Led by the church's recently formed Legion of Decency, the boycott cut movie attendance by 40 percent. The purpose of the action was to pressure the movie industry into censoring itself along lines suggested by Catholic moral teaching, and Philadelphia, with its large Catholic population, offered a demonstration of what the film moguls might expect if they ignored the church's demands. Soon afterward, the industry caved in and established its Production Code Administration, headed by a former seminarian. Written with the assistance of a Jesuit priest, Daniel A. Lord (whose role was unknown to the public), the code banned nudity, vulgar language, and any sympathetic treatment of sex outside marriage. Father Lord must not have been terribly well disposed toward sex *inside* marriage either, since movies were also forbidden to portray married couples occupying the same bed—a stricture that lasted into the 1950s. The code also pledged that no movie would be permitted to "throw ridicule on any religious faith."[1] It seems extraordinary that the industry accorded so much deference to one religious denomination, but money talked. Many Protestant leaders also favored censorship of movies, but only Catholics had organized a boycott; neither the WCTU nor the nineteenth-century Protestant framers of the Comstock laws had managed to attain such far-reaching national influence over the content of earlier entertainment media.

The rise of Catholic power in the thirties was a direct result of the importance of Catholic voters in the New Deal coalition, which also included Jews, labor, and the Solid South (solidly Democratic at the time). Roosevelt needed the Catholic vote, and it was assumed that there *was* a Catholic vote willing to take its cue from the church hierarchy—even though the hierarchy never endorsed political candidates. That assumption may well have been mistaken. American Catholics of the New Deal generation may have been much more willing to follow the lead of their priests and bishops on matters of faith and morals than Catholics are today, but their deference did not necessarily extend to political questions. A Catholic might follow his priest's instructions to boycott a dirty movie but consult his own conscience in the voting booth. Catholic voters, remembering Roosevelt's ringing endorsement of Smith, needed no encouragement from their church to vote for FDR in 1932, nor did they turn against the president when their church's hierarchy bitterly opposed the new administration's recognition of the Soviet Union in 1933. Possibly because they were more likely to belong to unions than other Americans, Catholics remained the staunchest component of the New Deal coalition. Although Roosevelt had recognized the godless Soviets, he did, after all, stand on the side of American labor. Even on more distant matters like the Spanish Civil War, public opinion polls, then in their infancy, showed a considerable divergence between the well-known positions of the Catholic bishops and the views of the American laity. As Thomas C. Reeves points out in a fascinating recent biography of Fulton J. Sheen—arguably the most famous and most admired American Catholic of the twentieth century—American church leaders followed the lead of the Vatican in their unanimous and ardent support for Francisco Franco, whose forces were backed by Nazi Germany, and their condemnation of the Soviet-supported but democratically elected Loyalists in Spain. But a 1938 Gallup poll showed that only 39 percent of American Catholics were firmly in the Franco camp; another 30 percent supported the Loyalists, and the rest had no opinion.[2] The fact that nearly two-thirds of lay Catholics either disagreed with the church or were unsure casts considerable doubt on the belief that there was a "Catholic vote" for the hierarchy to command. Even in the fifties, when millions of Democrats deserted the party to vote for the overwhelmingly popular war hero Dwight D. Eisenhower, a plurality of Catholics would cast their votes for Adlai E. Stevenson (who, with his Unitarian freethought heritage and a divorce in his past, was hardly an exemplar of traditional Catholic values).[3]

The true importance of burgeoning Catholic influence in the thirties was not directly political but cultural in the broadest sense. In the first two decades of the century, supporters of women's rights, birth control, and civil liberties were often seen as antireligious, and in the thirties, those who opposed Catholic attempts to turn church teachings into public policy were frequently accused of anti-Catholicism. This tactic placed secularists on the defensive, especially since anti-Catholicism was long associated with the ugliest sort of nativism and with violations of the First Amendment. Nevertheless, the young American civil liberties movement was composed almost entirely of liberal Protestants, Jews, and those who professed no religion at all: there were almost no Catholic civil libertarians in the thirties. One notable exception, Monsignor John A. Ryan, was a member of the ACLU board and had worked closely with Baldwin on issues involving labor and the rights of conscientious objectors. The Minnesota-born Ryan, a sociologist as well as a priest, was a product of the Progressive Era, and he had helped write Minnesota's first minimum wage law. As the first director of the Social Action Department of the National Catholic Welfare Conference, Ryan was the author of a 1919 policy statement by the bishops that called for progressive social legislation establishing a minimum wage, child labor restrictions, and federally sponsored health and old age insurance—in other words, programs that would become the cornerstone of the New Deal. In the early thirties, Ryan was dubbed the "Right Reverend New Dealer." But the clerical New Dealer was also the church's chief lobbyist in Washington, and he resigned from the ACLU in 1934 over the organization's support of birth control. Forty years would pass before another Catholic priest, the Reverend Robert F. Drinan, would serve on the ACLU's national advisory committee.

On both birth control and censorship, the Catholic hierarchy was continuously at odds with secularists. The church's success at establishing its own values as the standard for the movie industry confounded civil libertarians because, as an official history of the ACLU points out, the First Amendment guarantees the same free speech rights to religious leaders that it does to all other Americans. It does not allow the government to impose censorship, but it does allow private entities like the movie industry to censor themselves. Thus, the ACLU was forced "to draw the line between two competing civil liberties principles." While the organization conceded that private, voluntary boycotts were protected by the First Amendment, it opposed all attempts to use the law to impose religious standards on the public as a whole.[4] Since extralegal pressure tactics often worked so well, the church understandably preferred them to court battles.

Book, magazine, and newspaper publishers, however, made up a decentralized industry and were therefore somewhat less susceptible to demands for self-censorship. Here the church adopted a different strategy—encouraging Catholic police officials to suppress indecent publications. The ACLU did go to court in these instances, though it never raised the issue of local officials' religious motivation and affiliation. Catholic pressure was largely responsible for the banning of the April 11, 1938, issue of *Life* magazine in several cities with large Catholic populations. What offended the vigilant churchmen was *Life*'s publication of thirty-five pictures from a U.S. public health film titled *Birth of a Baby*. In 1931, the Supreme Court, in the case of *Near v. Minnesota*, had established, for the first time, the crucial legal principle that the equal protection clause of the Fourteenth Amendment prohibits states from overruling First Amendment guarantees of free speech and free assembly. More than one hundred and forty years after James Madison first suggested that First Amendment guarantees should bind the states as well as the federal government, Chief Justice Charles Evans Hughes declared that "it is no longer open to doubt that the liberty of the press and of speech is within the liberties safeguarded by the due process clause of the Fourteenth Amendment from invasion by state action."[5] In the same decision, the Court ruled that prior restraint—censoring or suppressing printed material in advance of publication—was unconstitutional. Nevertheless, Boston police commissioner Joseph F. Timilty, a Catholic, pressured New England magazine distributors into refusing to deliver any publication not approved by his personally selected board of censors. Needless to say, the board considered the *Life* photographs obscene. The same issue was also banned in heavily Catholic Pennsylvania and in St. Louis, Chicago, and New Orleans—all cities with Catholic police officials. In New York, Morris Ernst, general counsel for the ACLU, won an acquittal of *Life* publisher Roy Larsen, who had been charged with obscenity—but Larsen's acquittal could not, of course, return that particular magazine issue to newsstands in other cities.

On birth control, the ACLU squared off against the church even more frequently. Throughout the thirties, Catholic leaders campaigned against birth control with greater aggressiveness than they had in the twenties. That was understandable, because birth control was gaining much wider public acceptance even though the church usually won in court and always won in a Congress that quaked in fear of the so-called Catholic vote. Between 1930 and 1940, largely as a result of the unremitting efforts of Sanger and the American Birth Control Federation (renamed Planned Parenthood in 1942), the number of birth control clinics rose from 34 to 549. Both the tone and intensity of the Catholic hierarchy's opposition to birth control in the thirties can be gleaned from congressional hearings on a 1931 bill, the first of many to be squelched in committee, that would have allowed doctors to import contraceptives. Ryan testified that such a bill would open the "floodgates" to other kinds of "pornographic" and "obscene" materials. Articulating a theme that would appear with increasing frequency, another Catholic witness described the bill as a Soviet plot to undermine the morality of Americans. The American Federation of Labor, with its large Catholic membership, testified against the bill at the urging of the Catholic Welfare Conference.[6] In 1936, the ubiquitous and overworked Ernst finally won a landmark case (*U.S. v. One Package of Japanese Pessaries*) allowing doctors to import contraceptives. (Because so many Comstock-era state laws prohibited the distribution of contraceptives, manufacturing birth control devices was unprofitable in the United States.) It was the church's teaching on birth control—not censorship or communism—that finally erected an unbreachable barrier between civil libertarians and even the most socially liberal Catholics like Ryan. The barrier would not begin to crumble until that great soul Pope John XXIII ushered in a new era of *aggiornamento* and ecumenicism that began when he was elevated to the papacy in 1958 and was cut short by his death in 1965.

The church's labeling of birth control as a communist conspiracy, like the Protestant fundamentalists' linkage of evolutionism with bolshevism, was the product of a profoundly antimodernist mindset. But the American church's active commitment to anticommunism—a reflection of the Vatican's international stance—would prove to be unprecedented both in its duration and its influence throughout American society. Catholic opposition to "godless communism," disseminated throughout the tumultuous thirties to radio audiences of millions, laid the groundwork for increasing church influence that would reach the highest levels of government during the Cold War era. Moreover, the church's anticommunism, shared by large numbers of Americans of various religions, helped erode the longtime Protestant suspicion of Catholics—a slow cultural shift that began in the thirties and reached its conclusion with the election of John F. Kennedy as president in 1960. The equation of communism with atheism and anti-Americanism made the church itself seem more American to non-Catholics—at least to a fair number of Protestant non-Catholics. That equation also made Catholics seem more American *to themselves.* "In fighting the red peril," David O'Brien, a Catholic historian, observes, "the Catholic could dedicate himself to action which was both Catholic and American. Few would disagree that he was proving his worth as an American and demonstrating the compatibility of faith and patriotism."[7] As the bubble prosperity of the twenties gave way to a worldwide depression, bringing ominous news of political oppression and rumors of war from Europe, the American Catholic Church played a critical role in melding political with religious anticommunism. American Catholics, from cardinals on down, would become to grassroots anticommunism as evangelical Protestants had been to the American temperance movement.

Two priests, Fulton Sheen and Charles E. Coughlin, carried the anticommunist message of American Catholicism to millions of their non-Catholic countrymen as well as to their coreligionists.

Coughlin, an unknown parish priest in Detroit, made his radio debut on October 17, 1926. Four years later, with his first appearance on a program called *The Catholic Hour*, Sheen became the second priest—albeit with a very different, more spiritually focused message—to tap into an audience whose size offered an unprecedented opportunity for the mass marketing of both religion and anticommunism. Coughlin, dubbed "the father of hate radio" by a recent biographer, was destined to rise no higher in the church than the priesthood: his early populist message of Christian justice for the working man turned in the thirties into an anti–New Deal, pro-Nazi, and anti-Semitic—as well as anticommunist—platform.[8] Coughlin's diatribes were tolerated by Vatican officials and encouraged by his bishop for much of the thirties, but he was finally muzzled by an embarrassed hierarchy after Pearl Harbor. Sheen, by contrast, would die an archbishop and one of the most admired men in America, after making a smooth transition in 1952 from radio to his own television show, *Life Is Worth Living*. Sheen was everything Coughlin was not—well-educated, polished, able to fit not only in the wealthiest American Catholic circles but also in the WASP eastern establishment that Coughlin detested.

Born in 1896 in the small town of El Paso, Illinois, Sheen showed early academic promise, becoming the valedictorian of his Catholic high school class in nearby Peoria. He also earned a bachelor's degree from a four-year college before entering the seminary at age twenty-one (at a time when many Catholic boys began studying for the priesthood in their teens). Although raised by Catholic parents, Sheen came from an extended family whose relationship to Catholicism was anything but simple and straightforward. Some of his Irish immigrant ancestors had cut their ties with the church in the new world, married

Protestants, and even associated themselves with the freethought movement. Indeed, Sheen's father, Newt, joined the church only when he married Sheen's devoutly Catholic mother. Newt's first wife, a Protestant, had died after giving birth to a daughter—and the daughter was raised by her Protestant grandparents. The fact that the archbishop had a Protestant half sister became a closely guarded family secret. According to his biographer, Sheen never mentioned his half sister in public. One apostate family member, Sheen's great-uncle, Daniel, had been a partner in Robert Ingersoll's Peoria law firm. The historical irony was not lost on the nation's most admired twentieth-century Catholic cleric, who acknowledged that his black-sheep uncle had not been a Catholic. But Archbishop Sheen also insisted that the Great Agnostic's law partner had not gone so far as to embrace agnosticism.[9]

Coughlin and Sheen are rarely linked by historians, because Coughlin's direct involvement in politics, coupled with his unabashed fascist sympathies, marked him indelibly as a creature—a frightening creature to his liberal contemporaries—of the thirties and its fierce ideological and economic struggles. Sheen, by virtue of his stature as a television personality, is remembered as a man of the fifties and primarily as a religious presence—not as the anticommunist polemicist he was in the thirties. But the two belong together—and not only because of their common anticommunism. Sheen and Coughlin were the first members of the American clergy to combine the power of their status as men of the cloth with the full power of a new medium of communication. By doing so, they conferred a religious imprimatur on what was essentially a social agenda, blazing a trail for Protestant evangelicals, like Billy Graham, who would rise to prominence after the war as well as for the more recent electronic spokesmen of the Christian far right. Sheen, with his polish and spirituality, posed a much greater problem for secularist critics than Coughlin. It is more difficult to challenge the political ideas of a charismatic priest who also promises "peace of soul" and "the fulfillment of Christ" than it is to attack the ideas of one who uses the radio pulpit to praise

Hitler and fascism and to attack Jews and the president of the United States. Sheen himself was very cautious when asked to comment on Coughlin, though he did tell interviewers that there was "no conflict" between their radio messages. The main difference, he said in 1936, was that "Father Coughlin chooses to confine himself largely to the material. My sermons are confined to spiritual values."[10]

Certainly no one represented hard-line Catholic anticommunism more passionately and intemperately than Coughlin, who did not hesitate to criticize bishops and cardinals, as well as liberal politicians. Coughlin showed his true colors when he managed to achieve a modus vivendi in Detroit with the kind of right-wing fundamentalists who had made life hell on the campaign trail for Smith. The Ku Klux Klan, which had a considerable following in southeastern Michigan, initially objected to Coughlin's broadcasts, but he won them over when he joined a Klan funeral procession that was wending its way to the cemetery past his Shrine of the Little Flower. In 1970, the aging Coughlin would recall that "it was pouring rain and Woodward Avenue had turned to mud. I went out and walked with them [the Klan] at the head of the procession and helped them conduct their memorial service. After that we got along fine."[11] In 1930, Coughlin launched his first all-out attacks on bolshevism and socialism—which he, like many other Americans, considered indistinguishable. With the radio delivery of a sermon titled "Christ and the Red Fog," he was off and running, metamorphosing from a local into a national radio personality. Coughlin was nearly twenty years ahead of Joseph McCarthy in singling out individual university professors and public officials for "communistic" and "socialistic" leanings. By the end of the year, his show was so popular that it was picked up by the CBS radio network, with its audience of more than forty million. He soon launched a magazine, *Social Justice*, that followed the same political line as his radio broadcasts. Initially, the church hierarchy was so pleased by the response to Coughlin that the bishop of Detroit provided him with two priest assistants so that his duties as a pastor would not prevent him from fulfilling his responsibilities as a radio personality. Even after Coughlin became an outright fascist, having nothing but good to say about both Mussolini and Hitler, the church did not exercise its authority—the absolute authority it possessed and still possesses over every priest—to squelch him. Coughlin called the President "Franklin Double-crossing Roosevelt" and excoriated him as a "liar" and "betrayer" supported by communists, but still the church hierarchy did not act.[12]

Only after Pearl Harbor, when the United States entered the war as an ally of the evil atheistic Soviet communists, did Coughlin's ecclesiastical superiors put an end to his political writings and speeches. The church had a great deal to lose by allowing Coughlin to carry on with statements most Americans would have considered traitorous. Roosevelt had pleased American Catholics and angered civil libertarians by sending a personal envoy, Myron C. Taylor, to the Vatican. FDR had also appointed New York's Archbishop (and future Cardinal) Francis J. Spellman, the best-known Catholic prelate in the nation, military vicar of the U.S. armed forces. (One can only imagine what Jefferson and Madison would have had to say about the appointment of a "military vicar" to look after the spiritual welfare of the secular American army.) That Coughlin's *Social Justice* continued to publish until the spring of 1942 was, ironically, a tribute to the success of the ACLU in broadening the limits of free speech even during wartime. During the First World War, Coughlin would almost certainly have been jailed for the antiwar and antigovernment statements he published repeatedly. On March 16, 1942, he wrote: "We are becoming more and more convinced that the radicals who have seized our Federal Government care not one whit about driving Hitler from the face of the earth."[13] Roosevelt let it be known to Catholic authorities, through a close friend with high ecclesiastical connections, that if the church would not use its power to silence Coughlin, he would be prosecuted and his magazine shut down. On May 1, 1942, Archbishop Edward Mooney of Detroit gave Coughlin the choice of ceasing his nonreligious activities or being defrocked.[14] It is worth recalling, though, that the church silenced Coughlin only when faced by the wartime president with the threat of a public scandal. Astonishingly, Coughlin had gone unrebuked when he declared, as reported in the *Washington Post*, that "we are going to lose this war eventually. . . . I regarded Marxism as the parent of both Nazism and Communism. . . . Joseph Stalin is the father of pornographic literature in this country. He is the father of disruption on the campuses of this country, . . . he is the father of the the turmoil we are suffering."[15] That a normally cautious hierarchy— one that had, out of expediency, become as adept at operating within democracies as it had been within Catholic theocracies—would allow one of its priests to make such provocative, near-treasonous statements was a measure of the depth and tunnel vision of the church's anticommunism.

The cleric who carried the respectable mainstream anticommunist banner for American Catholicism was, of course, Fulton Sheen. By 1940, Sheen's *Catholic Hour* was broadcast over 106 radio stations. The National Council of Catholic Men, which sponsored the program, had mailed out 1.75 million copies of his radio talks, and Sheen received between 3,000 and 6,000 letters every day.[16] Unlike Coughlin, Sheen was an ornament to the church—an emissary to non-Catholics on radio and later on television, a close friend of J. Edgar Hoover, who promoted many Catholics to high positions in the FBI, and an effective proselytizer who snagged such high-profile converts as Clare Boothe Luce, the world-renowned violinist Fritz Kreisler, and Henry Ford II. (Ford's grandfather, as notoriously anti-Catholic as anti-Semitic, was said to have thought of disinheriting Henry II for converting before his marriage to Catholic socialite Anne McDonnell.) While Coughlin had appealed to the radically discontented, Sheen reached out to mainstream Americans of all faiths with his homilies on everything from the Virgin Mary to the evils of communism. Unlike Coughlin, Sheen gave many more talks on strictly religious subjects than on social issues—but that only strengthened the moral authority of his political preaching. Also unlike Coughlin, Sheen balanced his attacks on communism with criticism of fascism (though when it came to a battle between communism and fascism, as in the Spanish Civil War, Sheen was always on the side of the fascists).

But there is no question that Sheen's anticommunism was every bit as intense as Coughlin's. In September 1935, the up-and-coming Sheen told an audience of more than forty thousand in Cleveland:

> In the future there will be only two great capitals in the world: Rome and Moscow; only two temples, the Kremlin and St. Peter's; only two tabernacles, the Red Square and the Eucharist; only two hosts, the rotted body of Lenin and Christ Emmanuel; only two hymns, the Internationale and the Panis Angelicus—but there will be only one victory—if Christ wins, we win, and Christ cannot lose.[17]

As befitted a close friend of Hoover, Sheen supported early efforts to identify communist subversives—the precursor of the McCarthy-era blacklists. At a 1939 Communion breakfast for New York's Catholic elementary and secondary school teachers, Sheen delivered a speech that made no attempt to disguise his contempt for those who would impede the fight against communism with concern for civil liberties. He proposed the establishment of a "central clearing house" to which Jewish, Catholic, and Protestant teachers would be urged to forward "the names of any teacher who sends out their [*sic*] children to a Communist parade, or who turns over their classrooms to some member of a Communist organization, or a Nazi or Fascist organization." Sheen went on to express the opinion that any school teacher, "I care not whether she be Catholic, Jewish, or Protestant, who cooperates with any one of Stalin's agents, who sends children out of school to the next May Day parade, should thereby be considered ineligible to teach in American schools." Finally, Sheen advised his audience to "just watch the parade" in an effort to recognize children known to be students of communist-leaning teachers.[18] At the time of Sheen's speech, many American leftists—not only communists—still celebrated international labor day on May 1, rather than on the traditional American September holiday. There certainly were a fair number of political leftists among New York public school teachers, though it seems doubtful that any teacher would have independently ordered his or her students to skip classes to attend a May Day parade. In New York City, Sheen and his powerful boss, Spellman, commanded enormous deference from the city's non-Catholic business and civic establishment; the *Times* published a news story on Sheen's speech urging teachers to spy on one another but made no editorial comment.

Sheen also made an important contribution to the long-term pollution of American political dialogue, and to the demonization of secularism, by defining a liberal as the opposite of a reactionary. "Just as the reactionary defines every progressive movement as communistic," Sheen declared, "so, too, a liberal is one who brands every civilizing influence in civilization as fascist."[19] The antonymic pairing of "liberal" with "reactionary" is the work of a master propagandist; the analogy works only if one is prepared to accept the definition of a liberal as a person who rejects "every civilizing influence in civilization." Prominent among those civilizing influences were religion in general and Catholicism in particular. Sheen's observation is particularly telling because it was delivered during a period of American history when many Americans were proud to call themselves liberals; being a liberal meant being in favor of unions, the newly established Social Security program, and the idea that government could do good in society. Sheen might be considered a premature antiliberal—someone who pinned the extremist label on liberals fifty years before the New Right succeeded in cowing liberal Democrats into forsaking the L-word and hiding behind the wishy-washy "moderate."

One religious group that was profoundly alarmed by the Catholic attack on "Reds," and the equation of political radicalism with atheism, was the American Jewish community. Jews were sensitive in ways that other Americans were not to the anti-Semitism that emanated then from the highest levels of the Vatican, but the American Jewish distrust of the American church was also rooted in domestic politics.[20] Jews were a much smaller American religious minority than Catholics, and any challenge to the secularist basis of the American government was perceived as threatening to the rare and hard-won Jewish sense of security in a land where Christians were in the overwhelming majority. Jews, who did not then seek any tax support for their own religious schools, opposed Catholic attempts to obtain tax money, whether directly or indirectly, for the maintenance of parochial schools. The church's attacks on Reds were perceived as especially threatening because Jews were in fact represented on the American political left out of proportion to their numbers in the population. During the Red Scare, a large percentage of the arrested immigrants were Jews, and Jewish lawyers played an important role in civil libertarian attempts to have the Palmer-era convictions overturned. During the thirties, Jewish civil liberties lawyers were also in the forefront of efforts to defend the First Amendment rights of socialists, communists, and even Nazi sympathizers. On virtually every issue, Jews—whether observant or secular—lined up against the church. But no issue, including birth control, was more important to Jews than the continuing Catholic denigration of America's public schools.

If Catholic anticommunism made the church seem more American, the hierarchy's unrelenting hostility to public education kept alive both Jewish and Protestant suspicions of the Catholic relationship to traditional American values. In 1937, a pamphlet by Paul L. Blakely, S.J., an editor of the prominent Jesuit magazine *America*, appeared under the provocative title "May an American Oppose the Public School?" Blakely's answer, published under the imprimatur of New York's Cardinal Hayes, was a resounding yes. "Our first duty to the public school is not to pay taxes for its maintenance," he argued. "We pay that tax under protest; not because we admit an obligation in justice." The main obligation of every Catholic father toward the public school, he added acidly, was "to keep his children out of it." Blakely dismissed the notion that public education was a traditional American institution, noting that not "a single American who signed the Declaration of Independence, or fought in the Revolution, or sat at Philadelphia to draw up the Constitution, had ever been in a public school."[21] By that logic, it might also be argued that the Constitution was a bad idea because not a single one of its framers grew up under a constitutional government. It should be noted that on this issue, as on many other social questions, the Catholic laity did not necessarily agree with its priests, bishops, or Pope Pius XI, who had declared on many occasions that Catholics could not possibly support any school system, anywhere in the world, that did not provide religious instruction. By the thirties, when many American Catholics were only a generation or two removed from their immigrant roots, roughly half of all Catholic children attended public rather than parochial schools. The main reason, of course, was that parochial schools charged tuition and public schools did not. But there were other elements in the rejection of parochial schools by a substantial proportion of Catholics. Parochial schools, like the American church itself in the thirties, were staffed almost entirely by Irish American nuns and supervised by Irish American parish priests. Italian American Catholics resented the Irish domination of the American church, and many treated the church as the bestower of baptisms, weddings, and funerals but not as the moral arbiter of everyday life. Also, members of the educated Catholic upper middle class and the wealthy Catholic elite increasingly pursued upward mobility by sending their children to public or non-Catholic private schools. Joseph P. Kennedy, before enrolling his sons at prestigious Choate, sent them not to Boston parochial schools but to a neighborhood public school and then to nonsectarian private schools. For his sons to succeed in the non-Catholic world, Kennedy felt that they must be educated in non-Catholic institutions. (That he sent his daughters to Catholic schools reflected his different expectations for girls, who were to be educated only to become good Catholic wives and mothers.) Much of the hierarchy's animus toward public schools was surely rooted in the knowledge that American public education provided an attractive, free, maddeningly accessible alternative for Catholic parents who, for whatever reason, wanted secular rather than religious schooling for their children. To add insult to injury, Catholics themselves were being taxed to support the secularist schools that their bishops detested.

In spite of the nineteenth-century Blaine amendments prohibiting tax support of parochial schools in many states, the church had never stopped trying to obtain government funds, by the back door if not the front, for its school programs. During the New Deal, both states and the federal government inaugurated a wide variety of welfare programs, and these provided a wedge for the Catholic leadership to reopen an issue that seemed to have been settled a century earlier. While there was no direct federal aid to education until 1965, Catholic schools were eligible to participate in the New Deal school lunch program administered by the U.S. Department of Agriculture. In many instances, free textbooks and school bus transportation were also offered to Catholic school pupils. These forms of indirect aid would be cited as precedents after the war, when church officials made the case (at the time, unsuccessfully) that Catholic education served an important public as well as religious function and should therefore be eligible for government aid. The same argument has gained much more widespread public acceptance today, and it is made not only by Catholics but by all religious leaders who stake their claim to eligibility for public funds on grounds that their sectarian institutions also carry out a larger public mission. In the thirties and forties, though, secularist groups did not hesitate to point out that the religious activities of what today would be called "faith-based institutions" might and often did run counter to public purposes.

The battle between secularists and Catholic leaders over taxpayer support for religious institutions would not be fully joined until after the war, when the return of prosperity brought about an unprecedented expansion of health, education, and welfare programs at all levels of government. In the late thirties and throughout the war years, conflicts between religion and government fell within the traditional domain envisaged by the framers of the Constitution— attempts by the state to encroach on the consciences of those who adhered to unpopular minority faiths. As always, in one of the great and enduring ironies of American history, secularists stood in the forefront of efforts to uphold the constitutional rights of disdained religious minorities.

As Americans edged away from isolationism and began to see that their country's future was tied to the survival of the democratic states of Europe, the possibility of another war took on an increasing reality. It was inevitable that this shift in sentiment would produce a resurgence of demands for patriotic conformity, and pacifist religious minorities bore the brunt of those demands. The Jehovah's Witnesses, a growing, aggressively proselytizing sect that had managed to elicit outright hatred from large numbers of Americans belonging to mainstream religions, resisted participation in nearly all acts of symbolic allegiance to secular government. By the mid-thirties, the Witnesses were on the very short list of religious believers whose reputation in America was even lower than that of atheists. Nevertheless, the sect gained American converts during a decade when the Depression seemed like the end of the world to many who had lost their livelihoods. The Witnesses adhered to the apocalyptic visions laid out in the Book of Revelation, in which Armageddon was thought to be drawing near and only 144,000 people—Witnesses, naturally—were expected to be saved. Like many religious cults foolish enough to set a date for Armageddon, the Witnesses have had to constantly revise their forecasts. Much of the public antagonism to the Witnesses was generated by their proselytizing tactics; they accosted prospective converts on street corners and subjected entire communities to door-to-door, in-your-face harangues. They engaged in both anti-Semitic and anti-Catholic propaganda and—most damningly in the eyes of their fellow citizens of every faith—refused to salute the flag. For the Witnesses, any acknowledgment of the flag constituted a violation of the biblical prohibition against worshiping graven images. Witness children were taught not to recite the Pledge of Allegiance—a morning ritual in most American public schools—and many were already being expelled from schools long before the war. After Pearl Harbor, the Witnesses' stubborn resistance to flag ceremonies was seen by many as treasonous.

No one could have anticipated the mischief that would eventually be generated by the pledge when it was written in 1892, at the behest of the National Education Association, as an exercise designed to highlight the unity of children from many lands enrolled in American public schools. The author was Francis Bellamy, a member of the short-lived Christian Socialist movement. Bellamy, a former Baptist

minister, had been driven from his Boston pulpit for preaching against
the evils of capitalism (a biographical note never mentioned by right-
wing pledge worshipers today). As a Baptist and a socialist, Bellamy
believed in absolute separation of church and state: he would surely
have been horrified by the addition of "under God" to the pledge in
1954, at the height of the McCarthy era. The pledge was intended as a
straightforward statement of the American public school system's
commitment to assimilation of all immigrants—"one nation, indivisible, with liberty and justice for all." It was recited primarily in public
schools until the First World War, when Catholic educators, originally suspicious of the pledge's secular intent, decided that the words,
even without a nod to the deity, could do no harm and would help
demonstrate the Americanism of American Catholics. Well before the
Second World War, many states had passed laws requiring recitation
of the pledge in public schools. After Pearl Harbor, Congress got into
the act by codifying rules governing civilian display of the flag, and by
including the pledge in the display ceremony for the first time. The
new code replaced a rigid one-armed salute, first prescribed by Bellamy in his magazine, *The Youth's Companion*, with the now familiar
hand-on-heart posture. The old gesture, to a public by then all too
familiar with images of goose-stepping, straight-armed Nazis, looked
too much like the "Heil Hitler" salute.

Wartime patriotism did not change the attitude of the American
Witnesses, whose German counterparts were being sent to concentra-
tion camps for refusing to salute the swastika. Believers willing to
defy the Gestapo in defense of their faith were hardly likely to quail
before the demands of local American school boards, but the price for
students who acted on their faith was expulsion. The Supreme Court
took up the issue of compulsory pledge recitation for the first time in
1940, after school officials in Minersville, Pennsylvania, expelled
twelve-year-old Lillian Gobitis and her ten-year-old brother, William,
for refusing to salute the flag. In an 8–1 decision, the Court upheld the
school board. The *Gobitis* decision not only led to the expulsion of
more than two thousand Witness children from public schools in the
next two years but also was associated with a wave of mob violence

against the Witnesses. In Litchfield, Connecticut, usually a bastion of New England propriety, a mob assaulted approximately sixty Witnesses who had gathered on the town common to distribute their literature. In Nebraska, a Witness was castrated. Throughout the South, Witnesses were tarred and feathered. Between 1940 and 1942, an ACLU report detailed violent attacks on Witnesses in 355 local communities and forty-four states.[22]

In 1943, the Supreme Court—many of its members appalled by the wave of violence that had followed the *Gobitis* decision—took up a second flag case. This time, in *West Virginia Board of Education v. Barnette*, the Court reversed itself and struck down the state's pledge recitation requirement as a violation of the First Amendment's establishment clause. In an opinion all the more memorable because it was delivered in wartime, Justice Robert H. Jackson, who later became the chief American prosecutor at the Nuremberg war crimes trials, declared that "if there is any fixed star in our constellation, it is that no official, high or petty, can prescribe what shall be orthodox in politics, nationalism, religion, or other matters of opinion or force citizens to confess by word or act their faith therein." Justice Harlan Stone, the only dissenter from the majority opinion in the *Gobitis* case, had been strongly influenced by his experience during the First World War as a government-appointed investigator of conscientious objector claims. "It may well be questioned," he had written in 1919 after speaking with hundreds of conscientious objectors, "whether the state which preserves its life by a settled policy of violation of the conscience of the individual will not in fact ultimately lose it by the process."[23]

The importance of the *Barnette* decision cannot be overstated, not only because it barred the state from compelling displays of loyalty that violated religious belief but because it was based on the rights of individuals rather than on the privileges of religious institutions. Jackson's logic could and would be used to prevent schools from compelling Jewish children to participate in nondenominational Christian rituals; it would also be invoked in defense of the individual consciences of atheists as well as believers in minority religions.

Saluting the flag and pledging allegiance were purely symbolic acts, yet individuals risked violent reprisals if they refused to carry out the rituals. Conscientious objection, a morally based position with real consequences in a wartime society, might have been expected to provoke even more repressive responses from both the government and angry citizens. Yet the Roosevelt administration's policy on conscientious objectors, paralleling its willingness to tolerate a good deal of free speech even in wartime, was much less harsh than the Wilson administration's policies had been. There were many more conscientious objectors in the Second than in the First World War—a somewhat surprising development in that the war against Japan and Nazi Germany commanded much broader support from the American public than the earlier war against the kaiser's Germany. Part of the explanation was the oversight of an organized civil liberties movement that had not existed at the beginning of the First World War. The growth of the ubiquitous Witnesses was also a factor: Witness "lay ministers" accounted for nearly two-thirds of the 6,086 men jailed for refusing to serve even in noncombatant roles.[24] Many more conscientious objectors, from the traditionally pacifist Quaker and Mennonite denominations, agreed to serve their country in a nonmilitary capacity. Approximately 12,000 conscientious objectors worked in public-service camps run by the government with administrative aid from representatives of the leading pacifist sects (a collaboration considered a betrayal by absolutist objectors). Significantly, the wartime law signed by Roosevelt did not allow atheists or agnostics to claim conscientious objector status: pacifism had legal standing only if invoked in the name of God.

All of the nation's mainstream religions strongly endorsed the war effort, and none wished to identify themselves with loathed groups like the Witnesses. The attitude of American Catholics had changed dramatically since the First World War, when many German American and Irish American Catholics greeted America's entry into the war on the side of England with attitudes ranging from indifference to outright rebellion. Another generation of Americanization had done its work: the immigrant past, with its hatred between Irish Catholics and English

Protestants, meant nothing compared with the threat posed by the Axis powers. Catholics enlisted in the military in numbers higher than their proportion in the general American population, and church leaders, most notably New York's Spellman, demonstrated a firm commitment to American military action that would last through the Vietnam War. Spellman, a personal friend of Roosevelt's, had played a key role in the president's 1939 decision to send a personal emissary, over the objections of civil libertarians, to the Vatican. During the war, Spellman visited American troops so many times (often with a stopover at the Vatican to convey a message from Roosevelt to Spellman's mentor, Pius XII) that he became the best-known American church leader of any faith. The church's strong support of the American war effort was closely connected to its anticommunism; the fact that the Soviet Union was also fighting the Nazis made it all the more imperative, in the view of Catholic leaders, for the United States to prevent the Soviets from occupying European Catholic states. Not surprisingly, Spellman became deeply disillusioned with the president after the March 1945 Yalta Conference, where Roosevelt, Churchill, and Stalin laid out a formula for the United Nations—and where the United States and Britain basically agreed that the Russians, who already occupied Warsaw and had installed a communist government there, would shape the postwar government of Poland. (The details of the Yalta and Potsdam agreements are beyond the scope of this book, but the belief that the Democrats "gave away" eastern Europe to the Soviets has been a right-wing mantra since 1945. Many historians have argued that Roosevelt and Harry Truman could have done nothing else, in view of the fact that Soviet troops already occupied much of eastern Europe.)[25] U.S. acquiescence to communist control of Poland—the most devoutly Catholic country in Europe—was seen by the Catholic hierarchy as a blow and a betrayal. As Sheen's 1939 speech urging schoolteachers to ferret out communist colleagues demonstrated, the church hierarchy had been primed before the war to support any government hunt for subversives. After Yalta, the anticommunist predilections of leading American churchmen hardened into implacable opposition to anyone who tried to defend the First Amendment rights of American communists and other leftists. The church leadership would encourage the anticommunist passions of the McCarthy era and would, at every turn, insist on the linkage between communism and atheism. A new generation of fiery Protestant evangelicals, beginning with Billy Graham, would take up the same theme in the postwar years.

The public's acceptance of the idea that communism and atheism were inseparable evils was not really altered by America's wartime alliance with the Soviet Union. The use of mass communications media to preach the gospel of Christian anticommunism had strongly reinforced the free-floating warnings, promulgated by American religious conservatives since the 1790s, against the dangerous duo of religious infidelity and political radicalism. On the right, Enlightenment bashers were only too ready to place the responsibility for communism (and even Nazism) at the door of the violent French Revolution, while ignoring the Enlightenment beliefs of so many of the men who made the American Revolution. But the denigration of the Enlightenment did not come only from the right in an age of "ism"s. Many American leftists ridiculed Enlightenment-revering liberals as relics of a naive and overly idealistic age (although that naiveté and idealism, translated into law, provided the only recourse for political dissidents, including those on the extreme left, whose civil liberties had been violated). With the death of Clarence Darrow in 1938, American public life lost the last well-known secularist crusader who stood squarely in the Enlightenment freethought tradition of Thomas Paine and Robert Ingersoll. It would have taken an Ingersoll to hold his own against an impassioned clerical orator like Sheen and to make the case that Soviet-style communism, far from being the antithesis of religion, was merely a new form of blind faith, based not on the laws of nature but on the substitution of nonrational political dogma for nonrational religious dogma. The muting of the once-robust American dialogue between secularism and religion would set the stage for the postwar emergence of a civil faith that appropriated the language of patriotism, employed the tools of mass marketing, and realized the vision first set forth by the religious hucksters of the Roaring Twenties.

The Best Years of Our Lives

The prosperous Pax Americana between the end of the Second World War and the 1960 election of John Fitzgerald Kennedy was marked by a public religiosity that would not be outdone until the beginning of the next century, when George W. Bush would cite Jesus as his chief political adviser and begin his cabinet meetings with a prayer. Yet the postwar era was also characterized by a steady erosion of the power of church-supported cultural censorship as well as by a series of court decisions strengthening separation of church and state—two developments that cheered secularist civil libertarians but also reenergized religious conservatives.

Soon after the war, two cases—*Everson v. Board of Education* (1947) and *McCollum v. Illinois* (1948)—broke new ground by redefining the scope of the establishment clause of the First Amendment and making it more difficult to use tax money, directly or indirectly, for religious instruction. In *Everson*, the Supreme Court upheld, on narrow grounds, a New Jersey law that provided bus transportation for both public and parochial school students. But Justice Hugo Black wrote a memorable sentence in his majority opinion that provided a solid basis for opposition to a broadening of such subsidies in the future. "The First Amendment has erected a wall between church and state," he declared. "That wall must be kept high and impregnable."[1] The Court decided that transportation did not breach the wall of separation because the money did not go directly to religious schools.

A year later, in the *McCollum* case, the high court struck down an Illinois law allowing "released time" for religious teaching in public schools. In Champaign, Illinois, children had been released from regular classes for religious instruction to be delivered by Protestant, Catholic, and Jewish—though few rabbis participated—clergy. The religion classes were held in public school buildings, and parents who did not want their children to receive religious teaching could supposedly opt for a "secular" class during the released-time period. In fact, there was no secular instruction, because 99 percent of parents signed consent forms for their children to attend the religion classes. The plaintiff, Vashti McCollum, one of the few parents who did not sign, argued that her son had been cruelly taunted by other students for his nonattendance at religion classes. McCollum, the wife of a horticulture professor at the University of Illinois, came from a liberal Protestant background and described herself as a humanist, but she was labeled "the Atheist Mother" in countless newspaper headlines. (McCollum was named for Vashti, the first wife of King Ahasuerus in the Book of Esther. It is often forgotten that Esther, the Jewish heroine, was able to replace her predecessor only because Vashti had angered her husband by refusing to exhibit her charms before his drunken companions at a feast. McCollum's mother had chosen the name, she explained to her daughter, because the biblical Vashti was the first advocate of women's rights.) After the twentieth-century Vashti filed her lawsuit, her son was regularly beaten up, and his parents eventually had to send him out of town to a private school. In an unusual memoir describing the daily price paid by an individual plaintiff in an unpopular cause, McCollum quoted from the hate mail that she and her husband received for many years. A typical missive declared, "You would look so cute without an eye to offend you and without a tongue to offend me and mine. . . . We will make some lovely incisions in your filthy bellies and pull out those nervy Guts one by one, slow and easy. Just like the awful treatment you worldly ones have meted out to us generation after generation."[2] The contempt with which outspoken secularist dissidents like McCollum are treated by the religiously correct is evident today even in such distinguished scholarly works as the University of Chicago professor Martin E. Marty's massive history of American religion (its most recent volume published in 1996). To Marty, McCollum was nothing more than a discontented woman who had refused attempts by Champaign school authorities to "accommodate dissent like hers and also be attentive to the sensibilities of the larger public that wanted religion." But, Marty declares, "nothing satisfied Mrs. McCollum or the American Civil Liberties Committee," who "somehow worked the case up to the United States Supreme Court." *Somehow?* Is the use of public school facilities for religious teaching, and the ostracism of children who do not conform to the majority, an insignificant constitutional issue? Marty goes on to describe McCollum as a "militant person who took pleasure in being branded 'a wicked, godless woman, an emissary of Satan, a Communist and a fiend in human form,' just as she was being hailed by others as 'a courageous heroine, a champion of American liberty, a true pioneer, democrat, and patriot.' "[3] This passage provides an exemplary insight into the delegitimization, if not the outright demonization, of American secularism: to portray atheists and freethinkers as militant chronic troublemakers and publicity hounds is to trivialize the issues they raise.

In its 1948 decision, the Supreme Court took a very different view of McCollum's case. Justice Black, again writing the majority opinion, declared that the Champaign released-time program was a clear violation of the separation standard articulated in *Everson*. He emphasized the powerful pressure on schoolchildren to conform to the behavior advocated by their teachers and practiced by their peers:

> Religious education so conducted on school time and property is patently woven into the working scheme of the school. The Champaign arrangement thus presents powerful elements of inherent

pressure by the school system in the interest of religious sects. The fact that this power has not been used to discriminate is beside the point. Separation is a requirement to abstain from fusing functions of Government and of religious sects, not merely to treat them all equally. That a child is offered an alternative may reduce the constraint; it does not eliminate the operation of influence by the school in matters sacred to conscience and outside the school's domain. The law of imitation operates, and nonconformity is not an outstanding characteristic of children. . . . Again, while the Champaign school population represents only a fraction of the more than two hundred and fifty sects of the nation, not even all the practicing sects in Champaign are willing or able to provide religious instruction. The children belonging to these nonparticipating sects will thus have inculcated in them a feeling of separatism when the school should be the training ground for habits of community, or they will have religious instruction in a faith which is not that of their parents. As a result, the public school system of Champaign actively furthers inculcation in the religious tenets of some faiths, and in the process sharpens the consciousness of religious differences at least among some of the children committed to its care. These are consequences not amenable to statistics. But they are precisely the consequences against which the Constitution was directed when it prohibited the Government common to all from becoming embroiled, however innocently, in the destructive religious conflicts of which the history of even this country records some dark pages.

Thus, Black concluded, "Separation means separation, not something less. Jefferson's metaphor in describing the relation between Church and State speaks of a 'wall of separation,' not of a fine line easily overstepped. . . . In no activity of the State is it more vital to keep out divisive forces than in its schools, to avoid confusing, not to say fusing, what the Constitution sought to keep strictly apart. . . . It is the Court's duty to enforce this principle in its full integrity."[4]

Throughout the forties and fifties, even the staunchest civil libertarians were divided between "accommodationists"—those who believed that the First Amendment allowed some role for religion in public institutions—and strict separationists, who argued that the establishment clause prohibited both governmental support for and governmental intrusion on religion. *Everson* was an accommodation-ist decision, while *McCollum* moved the court toward a more strict separationist stance. Because it turned on tax reimbursement that chiefly benefited Catholic schools, *Everson* galvanized both Protes-tant and Jewish support for a firmer separationist position. Protes-tants and Other Americans United for Separation of Church and State was founded in 1948; the organization consisted primarily of main-stream to liberal Protestants, but it also had support from some theo-logically conservative Baptists whose suspicion of any government involvement with religion dated from the eighteenth century. (The group has long since lost its Protestant identity and is now Americans United for Separation of Church and State.)

The position of American Jews—particularly official Jewish organizations—regarding establishment clause cases was complicated by postwar fears of a resurgence of the anti-Semitism that had impelled the U.S. government to close its doors to Jewish refugees in the thirties. On the one hand, Jews did not wish to be seen as anti-Christian. On the other, Jews opposed policies—released time for religious instruction being the prime example—that inevitably singled out their children as members of a non-Christian minority. The American Jewish Congress took a strong separationist position, cooperating with the ACLU on many church-state cases, while the American Jewish Committee and the B'nai B'rith Anti-Defamation League, umbrella organizations that represented the Jewish establish-ment, took a more timid posture. Leo Pfeffer, a staff member of the Jewish Congress, became one of the leading authorities on the estab-lishment clause, writing many Supreme Court briefs and, in 1953, producing a massive history, *Church, State, and Freedom*, that remains the bible of American church-state legal issues from the revo-lutionary period through the first half of the twentieth century. Not only mainstream Jewish organizations but the ACLU itself feared that separation of church and state would become identified with anti-Christianity—and that did indeed happen. That so many ACLU attorneys were Jews, and that Jews were more often than not the plaintiffs in challenges to Christian ceremonies in schools, occasioned regular hostile comment in right-wing publications. In Champaign, McCollum had found that while the town's small Jewish community strongly opposed released-time instruction, no Jew was willing to support her case in public. One Jewish father, whose son had been beaten up after his parents refused to sign the consent form for religious instruction, was greeted by an antagonistic crowd at his store after it became known that he had attended the first hearing in McCollum's case. The townspeople warned him that he should be more careful about which causes he chose to support. As it happened, that first hearing in Champaign was held in July 1945, just two months after the end of the war in Europe. In a world in which the atrocities inflicted on European Jewry were just beginning to be revealed—and the American Jewish community was urging the United States to admit hundreds of thousands of survivors—it is hardly surprising that many individual Jews and official Jewish organizations were reluctant to associate themselves with anything that might be seen as anti-Christian.

The McCollum case, which turned not on financial issues but on the question of whether the Constitution could ever permit the use of public school facilities for religious teaching, posed a challenge to a practice that had originated with fundamentalist Protestants in downstate Illinois, a region then linked religiously and culturally with the southern Bible Belt. But cases that centered on the uses of public money, like *Everson*, nearly always involved the Catholic Church and its parochial schools. In the forties, accommodationists first charged— as the religious right does today with much greater vehemence—that the courts were inventing a new legal concept, the "wall of separation." In this view, the wall was merely an unfortunate Jeffersonian metaphor, never envisioned by the framers of the First Amendment as a legal standard. To accommodationists, the Supreme Court, beginning with *Everson* and continuing with even greater disregard for religion after Earl Warren was named chief justice by Eisenhower in 1954, was responsible for pulling a broad interpretation of the establishment clause out of thin air. However, the Court of the late forties was forced to break new ground precisely because of the proliferation of relatively recent laws, pushed through twenty state legislatures with the strong support of the Catholic Church, providing a variety of indirect tax subsidies for parochial schools. Such laws, of course, never existed in the era when the Constitution was written—or for most of American history. Indeed, whenever and wherever laws guaranteeing equality of religious denominations were passed in the postrevolutionary era, it was clear that the legislators intended not merely to prohibit a state-established church but to bar tax support for all religious sects. The 1786 Virginia religious freedom act turned on that very issue, and evangelicals gave up their own hopes for tax aid in return for the promise that there would be no established church. In postwar America, the Catholic Church alone operated a large system of religious schools (only a minuscule percentage of American Jews then sent their children to Orthodox day schools), and many Protestants and Jews suspected that the church intended to use indirect aid for transportation as the opening wedge in a campaign to obtain direct support for parochial schools.

Then, in 1948, came the publication of Paul Blanshard's *American Freedom and Catholic Power*, which set off a controversy that heightened Protestant, Jewish, and secularist fears about the church's intentions and intensifed the Catholic campaign against secularism and all its works. The Blanshard book, which originated as a series of articles in the *Nation* (a bête noire of the Catholic hierarchy and other conservative institutions), mounted a strong attack on the church's use of its political power to promote laws that made Catholic doctrine the standard for all Americans, most notably in such matters as birth control and divorce. Since the church was lobbying hard to obtain tax money for parochial school programs, the book also placed considerable emphasis on the many differences between Catholic and secular education and the dangers of using public funds to support a school system subject to the supposedly infallible moral teachings of a pope who was also the head of an independent state. Blanshard argued that "mutual silence about religious differences is a reasonable policy in matters of personal faith; but when it comes to matters of political, medical, and educational principle, silence may be directly contrary to public welfare. When a church enters the arena of controversial social policy . . . it must be reckoned with as an organ of political and cultural power."[5] Noting that any critic of church policies would inevitably be branded as "anti-Catholic" by the hierarchy, Blanshard took care to distinguish between the Catholic laity and the institutional church. "The American Catholic people themselves have no representatives of their own choosing, either in their own local hierarchy or in the Roman high command," Blanshard argued, "and they are compelled by the very nature of their church's authoritarian structure to accept nonreligious as well as religious policies that have been imposed upon them from abroad."[6] (In 2002, the writer Garry Wills, a practicing Catholic, pointed out that the Vatican's response to molestation scandals—in which Rome disagreed with the American bishops' decision to turn over accused pedophile priests to civil authorities—involved some of the same conflict-of-loyalty issues that Blanshard had raised in 1948.) Blanshard's book had many shortcomings—not the least of them his exaggerated notion of the degree to which individual American Catholics accepted the nonreligious opinions of their bishops and pope—but the American Catholic hierarchy reacted as if no one had a right to criticize the church in print.

New York Catholic leaders responded with outrage against the *Nation* articles, and the magazine was banned in 1948 from New York City and Newark, New Jersey, high school libraries as "offensive" to followers of the Catholic faith, often described as "a certain" faith in newspaper and magazine articles. This peculiar locution was also used to describe Jews in many publications at midcentury. Readers presumably understood that where Blanshard was concerned, Catholicism, not Judaism, was the offended "certain faith." The *New York Times*, which published the nation's most influential newspaper book review section, refused to advertise *American Freedom and Catholic Power* on grounds that it constituted "an attack upon faith—not upon church." In a letter to the Protestant *Christian Herald*, publisher

Arthur Hayes Sulzberger—cast in a very different mold from modern corporate executives who evade responsibility for controversial actions—declared that the ban had been his personal decision. He contended that Blanshard's chapter on "Sex, Birth Control, and Eugenics" was "particularly objectionable since it involved highly controversial matter of a religious nature."[7]

Then Cardinal Spellman did Blanshard the favor of attacking Eleanor Roosevelt for her opposition to tax subsidies for parochial schools. The controversy put the spotlight on *American Freedom and Catholic Power*, because Blanshard had devoted so much attention to the controversial subject of the role of parochial schools in a secular democracy. Mrs. Roosevelt, in her syndicated newspaper column, "My Day," was responding to a major speech by Spellman demanding that Catholic schools receive their share of federal aid to education. "The separation of church and state is extremely important to any of us who hold to the original traditions of our nation," Mrs. Roosevelt wrote. "To change these traditions by changing our traditional attitude toward public education would be harmful, I think, to our whole attitude of tolerance in the religious area."[8] Mrs. Roosevelt was herself an accommodationist rather than a strict separationist, and she suggested that public schools devise a prayer that would be acceptable to all denominations. Nevertheless, her relatively mild statement on the inadvisability of tax support for religious schools drove Spellman into a fury, which he expressed in an open letter printed in full in the *Times*. The Cardinal accused Mrs. Roosevelt of having compiled "a record of anti-Catholicism" and promoting "discrimination unworthy of an American mother." Spellman also intimated that her concern for separation of church and state was somehow linked with tolerance for communist suppression of religion in eastern Europe. "American freedom not only permits but encourages differences of opinion," he told Mrs. Roosevelt, "and I do not question your right to differ with me. But why I wonder do you repeatedly plead causes that are anti-Catholic? Even if you cannot find it within your heart to defend the rights of innocent little children and heroic, helpless men like Cardinal Martyr Mindszenty,* can you not have the charity not to cast upon them still another stone?"⁹

Mrs. Roosevelt, who initially responded to Spellman's letter with the acerbic comment that "I am sure the Cardinal has written in what seems to him a Christian and kindly manner,"¹⁰ went on to give as good as she got in a formal reply:

> You speak of the Mindszenty case. I spoke out very clearly against any unfair type of trial and anything anywhere in any country which might seem like an attack on an individual because of his religious beliefs. I can not, however, say that in European countries the control by the Roman Catholic Church of great areas of land has always led to happiness for the people of those countries. . . .
>
> I assure you I have no sense of being "an unworthy American mother." The final judgment, my dear Cardinal Spellman, of the unworthiness of all human beings is in the hands of God.¹¹

In the end, attacks by the Catholic hierarchy garnered more publicity for Blanshard than any number of advertisements could possibly have generated. The book wound up on national best-seller lists for six months, even though it was not reviewed by most publications until long after it became a bestseller. According to Blanshard, a fifty-cent paperback "quality," or "trade," paperback edition—then a much-admired new format for serious books—was never issued because his publisher, Beacon Press, had been warned by paperback

---

*In 1948, Cardinal Josef Mindszenty of Hungary had been sentenced to death for treason by a communist court—a judgment commuted to life imprisonment—after a show trial featuring a confession generally believed to have been coerced through torture and drugs. He became a symbol of communist persecution of religion in general and Catholicism in particular. In 1955, Mindszenty was released from prison owing to his ill health, and a year later he took refuge in the American embassy during the bloody uprising against Hungary's Soviet-controlled government. By 1971, the Hungarian government considered Mindszenty an embarrassing reminder of its Stalinist origins, and the cardinal was allowed to leave the country for Rome after diplomatic negotiations with the Vatican.

distributors that drugstores and newsstands would not stock the book for fear of Catholic boycotts.[12]

Blanshard's book *was* anti-Catholic, if anti-Catholicism is understood not as an attack on the constitutionally guaranteed right of all Catholics to practice their religion but as opposition to Catholic doctrine and its promulgation with public money. And Cardinal Spellman *was* speaking not only as an antisecularist but as an opponent of those Protestant and Jewish spokesmen who, grounded in their own religious traditions, wished to thwart Catholic influence not only on government but also on American society as a whole. By today's standards, the public arguments between Mrs. Roosevelt and Spellman, and between Blanshard and his Catholic critics, seem abrasive and intolerant. No mainstream religious leader today would dare to criticize a figure as prominent as Eleanor Roosevelt for harboring antireligious sympathies "unworthy of an American mother." At midcentury, American dialogue on the subject of faith retained a connection to the deeper religious passions of the American past, in which honest differences of belief had been considered so potentially disruptive to the fabric of society that only a secularist government could guarantee public stability and private liberty of conscience. From both a secularist and a religious perspective, there is a refreshing integrity about these fifty-year-old arguments, because they begin with the premise that religious differences are as important as religious commonalities. In that sense, even though there were wounded and angry feelings on all sides, the discourse was more respectful of both religion and secularism than the modern attempt to craft a nonsubstantive pansectarian public religion for everyone.

If secularists were winning more First Amendment battles in the postwar years, religious spokesmen, using every medium of mass communication, were successfully promoting a civil religion that worshiped both prosperity and Christianity. The sermons of Norman Vincent Peale, Billy Graham, and Fulton Sheen, delivered from television studios as well as traditional pulpits, proclaimed the doctrine of American exceptionalism, imbued with the conviction that God had selected America as the beneficiary of His special blessings. The pastor of Marble Collegiate Church on New York's Fifth Avenue, Peale gave voice to both the political and the religious implications of the exceptionalist faith in his foreword to the paperback edition of his *Power of Positive Thinking*, a best seller throughout the fifties and the prototype for the next, much larger generation of self-help books in the seventies and eighties. "I was born and reared in humble Midwestern circumstances in a dedicated Christian home," Peale told his readers. "The everyday people of this land are my own kind whom I know and love and believe in with great faith. When anyone of them lets God have charge of his life the power and glory are amazingly demonstrated."[13] These lines encapsulate much of the conventional religious and cultural wisdom of the late forties and the fifties. Real Americans—Peale's "own kind"—came not from the cities but from the small-town heartland, though, in the Horatio Alger mold, a humble midwestern boy might grow up to become the leader of one of the wealthiest churches in the richest and most sinful of American cities. "Everyday people" were not Jews, humanists, or atheists but Christians. A generation earlier, before the first stirrings of American ecumenicism, Peale would probably have specified Protestants rather than Christians as God's American anointed; a few years later, as Christians became more sensitized to the feelings of Jews, he would likely have used the more general "religious" or "God-fearing." At any rate, all that was required for Peale's countrymen to claim the happiness and success that was their birthright as Americans was to acknowledge the power of God.

Peale, Graham, and Sheen proved to be the most effective marketers of Christianity since the evangelist Paul—although Sheen, bound by the dogma that his was the one true church, was as interested in converting believers in other faiths to Catholicism as in spreading the more general Christian message expounded by Peale's bland self-help books and Graham's florid crusades. Graham, who grew more ecumenical as he aged, would eventually describe Sheen as "one of the greatest preachers of this century," but Peale never entirely discarded his suspicions of Catholic intentions.[14] Speaking from the pulpit of Marble Collegiate, he engaged in acrimonious exchanges with Sheen, who often preached at St. Patrick's Cathedral, twenty blocks to the north and a theological universe away. On one memorable occasion, after Sheen had asserted the supremacy of Catholic doctrine over all other faiths, a miffed Peale unecumenically proclaimed that "the Protestant Church needs a Martin Luther to drive another nail in the famous theses he tacked on the church door at Wittenberg; to tell the world that we believe in Protestantism and it is here to stay until the gates of St. Peter must rust on their hinges."[15] Like the thunderbolts hurled at each other by Cardinal Spellman and Mrs. Roosevelt, Sheen and Peale's scraps belong to another era—a time before the American civil religion prohibited criticism of anyone else's sincerely held faith.

Denominational spats notwithstanding, the postwar radio and television evangelists brought to fruition the partnership of government, business, advertising, and religion that Bruce Barton had envisioned in the twenties. The preachers of the fifties also shared an intense anticommunism and enjoyed access to business titans and top-level government officials, including Eisenhower, Hoover, and Secretary of State John Foster Dulles. By 1964, Graham would look back nostalgically at the Eisenhower era as "a time of spiritual awakening in America. The example he [Eisenhower] gave contributed much to this revival. Under him, I believe Americans felt a degree of security unknown under other presidents."[16] The closeness of the connection between business and religious leaders is strikingly evident in the list of luminaries on the executive committee that organized Graham's celebrated ninety-seven-day crusade in 1957 in New York's Madison Square Garden. They included Henry Luce (who, unlike his wife, had not succumbed to Sheen's charisma by converting to Catholicism); George Champion, president of the Chase Manhattan Bank; Edward V. (Eddie) Rickenbacker, an archconservative and a hero of both world wars; William Randolph Hearst, Jr., the newspaper publisher; and the ubiquitous Peale. In charge of fund-raising for the crusade was Howard E. Isham, vice president and treasurer of U.S. Steel.[17] The crusades of the postwar era were larger versions, amplified by radio broadcasts and sometimes by television, of the tent revival meetings, with nonstop preaching, that had been a staple of evangelical proselytizing since the eighteenth century. As Marshall Frady notes in an irreverent biography of Graham, the Garden was sold out for more than three months, but the response of New Yorkers—so many of them Jews and Catholics—was less than enthusiastic. Of the Garden's 19,000 seats, 11,200 were allotted to Christian tour groups from as far away as Oklahoma City and Houston; Graham had wisely exhorted his disciples throughout the country to take their summer vacations in New York and attend his crusade.[18] Like Peale, Graham vigorously proclaimed a gospel binding religion with true Americanism. For his final New York service, Graham spoke at a rally of 120,000 on Labor Day weekend in Times Square, then a center of peep shows and prostitution. He described the wicked square— "the spot that thousands of tourists think of as New York"—as having undergone a temporary transformation into a "great cathedral." Graham urged his listeners to "tell the whole world tonight that we Americans believe in God. Let us tell the world tonight that we are morally and spiritually strong as well as militarily and economically. Let us tonight make this a time of rededication—not only to God, but to the principles and freedoms that our forefathers gave us."[19]

Yet the mass media of the fifties were a double-edged sword, promoting both religious revivalism and the secularization of American popular culture. Sheen's *Life Is Worth Living*, which reached 5.5 million households a week by 1955, occupied the same television time slot as Milton Berle, who had even higher TV ratings (although it was Sheen, not Uncle Miltie, who made the annual list of the ten most-admired men in America). During this period of intense public interest in spiritual renewal, Americans were equally interested in seeing movies and reading books that only yesterday had been suppressed

by church-backed censorship laws. Although weekly church attendance was, according to polls, at an all-time high, many churchgoers
were not about to let ministers and priests determine the content of
their entertainment. In 1942, New York's Cardinal Spellman had told
the Knights of Columbus that the "fifth column of the saboteurs of
our factories and public utilities has its counterpart in the filth of
those who piously shout censorship if they are not permitted to freely
exercise their venal, venomous, diabolical debauching of the mind and
body of our boys and girls."[20] Only fifteen years later, the conservative religious linkage of anti-Americanism and pornography had
come to seem overwrought and outdated to a growing number of
educated Americans. Conservative stalwarts might picket movie theaters and accuse them of showing communist films, but to Americans
obsessed neither with the Red Menace nor with obscenity, the equation of sex and Stalinism looked ridiculous. The absurd strictures of
the dying movie production code, most ludicrously embodied in the
incarceration of movie husbands and wives in separate beds, reinforced
public disregard for religious spokesmen who lumped kitsch like *Forever Amber* (1947) with serious, albeit disturbing, movies like Otto Preminger's *The Man with the Golden Arm* (1955), a harrowing study of
drug addiction also targeted by many censorship boards; Elia Kazan's
Baby Doll (1956); and Preminger's *Anatomy of a Murder* (1959).

The sixties are generally remembered as the decade in which, for
good or ill, censorship of books and movies ceased in much of the
nation—in large measure as a result of the Warren Court's decisions
broadening the scope of the First Amendment. However, the edifice
of film censorship was already beginning to crumble in the more conservative early fifties, as a result of aggressive legal challenges by civil
libertarians and the greater sophistication of American audiences. The
decade began with a confrontation that would turn into a landmark
First Amendment case involving free expression in the movie industry. In 1950, the Italian director Roberto Rossellini's *The Miracle*, a
blasphemous and tedious film in which a peasant girl has sex with a
man she thinks is St. Joseph and bears a child she thinks is Jesus,
opened at Manhattan's Paris Theater. The ever-vigilant Spellman

denounced the film from the pulpit, and demonstrators picketed the theater with signs announcing, "This is a Communist Picture!" and "Buy American." Under intense pressure from Spellman, the state film licensing board withdrew legal permission for *The Miracle* to be shown. But the film's distributor took his case to court—a step that others in the movie business had been too intimidated to take in the past—and the Supreme Court ruled unanimously that movies were a form of expression protected by the First Amendment and could not be subject to prior restraint. The *Miracle* decision was the first in a long line of federal court rulings that would broaden the limits of expression for American-made mass-audience movies as well as for limited-distribution foreign films. The Chicago Board of Censors, one of the most conservative such bodies in the nation, tried to find a judge who would uphold its bans and lost seven cases in a row. One involved *Anatomy of a Murder*, which the watchful examiners had defined as obscene solely because the words *rape* and *contraceptive* were uttered in it.

Book censors, whether their concerns centered on political or erotic content, would also be on the run as soon as the fever of McCarthyism began to abate in the second half of the fifties. Professional librarians, who had supported the censorship activities of the WCTU at the start of the twentieth century, were more likely by 1960 to resist community attempts to dictate what could and could not be offered to users of their libraries. The Comstock postal law, still on the books, was dealt a decisive blow in 1959 when Grove Press brought out an unexpurgated edition of D. H. Lawrence's *Lady Chatterley's Lover*, a favorite target of both British and American censors since its publication in 1928. Eisenhower's postmaster general, Arthur Summerfield, tried to suppress the book, but a federal district judge, later upheld by the United States Court of Appeals, ruled that the book was not obscene. Religious conservatives were as appalled by the broadening of First Amendment free speech rights as they were by the attacks of civil libertarians on tax support for religious schools—or on religious activities in public schools. Men like Spellman and Graham saw secularism itself as the enemy, and they viewed

mainstream and liberal religious denominations as gutless and ineffec-
tual in the face of the increasing secularization of popular culture.

The promotion of symbolic public piety arose from a threefold
impulse on the part of conservative religious leaders. On one level,
religious boosterism was a response to what traditionalists saw as the
degradation and increasing sexual licentiousness of American culture.
Clerics also saw a need to find common ground amid the bitter erup-
tions of old sectarian conflicts over public support for parochial
schools. More important than either of these motives, however, was
the intense desire of both politicians and church leaders to identify
themselves with religious anticommunism, which, having taken root
well before the Second World War, had spread through every level of
American society with the advent of the Cold War and the era that
would always be associated with the name of Senator Joseph R.
McCarthy. The creation of a new, bland, and compulsory set of quasi-
religious rituals, exemplifed by the 1954 addition of "under God" to
the Pledge of Allegiance, was designed to emphasize America's religiosity—so different from Soviet godlessness!—without favoring any
particular religion. The Knights of Columbus, the most influential
Catholic laymen's association, spearheaded the movement to add God
to the pledge, and President Eisenhower and Congress readily
endorsed the proposal: this was one phrase upon which Protestants,
Catholics, and Jews—the Big Three—could all agree. The church's
galvanizing role in the sacralization of the secular pledge represented
another step in the rise of Catholic influence that dated from the
twenties. When the pledge was written in 1892, it was intended, at
least in part, as a statement of an assimilationist public school ethic
that stood in opposition to the separatist Catholic religious school
system. In the fifties, the church was still trying with great vehemence, though only limited success, to discourage Catholics from
attending public schools. The hierarchy's leadership of the movement
to insert God into the pledge represented a major tactical change
regarding public education: instead of fighting to banish Protestant

Bible reading and Protestant prayer from public schools—a mission already accomplished in most urban and suburban communities outside the South—the church hierarchy would support the inclusion of religious sentiment in the public school day as long as that sentiment did not violate Catholic doctrine.

The importance of such symbolic practices—the reason why secularists keep making a legal issue of them—is borne out by the current public misapprehension that the pledge dates from America's revolutionary beginnings, that it has always contained words acknowledging the nation's dependence on God, and that antireligious fanatics are responsible for trying to take away something that has always been a part of American tradition. The furor over a 2003 decision by the United States Court of Appeals for the Ninth Circuit declaring the phrase *under God* a violation of the establishment clause is a case in point. The lawsuit leading to the decision was brought by Michael Newdow, an atheist and San Francisco parent who would soon begin receiving hate mail of the sort that Vashti McCollum received a half century ago. Both President Bush and Attorney General John Ashcroft denounced the decision, and the case was immediately appealed to the Supreme Court.

During the second Red Scare, of the fifties, the equation of atheism and irreligion with communism was even more widely accepted by the public than it had been during the anti-immigrant and antibolshevik fervor after the First World War. There were several explanations for the intensified religious tone of the fifties campaign against communism. First, the Soviets had mounted an all-out attack on religion in the heavily Catholic countries of eastern Europe occupied by the Red Army after the war. These included Hungary, Poland, and Czechoslovakia, as well as the three Baltic states, Latvia, Lithuania, and Estonia, that had been absorbed outright into the Soviet Union. Large and vocal communities of first- and second-generation Catholic immigrants from these "captive nations" were deeply pained by the Soviet domination of their former homelands, and many immigrants had close ties to relatives trapped behind the frozen borders of postwar Europe. With backing from the Catholic Church in their new country, immigrant ethnic spokesmen emphasized the destruction of religious institutions in Soviet-dominated eastern Europe and saw the specter of bolshevism whenever American civil libertarians defended separation of church and state. In the years after the First World War, no such powerful and aggrieved immigrant community existed. Most Russian-born Americans in the twenties were Jews, and most Jews were not particularly concerned about Soviet repression of their long-time persecutor the Russian Orthodox Church.

The greater power of the American mass media also imparted a stronger religious cast to McCarthyite politics than had existed during the post–World War I anticommunist campaign. Radio was unavailable as a promoter of the first Red Scare, but in the fifties, both radio and television transmitted the preaching of anticommunist evangelists to millions. Paradoxically, the existence of a strong and organized civil liberties movement also fostered religious anticommunism during the McCarthy era. The ACLU's prominent role in both establishment-clause and free speech cases—many of which did involve communists and others on the political left—provided a handy link for conservatives who equated the defense of all First Amendment rights with atheism and communist sympathies. Even though many ACLU leaders took an accommodationist rather than a separatist position on church-state issues, civil libertarians could no more escape being classified as atheists than they could avoid being labeled "pinkos."

Finally, the conservative political views and clout of the most prominent members of the post–World War II Catholic hierarchy played a powerful role in shaping an association of atheism with communism, in ways unavailable to the more marginalized Catholic leadership of the twenties. Still, the connection between Catholicism and McCarthyism was frequently oversimplified, by contemporary political commentators as well as by subsequent historians, in part because the junior senator from Wisconsin was himself a Catholic. But, as Donald F. Crosby persuasively argues in *God, Church, and Flag* (1978), lay Catholics, as in the New Deal era, were not rubber stamps for the views of their priests, bishops, and cardinals. Public opinion polls showed that Catholics ran about 8 to 10 percentage points ahead of the rest of the American population in their support for McCarthy—not an insignificant gap—but the majority of Catholics, like Protestants, took a passive, noncommittal stance until the senator's reputation was destroyed in 1954 by the Army-McCarthy hearings. Differences among church leaders, who were not as inclined as they had been in the thirties to walk in lockstep on social and political issues, also affected the tone of Catholic responses to McCarthy. Polls consistently showed that support for McCarthy was strongest in Boston and New York, whose cardinals, Richard J. Cushing and Spellman, respectively, put all their resources, including diocesan newspapers, behind the hunt for communists. New York, it should be remembered, had a strong tradition of clerical anticommunist activity dating from the thirties, when Sheen was already urging Catholic schoolteachers to inform on colleagues suspected of having communist sympathies. In Chicago, the situation was very different. Bishop Bernard J. Sheil, a strong supporter of liberal social programs, was a vehement opponent of McCarthy, and Sheil's ecclesiastical superior, Cardinal Samuel J. Stritch, maintained a policy of strict neutrality and allowed all political points of view to be represented in the archdiocesan press. McCarthyism deepened a cultural divide that already existed between those American Catholics who still looked to the hierarchy for guidance in matters of nonreligious as well as religious opinion and those who wanted a less authoritarian church, based more on respect for individual conscience than on rules and dogmas laid down by the Vatican.

The most important American religious development of the fifties was the growing chasm between theological liberals and conservatives—a split within as well as between denominations. Graham, a son of the traditionally anti-Catholic Bible Belt, ultimately came to have much more in common with Spellman than he did with the scions of upper-class liberal Protestantism who founded Protestants and Other Americans United for Separation of Church and State. In 1954, Graham wrote an article, based on his sermons and elucidating his vision of the battle between Christianity and communism, for H. L. Mencken's old magazine, the *American Mercury*. The publication had been purchased in 1952 by the fiercely anticommunist, anti-Semitic financier Russell Maguire. In his article, Graham declared:

> Either Communism must die, or Christianity must die, because it is actually a battle between Christ and anti-Christ. . . . Satan began his revolution in the Garden of Eden. With Cain as his first devout follower, and with his brother Abel as a blood sacrifice upon the altar of totalitarianism, he has slaughtered, bludgeoned, and plundered his way through the centuries.[21]

Exactly why Abel is supposed to have been the first sacrifice to totalitarianism is unclear; if one espouses, as Graham generally did, a literal interpretation of the Bible, the only totalitarian government at the time was that of God himself, who, being the superior and creator of both Satan and Cain, allowed Abel to be set up for the primal murder and then served as Cain's judge and jury. No matter. Graham went on to declare that for communists, "the Devil is their God; Marx, their prophet; Lenin, their saint. . . . Karl Marx—a subtle, clever, degenerate materialist—having filled his intellectual craw with all the filth of Europe's gutters, . . . spewed this filthy, ungodly, unholy doctrine of world socialism over the gullible people of a degenerate Europe."[22]

The similarities between the religious anticommunist proselytizing of Graham and Spellman, as well as their shared conservatism on cultural issues such as censorship, created a moral basis for the political alliance that would emerge twenty years later between the most conservative faction of American Protestantism and the most conservative elements in the Catholic hierarchy. In the fifties, before John Kennedy convinced millions of southern fundamentalists that his first loyalty lay not with the Vatican but with the United States, the old mutual animosity was still too strong for conservative Protestants and the conservative wing of the Catholic Church to recognize their commonalities and the potential political power of those shared values.

Secularists, too, failed to fully appreciate the potential for a powerful alliance linking conservatives of different denominations. Yet there was already a de facto recognition, in the formation of a civil liberties coalition that included Jews and liberal Protestants as well as atheists and agnostics, of an emerging alliance—even stronger than the one envisioned by Ingersoll in the nineteenth century—between the forces of secularism and those of liberal religion. Indeed, conservative religious leaders were already pointing to the existence of such an alliance as one more piece of evidence that liberal religion and secularism were cut from the same ungodly mold.

American secularists' recognition of their common ground with religious liberals was (and is) tactically necessary in the pursuit of shared political, social, and legal aims. But that recognition, since the end of the Second World War, has precluded the kind of direct challenges to religion that freethinkers mounted in the nineteenth century. When secularists have spoken out against religious influence on government since the 1940s—as they do when they oppose pressure for tax support of parochial schools—they have avoided criticizing religious influence on society as a whole. Churches and their leaders have a perfect right, of course, to make the case for their moral views and social values, whether conservative or liberal, in both political and nonpolitical venues. But they do not have the right to do so with immunity from criticism simply because they are advancing their views in the name of religion. For the most part, the embattled secularists of the fifties were far more restrained in their criticism of reactionary social values promoted in the name of religion than they were when the same values were advanced by nonsectarian organizations. The John Birch Society, the well-financed ultrarightist organization founded by manufacturer Robert Welch in 1958, could be severely chastised for activities designed to undermine everything from the civil rights movement to American participation in the United Nations, while a right-wing minister expounding precisely the same positions from the pulpit would go unscathed.

One exception to the "speak no evil" approach to religion was Madalyn Murray O'Hair, the best-known American atheist of the late fifties and sixties, whose campaign against school prayer and Bible reading would earn her a place in the religious right's pantheon of demons. O'Hair (then Madalyn Murray), who stood almost alone in her willingness to call herself an atheist, was dubbed "Mad Madalyn" by her antagonists. A singleminded woman whose aggressive style made her sound unbalanced even to liberals who agreed with her on separation of church and state, she frequently described religion as lunacy and silliness. In her absolute intolerance for anyone who did not share her militant atheism, she was the antithesis of Ingersoll, whose cordial relations with clerical contemporaries like Henry Ward Beecher earned a respectful hearing for his views from those who might otherwise have assumed that they had nothing to learn from the Great Agnostic. O'Hair's abrasiveness—which seemed even more abrasive because she was a woman—discouraged people from listening to her even when she made perfect sense, as she did in a 1961 speech at the University of Maryland. She told the students that she was an atheist—"not an agnostic, nor a rationalist, nor a realist, nor a secularist, nor humanist, nor any other fancy name behind which people must hide in our society in order to be safe in our society. And isn't it an indictment of our society that we who do not believe—we nonbelievers of all stripes—must hide behind certain names since reprisals and sanctions would be put into effect against us if we said what we really believe."[23] O'Hair was, of course, right about what Americans thought of atheists and about the fear that induced dissenters like McCollum to call themselves humanists instead. But even committed secular humanists could easily be antagonized—and many were—by the suggestion that only atheism could serve as an honorable self-definition. O'Hair, along with a son and granddaughter, would meet an end grisly enough to satisfy the severest Calvinist. She disappeared in 1995, and her burned and dismembered body was found on a remote ranch in 2001. One of the prime suspects in her murder was a former office manager, fired by O'Hair for stealing $54,000 from her American Atheists Association. O'Hair's one surviving child, William, became a right-wing Christian evangelist.

The secularist victories of the postwar area were achieved mainly in courts of law rather than in the court of public opinion, and they were not followed by a sustained and candid appeal that challenged traditional beliefs and made a moral, as distinct from a legalistic, case on behalf of freedom of expression, secular public education, and rationalism itself. What was missing was an explicitly humanistic, nonreligious vision of personal ethics and social justice—a vision that could be understood even by Americans who had always believed that religion and morality were identical. In that respect, the guarded voice of twentieth-century American secularists presented a sharp contrast to the more forthright nineteenth-century freethinkers, who, at a time when even fewer Americans agreed with them, sought to persuade their countrymen that it was possible to work for the betterment of human beings without acknowledging the authority of God.

One of the most negative consequences of the taboo against any broad cultural criticism of religious influence was the failure of secularist liberals to conduct a thorough postmortem of the role of conservative religion, as distinct from conservative political ideology, in promoting McCarthyism. If the crucial role of religion during the Red Scare of the fifties had been better examined and more widely understood, the resurgence of religious conservatism after the Supreme Court legalized abortion in 1973 would not have come as such a shock to civil libertarians and feminists. But as McCarthy himself faded into history more swiftly than anyone might have imagined, it was more comfortable for many Americans—secularists included—to see McCarthyism as an aberration rather than as the complex product of a durable alliance between conservative religion and conservative politics. Just as fundamentalism was prematurely declared dead by many secularists after the Scopes trial, the support for McCarthy from right-wing clerics was written off by many hopeful secularists in the late fifties as an anachronism, the last gasp of a simplistic worldview that would soon seem as ludicrous to most Americans as witchcraft did to most New Englanders by the end of the eighteenth century.

As the fifties drew to a close, the loosely linked community of American secularists hardly knew what to call itself. Madalyn O'Hair may have regarded the word *secularist* as a cop-out for atheists too cowardly to own up to their real beliefs, but calling oneself a secularist provided little protection; the term had acquired many of the pejorative connotations attached to freethought and infidelity in the eighteenth and nineteenth centuries. Indeed, the word *secularist* was not commonly used by secularists themselves but was employed almost entirely as a pejorative by conservative preachers and theologians. Many closet atheists preferred to call themselves secular humanists, but "humanism without God" was also employed as a slur by conservative Christians.

At the same time, the sectarian animosities once exchanged by Catholic and Protestant clergy were slowly but surely being replaced by the fog of murky tolerance that has since become the defining characteristic of America's ecumenical public consensus. The fifties may have begun with a flare-up of old denominational hatreds, but they ended with the skin-deep civility that proclaims, "There's so much good in the worst of us/And so much bad in the best of us/That it ill behooves any of us/To talk about the rest of us." This spirit of bland tolerance was accompanied by a "tolerant" dismissiveness toward those who adhered to no faith. The new American civil religion did not exactly embrace secularists, agnostics, and atheists, but it did not persecute them either—unless they behaved like Mad Madalyn and aggressively challenged religious beliefs and believers. If right-wing believers still hated secularism and all its works, the majority tended to view self-proclaimed secularists as harmless cranks. At the end of the self-satisfied fifties, few were prescient enough to foresee that the social ferment of the sixties would reinvigorate American secularism—and its opponents—in a fashion harking back not only to the golden age of freethought but the much earlier nineteenth-century conjunction of abolition and feminism.

11

CULTURE WARS REDUX

In his celebrated speech to the Greater Houston Ministerial Association on September 12, 1960, Democratic presidential candidate John F. Kennedy declared unequivocally that he believed "in an America where the separation of church and state is absolute—where no Catholic prelate would tell the President (should he be Catholic) how to act, and no Protestant minister would tell his parishioners for whom to vote—where no church or church school is granted any public funds or political preference—and where no man is denied public office merely because his religion differs from the President who might appoint him or the people who might elect him." Kennedy went on to make it clear that he regarded the Jeffersonian wall of separation not as a flexible metaphor but as the foundation of the American system of government. He reminded his audience, composed heavily of evangelical Protestants, that Jefferson's religious freedom act in Virginia was strongly supported by Baptists who had endured persecution both in England and in America. With a nod to the nonreligious, the candidate also expounded his vision of America as a nation "where every man has the same right to attend or not attend the church of his choice." Kennedy's speech was widely regarded as one of the turning points of his campaign; he was addressing the fears not only of southern evangelicals, who in 1928 had rejected Al Smith because of his Catholicism, but of mainstream Protestants and Jews, who also had serious reservations about a Catholic in the White House. Norman Vincent Peale, the best-known Protestant cleric to voice his doubts, had flown in from New York for Kennedy's speech and press conference.

Kennedy was fortunate to have been a candidate for the presidency forty-four years ago instead of today. In 2004, his forthright support for a "wall of separation" would antagonize not only the evangelicals he won over in 1960 but the hierarchy of his own church. Kennedy's belief in an America where "no church or church school" would be eligible for tax support has been rejected by nearly all Republicans and a fair number of Democrats, fearful of being left behind as the faith-based bandwagon rolls on. As for the Catholic Church, the authoritarian Pope John Paul II has created problems for American Catholic politicans who thought that "dual loyalty" issues had been laid to rest in Kennedy's generation. In January 2003, the Vatican issued an innocuously titled "Doctrinal Note on Some Questions regarding the Participation of Catholics in Political Life," but the bland packaging was misleading. The "doctrinal note" was an order to Catholic officeholders to toe the line on abortion, physician-assisted suicide, and gay marriage—even if official church teaching conflicted with the politician's personal conscience and sense of public duty. (Senator Edward M. Kennedy, commenting on the Vatican effort to turn back the clock for American Catholic politicians, referred to his brother's Houston declaration that "I do not speak for my church on public matters—and the church does not speak for me."[1]) In 1960, John Kennedy faced no such Vatican-provoked tempests. Catholicism was being revitalized by John XXIII, who famously declared that he had no wish to claim infallibility. During the fall campaign, the pope—who was studying English and was well aware of the anti-Catholic charges that the U.S. government would be run from the Vatican should Kennedy be elected—drily told a visiting American

bishop, "Do not expect me to run a country with a language as difficult as yours."² It is impossible to overestimate the impact of John
XXIII, and the Second Vatican Council he convened in an effort to
reform his church, on American Catholics of all political and theological persuasions. One of his great admirers was Fulton Sheen, who, in
spite of his theological orthodoxy, approved of the pope's efforts to
open the church to new ideas. Sheen went through a metamorphosis
of his own in the sixties, when, in spite of his history of hard-line anticommunism, he became an outspoken opponent of the Vietnam War.
Indeed, the combination of John XXIII's papacy and Kennedy's presidency provided American Catholics with a new image of what it
could mean to be both American and Catholic—a self-definition
freed from the fervid anticommunism, as well as the one-note opposition to birth control, long identified with the church's leadership.

Kennedy, in both his personal style and his political philosophy,
was arguably the most secularist American president since Jefferson.
(He privately remarked that one of the worst aspects of having been
elected was that he would be obliged to attend mass every Sunday for
the next four years.) The period that began with Kennedy's election
and ended with the legalization of abortion is frequently viewed
today, especially by the religious right, as a time of rampant irreligion.
Many aspects of what the novelist Philip Roth has called the "de-
mythologizing decade" have been conflated into an image of the sixties as a time when all traditional religious values were trampled on
and ridiculed. In this view, irreligion is seen as the critical force behind
all the secularist sins of the decade: Supreme Court rulings on the
unconstitutionality of school prayer and Bible reading; the enthusiasm with which women began to use the newly developed birth control pill; the proliferation of movies and novels (Roth's 1969 *Portnoy's
Complaint* being a prime example) that would have been considered
the grossest obscenity a decade or two earlier; the emergence of a second wave of feminism far more militant than the nineteenth-century
women's movement; rising drug use; a growing tolerance of divorce;
and the loss of respect for authority implicit in demonstrations from

university campuses to the steps of the Pentagon. Many cultural conservatives saw a direct connection between the school prayer decisions of the early sixties and the rebellious youth culture of the late sixties. To those who were horrified by the social upheavals of the decade, it seemed logical to conclude that if children had only been forced to continue praying in school in 1962, they would not have turned into the hirsute young adults running around half naked (or altogether naked) and smoking marijuana at Woodstock in 1969.

The traumas of the late sixties are etched so dramatically and indelibly in the memories of Americans who had reached the age of reason by the time of President Kennedy's assassination that many cultural milestones between 1960 and 1963—with the exception of the Cuban missile crisis—have been largely forgotten. One of these was the 1962 Supreme Court decision *Engel v. Vitale*, which found a nondenominational school prayer authorized by the New York State Board of Regents to be unconstitutional. The decision made the front page of every major newspaper in the country and was the lead story on the television evening news. While education officials estimated that prayer was a routine practice in less than one-third of the nation's schools—mainly in southern and rural areas with homogeneous student bodies—the decision created an uproar among many who had never given the slightest thought to the question of whether the deity was receiving proper credit before teachers called their classes to order.[3]

The regents' prayer, drafted in 1958 after the ACLU protested the use of the Christian Lord's Prayer in schools, read simply: "Almighty God, we acknowledge our dependence upon Thee, and we beg thy blessings upon us, our parents, our teachers, and our country." New York school districts were not compelled to institute a daily prayer, and most did not, but they had to use the officially authorized wording if they did want students to pray. The case against the official prayer was brought by the New York Civil Liberties Union, which, unlike the national ACLU, took a strong separationist position on all church-state issues. Leo Pfeffer, the American Jewish Congress's expert on church and state, backed by a number of national ACLU leaders, had strongly opposed the challenge to the regents' prayer—in large measure because the plaintiffs were atheists. In the sixties as in the fifties, the ACLU always tried to cast its opposition to religious observance in schools as a matter of support for individual religious freedom—not as opposition to religion itself—and using atheists as plaintiffs undermined the attempt to create a proreligious, or at least a religiously neutral, image. Both the ACLU and religious leaders around the country were taken by surprise when the Court struck down the New York prayer. Justice Black, writing for the majority as he had in the *Everson* and *McCollum* cases, declared that it was "no part of the business of government to compose official prayers."⁴ A year later, the Court also declared Bible reading in schools unconstitutional. (One of the Bible cases was brought by Madalyn Murray.)

Conservative Protestant and Catholic leaders reacted furiously, as did many politicians, especially from the South. One Alabama congressman saw an atheist-integrationist conspiracy in the combination of *Engel* with the high court's 1954 school desegregation decision, *Brown v. Board of Education*. He charged that the justices had "put Negroes in the schools and now they've driven God out."⁵ Billy Graham called the ruling "a most dangerous trend" and "another step toward secularism in the United States." Cardinal James Francis McIntyre of Los Angeles pronounced the decision "shocking and scandalizing to one of American blood and principles, . . . not a decision according to law, but a decision of license." McIntyre declared that the high court was "biting the hand that feeds it . . . because all law comes from God. Yet the court presumes to deny the children of God in our schools the opportunity to speak to the Creator, the Lawmaker, the Preserver of mankind." In his closing blast, the cardinal connected communism with a decision that "puts shame on our faces, as we are forced to emulate Mr. Khrushchev." Jews, by contrast, reacted with almost unanimous approval of the high court's logic. The New York Board of Rabbis declared that "recitation of prayers in the public schools, which is tantamount to the teaching of prayer, is not in conformity with the American concept of the separation of church and state." Liberal Protestants, too, were pleased with the decision.

"It protects the religious rights of minorities," said Dean M. Kelly, director of the Department of Religious Liberty of the National Council of Churches, "and guards against the development of 'public school religion' which is neither Christianity nor Judaism but something less than either."[6]

In response to the decision, there were many proposals in Congress for a constitutional amendment to permit school prayer and Bible reading. At the beginning of the debate, it seemed that some form of prayer amendment might well pass. Protestant fundamentalists cared intensely about school prayer, but many Americans were less informed about and more indifferent to the entire subject, especially since most multiethnic, multireligious urban schools had long since dispensed with potentially controversial religious rituals. Fearful that the fundamentalists might carry the day as a result of public ignorance, the ACLU joined with other separationist and civil libertarian groups, including numerous Jewish organizations and Protestants and Other Americans United for Separation of Church and State, in a nationwide campaign against any prayer amendment. The National Council of Churches and all major Jewish organizations testified against such an amendment before the House Judiciary Committee, and the Catholic clergy no longer spoke with one voice. Spellman and McIntyre might pronounce themselves shocked by the court's ruling, but Father Robert F. Drinan, who later became a member of the ACLU national advisory committee, called for "cooperative separation" on establishment-clause issues. Furthermore, the Catholic hierarchy began to recall that it had expended a good deal of energy, over the course of more than a century, on a largely successful effort to remove Protestant prayer and the reading of the King James Bible from public schools. Who could say that a school prayer amendment might not reimpose Protestant words on Catholic schoolchildren? The difference between the "Protestant" and the "Catholic" Lord's Prayer, grounds for imprisonment or worse if you spoke the wrong words in the wrong venue in bad old pre-Enlightenment Europe, was still capable in twentieth-century America of inciting a war of words between the conservative Protestant and conservative Catholic faithful. Protestants, following the King James Version, end the prayer with, "For thine is the kingdom, the power, and the glory, for ever." Catholics end simply with, "And lead us not into temptation, but deliver us from evil." Protestants say, "And forgive us our debts, as we forgive our debtors," while Catholics say, "And forgive us our trespasses, as we forgive those who trespass against us." That religious leaders and school boards actually spent time arguing over such differences in wording argues powerfully on behalf of the Supreme Court's wisdom in banning all school prayer.

Little was heard at the time of *Engel* from the African American clergy, representing what was then and is now (according to public opinion polls) the most committed group of religious believers in the nation. Given the intensity of the battle for racial justice in the early sixties, it is hardly surprising that black ministers did not consider school prayer the preeminent moral issue of the day. To do so would have placed them on the side of Lyman Beecher, who saw Sunday postal service as a greater evil than slavery, rather than on the side of William Lloyd Garrison. (When I was a young reporter for the *Washington Post*, I asked a friend, a consultant on education to the Southern Christian Leadership Conference, whether the Reverend Martin Luther King, Jr., had strong views on the school prayer and Bible reading decisions. My friend laughed and said King had once remarked that it would be very nice if the school day across America could begin with a reading of the Bill of Rights. "After all," King told my friend, "we Negroes know our Bible. We don't need to have it read to us in school.")

Unlike the Civil War–era proposal to declare Jesus Christ the true head of the U.S. government, which politicians wisely bottled up in congressional committees, the twentieth-century prayer amendment received consideration by the full House and Senate. But the drive to sanction prayer in the Constitution never received the support of anything approaching a majority, in large measure because so many non-fundamentalist church leaders testified against it. Although the controversy receded from public view by the late sixties, it continued to fester for a large and angry minority that regarded the battle between secularism and religion as the most important issue in American life. In that respect, the split over school prayer was a precursor of the bitter division over the 1973 *Roe v. Wade* abortion decision: those who approved of the decision soon began to take legalized abortion for granted, while abortion opponents turned their initial shock into a concerted campaign to undo *Roe* by whatever means, however long it might take.

Fundamentalist sects continued to grow throughout the sixties—even as the courts held an increasingly separationist and secularist view on relations between government and religion. The expansion of religious fundamentalism, in membership and in financial resources, took place below the media radar line. Newspapers and television were covering civil rights and antiwar demonstrations as well as the sexual revolution, but the media largely overlooked one of the most important stories of the decade—the development of a powerful fundamentalist infrastructure of religious schools and communications outlets. The huge First Baptist Church of Dallas, for example, organized a system of schools, originally designed to evade desegregation, that served as a model for conservative Baptists throughout the South. Although the desegregation angle was covered by the press, the larger religious implications were ignored—especially by the northern media. Eventually, First Baptist, led by its charismatic ultraright pastor, W. A. Criswell, created a comprehensive structure of educational institutions that would play an important role in the rightward theological and political move of the entire Southern Baptist Convention in the 1980s. As a number of historians have now noted, the movement spearheaded by First Baptist "allowed the children of church members and likeminded people ... to move from kindergarten through graduate study in school environments ... considered theologically safe, unlike those found in the public schools and universities and in denominationally affiliated schools ... considered [theologically] wayward, such as Southern Methodist University and Baylor University."[7] The young people who belonged to conservative evangelical churches and graduated from their schools looked up not to John and Robert Kennedy and Martin Luther King but to Billy Graham and Strom Thurmond. Indeed, Graham was No. 2 on the 1969 list of the most admired men in America—after Richard Nixon. Trent Lott and Newt Gingrich were as much children of the sixties as their contemporaries who marched for civil rights and against the Vietnam War.

Throughout the first half of the sixties, the moral energies of committed American liberals—whether their morality was based on religion or godless humanism in the best secularist sense—were largely invested in the civil rights struggle in the South. Since 1955, when Rosa Parks refused to give up her bus seat to a white passenger in Montgomery, Alabama, the civil rights movement had held up an unforgiving mirror to the conscience of a nation. It was not, however, a mirror in which most white Americans, northern or southern, wished to see themselves. On October 21, 1963—five months after Martin Luther King delivered his unforgettable "I Have a Dream" speech from the steps of the Lincoln Memorial—*Newsweek* devoted a special issue to the response of white Americans to the civil rights movement. While the majority said they supported equal legal rights, nearly three-quarters of whites believed that Negroes were moving "too fast" in their drive for racial justice. Not surprisingly, only 3 percent of blacks agreed with that statement—a measure not only of the gap in perception between the races but of the depth of white resistance to change. Most whites outside the South were supportive *in theory* of the right of black Americans to eat a hamburger at a lunch counter, use a public toilet, or vote in elections without exposing themselves to insults, beatings, or murder. Nevertheless, a majority of whites strongly opposed most of the tactics civil rights demonstrators were using to bring about change. More than two-thirds said that lunch-counter sit-ins, consumer boycotts, and going to jail to fight discrimination were unjustified. Furthermore, nearly two-thirds of white clung to the illusion that the civil rights movement did not have the backing of "rank and file" Negroes—a belief refuted by more than 90 percent of black Americans in the same poll.[8] Like women's suffrage, the goals of the civil rights movement of the sixties—particularly the first half of the sixties—seem so uncontroversial today that it is easy to repress the knowledge that a majority of white Americans opposed even the nonviolent demonstrations of black Americans who wanted nothing more than basic dignity.

The Christian right would like today's public to forget exactly where religious conservatives stood on civil rights forty years ago. One of the more repellent ironies of modern religious correctness has been the attempt by fundamentalists to wrap themselves in the mantle of those men and women of faith who risked their lives to fight racism. In the sixties, right-wing fundamentalists were, almost without exception, hard-core segregationists. They attacked the twentieth-century civil rights movement as their spiritual actual ancestors had attacked the nineteenth-century abolitionist and feminist movements. What they saw was what their predecessors had seen—not a struggle for justice but a conspiracy of atheism, political radicalism, and sexual libertinism.

It is inarguable that the preeminent moral leadership of the early civil rights struggle came from the black churches of the South, but only those with an interest in concealing the sorry racial record of so many white churches, North and South, have the temerity to credit religion per se for inspiring the movement. The black ministers at the forefront of the battle could never have imagined that their history would one day be twisted to promote the attempts of conservatives to breach the First Amendment's barrier between church and state. There could be no more powerful argument against mixing religion and government than the success of independent African American churches in placing racial segregation and discrimination on a reluctant nation's social agenda. Would black churches have been able to take the lead in the struggle had they been dependent on funds doled out for "faith-based initiatives"—either by federal officials, who were at best lukewarm supporters of civil rights, or by southern satraps, who were usually the deadly adversaries of their black citizens?[9] Whites could bomb African American churches, but, thanks to the First Amendment, they could not control the activities of those institutions through anything short of murder.

By contrast, most faithful white southern churchgoers in the early civil rights era, and most of their ministers, were staunch defenders of segregation. Resistance to desegregation was particularly strong among evangelicals, whose silken ties to their brethren in the North had been severed by the Civil War. The tiny minority of white southern ministers who did speak out against racism were generally censured and abandoned by their churches—though that was hardly the worst that could happen. One of those embattled ministers, Edwin King (no relation to Martin Luther King), was arrested on May 28, 1963, in Jackson, Mississippi, after denouncing a violent police crackdown against sit-in demonstrators. He was bailed out by his friend Medgar Evers, the field secretary of the state NAACP, just in time to defend himself from an onslaught by his fellow clergymen at the annual meeting of the Mississippi Methodist Conference—which voted to bar the dissident minister from employment in any Methodist church in the state. Evers himself had less than two weeks to live; he was slain by a white supremacist assassin on June 12. In a dragnet in which state police scooped up many mourners who had attended Evers's funeral, King was arrested again. While the young minister was still in jail, someone tampered with the lug nuts on his car, causing a near-fatal "accident" after King was once again released.[10] Such was the support received from their religious brethren and superiors by courageous southern ministers who lived out the early Christian creed of nonviolent resistance to tyranny and injustice. In *Pillar of Fire* (1998), the civil rights historian Taylor Branch tells a story about King that shows exactly what sort of religion was acceptable to the enemies of racial equality. In 1961, while visiting freedom riders jailed in a notorious state prison, the minister brought copies of Mohandas K. Gandhi's books as gifts for the prisoners. Knowing that Gandhi's writings would not be allowed inside the jail, King had the foresight to wrap the subversive literature in Billy Graham's book jackets.[11]

On civil rights, the Catholic Church in the South had a much better, though still mixed, record than southern Protestants. In 1958, the U.S. Conference of Catholic Bishops issued a strong statement condemning racial prejudice and discrimination, but American bishops differed greatly in their willingness to translate the principle into action. There were mavericks like Bishop Vincent S. Waters of Raleigh, North Carolina, who as early as 1953 wrote a pastoral letter declaring that "no segregation of races" would be tolerated in any church in his diocese. Furthermore, he told the Catholic faithful that if "Christ had said love our enemies, we certainly can love our friends. These [Catholics of all races] are our friends and members of our own body." In New Orleans, the most Catholic city in the Deep South, Archbishop Joseph F. Rummel was much slower to take a stand, especially on the inflammatory issue of school desegregation. Under strong pressure from a biracial committee of pro–civil rights Catholic laity (unlike most of the South, Louisiana had a large population of black Catholics), Rummel acted to desegregate the city's parochial schools only in 1962. Soon afterward, though, he excommunicated three prominent Catholic laymen—including Leander Perez, the notoriously racist district attorney of Plaquemines Parish, for urging Catholics to protest school desegregation by disrupting Sunday Mass.[12] One can only imagine how different—how much less bloody—the civil rights struggles of the next few years might have been if equally prominent white Baptist preachers, speaking to a much larger white constituency than Catholics commanded in the South, had consistently condemned segregation from their pulpits. Most Southern rabbis were extremely cautious about speaking out against racism (though they did not endorse segregation as so many Protestant fundamentalists did). They feared drawing attention to themselves, particularly because anti-Semitic segregationists were constantly alluding to the disproportionate presence of Jews among northern white civil rights workers.

Nor was the posture of northern churches and their leaders uniformly favorable toward civil rights—especially when it came to direct action to support the movement. Not only the Christian right but many representatives of mainstream religions have retrospectively exaggerated the level of their coreligionists' support for racial equality. Rabbi Marc Schneier, in *Shared Dreams: Martin Luther King, Jr. and the Jewish Community* (1999), offers an unusually honest look at what men of his faith did, and did not, do. In June 1964, the Central Congregation of American Rabbis—which included many prominent Reform Jewish supporters of the civil rights movement—was holding its annual convention in Atlantic City, New Jersey. Atlantic City just happens to be a relatively short plane ride from beautiful four-hundred-year-old St. Augustine, Florida, the oldest town in the nation, where some of the most violent clashes between the Klan and civil rights demonstrators were taking place during that blood-soaked "freedom summer." On May 28, the Reverend Andrew Young had been leading a march toward St. Augustine's one-time slave market, by then considered a picturesque tourist attraction, when he was beaten unconscious by Klansmen as local police looked on and did nothing. Under a court order not to interfere with the marchers, city officials once again stood by, on June 9, as peaceful demonstrators were bloodied by Klansmen on St. Augustine's famous white sand beaches. At that point, King sent a telegram to the rabbinical convention asking the assembled rabbis to join him in St. Augustine. As Schneier recounts, only sixteen of several hundred rabbis responded to the call. The rabbis naturally feared for their own safety, but that, as Rabbi Arnold Jacob Wolf—one who stayed behind—admitted, was far from the only reason for their decision. A leading social activist who declined to go to St. Augustine, Wolf proffered a painfully candid self-analysis not long afterward:

> I must ask myself what the meaning of my refusal to answer Dr. King's call was, a refusal shared by nearly all my colleagues on this and nearly every other occasion. . . . The real reason for my refusal is more than the sum of my personal inadequacies. . . . When I said no, I meant it. No—I do not really wish to work with you! I do

not wish to swim with you! I do not wish to go to jail with you! I do not wish to eat your food or be one of you![13]

Before the sixties, northern whites—whether of a secularist or a religious bent—had played almost no role in the boycotts and other nonviolent demonstrations that began in Montgomery and first brought King to national prominence. But as the conscience of the nation was slowly stirred by the sight of black children being escorted into schools past jeering mobs and, later, by the bloody spectacle of demonstrators being clubbed and set upon by police dogs, more whites—and more northerners of both races—went South. The civil rights movement then became a collaboration among Americans of many religions, and of no religion, moved by the same moral imperatives. It was a coalition the nation had not seen since the abolitionist movement, when iconoclastic religious believers and freethinkers were united by the conviction that slavery was immoral, when Garrison declared his belief that membership in the human race—not membership in a church—was all that was required to recognize the evil of slavery. The new civil rights coalition included black leaders, many of them ordained clergymen, of King's generation; representatives of the Catholic left, energized by the new spirit of reform in the church; liberal Protestants, heirs to all who had rebelled against rigid Calvinism; both observant and secular Jews; and agnostics and atheists who rejected all religion except the religion of humanity. But the white members of that dedicated coalition never spoke for middle-of-the-road white church members in the North or the South.

The extensive participation in the movement of nonreligious civil rights advocates and civil libertarians was a delicate issue for those who wished the cause of racial justice to be seen not as a radical departure from but as the embodiment of American tradition at its best. Like the image-conscious suffragists at the turn of the century, civil rights leaders had good reason not to draw attention to the importance of the nonreligious, and even the unconventionally religious, in their movement. King's personal association with Jews, who were regarded by most segregationists as indistinguishable from atheists, gave white racists another reason to hate him. As was well known in the sixties, King's closest white friend and personal lawyer was Stanley Levison, a nonobservant, nonbelieving Jew who was a veteran of the "Old Left" of the thirties and a defense lawyer for communists, socialists, and labor unions throughout the McCarthy era. King and Levison were such good friends that they reportedly spoke on the telephone nearly every night—and one of the topics they discussed was religion. Deeply rooted in his Baptist faith, King found it impossible to imagine that someone could be as morally committed to the betterment of humanity as Levison without believing in any god or any religion. "You believe in God, Stan," King would tease his friend. "You just don't know it."[14]

Clerical collars, nuns' habits, and rabbis' yarmulkes provided some, though not much, insulation from constant charges that the "atheistic" and "communistic" volunteers had descended upon the South in order to engage in promiscuous interracial sex. On the second day of the 1965 voting rights march from Selma to Montgomery, Alabama's Representative William Dickinson declared in a speech on the floor of the House that the marchers were nothing but "human flotsam, adventurers, beatniks, prostitutes, and similar rabble hired to march at $10 a day, free room and board, and all the sex they wanted. Free love among this group is not only condoned, it is encouraged. . . . Only the ultimate sex act with one of another color can demonstrate that they have no prejudice."[15] Julian Bond, then a spokesman for the Student Non-Violent Coordinating Committee (SNCC), replied that he hoped the congressman realized "that he is accusing nuns, priests, rabbis, and other responsible citizens of misconduct."[16] What civil rights leader would wish to underscore the religious unconventionality of so many volunteers, given the omnipresent suggestions that even longtime members of the clergy were nothing but imposters? A typical comment, overheard by a reporter covering the march for the *New Yorker*, was made by a middle-aged white woman to an Alabama state trooper. "Look at them so-called white men," she said, "them with their church collars that they bought for fifty cents! And them de-virginated nuns! I'm a Catholic myself, but it turns my stomach to see them!"[17]

The irreligion of many of the younger white volunteers was a sore point not only with white segregationsts but also with many respected elders in southern black communities. One such man was Albert Jones, an NAACP leader in Meridian, Mississippi and a friend of Michael Schwerner, a Jewish volunteer from New York who was murdered by Klansmen in the summer of 1964 along with Andrew Goodman, a fellow New Yorker, and James Chaney, a local black volunteer. Jones explained in a 1965 interview:

> The church is important to Mississippi Negroes. Even as we become militant and fight for our rights, we still want to retain our religion. Some of the white ones who come in here are not reverent and religious, so they have a limited understanding of our people. I want to fight as much as anybody for Negro advancement. My windows have been shot out and blasted out. I want the ballot for Negroes, better jobs, better education, and I don't want Negroes looked down on any more. But the church is still our mighty fortress, and I want it to stay that way.[18]

Religion could also be an issue between many members of the older generation of black ministers (though "old" is relative: King was only thirty-nine when he was assassinated in 1968) and the younger generation of more militant blacks like Bond and Stokely Carmichael. Many of the younger men held views on religion more in line with those of W. E. B. Du Bois—who had almost as little respect for the black church as he did for white churches—than with those of King. Du Bois, who renounced his American citizenship in 1963 and died in Ghana, had excoriated the black ministry in the early decades of the twentieth century for being "choked with pretentious, ill-trained men and in far too many cases with men dishonest and otherwise immoral." In 1912, he called for reforms "to make the Negro church a place where colored men and women of education and energy can work for the best things regardless of their belief or disbelief in unimportant dogmas and ancient and outworn creeds."[19] It could well be argued that the leadership of the black church in the civil rights movement was the fulfillment of Du Bois's vision, but the younger nonreligious blacks did not always display the respect for devout African American believers that King and his clerical contemporaries displayed toward those whose humanism was the sole moral basis of their commitment to civil rights.

Nonobservant Jews, motivated not by Judaism as a religion but by the secular Jewish tradition of social activism, made up the largest group among college-age whites who volunteered in the South during the dangerous summers between 1960 and 1965. *Nigger* was the only epithet hurled more frequently at marchers than *kike* and *Jew-boy*. Goodman and Schwerner espoused the secular humanism that motivated so many of the young Jewish volunteers. The twenty-four-year-old Schwerner, a graduate of the Columbia University School of Social Work; his twenty-two-year-old wife, Rita, a Queens College graduate; and the twenty-year-old Goodman, still a student at Queens, had been raised by their parents on secularist Jewish social ideals. Schwerner was an atheist and a humanist who, his wife later told interviewers, believed in all men rather than in one God. His European-born grandparents were believing Jews, but his parents had moved away from traditional religious observance. At thirteen, Schwerner had decided not to have a bar mitzvah, showing considerable resolve, since even the most secular Jews at the time were generally unwilling to forgo the traditional ceremony in which a boy becomes a man in the eyes of the Jewish community. Schwerner intended to devote his life to some form of work on behalf of the poor and dispossessed; since January 1964 he and his wife had run a community center in Meridian under the auspices of the Congress of Racial Equality. "Mickey was human, intensely human," his wife said later. "He had this wonderful conviction that every human being is essentially good—that every individual knows what is good for himself and, if given a fair chance, will eventually choose what is good."[20] Goodman was a product of the same secular Jewish tradition; like

Schwerner, he declined to have a bar mitzvah. The son of parents who met as students at Cornell University and whose youthful politics in the thirties were defined by antifascism, Goodman was raised on Manhattan's liberal Upper West Side. His mother, Carolyn, a clinical psychologist, and his father, Robert, an engineer, were nonobservant Jews who raised their three sons to believe in humanism. "That was the key word for us," said eighty-eight-year-old Carolyn Goodman in 2003. "And it's a positive word—not the negative that conservatives have tried to make it. To me, a good Jew is someone who believes in the equality of human beings and reaches out to those in need. That's what Andy believed—and that's why he went to Mississippi. Not because God told him to do it but because he believed in human beings helping other human beings."[21] Goodman had been in Mississippi just one night when he drove off toward the tiny town of Longdale with Schwerner and Chaney, on a mission to see what they could do to help black farmers whose church had just been burned down by the Klan. The three were murdered on June 21, 1964—a day after the U.S. Senate passed the landmark civil rights act outlawing discrimination in public accommodations and employment. Their bodies were entombed beneath a dam under construction in Neshoba County, and the decomposing remains were excavated forty-four days later, after an informer revealed the location to the FBI. The conspirators had only planned to murder Schwerner, who was well known to them because he had been working in Meridian since January. The killers were baffled because Goodman, unlike Schwerner, was clean-shaven. "The other Jew don't look much like a Jew" was the verdict on Goodman's beardlessness. In the end, he was killed because he was with Schwerner and was, after all, only "another atheist, Communist, nigger-loving Jew."[22]

Nine months after the slayings in Mississippi, another murder of another civil rights worker made front-page news. Viola Gregg Liuzzo, a thirty-nine-year-old Detroit wife and mother of five, was shot on a lonely stretch of highway between Selma and Montgomery. Liuzzo, a lapsed Catholic, was neither an atheist nor an agnostic, but she represented many in the movement who were motivated by humanistic rather than theistic spiritual beliefs. Many of the "spiritual humanists"—as distinct from absolutely secular humanists—were middle-aged women who had turned to religion to sustain them during a life crisis, only to find that orthodox faith no longer had answers that made sense. Liuzzo's crisis came when one of her babies was born dead. In *From Selma to Sorrow* (1998), her biographer, Mary Stanton, describes a painful scene in which Liuzzo was informed that, according to Catholic doctrine, a stillborn baby could never go to heaven because it had not been baptized. Liuzzo asked her husband, "Why would a loving God do that. . . . I can't believe it's true."[23] In 1965, she began attending Detroit's First Unitarian Universalist Church, a center of civil rights activism with many former freedom riders in its congregation.

After the murder, J. Edgar Hoover's FBI orchestrated a campaign to stigmatize Liuzzo as a bad mother and a mentally unstable woman of loose morals. The slanderous publicity was based on remarkably persistent social stereotypes used to label female social activists as libertines and opponents of God Himself. (An FBI informer was in the car with the men charged with actually shooting Liuzzo—reason enough for a disinformation campaign aimed at blaming the victim.) In the 1830s, when Angelina and Sarah Grimké began to speak out about the sexual degradation of black women under slavery, the sisters were constantly accused of having an unnatural interest in interracial sex—an accusation all the more potent in an era when respectable women were not supposed to be interested in sex at all. Lucretia Mott, whose personal reputation was so spotless that she could not be charged with sexual prurience, was attacked instead as a "bad woman," "female fanatic," and "brazen infidel" whose antislavery mission amounted to nothing less than a "sacrilegious condemnation of the Holy Bible."[24] The posthumous denigration of Liuzzo, the only woman to be murdered for her participation in the civil rights movement, took a similar tack, employing far more vulgar and graphic terms than those available to nineteenth-century gentlemen.

"Acquittal is certain," predicted Matt Murphy, the attorney representing the Klansmen charged with Liuzzo's killing. "All I need to use is the fact that Mrs. Liuzzo was in the car with a nigger man and she wore no underpants."[25] Liuzzo had been accompanied by a nineteen-year-old local black volunteer, and they were heading for Montgomery to pick up tired marchers and drive them back to Selma. By 1965, the image of female civil rights workers sans underpants had become a cliché throughout the South. A toxicologist's report showed no evidence that Liuzzo had recently engaged in sexual intercourse— a finding that the self-styled "Klonsel" Murphy repeatedly challenged. At the trial, Murphy also took aim at Liuzzo's religious beliefs. "Mrs. Liuzzo was up there singing, 'we will overcome, we will overcome, we will overcome,' " he ranted. "What in God's name were they trying to overcome? God himself? . . . Integration breaks every moral law God wrote. Noah's son was Ham [and he] committed adultery and his sons were the Hamites and God banished them and they went to Africa and the only thing they ever built was grass huts. No white woman can ever marry a descendant of Ham."[26] Liuzzo's status as a mother of five was used not to gain sympathy for her but to impeach her character; national opinion polls showed that a majority of Americans—women as well as men, northerners as well as southerners—felt that no mother had a right to leave her children, even for a few days, to work for a social cause. That Liuzzo had not expected to be murdered was beside the point in the view of a public that still believed a woman's place was in the home. The participation in the civil rights movement of many white women of Liuzzo's generation—and even more women in their twenties—elicited vicious epithets that proved to be a precursor of later right-wing attacks on the reborn feminist movement. Black female volunteers were thought to be sleeping with white male volunteers, but that was more acceptable to southern segregationists than the ravishing of white women by the descendants of Ham. Betty Friedan, in her 1963 bestseller *The Feminine Mystique*, drew a telling connection between contemporary attacks on civil rights workers and nineteenth-century attacks on advocates of women's suffrage. Her analysis would prove just as true in relation to the twentieth-century women who participated in both the civil rights and the feminist movements:

> The myth that these women [nineteenth-century feminists] were "unnatural monsters" was based on the belief that to destroy the God-given subservience of women would destroy the home and make slaves of men. Such myths arise in every kind of revolution that advances a new portion of the family of man to equality. The image of the feminists as inhuman, fiery man-eaters, whether expressed as an offense against God or in the modern terms of sexual perversion, is not unlike the stereotype of the Negro as a primitive animal or the union organizer as an anarchist.[27]

Liuzzo, a coal miner's daughter and a high school graduate who had only recently begun attending college, had read *The Feminine Mystique*. Although the killings of Goodman and Schwerner prompted the usual segregationist complaints that outside agitators had no business intruding on the southern way of life, there was no suggestion that the two had unmanned themselves by their actions. Liuzzo, by contrast, was attacked not only as a northern busybody but, as Friedan might have predicted, as an unnatural woman who had stepped out of her God-ordained place in society. In the view of hardcore segregationists, she deserved to die for that transgression; in the eyes of less biased Americans, she may not have deserved to die but was certainly responsible for placing herself in harm's way. Young Rita Schwerner, waiting in Mississippi for her husband's body to be found, had been denigrated on precisely the same grounds. She, too, had violated the traditional code for women, not by leaving her husband behind in the North but by coming to Mississippi to work with him side by side and by aggressively challenging state officials for their complicity in his death. Not to mention the fact that the couple had slept in the homes of black Mississippians—the implication being that the Schwerners had been availing themselves of the opportunity to engage in interracial sex rather than simply taking advantage of the only shelter available to northern civil rights workers. Such a woman, in the view of many white Mississippians, deserved to be widowed at a young age.[28]

It takes nothing away from the heroism of civil rights volunteers animated by religious ideals to point out that the movement also had many heroes animated by nonreligious humanism. One of the greatest strengths of the movement was that it had room enough, as there had been in the ranks of nineteenth-century abolitionists, for every strand of religious and nonreligious belief: the devout Christianity of a King, the individualistic and humanistic spirituality of a Liuzzo, the atheism of a Schwerner or a Goodman. In the era of its greatest successes, which included passage of the 1964 and 1965 laws attempting to undo nearly a century of Jim Crow, the civil rights movement became an overarching moral force that embraced and transcended both religion and secularism. But the laws that emerged from the civil rights struggle, though assuredly written in the blood of martyrs, were based not on the duties of humans to their gods but on the obligations of citizens to one another. The desire of the apostles of religious correctness to recast the civil rights struggle as a purely religious movement is of a piece with their insistence that the secularist framers of the Constitution really intended to found a Christian nation. The attempt of the religious right to sacralize the civil rights struggle has nothing to do with historical truth and everything to do with the time that has passed since those passionate days—time enough to engender the sentimentality that breeds forgetting.

Although the civil rights and the later antiwar movement were grounded in both religious and secularist impulses, the third great social movement originating in the sixties—the renewal of the struggle for women's rights—was thoroughly and fundamentally secularist. Religious feminists, who have labored for years with varying degrees of success to transform Protestantism, Catholicism, and Judaism into faiths that respect the equality of women both as members and as spiritual leaders, will no doubt quarrel with any definition of feminism as essentially secularist. On this issue, however, the religious right is right: true belief in and commitment to the equality of women and men shakes the foundations of all religions. Religion and feminism can be reconciled only through a radical reconstruction of traditional religious practices and beliefs. By admitting women to the clergy, much of American Protestantism and Reform and Conservative Judaism have adapted to what is essentially a secularist demand—that women be treated within their religious institutions as equal moral and intellectual beings. It is reasonable to argue, as religious conservatives do, that mainstream American religion has become more secularized as a result of its accommodation to feminism—just as mainstream nineteenth-century Protestantism was secularized by its accommodation to evolutionism and eighteenth-century Protestantism by its exposure to Enlightenment thought. Whether one views the secularization of religion as good or bad is another matter. For extremist conservatives of all faiths, the status of women is a line in the sand, a measure of their unwillingness to let secular laws and new secular customs overturn centuries of religious dogma and tradition. The real enemies of fundamentalism are rationalism and the modern world, and while this observation is most frequently applied by American pundits to radical Islamist theocracies, it also applies in some measure to any religion, fundamentalist or not, that treats women as the inferiors of men.

Pope John Paul II's absolute refusal to consider admitting women to the Catholic priesthood—although the majority of American and European Catholics strongly support the ordination of women—baffles many non-Catholics, in part because the church espouses increasingly liberal positions on matters of social and economic justice. But the pope's resistance is based on theology, not sociology, and is perfectly comprehensible within his historical frame of reference. The church is not a democracy—yet another secularist idea—and its practices are not determined by the opinions of its communicants. For the men who run the church today, allowing women to take center stage in what faithful Catholics believe to be the literal transformation of bread and wine into the body and blood of the savior—the doctrine known as transubstantiation—represents not merely a loss of male hierarchical power but the desacralization of Catholicism's fundamental mystery. The essence of a secularist and rationalist worldview *is* the desacralization of mysteries and taboos that defy logic and the laws of nature, and that is why American feminism has elicited such fierce and enduring enmity from the religious right. At its core, feminism can only be understood as an attack on the sacralization of man-made customs governing relations between the sexes.

Most of the women who led the resurgence of American feminism in the late sixties were veterans of both the civil rights and the antiwar movements, and an extraordinarily large proportion were secular Jews who, like Schwerner and Goodman, identified themselves with Jewish social activism rather than with Judaism as a religion. Many Jewish feminists, fearful of the anti-Semitism that had been used historically to besmirch social reform movements with a strong Jewish presence, tried to downplay the importance of Jews in the movement. The long-standing rightist equation of Jews with atheists made the visibility of Jews as feminist theorists and tactical leaders even more problematic from a public relations standpoint. Betty Friedan and Gloria Steinem, the most recognizable feminists to mainstream Americans by the early seventies, were both Jews (actually, Steinem was Jewish only on her father's side). On her lecture tours around the country, Steinem usually teamed up with a black speaker in a strategy designed to defuse charges that feminists were white elitists unconcerned with either black or working-class white women. The full story of African American feminism has yet to be written, but black women not only benefited from but shaped some of the most important feminist advances in education and employment. Beginning in the early seventies, which produced the first generation of prominent female attorneys and officeholders elected on their own instead of as widows of lawmakers, black political pioneers like Representatives Barbara Jordan of Texas and Shirley Chisholm of New York were powerfully supportive of feminist causes. Women's rights never took precedence over the drive for racial justice for black feminists, but for many, especially in public life, the two causes complemented each other. There were too many similarities between the justifications for discrimination based on race and on sex for successful African American women to dismiss feminism as a white woman's cause.

Just as the civil rights movement took up the unfinished work of emancipation, the feminist movement took up the unfinished business begun at Seneca Falls in 1848. The feminists of the sixties and seventies were a throwback not to the middle-of-the-road suffragists who took over the women's movement at the end of the nineteenth century but to the more radical feminism of the founding mothers. Time had proved Stanton correct in her contention that the vote alone was not enough to achieve equal rights for women. Many of the issues that mattered to the new feminists, such as discrimination in employment and education, had been just as important to the early-nineteenth-century advocates for women's equality. These bread-and-butter demands for fair treatment, which have now become as uncontroversial as suffrage, were resisted fiercely when first broached to employers at the beginning of the 1970s. A pro forma ban on sex discrimination in employment had been added to the ban on racial and religious bias in Title VII of the Civil Rights Act, largely because segregationist lawmakers hoped that some of their male colleagues would find the inclusion of women so outlandish that they might vote against the whole bill. Most business leaders never dreamed that women would one day actually sue to gain access to jobs and salaries that had been reserved for men. There was no organized women's movement to press such demands in 1964, although if more men of power had read Friedan's feisty *Feminine Mystique*, some of them might have seen the handwriting on the kitchen wall. Demands for equal job opportunities and equal pay might and did irritate, even incense, those accustomed to relying on and profiting from the work of women restricted to poorly paid secretarial and "pink-collar" jobs like waitressing. However, bread-and-butter feminism was not so fundamentally threatening as to arouse the full ire of the religious right. It took the legalization of abortion, with its negation of sacral rationales for strict social control of women's childbearing decisions, to join the battle between conservative religion and secularist feminism.

Abortion was the first issue to unify feminists who were fighting among themselves about everything from the "bourgeois" makeup of the movement's participants to the importance of gay concerns. The latter was no trivial matter for feminism's public image: "dyke" was the epithet of choice hurled at feminists from the first protest that attracted public notice—the picketing of the 1968 Miss America pageant by a group of New York women. "Kikes and dykes" soon followed, proving that efforts to divert attention from the Jewish presence in the movement had not been entirely successful. In a year that had seen the assassinations of King and Robert F. Kennedy, rioting in urban ghettos after King's murder, and bloody clashes between police and antiwar demonstrators protesting at the Democratic National Convention in Chicago, a challenge to the values embodied by Miss America was treated by the press more as comic relief than as a serious harbinger of any broader women's activism. That dismissive attitude changed sooner than anyone would have predicted in a country torn by racial strife and deeply divided over the Vietnam War. The seriousness of the feminist campaign for liberalization of abortion laws was in large measure responsible for a shift in the attitude of superior amusement that the media had initially adopted toward "women's libbers." Abortion also served as a strong, albeit temporary, bridge between "rationalist feminists," who focused on specific goals attainable within the structure of American society, and a profoundly irrational element, also present on the wilder fringes of the New Left, whose ideas about how to gain justice for women eventually came to encompass violence, anarchy, and hatred of men. As the feminist author Susan Brownmiller notes in her memoir *In Our Time* (1999), "an imaginative campaign—rash, impudent, decentralized, yet interconnected by ideas and passion—successfully altered public perception to such an extent that a 'crime,' as the law defined it, became a 'woman's constitutional right.' "[29] The climax of the campaign was, of course, the *Roe* decision in 1973. The feminist drive to overturn restrictive abortion laws took many forms—lobbying state legislatures, helping women across the country to obtain abortions in the few states that permitted them, and educating the press about injuries and deaths resulting from more than one million illegal abortions performed each year. In the four years leading up to the Supreme Court decision—an astonishingly short time for any public education campaign to succeed—feminists, with support from a handful of courageous doctors, helped to create a widespread public awareness of an issue that had scarcely existed in the consciousness of anyone other than women who had themselves faced the desperate choices necessitated by an unwanted pregnancy. (In 1968, when I was twenty-three and first became aware of the new women's movement, I identified myself as a feminist but had never given a moment's thought to the subject of abortion.) In 1968, a Gallup poll found that only 15 percent of Americans favored liberalizing abortion laws; by 1972, 64 percent did.

The most important achievement of feminists who fought for the legalization of abortion—one that particularly enraged the religious right—was the stripping away of at least some of the secrecy and shame that had long surrounded the experience for women themselves. In the first issue of *Ms.* magazine in 1972, fifty-three women signed a declaration, addressed to the Nixon White House, under the simple headline WE HAVE HAD ABORTIONS. The prominent signers included Pulitzer Prize–winning historian Barbara Tuchman, folksinger Judy Collins, tennis star Billie Jean King, and Steinem, editor in chief of the new magazine and a media darling. Signing the statement was an act of considerable courage for women who had careers and reputations to protect; they were admitting to an act that was still a crime in most parts of the nation and was considered a grievous sin by many of their fellow Americans. Their refusal to accept the burden of sin and shame, coupled with the belief that decisions about abortion fall within the domain of individual conscience rather than of religious dogma, laid bare the secularist underpinnings of the new feminist ideals.

The insistence that abortion was and should be a private and individual matter is a classic example of moral relativism—an honorable concept that has been poisoned by cultural conservatives and insufficiently defended by secularists. Supporters of legal abortion say, in essence, "You think abortion is wrong, and I respect that, but I think abortion is right in some circumstances—so neither of us should decide for the other." To understand why that position is so repellent to the religious right, and why it has given rise to a powerful thirty-year movement aimed at overturning *Roe*, it is necessary to examine the ways in which the meaning of moral relativism, both in a philosophical sense and in terms of its influence on public policy, has been distorted. The stereotypical conservative image of relativism is that it amounts to nothing more than the notion that all morality is merely a matter of personal opinion. On a deeper level, theological and social conservatives define relativism as an "end justifies the means" ethic used to rationalize acts that should always, in any circumstance, be deemed both sinful and criminal. A murder is a murder, say the moral absolutists. The fallacy in this logic is that while all decent societies do indeed prohibit murder, they disagree on the definition of murder—and such disagreement exists even within a specific society at a specific time. Indeed, every dictionary defines murder as "the unlawful killing of a human being with malice aforethought." *Unlawful.* That one word turns the supposedly sacrosanct, eternal concept of murder into a thoroughly relativist notion. Whether the act is, or is not, unlawful is the heart of the matter. Is it murder to execute criminals? The Christian right says no, capital punishment is a *lawful* form of societal self-defense, while opponents of capital punishment say that executions are nothing more than state-sanctioned murder. The law, made by men and not by God, is what makes the difference. Abortion poses precisely the same problem of definition. The Protestant right and the Catholic hierarchy say that abortion is murder because they regard even a day-old collection of cells as a human being—a person capable of being murdered. Most Jews, mainstream Protestants, liberal Catholics, and atheists do not regard abortion as murder because they do not believe that the embryo or fetus—at least not before it can survive outside the mother's body—is a person. The battle over abortion is a quarrel not between relativists who favor murder and absolutists who oppose it but between competing definitions of whether a fetus is a person to whom the term *murder* can even be applied. The absolutists, speaking out of their own subjective religious beliefs, insist that their definition is the one that should serve for all. The secularist and relativist positions—and they are, for all practical purposes, identical—is that one subjective religious viewpoint cannot serve all in a democratic society.

Justice Harry Blackmun's eloquent opinion in *Roe* epitomizes both secularism and relativism in its assertion that the Constitution "is made for people of fundamentally differing views, and the accident of our finding certain opinions natural and familiar or novel and even shocking ought not to conclude our judgment upon the question whether statutes embodying them conflict with the Constitution of the United States." Blackmun, whose wife, Dottie, was in attendance on January 22, 1973, when he read an eight-page summary of his opinion, opened with a revealing statement that explicitly elaborated on the relativist nature of his thinking:

> We forthwith acknowledge our awareness of the sensitive and emotional nature of the abortion controversy, of the vigorous opposing views, even among physicians, and of the deep and seemingly absolute convictions that the subject inspires. One's philosophy, one's experiences, one's exposure to the raw edges of human existence, one's religious training, one's attitudes toward life and family and their values, and the moral standards one establishes and seeks to observe, are all likely to influence and to color one's thinking and conclusions about abortion.

Blackmun went on to state unequivocally that "the word 'person,' as used in the Fourteenth Amendment, does not include the unborn."[30]

Grounded in the controversial assertion of a constitutional right to privacy, *Roe* was the product not only of the new feminist consciousness but of a half century of struggle by civil libertarians and centrist birth control crusaders. On this issue, the radical feminists and the more "bourgeois" representatives of the ACLU and Planned Parenthood were united. Harriet Pilpel, general counsel for both the ACLU and Planned Parenthood, pushed hard and successfully to make reproductive rights a part of the ACLU's agenda; her mentor and predecessor as counsel for both groups was Morris Ernst, who had been fighting for the legalization of birth control since the thirties. In the early sixties, many within the ACLU had feared that being identified with abortion would remarginalize the organization just as the nation emerged from the fear-filled legacy of the McCarthy era. Moreover, abortion rights activists, whether they came from the legalistic civil libertarian community or from more radical feminist groups, were constantly attacked as enemies of religion—and the ACLU's antireligious image had long been a matter of great concern to many of its board members.

In 1973, those who celebrated the *Roe* decision had no idea that it would become the touchstone of conservative religious and political activism for the rest of the century. As Brownmiller observes, feminists responded to the decision with "the euphoric delusion that the women's revolution was an unstoppable success."[31] Even those less given to euphoria—including some old ACLU hands who anticipated a proliferation of state laws designed to evade the intent of *Roe*—had reason to believe that legal abortion, like the desegregation of public facilities, would eventually be tolerated by those who detested the practice. The delusion that the abortion battle was over was fueled by the inability of many secularists, whether atheists or adherents of a liberal faith, to comprehend the absolute conviction that animates orthodox believers. Like the soon to be revived fundamentalist campaign against evolution, the antiabortion crusade set off by *Roe* was seen by its Christian soldiers not as a political battle—though it was certainly that too—but as a stark confrontation between absolute good and absolute evil. Just as William Jennings Bryan had considered evolutionism inseparable from atheism, bolshevism, and perverted science and technology, the religious right saw the legalization of abortion as the culmination of everything loathsome in the social upheavals not only of the previous decade but of the previous two centuries. Belief in the divinely ordained rights of the unborn overcame centuries of theological enmity between Protestant fundamentalists and the American Catholic hierarchy and bridged the gap between the economic conservatism of the Protestant right and the liberal commitment to social justice of the Catholic Church. Although American Catholic bishops favored generous government spending to aid the poor, and the Protestant right tended to see government as an accomplice of Satan, the common commitment to the battle against abortion trumped all differences.

The battle would not be short or easy, for the task that religious conservatives set for themselves was not merely the undoing of *Roe* but the dismantling of two centuries of safeguards written into the nation's godless Constitution. For the past four decades, the militant religious right has mounted a tireless assault on separation of church and state—a principle deeply inculcated in though seldom reflected upon by a public that takes religious freedom for granted. For the religiously correct, it is not enough for Americans to believe, as they always have and do today, that government interference with religion is a bad thing. The public must also be persuaded that religious interference with government is a good thing—that it is not interference at all but a beneficent and harmonious manifestation of God's blessings upon America.

Reason Embattled

In January 2002, Supreme Court Associate Justice Antonin Scalia made a major speech so sweeping and extreme in its contempt for democracy, and so willfully oblivious to the Constitution's grounding in human rather than divine authority, that it might well, in an era when American secularists were less intimidated by the forces of religion, have elicited calls for impeachment. Delivered at the University of Chicago Divinity School and revealingly titled "God's Justice and Ours," Scalia's address opened with an overview of the death penalty in America but moved quickly to the justice's disdain for secular government.[1] Scalia is an outspoken judicial supporter of capital punishment, to the point of upholding state laws that permit the execution of minors and the mentally retarded. The death penalty does not violate the Eighth Amendment's prohibition of cruel and unusual punishment, in Scalia's opinion, because executions were not considered "cruel and unusual" when the Constitution was written. Indeed, as the justice pointed out, the death penalty could be imposed in the eighteenth century not only for murder but for many other felonies, like horse thieving. To Scalia, the Constitution is "not living but dead—or, as I prefer to put it, enduring. It means today not what current society (much less the Court) thinks it ought to mean, but what it meant when it was adopted." If this line of thought is followed to its logical and unsettling conclusion—if the Constitution can mean only what it meant in 1791—courts should be free to hand down death sentences for grand theft auto, the modern equivalent of horse theft.

But the real underpinnings of Scalia's support for the death penalty are to be found not in constitutional law but in the justice's religious convictions. He believes that the state derives its power not from the consent of the governed—"We, the People," as the "dead" document plainly states—but from God. God has the power of life and death, and therefore lawful governments also have the right to exact the ultimate penalty. Democracy, with its pernicious idea that citizens are the ultimate arbiters of public policy, is responsible for the rise of opposition to the death penalty in the twentieth century. "Few doubted the morality of the death penalty in the age that believed in the divine right of kings," Scalia noted in his speech. He would have been just as accurate had he pointed out that most subjects in absolute monarchies also supported the right of kings to torture and to impose the death penalty by drawing and quartering. To bolster his argument, Scalia turned to that perennial favorite of conservative politicians and theologians the evangelist Paul:

> Let every soul be subject unto the higher powers. For there is no power but of God: the powers that be are ordained of God. Whosoever therefore resisteth the power, resisteth the ordinance of God: and they that resist shall receive to themselves damnation. For rulers are not a terror to good works, but to the evil. Wilt thou then not be afraid of the power? Do that which is good, and thou shalt have praise of the same: for he is the minister of God to thee for good. But if thou do that which is evil, be afraid; for he beareth not the sword in vain: for he is the minister of God, a revenger to execute wrath upon him that doeth evil. (Romans 13:1–4)

The justice then reminded his divinity school audience, "This is not the Old Testament, I emphasize, but St. Paul." His disclaimer is significant, because it implies that New Testament justice is morally superior to "Old Testament vengeance": the divine authority claimed by Scalia for the death penalty is not the law of Moses but Christian (conservative Christian) doctrine. That is a common enough Christian prejudice, even in our enlightened ecumenical age, but one with limitless potential for mischief when it issues from the lips of a Supreme Court justice who sees civil government through a theological lens:

> It is easy to see the hand of the Almighty behind rulers whose forebears, in the dim mists of history, were supposedly anointed by God, who at least obtained their thrones in awful and unpredictable battles whose outcome was determined by the Lord of Hosts, that is, the Lord of Armies. It is much more difficult to see the hand of God—or any higher moral authority—behind the fools and rogues (as the losers would have it) whom we ourselves elect to do our own will. How can their power to avenge—to vindicate the "public order"—be greater than our own?

In other words, if our elected leaders are merely human, with power that can be granted and rescinded only by humans, there is no reason for the rest of us to respect their authority. That citizens might respect themselves enough to respect the authority of their elected officials—even without being threatened by the sword of the Lord of Hosts—is a possibility that Scalia does not even consider. If there were any doubt about the explicitly Christian nature of Scalia's vision, he erased it with his contention that "the more Christian a country is the *less* likely it is to regard the death penalty as immoral. Abolition [of capital punishment] has taken its firmest hold in post-Christian Europe, and has least support in the church-going United States. I attribute that to the fact that, for the believing Christian, death is no big deal."

As a practicing and theologically conservative Catholic, Scalia has just one problem with the death penalty: it has been denounced by his church, in John Paul II's 1995 encyclical *Evangelium Vitae* (a document that also condemns euthanasia and abortion). But Scalia was relieved to learn, after consulting with experts in canon law, that the pope's views on the death penalty—unlike his views on abortion—are not binding upon Catholics but must merely be given serious and respectful consideration. That is fortunate for the justice, because he believes that American Catholics should resign from public office if they are asked in their role as public officials to uphold government policies that contradict the doctrines of the church. Indeed, Scalia's problem with the church's "new" (a word he equates with bad) teaching on capital punishment offers a perfect illustration of the danger of looking for heavenly instructions to solve earthly political disputes. If popes of different generations can interpret God's will in different ways in response to changing social circumstances—and John Paul's views about the immorality of the death penalty would surely confound his predecessors who presided over the Inquisition—it seems presumptuous for a mere judge to cite unchanging divine orders in support of his opinions.

As evidence of the religious faith on which the United States was supposedly founded, Scalia cited the inscription "In God We Trust" on coins; the phrase "one nation, under God" in the Pledge of Allegiance; and the "constant invocations of divine support in the speeches of our political leaders, which often conclude, 'God bless America.'" Scalia failed, however, to mention the relatively recent and opportunistic origins of these supposedly sacred symbols and practices. The affirmation on coins of America's trust in the deity was intended as a harmless sop to ministers who, during the Civil War, wanted to bully Congress and the president into amending the Constitution to include God, while "under God" found its way into the pledge only as a belated slap in the face to the godless Soviets. As for the endless repetitions of "God bless America," it is fair to say that the first six presidents of the United States did not invoke the blessings of the deity as frequently in their entire public careers as President Bush does each month. And somehow, the republic survived. Far from representing a tradition that goes back to the founding fathers, the ubiquitous and obligatory invocations of God by American public officials today represent a radical break with the secularist ideals that formed the basis of the American constitutional government. In

Scalia's pantheon of American religious symbols, there is one conspicuous exception—the Constitution itself. He did not explain to the
Chicago divines exactly how he reconciles the Constitution's deliber-
ate omission of any reference to God with the contention that the
American government derives its ultimate power not from the people
but from the divinity. Of course, the two cannot be reconciled. The
founders were fully aware of all the ministerial predictions that the
deity, furious at being left out of the Constitution, would "crush us to
atoms in the wreck"—and still they chose to invoke the authority of
the people. Self-styled strict constructionists like Scalia have no alternative but to ignore what the Constitution actually says—or rather,
does not say.

Astonishingly, Scalia's radical speech attracted little public notice
until it was reprinted five months later in *First Things: The Journal of
Religion and Public Life* and then dissected in a column on the op-ed
page of the *New York Times*. "Chilling" was the word used in the
Times by Sean Wilentz, director of Princeton University's American
studies program, to describe Scalia's views.[2] The initial absence of any
consternation over Scalia's broadside against secular government is
one measure of the religious right's success in placing liberals and secularists on the defensive—and of the cowardice of politicians who fear
being maligned as antireligious when they stand up for separation of
church and state.

The virtue of the justice's extremism is that it lays bare the mes-
sianic radicalism at the heart of the current assault on separation of
church and state. This assault is not only an attempt to rewrite secular
law; it is also intended to undermine all secularist and nonreligious
humanist values. For the warriors of the religious right, governmental
power is not an end in itself but merely one more mechanism, along
with institutions of education, communications, and finance, for
advancing their values within society. The official White House Web
site says it all: the Office of Faith-Based and Community Initiatives
offers a long list of "do's and don'ts for faith-based organizations"
attempting to negotiate the federal grant system. The White House
helpfully documents an ever-expanding array of grant possibilities

deemed particularly suitable for religious organizations. Heading the list is abstinence education, the pet program of those who oppose both birth control and abortion and insist that preaching chastity is the only way to prevent unwanted pregnancies. Fifty-six years ago in his *McCollum* opinion, Justice Hugo Black asserted that "Jefferson's metaphor in describing the relation between Church and State speaks of a 'wall of separation,' not of a fine line easily overstepped." Reasonable people may disagree about how high the wall should rise in specific situations, but the White House's checklist inviting churches to begin feeding at the federal trough—and providing detailed instructions on how to strike the best deal—does not even acknowledge the existence of a line, much less a wall. Short of erecting a cross atop the White House (and perhaps a menorah, a crescent, and a statue of Buddha to show that America respects all faith-based institutions), the current administration could hardly do more to demonstrate its commitment to pulverizing a constitutional wall that has served both religion and government well for more than two hundred years.

It is demoralizing, and a measure of the intimidating power of religiously correct rhetoric, that so many Democrats have jumped on the faith-based bandwagon. During the 2000 presidential campaign, Democratic presidential candidate Al Gore told reporters that he would precede every major executive decision with the question "What would Jesus do?" His running mate, Joseph Lieberman, a strong supporter of faith-based funding, pooh-poohed First Amendment concerns. "The line between church and state is an important one and has always been hard for us to draw," he said, "but in recent years we have gone far beyond what the Framers ever imagined in separating the two . . . and constructed a 'discomfort zone' for even discussing our faith in public settings—ironically making religion one of the few socially acceptable targets of intolerance." Lieberman is a historical amnesiac: his grandparents and great-grandparents, mindful of their people's experience in Europe, would likely have been more concerned about what erosion of the church-state barrier might do to Jews than about allowing any religion, including their own, a share of government largesse. Moreover, American Jewish organizations have always viewed attacks on the establishment clause as potentially "bad for the Jews"—understandably so, since the success story of American Jews is one of the great testaments to the beneficent effect of secularist government on religious minorities. Had the founding secularists not won the battle over prohibiting religious (aka Christian) tests for public office, a constitutional amendment would have been required at some point for Lieberman to run for any national position. Lieberman's statement also follows the religiously correct line that religion, not secularism, is embattled in the public square in America. If that is true, it is difficult to understand why the president feels free to offer biblical references in support of his foreign and domestic policies and why nearly every candidate for national office emphasizes the supposed centrality of religion in American life, why television anchors now routinely assure grieving relatives of crime victims and fallen soldiers, "Our prayers are with you."

Religion is so much a part of the public square that a majority of Americans say they would refuse to vote for an atheist for president, even though they would consider voting for an African American, a woman, a Jew, or a homosexual.[3] Americans are probably not telling the truth on this issue to pollsters; it is difficult to credit the assertion that a majority of citizens, in the privacy of the voting booth, would cast their ballots for a gay or a black presidential candidate, and I also have my doubts that either a Jew or a woman could be elected at this time. It is clear, however, that Americans find it much more socially acceptable to express prejudice against atheists than against other groups. One can only imagine the outcry from the religiously correct if, say, the Council for Secular Humanism applied for a grant to provide pregnancy counseling for teenagers.

The Christian right, with its financial power and its stranglehold on the Republican Party, is a now familiar actor in the embattlement of American secularism. Initially brought together by their fury over *Roe*, right-wing political action committees have over a thirty-year period channeled millions of dollars in every election into the coffers of candidates pledged to promote legislative abortion restrictions and to support the appointment of antiabortion judges. The capture of the Republican Party by a militant religious minority, and the marginalization of libertarian conservatives like Senator John McCain of Arizona and the late Senator Barry Goldwater (also from Arizona, a state that admires rugged individualism in its politicians), has produced decades of judicial appointments that have moved the entire federal bench to the right. The Supreme Court now decides most abortion cases by a 5-4 vote, and the resignation of just one prochoice justice would give Bush the chance to make an appointment that could finally fulfill the most cherished dream of the religious right—the overturning of *Roe*. However, the initial right-wing focus on abortion has long since been expanded into a much larger agenda designed to obliterate the distinction, to borrow Scalia's words, between "God's justice and ours." From well-publicized campaigns such as the revived battle against the teaching of evolution—with antievolutionism repackaged as "creation science"—to quieter efforts like the push by fundamentalist broadcasters to drive "liberal" public radio stations from the airwaves, the Christian right tirelessly works to insinuate its values into every aspect of public policy at every level of government.

Yet it is a mistake to view the rise of religious correctness as a phenomenon driven exclusively by right-wing money and political clout. An equally important factor—indeed, an indispensable condition for the successes of the ultraconservative minority—is the larger American public's unexamined assumption that religion per se is, and always must be, a benign influence on society. The extreme right has exploited that assumption brilliantly and succeeded in tarring opponents of faith-based adventurism as enemies of all religion, as atheists, as "relativists." It takes a drastic example of religion's potential to do either public or private harm—say, a Christian Scientist parent's denial of a life-saving blood transfusion to his child or the transformation of a plane into a death-dealing weapon in the name of the extreme fundamentalist wing of Islam—to shake the general American faith in all religion as a positive social force. Indeed, religious correctness demanded that President Bush deny the existence of any connection between the events of September 11 and "real" Islam, just as far-right religious antiabortion organizations invariably deny any connection between their demonization of abortion and the assassinations of doctors who perform abortions. The problem, of course, is not religion, of whatever brand, as a spiritual force but religion melded with political ideology and political power. Since the religiously correct do not acknowledge any danger in mixing religion and politics, evil acts committed in the name of religion must always be dismissed as the dementia of criminals and psychopaths.

Embattled secularists have done a particularly poor job of educating mainstream religious believers about the religious right's effort to vitiate the First Amendment. Most Americans do not read conservative intellectual journals like *First Things*, and it is highly doubtful that the majority of citizens, religious or nonreligious, would agree with Scalia's more extreme views—if they were aware of them. Nor is it likely that they would approve of a broad faith-based initiative if the implications had been explained to them by respected public figures, from the worlds of business, religion, and private charities as well as politics, with the courage and integrity to defend secularist values. A 2001 poll by the Pew Forum on Religion and Public Life, a respected organization that regularly queries Americans on religious issues, revealed an astonishing disconnect between Americans' general approval of faith-based funding and their deep reservations about what specific churches might actually do with government money.[4] While 70 percent said that they support faith-based funding for social services—a figure repeatedly cited by proponents of such plans— nearly 80 percent opposed tax support of religious organizations that hire only members of their own faith. Yet Bush ignored the overwhelming public sentiment against discriminatory hiring in an executive order issued in late 2002, in which he told federal agencies that religious groups could qualify as public contractors even if they refuse to hire workers of other faiths. One reason the president may have felt free to disregard public disapproval of religious discrimination in hiring was the near-total absence of press coverage highlighting the kinds of reservations expressed in the Pew poll.

The public also indicated that it has grave doubts about the ability of religious organizations to deliver services in areas clearly affected by religious doctrine. Only 39 percent queried by the Pew researchers felt that religious groups were best qualified to provide pregnancy counseling. Secular community-based groups were favored by 42 percent, and another 16 percent chose the government. Government—neither private religious nor secular organizations—was seen by a large majority as the most effective provider of health care, job training, and literacy programs. Faith-based organizations were viewed as most effective only for feeding the homeless and counseling prisoners (who may be seen by the public as one group that could benefit from a strong dose of hellfire).

Moreover, nearly 60 percent of Americans oppose any federal funding for groups that encourage religious conversions. That is significant, because among America's major religions, Judaism is the only faith that does not have a tradition of proselytizing. Christian evangelicals, the staunchest supporters of faith-based funding, constantly seek converts via the mass media as well as through outreach from individual congregations. It is hardly likely, though, that the government will deny funds to the evangelical Christian community of which the born-again president is a member. Indeed, the public's fears about discriminatory hiring and religious proselytizing have already been borne out in at least one fundamentalist Christian program for prisoners, operating in four states under the auspices of a foundation headed by Charles Colson, a born-again Christian and convicted Watergate felon. In 2003, Americans United for Separation of Church and State sued to halt the "Christ-centered" program, under which prisoners are offered privileges that include access to big-screen televisions, computers, and private bathrooms in return for a hefty dose of Bible study and "Christian counseling." Furthermore, the program's employees, as a condition of being hired, are required to sign a statement affirming their belief in a literal interpretation of the Bible. That is precisely the sort of religious discrimination in hiring rejected by four out of five Americans in the Pew poll.

Finally, the poll results underline the most obvious peril inherent not only in faith-based funding for social services but in many plans (spurred by the ill-advised 2002 Supreme Court decision *Zelman v. Simmons-Harris*, upholding an Ohio school voucher program) to provide tax breaks for parents whose children attend religious schools. The danger in such subsidies, recognized by the men who wrote Virginia's religious freedom act in the 1780s, is that they make it the government's business to decide which religions are worthy of public support and which are not. Americans may give a general nod of approval to faith-based funding, but the faiths they approve by a convincing majority are limited to mainstream Protestantism, Judaism, and Catholicism. While more than 60 percent in the Pew survey said that conventional Protestant and Catholic churches and synagogues should be able to apply for government money, only a bare majority—51 percent—wanted evangelical Protestant churches to be eligible. (This result might be a reflection of mainstream America's distrust of right-wing television evangelists.) As for Islam, only 38 percent of Americans thought mosques should be eligible—and the Pew poll was taken before September 11. On what basis do we decide which religions—and which factions within religions—are "moderate" enough to be eligible for tax money? That is precisely the question that the framers of the Constitution never wanted to fall within the authority of any government agency or official.

Americans' strong reservations when presented with specific questions about faith-based funding—as distinct from a general question that does not raise the matter of exactly which religions will get money and for what purpose—suggest that many would respond positively to a strong secularist defense of the godless constitution. For secularists to mount such an effective challenge, they must first stop pussyfooting around the issue of the harm that religion is capable of doing. In a peculiar essay in the *Atlantic* titled "Kicking the Secularist Habit," David Brooks (now an op-ed columnist for the *New York Times*) admits to having discovered the astonishing fact, in the wake of September 11, that "human beings yearn for righteous rule, for a just world or a world that reflects God's will—in many cases at least as strongly as they yearn for money or success."[5] To understand the yearning for a world that reflects God's will, Brooks argues, it is necessary to move "away from scientific analysis and into the realm of moral judgment." The crucial questions are, "Do individuals pursue a moral vision of righteous rule? And do they do so in virtuous ways, or are they, like Saddam Hussein and Osama bin Laden, evil in their vision and methods?" Whether Brooks ever was a genuine secularist or whether he merely set up a straw man in his essay, the crucial question in judging such matters is not whether individuals pursue a "moral vision of righteous rule": fanatics throughout history have always been convinced of the virtuousness of their visions. The fundamental issue is whether fanatics possess the power to pursue their particular religious/political vision with devastating consequences for those who do not share it. If bin Laden did not have political and financial support from radical Islamists dedicated to extending the sweep of their theocracies, the morality or immorality of his personal vision would be of little consequence: he would be just another aggrieved prophet crying in the wilderness.

It is precisely because secularists do understand the power of religion, and the possibility that any intensely felt drive for righteousness may overwhelm dissenters in its path, that they insist on the fundamental importance of separation between church and state. Bin Laden, with his clear-cut evil aims, is an easy case; the hard cases, which the Constitution was designed to prevent, involve political decisions in which both virtue and evil may be in the eye of the beholder. There is no doubt that Bush, in many areas of foreign and domestic policy, is pursuing his vision of righteous rule in a fashion compatible with his religion-based personal morality—but he is pursuing it through a governmental mechanism that represents millions of Americans who do not share his religion or his personal idea of righteousness.

Nor is it enough for secularists to speak up in defense of the Constitution; they must also defend the Enlightenment values that produced the legal structure crafted by the framers. Important as separation of church and state is to American secularists, their case must be made on a broader plane that includes the defense of rational thought itself. The great nineteenth-century freethinkers, heirs of the Enlightenment, are often mocked today for their faith in human progress and the ascendancy of science and for their predictions that a secular religion combining humanism and scientific rationalism would soon replace the orthodox creeds of the day. Men like Ingersoll were certainly wrong in their predictions of the imminent demise of religion—even in its most retrograde and cruel forms—but whether they were wrong under the long arc of the moral universe remains to be seen. The need for a strong secularist defense of science is especially urgent today, as many of the antisecularist right's policy goals are intimately linked to an irrational distrust of science and scientists. There is a particularly strong connection between the revival of antievolutionism since 1980 and the political attack on separation of church and state, because the Christianization of secular public education has long been a goal of the forces of conservative religion. Indeed, the teaching of evolution is often cited by right-wing politicians as a major cause of school violence. Soon after the 1999 shootings at Columbine High School, Representative Tom DeLay of Texas (now House majority leader) suggested that the theory of evolution, which places humans within the animal kingdom, is responsible for influencing children to behave like lower animals. Quoting a letter published in a Texas newspaper, DeLay observed that American schoolchildren are being indoctrinated in the notion "that they are nothing but glorified apes who have evolutionized out of some primordial soup of mud." This sort of know-nothingism is often dismissed by secularist intellectuals as too absurd to merit a reply, but similar arguments are being advanced on a regular basis, at local school board meetings throughout the nation, as a justification for teaching "creation science" in biology classes.

There is also a connection between the antievolution campaign and the lamentable state of American scientific literacy. During the past two decades, study after study has documented the decreasing knowledge of basic scientific facts among American public school students and their teachers. This ignorance is generally attributed to lax American educational standards, and there is of course a great deal of truth in the charge. But fundamentalist, antimodernist religion has, since the twenties, been a significant player in the dumbing down of the scientific curriculum at the elementary and secondary school level. Because knowledge of biology has increased exponentially since the midpoint of the twentieth century, and understanding of biology is critical to understanding science in general, antievolutionists have the potential to inflict much greater damage on schools today than they did in the past. It is safe to say that in no outpost of "secular Europe" would one out of four public school biology teachers have said, as American teachers did in a 1988 survey by researchers from the University of Texas, that humans and dinosaurs may have inhabited the earth simultaneously. A similar proportion of high school science teachers believed that it was possible for the living to communicate with the dead.[6] It is hard to imagine that accurate information is being conveyed to students by teachers whose heads are in such a muddle. One may hope that a teacher who believes in communication with "the other side" will keep her spiritualist faith out of the classroom, but a teacher who does not know that dinosaurs were extinct eons before humans arrived on the scene can hardly be deemed fit to instruct her students in modern biology (or, for that matter, in late-nineteenth-century biology). Just as the word *evolution* was removed from many textbooks in the twenties, evolutionary development as a scientific fact began to be downplayed in the nineties in school districts where organized fundamentalists brought pressure to bear on school administrators and elected school boards. Many teachers, fearful of being targeted for taking a strong stand on evolution (presumably not the same teachers who believe dinosaurs roamed the earth with man), now try to avoid using the E-word in their classrooms.

The obfuscation of scientific terminology to placate the religiously correct cannot help but undermine Americans' ability to make crucial distinctions between scientific fact and theological opinion. Fundamentalists would have great success in convincing a significant portion of the public that science has no more of a factual basis than any religion and that the evolution of man from lower life forms is as unproven as the special creation of man in the Garden of Eden. While most Americans today continue to reject the fundamentalists' outright opposition to the teaching of evolution in public schools, opinion polls have also shown that the majority of the public sees no problem with schooling that places a religious version of God-guided evolution—"intelligent design"—on an equal footing with scientific evolutionary theory. The fundamentalists' successful campaign to blur the distinction between scientific and religious concepts—the oxymoronic "creation science" is the most brilliant example—has impaired the ability of the public, and its elected representatives, to bring rational analysis to bear on nearly every public policy issue involving bioethics. The heated political debate over embryonic cloning, for example, has been characterized by the stunning inability of many in Congress to distinguish between duplicating embryos for the purpose of extracting their cells to treat disease and cloning humans by nursing embryos and fetuses in hatcheries à la *Brave New World*. Lack of scientific understanding on the part of legislators and the public has enabled religious opponents of the research (who on this issue include both Protestant fundamentalists and the Catholic hierarchy) to obscure the fact that their real objection to all medical uses of embryonic stem cells is that they consider any interference with the embryo a form of abortion. That is a perfectly legitimate position, but it is a theological position that should not be permitted to masquerade as a general ethical principle.

The attack on science is a prime secularist issue not because religion and science are incompatible but because particular forms of religious belief—those that claim to have found the one true answer to the origins and ultimate purpose of human life—are incompatible not only with science but with democracy. Those who rely on the perfect hand of the Almighty for political guidance, whether on biomedical research or capital punishment, are really saying that such issues can never be a matter of imperfect human opinion. If the hand of the Almighty explains and rules the workings of nature, it can hardly fail to rule the workings of the American political system.

The fact that an overwhelming majority of Americans say they believe in God and (in much smaller numbers) regularly attend church does not mean that a coherent secularist message will fall on deaf ears. As the Pew poll results show, most Americans, whatever their religious views, have a healthy respect for the constitutional principle of separation of church and state. And most oppose the religious right's attempts to sacralize decisions on such matters as biomedical research. Polls consistently show that a majority, among Catholics and evangelical Christians as well as others, disagree with their church leaders on stem-cell studies. The problem is that religious fundamentalists care more about religious issues than the rest of the public does, and they do more to see that their views are heard. They have dominated public discourse and have trapped American secularists between two poles. On the one hand, secularists are credited with exaggerated importance by those who have swallowed the argument that the nonreligious have already won the day; on the other, secularists are attacked (sometimes by the same people) as enemies of majoritarian, by definition religious, American values. The antisecularists cannot have it both ways. If secularists are in charge of everything, then America is not as religious as the religiously correct claim; if secularists are an insolent minority trying to erode the values of the majority, then they are not in charge of everything.

To make an effective case to their fellow Americans, secular humanists must reclaim the language of passion and emotion from the religiously correct. No one is a more pedestrian orator in ordinary circumstances than Bush, but when he drew on the words of Paul to assure a grieving nation that "nothing can separate us from God's love," he gained a new stature not only from the gravity of the situation but from the passion and grace of the words written in that most emotional of books, the Bible. Secularists frequently present themselves, and are perceived by others, as a cool lot, applying intellectual theories to social questions but ignoring the emotions that move religious believers. In August 2003, when federal courts ordered the removal of a hefty Ten Commandments monument from the Alabama State Supreme Court building, thousands of Christian demonstrators converged on Montgomery from as far away as California. They were not only outraged but visibly grief-stricken when the monument was moved out of sight. It was, one demonstrator said with tears in his eyes, like a death in the family. Secularist civil libertarians who had brought the lawsuit, by contrast, spoke in measured, objective tones about the importance of the First Amendment's separation of church and state. The language and gestures of emotion do not lend themselves to the communication of rationalist values. In Montgomery, Christian demonstrators kissed their Bibles; for a secularist, kissing a copy of the Constitution would be a form of idolatry.

Yet it is crucial for today's secularists to find a way to convey the passions of humanism as Ingersoll once did, to move hearts as well as to change minds. In a speech (appropriately titled "A Lay Sermon") before the American Secular Union in 1886, Ingersoll quoted "the best prayer I have ever read"—the soliloquy Lear delivers when, after raging on the heath, he stumbles on a place of shelter:

> *Poor naked wretches, wheresoe'er you are,*
> *That bide the pelting of this pitiless storm,*
> *How shall your houseless heads and unfed sides,*
> *Your loop'd and window'd raggedness, defend you*
> *From seasons such as these? Oh, I have ta'en*
> *Too little care of this! Take physic, pomp;*
> *Expose thyself to feel what wretches feel,*
> *That thou mayst shake the superflux to them,*
> *And show the heavens more just.*

This is the essence of the secularist and humanist faith, and it must be offered not as a defensive response to the religiously correct but as a robust creed worthy of the world's first secular government. American secularists have trouble deciding what to call themselves today, in part because the term has been so denigrated by the right and in part because identifying oneself as a secular humanist—unlike, say, calling oneself a Jew, a Catholic, or a Baptist—has a vaguely bureaucratic ring. It is time to revive the evocative and honorable *freethinker*, with its insistence that Americans think for themselves instead of relying on received opinion. The combination of *free* and *thought* embodies every ideal that secularists still hold out to a nation founded not on dreams of justice in heaven but on the best human hopes for a more just earth.

<hr />

Robert Ingersoll's Eulogy for Walt Whitman, March 30, 1892

My friends: Again we, in the mystery of Life, are brought face to face with the mystery of Death. A great man, a great American, the most eminent citizen of this Republic, lies dead before us, and we have met to pay a tribute to his greatness and his worth.

I know he needs no words of mine. His fame is secure. He laid the foundations of it deep in the human heart and brain. He was, above all I have known, the poet of humanity, of sympathy. He was so great that he rose above the greatest that he met without arrogance, and so great that he stooped to the lowest without conscious condescension. He never claimed to be lower or greater than any of the sons of men.

He came into our generation a free, untrammeled spirit, with sympathy for all. His arm was beneath the form of the sick. He sympathized with the imprisoned and despised, and even on the brow of crime he was great enough to place the kiss of human sympathy.

One of the greatest lines in our literature is his, and the line is great enough to do honor to the greatest genius that has ever lived. He said, speaking of an outcast: "Not till the sun excludes you do I exclude you."

His charity was wide as the sky, and wherever there was human suffering, human misfortune, the sympathy of Whitman bent above it as the firmament bends above the earth.

He was built on a broad and splendid plan—ample, without appearing to have limitations—passing easily for a brother of mountains and seas and constellations; caring nothing for the little maps and charts with which timid pilots hug the shore, but giving himself freely with recklessness of genius to winds and waves and tides; caring for nothing as long as the stars were above him. He walked among men, among writers, among verbal varnishers and veneerers, among literary milliners and tailors, with the unconscious majesty of an antique god.

He was the poet of that divine democracy which gives equal rights to all the sons and daughters of men. He uttered the great American voice; uttered a song worthy of the great Republic. No man ever said more for the rights of humanity, more in favor of real democracy, of real justice. He neither scorned nor cringed, was neither tyrant nor slave. He asked only to stand the equal of his fellows beneath the great flag of nature, the blue and stars.

He was the poet of Life. It was a joy simply to breathe. He loved the clouds; he enjoyed the breath of morning, the twilight, the wind, the winding streams. He loved to look at the sea when the waves burst into the whitecaps of joy. He loved the fields, the hills; he was acquainted with the trees, with birds, with all the beautiful objects of the earth. He not only saw these objects, but understood their meaning, and he used them that he might exhibit his heart to his fellow-men.

He was the poet of Love. He was not ashamed of that divine passion that has built every home in the world; that divine passion that has painted every picture and given us every real work of art; that divine passion that has made the world worth living in and has given some value to human life.

He was the poet of the natural, and taught men not to be ashamed of what is natural. He was not only the poet of democracy, not only the poet of the great Republic, but he was the poet of the human race.

He was not confined to the limits of this country, but his sympathy went out over the seas to all the nations of the earth.

He stretched out his hand, and felt himself the equal of all kings and all princes, and the brother of all men, no matter how high, no matter how low.

He has uttered more supreme words than any writer of our century, possibly of almost any other. He was, above all things, a man, and above genius, above all the snow-capped peaks of intelligence, above all art, rises the true man. Greater than all is the true man, and he walked among his fellow-men as such.

He was the poet of Death. He accepted all life and all death, and he justified all. He had the courage to meet all, and was great enough and splendid enough to harmonize all and to accept all there is of life as a divine melody.

You know better than I what his life has been, but let me say one thing. Knowing, as he did, what others can know and what they cannot, he accepted and absorbed all theories, all creeds, all religions, and believed in none. His philosophy was a sky that embraced all clouds and accounted for all clouds. He had a philosophy and a religion of his own, broader, as he believed—as I believe—than others. He accepted all, he understood all, and he was above all.

He was absolutely true to himself. He had frankness and courage, and he was as candid as light. He was willing that all the sons of men should be absolutely acquainted with his heart and brain. He had nothing to conceal. Frank, candid, pure, serene, noble, and yet for years he was maligned and slandered, simply because he had the candor of nature. He will be understood yet, and that for which he was condemned—his frankness, his candor—will add to the glory and greatness of his fame.

He wrote a liturgy for mankind; he wrote a great and splendid psalm of life, and he gave to us the gospel of humanity—the greatest gospel that can be preached.

He was not afraid to live, not afraid to die. For many years he and death were near neighbors. He was always willing and ready to meet and greet this king called death, and for many months he sat in the deepening twilight waiting for the night, waiting for the light.

He never lost his hope. When the mists filled the valleys, he looked upon the mountain tops, and when the mountains in darkness disappeared, he fixed his gaze upon the stars.

In his brain were blessed memories of the day, and in his heart were mingled the dawn and dusk of life.

He was not afraid; he was cheerful every moment. The laughing nymphs of day did not desert him. They remained that they might clasp the hands and greet with smiles the veiled and silent sisters of the night. And when they did come, Walt Whitman stretched his hand to them. On one side were the nymphs of the day, and on the other the silent sisters of the night, and so, hand in hand, between smiles and tears, he reached his journey's end.

From the frontier of life, from the western wave-kissed shore, he sent us messages of content and hope, and these messages seem now like strains of music blown by the "Mystic Trumpeter" from Death's pale realm.

To-day we give back to Mother Nature, to her clasp and kiss, one of the bravest, sweetest souls that ever lived in human clay.

Charitable as the air and generous as Nature, he was negligent of all except to do and say what he believed he should do and say.

And I to-day thank him, not only for you but for myself, for all the brave words he has uttered. I thank him for all the great and splendid words he has said in favor of liberty, in favor of man and woman, in favor of motherhood, in favor of fathers, in favor of children, and I thank him for the brave words he has said of death.

He has lived, he has died, and death is less terrible than it was before. Thousands and millions will walk down into the "dark valley of the shadow" holding Walt Whitman by the hand. Long after we are dead the brave words he has spoken will sound like trumpets to the dying.

And so I lay this little wreath upon this great man's tomb. I loved him living, and I love him still.

Notes

INTRODUCTION

1. ROBERT GREEN INGERSOLL, *The Works of Robert Ingersoll* (New York, 1900), vol. 9, pp. 74, 76.
2. ISAAC KRAMNICK and R. LAURENCE MOORE, *The Godless Constitution: The Case against Religious Correctness* (New York, 1996).
3. THEODORE ROOSEVELT, *Gouverneur Morris* (Oyster Bay, 1975), p. 174.
4. The Graduate Center, City University of New York, *American Religious Identification Survey, 2001*, exhibits 1, 3. All figures in this survey are based strictly on self-reported religious identification or affiliation. The population of ethnic Jews in America, for example, is significantly larger than the population of those who identified themselves as religiously observant Jews in the CUNY survey.
5. The Pew Forum on Religion and Public Life (www.pewforum.org), "Religion and Politics: Contention and Consensus," July 24, 2003.
6. The phrase was coined by RICHARD JOHN NEUHAUS, *The Naked Public Square* (Grand Rapids, 1984).
7. STEPHEN L. CARTER, *The Culture of Disbelief* (New York, 1993), p. 67.
8. INGERSOLL, *Works*, vol. 8, pp. 393–94.

CHAPTER I: REVOLUTIONARY SECULARISM

1. *The Adams-Jefferson Letters*, ed. LESTER J. CAPPON (Chapel Hill, 1959), vol. 2, p. 373.
2. JOHN A. DIX, *History of the Parish of Trinity Church in the City of New York* (New York, 1889–1950), vol. 1, p. 304, in JON BUTLER, *Awash in a Sea of Faith* (Boston, 1990), p. 177.
3. I. WOODRIDGE RILEY, *American Philosophy in the Early Schools* (New York, 1907), p. 217, from folio volume of Stiles manuscripts at Yale University, p. 460.
4. Quoted in BROOKE HINDLE, *The Pursuit of Science in Revolutionary America, 1735–1789* (Chapel Hill, 1956), p. 255.
5. *The Papers of Thomas Jefferson*, ed. JULIAN P. BOYD (Princeton, 1950), vol. 8, p. 269.
6. ETHAN ALLEN, *Reason the Only Oracle of Man* (New York, 1940), p. 119.
7. TIMOTHY DWIGHT, *Travels in New-England and New-York* (London, 1823), vol. 2, p. 388.
8. See G. ADOLPH KOCH, *Republican Religion* (New York, 1933), p. 33.
9. ALLEN, *Reason*, p. 457.
10. *The Life and Selected Writings of Thomas Jefferson*, ed. ADRIENNE KOCH and WILLIAM PEDEN (New York, 1988), p. 46.
11. *The Complete Madison*, ed. SAUL K. PADOVER (New York, 1953), p. 303.
12. Ibid., p. 300.
13. See THOMAS E. BUCKLEY, S.J., *Church and State in Revolutionary Virginia* (Charlottesville, 1977), pp. 179–80.
14. Ibid., p. 148. By the "Bill of Rights," the petitioner meant the Virginia Declaration of Rights, written by George Mason and adopted by the Virginia Constitutional Convention of June 12, 1776. Thomas Jefferson drew on the opening paragraphs of Virginia's Declaration of Rights in the Declaration of Independence. In 1789, the Virginia declaration became the model for the federal Constitution's Bill of Rights.
15. DAVID BENEDICT, *A General History of the Baptist Denominations in America* (Boston, 1813), vol. 2, p. 479.
16. Quoted in BUCKLEY, *Church and State*, p. 150.
17. Ibid.
18. Ibid., p. 147.
19. *Life and Selected Writings of Thomas Jefferson*, p. 46.
20. See BUCKLEY, *Church and State*, p. 191.

21. *Life and Selected Writings of Thomas Jefferson,* p. 378.
22. Quoted in MORTON BORDEN, *Jews, Turks, and Infidels* (Chapel Hill, 1984), p. 12.
23. Quoted in RUSSELL NYE, *The Cultural Life of the New Nation* (New York, 1960) p. 198.
24. Quoted in *The Debates in the Several State Conventions on the Adoption of the Federal Constitution,* ed. JONATHAN ELIOT (Philadelphia, 1891), p. 41.
25. Quoted in BORDEN, *Jews, Turks, and Infidels,* p. 16.
26. D. M'ALLISTER, "Testimonies to the Religious Defect of the Constitution" (Philadelphia, 1784), in BORDEN, *Jews, Turks, and Infidels,* p. 41.
27. Ibid., pp. 35–36.
28. Ibid., pp. 39–40.
29. *Adams-Jefferson Letters,* vol. 2, p. 512.
30. Ibid.
31. *Papers of George Washington,* Library of Congress, vol. 325, pp. 19–20. A facsimile of Washington's letter is available online at www.tourosynagogue.org.

CHAPTER 2: THE AGE OF REASON AND UNREASON

1. "Thomas Paine's Second Appearance in the United States," *Atlantic Monthly,* vol. 4, no. 21, July 1859.
2. *The Thomas Paine Reader,* ed. MICHAEL FOOT and ISAAC KRAMNICK (New York, 1987), p. 402.
3. Quoted in KOCH, *Republican Religion,* p. 272.
4. *Life and Selected Writings of Thomas Jefferson,* p. 254.
5. Ibid., pp. 255–56.
6. "The Voice of Warning, to Christians, on the Ensuing Election of a President of the United States" (New York, 1800), p. 8, in KOCH, *Republican Religion,* p. 270.
7. KOCH, *Republican Religion,* p. 275.
8. Quoted in NYE, *Cultural Life,* p. 213.
9. LYMAN BEECHER, *Autobiography, Correspondence, Etc.,* ed. CHARLES BEECHER (New York, 1864), vol. 1, p. 43.
10. TIMOTHY DWIGHT, *Sermons* (New Haven, 1828), vol. 1, p. 355.
11. Ibid., p. 43.
12. For a fuller discussion, see FRANCES HILL, *A Delusion of Satan* (New York, 1995), pp. 53–59.

13. WILLIAM BENTLEY, *The Diary of William Bentley* (Salem, 1905) vol. 1, p. 82.

14. Ibid., p. 88.

15. BUTLER, *Awash in a Sea of Faith*, p. 220.

16. JAMES RIKER, *The Annals of Newtown, in Queens County, New-York* (New York, 1852), in KOCH, *Republican Religion*, p. 232.

17. JOHN FELLOWS, "Memoir of Mr. Palmer" (London, 1828), p. 4, in KERRY S. WALTERS, *Elihu Palmer's "Principles of Nature"* (Wolfboro, N.H., 1990), p. 9.

18. Quoted in WALTERS, *Elihu Palmer's*, pp. 101–03.

19. KOCH, *Republican Religion*, pp. 290–91.

20. Quoted in WALTERS, *Elihu Palmer's*, p. 180.

21. BENJAMIN FRANKLIN, *Representative Selections*, ed. CHESTER E. JORGENSEN and FRANK LUTHER MOTT (New York, 1936), p. 485.

22. ROBERT HALL, *Modern Infidelity Considered with Respect to Its Influence on Society* (Charlestown, Mass., 1801), in WALTERS, *Elihu Palmer's*, p. 13.

23. TIMOTHY DWIGHT, *The Duty of Americans at the Present Crisis*, July 4, 1798, p. 11.

24. WILLIAM MEADE, *Old Churches, Ministers and Families of Virginia* (Philadelphia, 1872), vol. 1, p. 175.

25. "Thomas Paine's Second Appearance in the United States."

26. NATHAN BANGS, *A History of the Methodist Episcopal Church* (New York, 1845), vol. 2, p. 21.

27. THOMAS PAINE, "Common Sense," *The Complete Writings of Thomas Paine*, ed. PHILIP S. FONER (New York, 1945), vol. 1, p. 13.

28. THOMAS PAINE, *The Age of Reason: Part I, Complete Writings of Thomas Paine*, vol. 1, p. 506.

29. "Thomas Paine's Second Appearance in the United States."

30. Ibid.

31. Ibid. Zoar was the city where Lot and his daughters took refuge after fleeing Sodom. In the biblical account, Zoar was the only city righteous enough to merit surviving the Lord's destruction of all other sinful communities in the vicinity.

32. The *Complete Writings of Thomas Paine*, vol. 2, p. 1433.

33. Ibid., pp. 1435–38.

34. BENTLEY, *Diary*, vol. 3, p. 442.

35. Quoted in ALFRED OWEN ALDRIDGE, *Man of Reason: The Life of Thomas Paine* (Philadelphia, 1959), p. 316.

36. *Beacon*, August 10, 1844, in CAROL A. KOLMERTEN, *The American Life of Ernestine Rose* (Syracuse, 1999), p. 40.

37. MONCURE DANIEL CONWAY, *The Life of Thomas Paine* (New York, 1892), vol. 2, p. 428.

CHAPTER 3: LOST CONNECTIONS: ANTICLERICALISM, ABOLITION-
ISM, AND FEMINISM

1. *Adams-Jefferson Letters*, vol. 2, p. 515.

2. W. J. CASH, *The Mind of the South* (New York, 1941), p. 57.

3. Ibid., p. 81.

4. THOMAS BACON, *Four Sermons Preached at the Parish Church of St. Peter, in Talbot County . . .*, (London, 1853), in BUTLER, *Awash in a Sea of Faith*, pp. 144–45.

5. *Liberator*, August 6, 1836, in *Documents of Upheaval: Selections from William Lloyd Garrison's "The Liberator," 1831–1865*, ed. TRUMAN NELSON (New York, 1966), p. 108.

6. Quoted in CASH, *Mind of the South*, p. 80.

7. HENRY MAYER, *All on Fire* (New York, 1998), p. xix.

8. Quoted in Ibid., p. 18.

9. Quoted in Ibid., p. 30.

10. *Liberator*, November 21, 1845, in AILEEN S. KRADITOR, *Means and Ends in American Abolitionism* (New York, 1969), pp. 92–93.

11. Ibid.

12. CATHERINE H. BIRNEY, *Sarah and Angelina Grimké: The First American Women Advocates of Abolition and Women's Rights* (Westport, 1885), p. 190.

13. Quoted in Ibid., p. 182.

14. *History of Woman Suffrage*, ed. ELIZABETH CADY STANTON, SUSAN B. ANTHONY, and MATILDA JOSLYN GAGE (Rochester, 1881), vol. 1, p. 81.

15. Ibid., pp. 82–83.

16. In *Documents of Upheaval*, p. 97.

17. BENTLEY, *Diary*, vol. 4, p. 311.

18. Quoted in KRAMNICK and MOORE, *Godless Constitution*, p. 139.

19. Ibid., p. 141.

20. RICHARD H. JOHN, *Spreading the News: The American Postal System from Franklin to Morse* (Cambridge, 1995), p. 201.

21. Quoted in KRAMNICK and MOORE, *Godless Constitution*, p. 142.

22. *Liberator*, July 23, 1836, in *Documents of Upheaval*, pp. 97–98.

23. Ibid., July 30, 1836, pp. 101–102.

24. Ibid., August 6, 1836, p. 107.

25. *James and Lucretia Mott: Life and Letters*, ed. ANNA DAVIS HALLO-WELL (Boston, 1884), pp. 186–87.

26. *History of Woman Suffrage*, vol. 1, p. 419.

27. Ibid., p. 191.

28. MAYER, *All on Fire*, p. 290.

29. *Liberator*, August 28, 1840, in *Documents of Upheaval*, p. 170.

30. ELIZABETH CADY STANTON, *Eighty Years and More* (Boston, 1898), pp. 147–48.

31. Ibid.

32. ELISABETH GRIFFITH, *In Her Own Right: The Life of Elizabeth Cady Stanton* (New York, 1984), p. 55.

33. *History of Woman Suffrage*, vol. 1, p. 70.

34. GRIFFITH, *In Her Own Right*, p. 56.

35. *History of Woman Suffrage*, vol. 1, p. 72.

36. Ibid., p. 73.

37. *New York Herald*, October 25, 1850.

38. Quoted in MAYER, *All on Fire*, p. 391.

39. *James and Lucretia Mott: Life and Letters*, p. 485.

40. *History of Woman Suffrage*, vol. 1, p. 431.

41. Ibid., p. 341.

42. KOLMERTEN, *American Life*, p. xviii. There is only one other full-length biography of Rose, Yuri Suhl's 1959 *Ernestine L. Rose and the Battle for Human Rights*, commissioned by the Emma Lazarus Federation of Jewish Women's Clubs. Written from à Jewish perspective before the beginning of the late-twentieth-century feminist movement, the book was reissued in 1990 under the title *Ernestine L. Rose: Woman's Rights Pioneer*.

43. Quoted in Ibid., p. 153.

44. Quoted in Ibid., p. 107.

45. *Boston Investigator*, December 12, 1855, in KOLMERTEN, *American Life*, p. 153.

46. *History of Woman Suffrage*, vol. 1, pp. 608–09.

47. *Albany Express*, March 1, 1854, in KOLMERTEN, *American Life*, p. 137.

48. Quoted in DIANNE ASHTON, *Rebecca Gratz: Women and Judaism in Antebellum America* (Detroit, 1977), p. 228.

49. SARA A. UNDERWOOD, *Heroines of Free Thought* (New York, 1876), p. 259.

CHAPTER 4: THE BELIEF AND UNBELIEF OF ABRAHAM LINCOLN

1. *Pittsburgh Dispatch*, Jan. 28–29, 1864, in BORDEN, *Jews, Turks, and Infidels*, p. 63.

2. *Proceedings of the National Convention to Secure the Religious Amendment of the Constitution of the United States, Held in Cincinnati, January 31 and February 1, 1872* (Philadelphia, 1872), pp. viii–x, in BORDEN, *Jews, Turks, and Infidels*, p. 69.

3. The Emancipation Proclamation did not free all slaves, only those in states in rebellion against the Union. Slaves in states like Kentucky, which had remained loyal to the Union even though their laws permitted slavery, were not freed until the Thirteenth Amendment was passed in 1865.

4. BENJAMIN P. THOMAS, *Abraham Lincoln* (New York, 1952), p. 359.

5. Director of the U.S. Mint, *Fourth Annual Report* (Washington, 1896), in *Truth Seeker*, vol. 34, November 30, 1907.

6. RONALD C. WHITE JR., *Lincoln's Greatest Speech* (New York, 2002), p. 102.

7. Quoted in WILLIAM J. WOLF, *The Religion of Abraham Lincoln* (New York, 1963), p. 201.

8. JOHN E. REMSBURG, *Six Historic Americans* (New York, 1906), pp. 34–35.

9. Ibid., p. 83.

10. WARD HILL LAMON, *Life of Lincoln* (Boston, 1872), p. 487.

11. JOSIAH GILBERT HOLLAND, *Life of Lincoln* (Springfield, Mass., 1866), p. 542.

12. Ibid., pp. 235–39.

13. LAMON, *Life of Lincoln*, p. 486.

14. Ibid.

15. WARD HILL LAMON, *Recollections of Abraham Lincoln: 1847–1865*, ed. DOROTHY LAMON TEILLARD (New York, 1895), pp. 335–36. After Ward Hill Lamon died in 1893, his daughter edited and published the personal notes and documents that her father had originally intended to use in a second volume of his 1872 *Life of Lincoln*—a project Lamon abandoned when the first volume sold poorly.

16. ELTON TRUEBLOOD, *Abraham Lincoln: Theologian of American Anguish* (New York, 1973), p. 14.

17. ABRAHAM LINCOLN, *The Collected Works of Abraham Lincoln* (New Brunswick, 1953), vol. 5, pp. 419–20.

18. WOLF, *Religion of Abraham Lincoln*, p. 186.

19. WHITE, *Lincoln's Greatest Speech*, p. 201.
20. Quoted in Ibid., p. 182.
21. Ibid., pp. 202–03.
22. *New York World*, March 6, 1865.
23. Quoted in JAY WINIK, *April 1865* (New York, 2001), p. 163.

CHAPTER 5: EVOLUTION AND ITS DISCONTENTS

1. INGERSOLL, *Works*, vol. 1, p. 393.
2. ASA GRAY, *Darwiniana* (Cambridge, Mass., 1963), p. 16.
3. *New York Times*, September 5, 1873.
4. CHARLES DARWIN, *The Origin of Species* and *The Descent of Man*, Modern Library combined ed. (New York, 1948), p. 911.
5. Ibid., pp. 411–12.
6. SAMUEL CLEMENS to OLIVIA LANGDON, January 8, 1870, in *The Bible according to Mark Twain*, ed. HOWARD G. BAETZHOLD and JOSEPH B. MCCULLOUGH (New York, 1996), p. xv.
7. INGERSOLL, *Works*, vol. 1, pp. 394–95.
8. P. R. RUSSELL, *Advent Review and Sabbath Herald*, no. 47 (1876), p. 153, in RONALD L. NUMBERS, *The Creationists* (New York, 1992), p. 5.
9. Quoted in STEPHEN JAY GOULD, *Rocks of Ages* (New York, 1999), pp. 119–20.
10. JAMES TURNER, *Without God, Without Creed: The Origins of Unbelief in America* (Baltimore, 1985), p. 180.
11. See GEORGE E. WEBB, *The Evolution Controversy in America* (Lexington, 1994) p. 16.
12. *Life and Letters of Thomas Henry Huxley*, ed. LEONARD HUXLEY (London, 1900), p. 461.
13. *American Journal of Science*, vol. 1, August 1895, in HUXLEY, *Life and Letters*, p. 461.
14. *New York Times*, September 23, 1876.
15. Ibid., September 24, 1876.
16. RICHARD HOFSTADTER, *Social Darwinism in American Thought* (Boston, 1955), p. 32.
17. Ibid., p. 10.
18. JAMES R. MOORE, *The Post-Darwinian Controversies* (London, 1979), pp. 164–65, from Spencer's 1858 prospectus.
19. HERBERT SPENCER, *Social Statics* (New York, 1864), p. 415.
20. MOORE, *Post-Darwinian Controversies*, p. 167.

21. JOHN FISKE, *Essays Historical and Literary* (New York, 1907), pp. 275–76.

22. Ibid., pp. 235–36.

23. DARWIN, *Descent of Man*, pp. 500–01.

24. Ibid., p. 501.

25. Quoted in Webb, *Evolution Controversy*, p. 34.

26. SUSAN B. ANTHONY, *Diary*, April 14, 1854, in KOLMERTEN, *American Life*, p. 155.

27. GEORGE E. MACDONALD, *Fifty Years of Freethought* (New York, 1931), vol. 2, p. 330.

28. THOMAS HUXLEY to CHARLES KINGSLEY, September 23, 1860, in L. HUXLEY, *Life and Letters*, vol. 1, pp. 237–38.

29. INGERSOLL, *Works*, vol. 12, p. 400.

30. J. G. OLIVER, *Proceedings and Addresses at the Freethinkers Convention Held in Watkins* (New York, 1878), p. 178, in TURNER, *Without God*, p. 247.

CHAPTER 6: THE GREAT AGNOSTIC AND THE GOLDEN AGE OF
FREETHOUGHT

1. *Ingersoll: Immortal Infidel*, ed. ROGER E. GREELEY (Buffalo, 1977), p. 127.

2. Quoted in Ibid., p. 133.

3. KENNETH S. LATOURETTE, *A History of the Expansion of Christianity* (New York, 1937–45) vol. 4, p. 177.

4. MACDONALD, *Fifty Years*, vol. 1, p. 276.

5. *Cass County Republican*, October 22, 1874.

6. INGERSOLL, *Works*, vol. 1, pp. 377–79.

7. Ibid., pp. 374–75.

8. Ibid., vol. 12, pp. 172–73.

9. The Fugitive Slave Act of 1850 ordered "all good citizens," under penalty of prosecution, to assist federal marshals in finding escaped slaves and returning them to their owners. Federal law had provided for the return of escaped slaves since 1793, but the stiff penalties for those who assisted the escapees were new. The law was widely defied by abolitionists, although many blacks were captured and returned to slavery during the 1850s. Intended to placate the South, the act may well have hastened the coming of civil war, since it pushed many more northern whites into the abolitionist camp.

10. Quoted in C. H. CRAMER, *Royal Bob: The Life of Robert G. Ingersoll* (New York, 1952), p. 30.

11. HARRY THURSTON PECK, *"What Is Good English?" and Other Essays* (New York, 1899), p. 236.

12. INGERSOLL, *Works*, vol. 10, pp. 592–93.

13. *New York Times*, July 22, 1899.

14. *New York Sun*, August 26, 1876.

15. Quoted in CRAMER, *Royal Bob*, p. 218.

16. PECK, *"What Is Good English?"* pp. 234–35.

17. Quoted in CRAMER, *Royal Bob*, p. 102.

18. INGERSOLL, *Works*, vol. 1, p. 371.

19. *Mason City Republican*, June 11, 1885, in CRAMER, *Royal Bob*, p. 11.

20. INGERSOLL, *Works*, vol. 2, pp. 130–31.

21. *New York Times*, May 24, 1880.

22. *New York Times*, July 22, 1899.

23. INGERSOLL, *Works*, vol. 1, pp. 86–90.

24. FRED WHITEHEAD and VERLE MUHRER, *Freethought on the Frontier* (Buffalo, 1992), pp. 15–36.

25. MERIDEL K. LESUEUR, *North Star Country* (Lincoln, 1984), pp. 205, 219.

26. MACDONALD, *Fifty Years*, vol. 2, pp. 123–24.

27. Quoted in GREELEY, *Ingersoll*, p. 154.

28. *American Magazine*, October 1911.

29. INGERSOLL, *Works*, vol. 8, pp. 135–36.

30. Quoted in PAUL AVRICH, *The Haymarket Tragedy* (Princeton, 1986), p. xii.

31. FRANK HARRIS, "Emma Goldman, the Famous Anarchist," *Contemporary Portraits*, 4th ed. (New York, 1923), p. 225, in MARTHA SOLOMON, *Emma Goldman* (Boston, 1987) p. 1.

32. Quoted in AVRICH, *Haymarket Tragedy*, pp. 217–19.

33. INGERSOLL, *Works*, vol. 8, p. 292.

34. *The Letters of Robert G. Ingersoll*, ed. EVA INGERSOLL WAKEFIELD (New York, 1951), pp. 627–28.

35. Ibid., p. 220.

36. Quoted in ORVIN K. LARSON, *American Infidel: Robert G. Ingersoll*, ed. EVA INGERSOLL WAKEFIELD (New York, 1962) p. 277.

37. INGERSOLL, *Works*, vol. 1, p. 201.

CHAPTER 7: DAWN OF THE CULTURE WARS

1. GERTRUDE HIMMELFARB, *The De-Moralization of Society: From Victorian Virtues to Modern Values* (New York, 1994), p. 267.
2. *The Fundamentals*, edited by the Reverend A. C. DIXON, was published by the Testimony Publishing Company in Chicago.
3. INGERSOLL, *Works*, vol. 8, pp. 136–37.
4. W. E. B. DU BOIS, *The Autobiography of W. E. B. Du Bois* (New York, 1968), p. 285.
5. Ibid., p. 159.
6. Ibid., pp. 285–86. Du Bois was referring to the aggressive anticommunist activities of New York's Cardinal Patrick Hayes, who preceded Francis J. Spellman as head of the nation's largest Catholic diocese. By the "Communism of Christianity," Du Bois meant the egalitarianism of the early church.
7. Ibid., p. 285.
8. "Speech to the 'Opening Convention of the National Woman Suffrage Association, January 19 and 20, 1869,' " Elizabeth Cady Stanton Papers, Library of Congress, Washington, D.C.
9. GRIFFITH, *In Her Own Right*, p. 140.
10. MACDONALD, *Fifty Years*, vol. 2, p. 107.
11. *History of Woman Suffrage*, vol. 4, pp. 60–61.
12. Ibid., p. 59.
13. Ibid., p. 199.
14. Ibid., p. 209.
15. Quoted in IDA HUSTED HARPER, *Life and Work of Susan B. Anthony* (Indianapolis, 1901), vol. 2, p. 847.
16. GRIFFITH, *In Her Own Right*, p. 297.
17. ELIZABETH CADY STANTON, *The Woman's Bible* (Boston, 1993), pp. 161–62.
18. Ibid., p. 113.
19. STANTON to ELIZABETH SMITH MILLER, April 19, 1897, Elizabeth Cady Stanton Papers, Library of Congress.
20. STANTON, *Woman's Bible*, p. 11.
21. Quoted in Ibid., p. 217.
22. GRIFFITH, *In Her Own Right*, p. xv.
23. Ibid., p. xvi.
24. Quoted in CRAMER, *Royal Bob*, p. 172.
25. HEYWOOD BROUN and MARGARET LEECH, *Anthony Comstock: Roundsman of the Lord* (New York, 1927), p. 15.

26. Quoted in BROUN and LEECH, *Anthony Comstock*, p. 17.

27. CHARLES C. MOORE, *Behind the Bars: 31498* (Lexington, 1899), p. 87.

28. *Lexington Leader*, July 9, 1899, in MOORE, *Behind the Bars*, pp. 259–60.

29. ALISON M. PARKER, *Purifying America* (Chicago, 1998), p. 69.

30. Quoted in FRANK GRANGER, "Unfit to Print—Censorship of Printing," Graphic Comm Central, 1997, www.teched.vt.edu/gcc.

31. WALT WHITMAN, *Leaves of Grass* Modern Library ed. (New York, 1940), pp. 314–15.

32. *Boston Intelligencer*, May 3, 1856.

33. EMMA GOLDMAN, *Red Emma Speaks*, ed. ALIX KATES SHULMAN (New York, 1983), p. 211.

34. Quoted in JUSTIN KAPLAN, *Walt Whitman: A Life* (New York, 1980), p. 34.

35. JEROME M. LOVING, *Walt Whitman's Champion: William Douglas O'Connor* (College Station and London, 1976), p. 57. For a full discussion of the incident, see pp. 57–84.

36. WILLIAM DOUGLAS O'CONNOR, "The Good Gray Poet: A Vindication," in Loving, *Walt Whitman's Champion*, p. 168.

37. WILLIAM DOUGLAS O'CONNOR, "Suppressing Walt Whitman," *New York Tribune*, May 25, 1882.

38. Quoted in BROUN AND LEECH, *Anthony Comstock*, p. 170.

39. LOVING, *Walt Whitman's Champion*, p. 138.

40. ELIZABETH CADY STANTON, *Elizabeth Cady Stanton, as Revealed in Her Letters, Diaries, and Reminiscences*, ed. THEODORE STANTON and HARRIET STANTON BLATCH (New York, 1922), p. 210.

41. Quoted in SHERRY CENIZA, *Walt Whitman and 19th-Century Women Reformers* (Tuscaloosa, 1998), p. 237.

42. Ibid.

43. *New York Herald*, March 31, 1892.

44. INGERSOLL, *Works*, vol. 12, pp. 475–76.

CHAPTER 8: UNHOLY TRINITY: ATHEISTS, REDS, DARWINISTS

1. Quoted in LAWRENCE W. LEVINE, *Defender of the Faith: William Jennings Bryan. The Last Decade, 1915–1925* (New York, 1965), p. 279.

2. Quoted in WEBB, *Evolution Controversy*, p. 63.

3. MAYNARD M. METCALF, *An Outline of the Theory of Organic Evolution* (New York, 1904), pp. xix–xx, in Numbers, *Creationists*, p. 37.

4. *Truth Seeker*, August 20, 1904.

5. "Socialism, Communism, and Nihilism," *The Great Encyclical Letters of Leo XIII* (New York, 1903), p. 23.

6. ROGER BALDWIN, *New York Herald Tribune Books*, October 25, 1931.

7. BALDWIN, "Reminiscences," in ROBERT C. COTTRELL, *Roger Nash Baldwin and the American Civil Liberties Union* (New York, 2000), p. 30.

8. EMMA GOLDMAN, "Rebel Thoughts," *Woman Rebel*, June 1914.

9. GOLDMAN, *Mother Earth*, May 1916, pp. 426–430.

10. ELLEN CHESLER, *Woman of Valor* (New York, 1992), p. 87.

11. CLARENCE DARROW, *The Story of My Life* (New York, 1932), p. 218.

12. Quoted in PETER IRONS, *A People's History of the Supreme Court* (New York, 1999), p. 268.

13. *New York Times*, December 22, 1919.

14. Ibid., December 23, 1919.

15. FREDERICK LEWIS ALLEN, *Only Yesterday* (New York, 1959), pp. 48–49.

16. WILLIAM JENNINGS BRYAN, "The Menace of Darwinism," *Commoner*, April 1921, p. 5.

17. DARROW, *Story*, p. 32.

18. Quoted in LESLIE HENRI ALLEN, *Bryan and Darrow at Dayton* (New York, 1967), pp. 7–9.

19. *New York Times*, August 14, 1926.

20. ALLEN, *Only Yesterday*, p. 171.

21. Quoted in WEBB, *Evolution Controversy*, p. 101.

22. *New York Times*, July 13, 1926.

23. See WEBB, *Evolution Controversy*, pp. 110–34.

24. SINCLAIR LEWIS, *Babbitt* (New York, 2002), p. 16.

25. BRUCE BARTON, preface to *The Man Nobody Knows* (New York, 1924), n.p.

26. BARTON, *Man Nobody Knows*, p. 129.

27 Ibid., pp. 179–80.

28. National Education Association, *Journal of Proceedings and Address . . . 1888* (Topeka, 1888), p. 158, in PHILIP GLEASON, *Keeping the Faith: American Catholicism Past and Present* (Notre Dame, 1986), p. 124.

29. Quoted in VINCENT P. LANNIE, *Public Money and Parochial Education* (Cleveland, 1968), p. 253.

30. See CHESLER, *Woman of Valor*, pp. 201–05.

31. INGERSOLL, *Works*, vol. 4, p. 505.

32. Quoted in CHESLER, *Woman of Valor*, p. 212.

33. EMANUEL HALDEMAN-JULIUS, *The World of Haldeman-Julius* (New York, 1960), p. 28.

34. Ibid., p. 30.

35. HARRY GOLDEN, in HALDEMAN-JULIUS, *The World*, p. 5.

36. ALLAN NEVINS, preface to *American Freethought: 1860–1914*, by Sidney Warren (New York, 1943), p. 9.

37. MACDONALD, *Fifty Years*, vol. 2, pp. 609–10.

38. DARROW, *Story*, p. 279.

CHAPTER 9: ONWARD, CHRISTIAN SOLDIERS

1. GARTH JOWETT, *Film: The Democratic Art. A Social History of American Film* (Boston, 1976), pp. 233–59.

2. THOMAS C. REEVES, *America's Bishop: The Life and Times of Fulton J. Sheen* (San Francisco, 2001), p. 102.

3. DONALD F. CROSBY, *God, Church, and Flag: Senator Joseph R. McCarthy and the Catholic Church* (Chapel Hill, 1978), p. 24.

4. SAMUEL WALKER, *In Defense of American Liberties: A History of the ACLU* (Carbondale, 1990), p. 100.

5. *Near v. Minnesota*, 283 US 697.

6. See CHESLER, *Woman of Valor*, p. 330.

7. DAVID O'BRIEN, *American Catholics and Social Reform* (New York, 1960), p. 96.

8. DONALD WARREN, *Radio Priest: Charles Coughlin, the Father of Hate Radio* (New York, 1996).

9. See REEVES, *America's Bishop*, pp. 10–11.

10. *Boston Post*, May 3, 1936, in REEVES, *America's Bishop*, p. 107.

11. Quoted in SHELDON MARCUS, *Father Coughlin: The Tumultuous Life of the Priest of the Little Flower* (Boston, 1973), p. 28.

12. *Detroit News*, July 17, 1936.

13. Quoted in MARCUS, *Father Coughlin*, p. 213.

14. For a fuller discussion of Roosevelt's role, see MARCUS, *Father Coughlin*, pp. 208–24.

15. *Washington Post*, March 26, 1942.

16. See REEVES, *America's Bishop*, pp. 108–10.

17. Quoted in Ibid., p. 100.

18. *New York Times*, April 23, 1939.

19. Ibid.

20. See DAVID I. KERTZER, *The Popes against the Jews: The Vatican's Role in the Rise of Modern Anti-Semitism* (New York, 2001); JAMES CARROLL, *Constantine's Sword* (Boston, 2001); and GARRY WILLS, *Papal Sin: Structures of Deceit* (New York, 2000).

21. Quoted in PAUL BLANSHARD, *American Freedom and Catholic Power* (Boston, 1958), p. 104.

22. WALKER, *In Defense*, p. 109.

23. HARLAN F. STONE, "The Conscientious Objector," *Columbia University Quarterly*, vol. 21, no. 4 (October 1919), p. 269.

24. WALKER, *In Defense*, p. 151.

25. See JAMES MACGREGOR BURNS, *Roosevelt: The Lion and the Fox* (New York, 1956) and *Roosevelt: The Soldier of Freedom* (New York, 1970).

CHAPTER 10: THE BEST YEARS OF OUR LIVES

1. 330 US 1, 1947.

2. VASHTI CROMWELL MCCOLLUM, *One Woman's Fight* (Boston, 1961), p. 98.

3. MARTIN E. MARTY, *Modern American Religion: Under God, Indivisible, 1941–1960* (Chicago, 1996), vol. 3, pp. 225–26.

4. 333 US 203.

5. BLANSHARD, *American Freedom*, p. 1.

6. Ibid., p. 3.

7. ARTHUR HAYES SULZBERGER to *Christian Herald*, May 10, 1949, in the *Herald*, September 1950.

8. ELEANOR ROOSEVELT, "My Day," June 23, 1949.

9. SPELLMAN TO ROOSEVELT, *New York Times*, July 26, 1949.

10. *New York World-Telegram*, July 26, 1949.

11. ROOSEVELT TO SPELLMAN, *New York Times*, July 28, 1949.

12. BLANSHARD, *American Freedom*, p. 7.

13. NORMAN VINCENT PEALE, *The Power of Positive Thinking* (New York, 1963), p. viii. The first edition of Peale's book was published by Prentice-Hall in 1952.

14. REEVES, *America's Bishop*, p. 1.

15. *New York Times*, March 12, 1934.

16. BILLY GRAHAM, "Billy Graham's Own Story: 'God Is My Witness,' " *McCall's*, May 1964.

17. MARSHALL FRADY, *Billy Graham: A Parable of American Righteousness* (Boston, 1979), p. 292.

18. Ibid., p. 310.

19. Quoted in GEORGE BURNHAM and LEE FISHER, *Billy Graham and the New York Crusade* (Grand Rapids, 1957), pp. 189–90.

20. Quoted in ROBERT I. GANNON, *The Cardinal Spellman Story* (London, 1962), p. 330.

21. Quoted in FRADY, *Billy Graham*, p. 237.

22. Ibid.

23. MADALYN O'HAIR, *Why I Am an Atheist* (Austin, 1991), p. 5.

CHAPTER 11: CULTURE WARS REDUX

1. *New York Times*, January 26, 2003.

2. Quoted in THEODORE C. SORENSEN, *Kennedy* (New York, 1971), p. 194.

3. *New York Times*, June 26, 1962.

4. 370 US 421.

5. Quoted in WALKER, *In Defense*, p. 225.

6. *New York Times*, June 26, 1962.

7. "Fundamentalism," Handbook of Texas Online, a project of the General Libraries at the University of Texas at Austin and the Texas State Historical Association (Austin, 2002), www.tsha.utexas.edu.

8. "How Whites Feel about Negroes," *Newsweek*, October 21, 1963, pp. 45–57.

9. I am indebted for this observation to the Reverend CARLTON W. VEAZEY, for many years pastor of a predominantly black Baptist church in Washington, D.C., and now president of the Religious Coalition for Reproductive Choice, a national interfaith organization based in Washington.

10. See TAYLOR BRANCH, *Pillar of Fire: America in the King Years, 1963–1965* (New York, 1998), p. 121–22.

11. Ibid., p. 122.

12. See JAMES J. HENNESEY, *American Catholics: A History of the Roman Catholic Community in the United States* (New York, 1981), p. 306.

13. ARNOLD JACOB WOLF, "The Negro Revolution and Jewish Theology," *Judaism*, 13:4 (1964), pp. 478–79, in MARC SCHNEIER, *Shared Dreams: Martin Luther King, Jr. and the Jewish Community* (Woodstock, Vt., 1999), p. 126.

14. ALEX AYRES, *The Wisdom of Martin Luther King, Jr.* (New York, 1993), p. 139, in SCHNEIER, *Shared Dreams*, p. 55.

15. *New York Times*, March 30, 1965.

16. Ibid.
17. RENATA ADLER, "Letter from Selma," *New Yorker*, April 10, 1965.
18. Quoted in WILLIAM BRADFORD HUIE, *Three Lives for Mississippi* (New York, 1965), p. 237.
19. W. E. B. DU BOIS, *The Crisis Writings*, ed. DANIEL WALDEN (Greenwich, 1972), pp. 352–53.
20. See HUIE, *Three Lives*, pp. 110–11.
21. Interview with author, February 12, 2003.
22. See HUIE, *Three Lives*, pp. 167–92.
23. MARY STANTON, *From Selma to Sorrow: The Life and Death of Viola Liuzzo* (New York, 1998) p. 135. This anecdote is based on an interview with Liuzzo's daughter, MARY. At the time, Catholic teaching did maintain that the souls of unbaptized infants must remain in limbo—a state which, unlike hell, involves no physical suffering but which deprives the unbaptized soul of the presence of God. However, the Second Vatican Council revised that doctrine, and Catholics now believe that an unbaptized, stillborn infant—who cannot have committed any sin—goes straight to heaven.
24. *JAMES and LUCRETIA MOTT: Life and Letters*, p. 341.
25. *Time*, May 14, 1965.
26. Quoted in RICHARD K. TUCKER, *The Dragon and the Cross: The Rise and Fall of the Ku Klux Klan in Middle America* (Hamden: 1991), pp. 189–90.
27. BETTY FRIEDAN, *The Feminine Mystique* (New York, 1970), p. 80.
28. See HUIE, *Three Lives*, pp. 201–09.
29. SUSAN BROWNMILLER, *In Our Time: Memoir of a Revolution* (New York, 1999), p. 102.
30. 410 US 113.
31. BROWNMILLER, *In Our Time*, p. 135.

CHAPTER 12: REASON EMBATTLED

1. The address was reprinted in *First Things: The Journal of Religion and Public Life*, May 2002.
2. SEAN WILENTZ, "From Justice Scalia, a Chilling Vision of Religion's Authority in America," *New York Times*, July 8, 2002.
3. 1999 Gallup Poll, cited in NATALIE ANGIER, "Confessions of a Lonely Atheist," *New York Times Magazine*, January 14, 2001.

4. See "Faith-Based Plans Backed, but Church-State Doubts Abound," April 10, 2001, Pew Forum on Religion and Public Life (www.pew-forum.org).

5. *Atlantic*, March 2003.

6. WEBB, *Evolution Controversy*, p. 254.

Selected Bibliography

ADAMS, JOHN, and THOMAS JEFFERSON. *The Adams-Jefferson Letters.* Vols. 1–2. Ed. Lester J. Cappon. Chapel Hill: University of North Carolina Press, 1959.

ALDRIDGE, ALFRED OWEN. *Man of Reason: The Life of Thomas Paine.* Philadelphia: Lippincott, 1959.

ALLEN, ETHAN. *Reason the Only Oracle of Man.* New York: Scholars' Facsimiles & Reprints, 1940.

ALLEN, FREDERICK LEWIS. *Only Yesterday.* New York: Harper & Brothers, 1931.

ASHBY, LEROY. *William Jennings Bryan: Champion of Democracy.* Boston: Twayne Publishers, 1987.

ASHTON, DIANNE. *Rebecca Gratz: Women and Judaism in Antebellum America.* Detroit: Wayne State University Press, 1977.

AVRICH, PAUL. *The Haymarket Tragedy.* Princeton: Princeton University Press, 1984.

BALDWIN, NEIL. *Henry Ford and the Jews.* New York: Perseus Books, 2001.

BANGS, NATHAN. *A History of the Methodist Episcopal Church.* Vol. 2. New York: T. Mason and G. Lane, 1838–41.

BARTON, BRUCE. *The Man Nobody Knows.* Indianapolis: Bobbs-Merrill, 1925.

BEECHER, LYMAN. *Autobiography, Correspondence, Etc.* Ed. Charles Beecher. New York: Harper, 1865.

BELLAH, ROBERT N. *The Broken Covenant: American Civil Religion in a Time of Trial.* Chicago: University of Chicago Press, 1975.

BENEDICT, DAVID. *A General History of the Baptist Denomination in America and Other Parts of the World.* Vol. 2. Gallatin: Church History Research and Archives, 1985.

BENTLEY, WILLIAM. *The Diary of William Bentley.* Vols. 1–4. Salem: Essex Institute, 1905.

BIRNEY, CATHERINE H. *The Grimké Sisters: Sarah and Angelina Grimké, the First American Women Advocates of Abolition and Women's Rights* (1885). Westport: Greenwood Press, 1969.

BLANSHARD, PAUL. *American Freedom and Catholic Power.* Boston: Beacon Press, 1958.

BORDEN, MORTON. *Jews, Turks, and Infidels.* Chapel Hill: University of North Carolina Press, 1984.

BOSTON, ROBERT. *Why the Religious Right Is Wrong about Separation of Church and State.* Buffalo: Prometheus Books, 1993.

BRANCH, TAYLOR. *Pillar of Fire: America in the King Years, 1963–1965.* New York: Simon and Schuster, 1998.

BRAUDE, ANN. *Radical Spirits: Spiritualism and Women's Rights in Nineteenth-Century America.* Boston: Beacon Press, 1989.

BROUN, HEYWOOD, and MARGARET LEECH. *Anthony Comstock: Roundsman of the Lord.* New York: Albert and Charles Boni, 1927.

BROWNMILLER, SUSAN. *In Our Time: Memoir of a Revolution.* New York: Dial Press, 1999.

BUCKLEY, THOMAS E. *Church and State in Revolutionary Virginia.* Charlottesville: University Press of Virginia, 1977.

BURNHAM, GEORGE, and LEE FISHER. *Billy Graham and the New York Crusade.* Grand Rapids: Zondervan Publishing House, 1957.

BURNS, JAMES MACGREGOR. *Roosevelt: The Lion and the Fox.* New York: Harcourt Brace, 1956.

———. *Roosevelt: The Soldier of Freedom.* New York: Harcourt Brace Jovanovich, 1970.

BUTLER, JON. *Awash in a Sea of Faith.* Cambridge: Harvard University Press, 1990.

CARROLL, JAMES. *Constantine's Sword: The Church and the Jews.* Boston: Houghton Mifflin, 2001.

CARTER, STEPHEN L. *The Culture of Disbelief.* New York: Basic Books, 1993.

CASH, W. J. *The Mind of the South.* New York: Knopf, 1941.

CENIZA, SHERRY. *Walt Whitman and 19th-Century Women Reformers.* Tuscaloosa: University of Alabama Press, 1998.

CHESLER, ELLEN. *Woman of Valor: Margaret Sanger and the Birth Control Movement in America.* New York: Simon and Schuster, 1992.

CONWAY, MONCURE DANIEL. *The Life of Thomas Paine.* Vols. 1–2. New York: G. P. Putnam's Sons, 1892.

———. *Autobiography: Memories and Experiences.* Vols. 1–2. New York: Cassell and Company, 1892.

COTTRELL, ROBERT C. *Roger Nash Baldwin and the American Civil Liberties Union.* New York: Columbia University Press, 2000.

CRAMER, C. H. *Royal Bob: The Life of Robert G. Ingersoll.* Indianapolis: Bobbs-Merrill, 1952.

CROSBY, DONALD F. *God, Church, and Flag: Senator Joseph R. McCarthy and the Catholic Church, 1950–1957.* Chapel Hill: University of North Carolina Press, 1978.

DARWIN, CHARLES. *On the Origin of Species: The Origin of Species by Means of Natural Selection; or, the Preservation of Favoured Races in the Struggle for Life* and *The Descent of Man and Selection in Relation to Sex.* New York: Modern Library, 1948.

DARROW, CLARENCE. *The Story of My Life.* New York: Grosset and Dunlap, 1932.

DU BOIS, W.E.B. *The Autobiography of W.E.B. Du Bois.* New York: International Publishers, 1968.

———. *W.E.B. Du Bois: The Crisis Writings.* Ed. Daniel Walden. Greenwich: Fawcett Publications, 1972.

DWIGHT, TIMOTHY. *Travels in New-England and New-York.* Vol. 2. London: W. Barnes and Son, 1823.

———. *Sermons.* Vol. 1. New Haven: H. Howe, 1828.

ELLIS, JOSEPH J. *Founding Brothers.* New York: Knopf, 2000.

FALK, CANDACE. *Love, Anarchy, and Emma Goldman.* New York: Holt, Rinehart and Winston, 1984.

FINAN, CHRISTOPHER M., *Alfred E. Smith: The Happy Warrior.* New York: Hill and Wang, 2002.

FISKE, JOHN. *Essays Historical and Literary.* New York: Macmillan, 1907.

FRADY, MARSHALL. *Billy Graham: A Parable of American Righteousness.* Boston: Little, Brown, 1979.

FRANKLIN, BENJAMIN. *Representative Selections.* Ed. Frank Luther Mott and Chester E. Jorgenson. New York: American Book Company, 1936.

———. *The Autobiography*. New York: Vintage, 1990.

———. *Poor Richard's Almanack*, 1751.

FRASER, CAROLINE. *God's Perfect Child: Living and Dying in the Christian Science Church*. New York: Metropolitan Books, 1999.

FRIEDAN, BETTY. *The Feminine Mystique*. New York: Norton, 1963.

FRUCHTMAN, JACK, JR. *Thomas Paine: Apostle of Freedom*. New York: Four Walls Eight Windows, 1994.

GARRISON, WILLIAM LLOYD. *Documents of Upheaval: Selections from William Lloyd Garrison's "The Liberator," 1831–1865*. Ed. Truman Nelson. New York: Hill and Wang, 1966.

GLEASON, PHILIP. *Keeping the Faith: American Catholicism Past and Present*. Notre Dame: University of Notre Dame Press, 1987.

GOLDMAN, EMMA. *Living My Life*. New York: Meridian Books, 1977.

———. *Red Emma Speaks: Selected Writings and Speeches*. Comp. and ed. Alix Kates Shulman. New York: Random House, 1972.

GOLDSMITH, BARBARA. *Other Powers: The Age of Suffrage, Spiritualism, and the Scandalous Victoria Woodhull*. New York: Knopf, 1998.

GOULD, STEPHEN JAY. *Rocks of Ages: Science and Religion in the Fullness of Life*. New York: Ballantine, 1999.

GRAY, ASA. *Darwiniana*. Cambridge: Belknap Press of Harvard University Press, 1963.

GRIFFITH, ELISABETH. *In Her Own Right: The Life of Elizabeth Cady Stanton*. New York: Oxford University Press, 1984.

HALDEMAN-JULIUS, EMANUEL. *Snapshots of Modern Life*. Girard: Haldeman-Julius Publications, 1927.

———. *The Militant Agnostic*. Amherst, N.Y.: Prometheus Books, 1995.

———. *The World of Haldeman-Julius*. Comp. Albert Mordell. New York: Twayne Publishers, 1960.

HARPER, IDA HUSTED. *The Life and Work of Susan B. Anthony*. Vols. 1–3. Indianapolis: Bowen-Merrill Company (vols. 1–2), Hollenbeck Press (vol. 3), 1899–1908.

HENNESEY, JAMES T. *American Catholics: A History of the Roman Catholic Community in the United States*. New York: Oxford University Press, 1981.

HERNDON, WILLIAM H., and JESSE W. WEIK. *Abraham Lincoln: The True Story of a Great Life*. New York: D. Appleton and Company, 1896.

HESSELTINE, WILLIAM B. *Ulysses S. Grant: Politician*. New York: Frederick Ungar, 1935.

HESTON, WATSON. *Old Testament Stories Comically Illustrated*. New York: Truth Seeker Company, 1892.

HILL, FRANCES. *A Delusion of Satan*. New York: Doubleday, 1995.

HIMMELFARB, GERTRUDE. *The De-Moralization of Society*. New York: Knopf, 1995.

HINDLE, BROOKE. *The Pursuit of Science in Revolutionary America*. Chapel Hill: University of North Carolina Press, 1956.

History of Woman Suffrage. Vols. 1–6. Ed. Susan B. Anthony, Matilda Joslyn Gage, and Elizabeth Cady Stanton. New York: Source Book Press, 1970. Reprint of 1881–1922 eds.

HOFSTADTER, RICHARD. *Social Darwinism in American Thought*. New York: George Braziller, 1959.

HOLLAND, J. G. *Life of Abraham Lincoln*. Springfield: G. Bill, 1866.

HUXLEY, THOMAS HENRY. *Life and Letters of Thomas Henry Huxley, by His Son, Leonard Huxley*. New York: D. Appleton and Company, 1900.

INGERSOLL, ROBERT GREEN. *The Works of Robert Ingersoll*. Vols. 1–12. New York: *Dresden Publishing Company*, C. P. Farrell, 1900.

———. *Ingersoll: Immortal Infidel*. Ed. Roger E. Greeley. Buffalo: Prometheus Books, 1977.

———. *Letters*. With a biographical introduction by Eva Ingersoll Wakefield. New York: Philosophical Library, 1951.

IRONS, PETER. *A People's History of the Supreme Court*. New York: Penguin Books, 2000.

IVERS, GREGG. *To Build a Wall: American Jews and Separation of Church and State*. Charlottesville: University Press of Virginia, 1995.

JEFFERSON, THOMAS. *The Life and Selected Writings of Thomas Jefferson*. Ed. Adrienne Koch and William Peden. New York: Modern Library, 1944.

JOHN, RICHARD H. *Spreading the News: The American Postal System from Franklin to Morse*. Cambridge: Harvard University Press, 1995.

KAPLAN, JUSTIN. *Walt Whitman: A Life*. New York: Simon and Schuster, 1980.

KERTZER, DAVID I. *The Popes against the Jews: The Vatican's Role in the Rise of Modern Anti-Semitism*. New York: Knopf, 2001.

KOCH, G. ADOLF. *Republican Religion: The American Revolution and the Cult of Reason*. New York: Henry Holt and Company, 1933.

KOLMERTEN, CAROL A. *The American Life of Ernestine L. Rose*. Syracuse: Syracuse University Press, 1999.

KONVITZ, MILTON R. *First Amendment Freedoms: Selected Cases on Freedom of Religion, Speech, Press, Assembly*. Ithaca: Cornell University Press, 1963.

KRADITOR, AILEEN S. *Means and Ends in American Abolitionism*. New York: Pantheon, 1969.

KRAMNICK, ISAAC, and R. LAURENCE MOORE. *The Godless Constitution*. New York: W. W. Norton, 1996.

LAMON, WARD HILL. *The Life of Abraham Lincoln; from His Birth to His Inauguration as President*. Boston: J. R. Osgood and Company, 1872.

———. *Recollections of Abraham Lincoln*. Ed. Dorothy Lamon Teillard. Lincoln: University of Nebraska Press, 1994.

LANNIE, VINCENT P. *Public Money and Parochial Education: Bishop Hughes, Governor Seward, and the New York School Controversy*. Cleveland: Press of Case Western Reserve University, 1968.

LARSON, ORVIN. *American Infidel: Robert G. Ingersoll*. New York: Citadel Press, 1962.

LATOURETTE, KENNETH S. *A History of the Expansion of Christianity*. Vols. 4–7. New York: Harper & Brothers, 1937–45.

LEO XIII. *The Great Encyclical Letters of Pope Leo XIII*. New York: Benziger Brothers, 1903.

LE SUEUR, MERIDEL K. *North Star Country*. Lincoln: University of Nebraska Press, c 1945, 1984.

LEWIS, SINCLAIR. *Babbitt*. New York: Harcourt Brace, 1922.

LINCOLN, ABRAHAM. *Collected Works of Abraham Lincoln*. Vols. 5–8. Ed. Roy P. Basler, Marion Dolores Pratt, and Lloyd A. Dunlap. New Brunswick: Rutgers University Press, 1953–55.

LOVING, JEROME. *Walt Whitman's Champion: William Douglas O'Connor*. College Station: Texas A & M University Press, 1978.

MACDONALD, GEORGE E. *Fifty Years of Freethought*. Vols. 1–2. New York: Truth Seeker Company, 1929.

MADISON, JAMES. *The Complete Madison: His Basic Writings*. Ed. Saul K. Padover. New York: Harper and Brothers, 1953.

MARCUS, SHELDON. *Father Coughlin: The Tumultuous Life of the Priest of the Little Flower*. Boston: Little, Brown, 1973.

MARTY, MARTIN E. *Modern American Religion*. Vols. 1–3. Chicago: University of Chicago Press, 1986–96.

MAYER, HENRY. *All on Fire*. New York: St. Martin's Press, 1998.

MCCOLLUM, VASHTI CROMWELL. *One Woman's Fight*. Boston: Beacon Press, 1961.

MEADE, WILLIAM. *Old Churches, Ministers, and Families of Virginia*. Bowie, Md.: Heritage Books, 1992.

MEDVEDEV, ZHORES A. *A Question of Madness*. Trans. Ellen de Kadt. London: Macmillan, 1971.

———. *The Rise and Fall of T. D. Lysenko.* Trans. I. Michael Lerner, with the editorial assistance of Lucy G. Lawrence. New York: Columbia University Press, 1969.

MONAHAN, MICHAEL. *Palms of Papyrus.* East Orange: Papyrus Publishing Company, 1909.

MOORE, CHARLES C. *Behind the Bars: 31498.* Lexington: Blue Grass Printing Company, 1899.

MOTT, JAMES R. *The Post-Darwinian Controversies.* Cambridge: Cambridge University Press, 1979.

MORTON, MARIAN J. *Emma Goldman and the American Left: "Nowhere at Home."* New York: Twayne Publishers, 1992.

MOTT, JAMES, and LUCRETIA MOTT. *James and Lucretia Mott: Life and Letters.* Ed. Anna Davis Hallowell. Boston: Houghton, Mifflin, 1884.

NEUHAUS, RICHARD JOHN. *The Naked Public Square.* Grand Rapids: W. B. Erdmans, 1984.

NUMBERS, RONALD. *The Creationists.* New York: Knopf, 1992.

NYE, RUSSEL BLAINE. *The Cultural Life of the New Nation, 1776–1830.* New York: Harper and Row, 1960.

O'HAIR, MADALYN MURRAY. *Why I Am an Atheist.* Austin: American Atheist Press, 1991.

O'NEILL, J. M. *Religion and Education under the Constitution.* New York: Harper and Brothers, 1949.

PAINE, THOMAS. *The Thomas Paine Reader.* Ed. Michael Foot and Isaac Kramnick. New York: Penguin Books, 1987.

———. *The Complete Writings of Thomas Paine.* Ed. Philip S. Foner. New York: Citadel Press, 1945.

PARKER, ALISON M. *Purifying America: Women, Cultural Reform, and Pro-Censorship Activism: 1873–1933.* Chicago: University of Illinois Press, 1997.

PEALE, NORMAN VINCENT. *The Power of Positive Thinking.* New York: Fawcett Crest, 1963.

PECK, HARRY THURSTON. *What Is Good English? and Other Essays.* New York: Dodd, Mead, 1899.

PFEFFER, LEO. *Church, State, and Freedom.* Boston: Beacon Press, 1953.

PLUMMER, MARK. *Robert G. Ingersoll: Peoria's Pagan Politician.* Macomb: Western Illinois Monograph Series, 1984.

RAY, SISTER MARY AUGUSTINA. *American Opinion of Roman Catholicism in the Eighteenth Century.* New York: Columbia University Press, 1936.

REMSBURG, JOHN E. *Six Historic Americans.* New York: Truth Seeker Company, 1906.

ROOSEVELT, THEODORE. *Gouverneur Morris*. Oyster Bay: Theodore Roosevelt Association. 1975.

SCHNEIER, MARC. *Shared Dreams: Martin Luther King, Jr. and the Jewish Community*. Woodstock, Vt.: Jewish Lights Publishing, 1999.

SCHWARTZ, BERNARD. *The New Right and the Constitution: Turning Back the Legal Clock*. Boston: Northeastern University Press, 1990.

SOLOMON, MARTHA. *Emma Goldman*. Boston: Twayne Publishers, 1987.

SORAUF, FRANK. *The Wall of Separation: The Constitutional Politics of Church and State*. Princeton: Princeton University Press, 1976.

SORENSEN, THEODORE C. *Kennedy*. New York: Harper and Row, 1965.

SPENCER, HERBERT. *Social Statics*. New York: D. Appleton and Company, 1893.

STANTON, ELIZABETH CADY. *Eighty Years and More: Reminiscences, 1815–1897*. Boston: Northeastern University Press, 1993.

———. *The Woman's Bible*. Boston: Northeastern University Press, 1993.

STANTON, MARY. *From Selma to Sorrow: The Life and Death of Viola Liuzzo*. Athens: University of Georgia Press, 1998.

THOMAS, BENJAMIN PLATT. *Abraham Lincoln: A Biography*. New York: Knopf, 1952.

TOCQUEVILLE, ALEXIS DE. *Democracy in America*. Vols. 1–2. New York: Knopf, 1960.

TROLLOPE, FRANCES. *Domestic Manners of the Americans*. Vol. 2. Ed. Pamela Neville-Sington. New York: Penguin, 1997.

TRUEBLOOD, ELTON. *Abraham Lincoln: Theologian of American Anguish*. New York: Harper and Row, 1973.

Truth Seeker. Vols. 10–37. New York: Truth Seeker Company, 1883–1910.

TUCKER, RICHARD. *The Dragon and the Cross: The Rise and Fall of the Ku Klux Klan in Middle America*. Hamden: Archon Books, 1991.

TURNER, JAMES. *Without God, without Creed: The Origins of Unbelief in America*. Baltimore: Johns Hopkins University Press, 1985.

TWAIN, MARK. *The Bible according to Mark Twain*. Ed. Howard G. Baetzhold and Joseph B. McCullough. New York: Touchstone Books, 1996.

———. *The Adventures of Huckleberry Finn*. New York: Random House, 1996.

UNDERWOOD, SARA A. *Heroines of Freethought*. New York: C. P. Somerby, 1876.

WALDSTREICHER, DAVID. *In the Midst of Perpetual Fetes: The Making of American Nationalism, 1776–1820.* Chapel Hill: University of North Carolina Press for the Omohundro Institute of Early American History and Culture, Williamsburg, Va., 1997.

WALKER, SAMUEL. *In Defense of American Liberties: A History of the ACLU.* Carbondale: Southern Illinois University Press, 1999.

WALTERS, KERRY S. *Elihu Palmer's Principles of Nature.* Wolfeboro: Longwood Academic, 1990.

WARREN, DONALD. *Radio Priest: Charles Coughlin, the Father of Hate Radio.* New York: Free Press, 1996.

WARREN, SIDNEY. *American Freethought: 1860–1914.* New York: Columbia University Press, 1943.

WEBB, GEORGE E. *The Evolution Controversy in America.* Lexington: University Press of Kentucky, 1994.

WEINBERG, ARTHUR, and LILA WEINBERG. *Clarence Darrow: A Sentimental Rebel.* New York: G. P. Putnam's Sons, 1980.

WHITE, RONALD C. *Lincoln's Greatest Speech: The Second Inaugural.* New York: Simon and Schuster, 2002.

WHITEHEAD, FRED, and VERLE MUHRER. *Free-Thought on the American Frontier.* Buffalo: Prometheus Books, 1992.

WHITMAN, WALT. *Leaves of Grass.* New York: Modern Library, 1921.

———. *Leaves of Grass. Facsimile of the 1855 Text.* Ed. Thomas Bird Mosher. Portland: Thomas Bird Mosher, William Francis Gable, 1920.

———. *Leaves of Grass: Preface to the Original Edition.* London: Trübner, 1881.

WILLS, GARRY. *Papal Sin: Structures of Deceit.* New York: Doubleday, 2000.

WINIK, JAY. *April 1865.* New York: Perennial, 2002.

WOLF, WILLIAM J. *The Religion of Abraham Lincoln.* New York: Seabury Press, 1963.

Acknowledgments

During the years it took to complete this book, I received extraordinary support from a number of institutions and individuals. Above all, I am indebted to the Dorothy and Lewis B. Cullman Center for Scholars and Writers of that great institution, the New York Public Library, for providing me with a year in research paradise as a 2001–02 fellow. I am especially grateful to Peter Gay, the center's former director, for his consistently wise counsel and to Pamela Leo, assistant director, for her troubleshooting skills.

Bob and Blaikie Worth provided several grants, as well as personal encouragement, that enabled me to go on working at crucial points in this project. Bob was one of the first readers of the book in manuscript.

Aaron Asher, my editor for many years before his retirement from publishing, believed in this book before I began to write it. Through early drafts of the manuscript, he gave me the benefit not only of his editorial skills but of his passionate commitment to all of the values implicit in the words *freethought* and *freethinker*. His suggestions were imbued with the rare combination of a friend's empathy and a rigorous professional's detached editorial judgment.

The Council for Secular Humanism and Tom Flynn, editor of *Free*

Inquiry magazine, offered both encouragement and practical assistance. Tom opened up the Robert G. Ingersoll Birthplace Museum to me for a private tour and provided a rare photograph of the Great Agnostic speaking to a crowd.

My colleagues from my fellowship year at the Center for Scholars and Writers have taken a continuing and unfailing interest in my work. David Waldstreicher offered endlessly useful suggestions for research on eighteenth- and early-nineteenth-century American history. Carmen Boullosa, James Morris, Carla Peterson, and Thadious Davis gave both scholarly advice and sustaining personal friendship.

Several members of the New York Public Library staff have been particularly helpful: Beth Diefendorf, who oversees the splendid third-floor Main Reading Room; Wayne Furman of the Office of Special Collections; and Carolyn Oyama and Herbert Scher of the communications office. I began writing *Freethinkers* at the Scholars' Center and finished the book in the library's Frederick Lewis Allen Room, a haven for nonfiction authors.

It is impossible to thank all the friends and professional colleagues who have served as sounding boards for my ideas, but I am especially grateful for the interest of Adam Hochschild, Angeline Goreau, Johanna Kaplan, and Jack Schwartz.

As always, I am indebted to my longtime literary agents, Georges and Anne Borchardt.

As is well know, editors today do not always get to finish what they start. But I would be remiss not to acknowledge Jane Rosenman, who bought the original book proposal, and Ileene Smith.

Sara Bershtel, my editor at Metropolitan Books, gives the lie to the widely touted notion that no one in modern publishing actually reads and edits manuscripts. Her scrupulous line-by-line editing and meticulous attention to every aspect of the book production process are the marks of a great editor. Having a perfectionist for an editor draws the best out of a writer.

At Metropolitan, I also wish to thank Riva Hocherman for her invaluable suggestions on the book's early chapters and Roslyn Schloss for her meticulous and sensitive copyediting throughout. I am grateful to Fritz Metsch and John Candell for the book's and the jacket's elegant designs and to Shara Kay for making everything work better.

Index

About the Author

Susan Jacoby is the author of six previous books, including *Wild Justice: The Evolution of Revenge*, a *New York Times* Notable Book and Pulitzer Prize finalist. She has received numerous research grants, including fellowships from the Guggenheim Foundation, National Endowment for the Humanities, and the Center for Scholars and Writers of the New York Public Library. A contributor to the *New York Times*, the *Washington Post*, TomPaine.com, and the *AARP Bulletin*, among other publications, she lives in New York City.